1989
15th EDITION
THE COMPLETE HANDBOOK OF
PRO BASKETBALL

1989
15th EDITION
THE COMPLETE HANDBOOK OF
PRO BASKETBALL

EDITED BY ZANDER HOLLANDER

AN ASSOCIATED FEATURES BOOK

A SIGNET BOOK
NEW AMERICAN LIBRARY

ACKNOWLEDGMENTS

When *The Complete Handbook of Pro Basketball* was born 15 years ago, the NBA had 18 teams, including Buffalo, New Orleans and KC-Omaha, and there was the eight-team ABA. The ABA is long gone, Buffalo is now the Los Angeles Clippers via San Diego, New Orleans is Utah and KC-Omaha is Sacramento. And this year, with the addition of the Charlotte Hornets and Miami Heat, the flourishing NBA is up to 25 teams. In addition to expansion, the new season is marked by the introduction of three referees. At least there are no plans for instant replay to settle questionable calls.

We acknowledge those who helped make the new edition happen: contributing editor David Kaplan, the writers listed on the contents page and Lee Stowbridge, Eric Compton, Fred Cantey, Richard Rossiter, Linda Spain, Alex Sachare, Brian McIntyre, Terry Lyons, Marty Blake, the NBA team publicity directors, Elias Sports Bureau, Dot Gordineer of Libra Graphics and Westchester Book Composition.

PHOTO CREDITS: Covers—Andrew Bernstein. Inside photos—Ira Golden, Michael Hirsch, Vic Milton, Mitch Reibel, Richard Reiss, N.Y. Daily News, Wide World, UPI and the NBA team photographers.

Zander Hollander

 SIGNET TRADEMARK REG. U.S. PAT. OFF. AND FOREIGN COUNTRIES REGISTERED
TRADEMARK—MARCA REGISTRADA
HECHO EN CHICAGO, U.S.A.

SIGNET, SIGNET CLASSIC, MENTOR, ONYX, PLUME, MERIDIAN AND NAL BOOKS are published by NAL PENGUIN, 1633 Broadway, New York, New York 10019

First Printing, November, 1988

1 2 3 4 5 6 7 8 9

PRINTED IN THE UNITED STATES OF AMERICA

CONTENTS

Editor's Note: The material herein includes trades and rosters up to final printing deadline.

Great Love Matches...
Starting with
Magic & Isiah

By JOE GERGEN

Once upon a time, there was a code of conduct that covered this sort of thing. Much as the old cowboy stars confined public displays of affection to their trusty steeds, our athletic heroes were content—at least within camera range—to kiss inanimate objects. Thus were we treated to pictures of baseball players bussing their bats after a game-winning home run, tennis champions embracing their trophies and bottom-line oriented golfers paying lip service to a winner's check.

Nobody was shocked. It was considered acceptable behavior in the world of sports. As recently as the spring of 1975, a young netminder named Glenn (Chico) Resch made a name for himself by kissing the goalposts after another improbable victory by the young New York Islanders in the midst of an amazing comeback from three games down in the Stanley Cup playoffs. In time, the Islanders grew up to win four National Hockey League championships in succession and Resch grew up to become a well-traveled veteran in need of a hairpiece. Still, we remember them for their youthful exuberance in a more innocent age.

It's uncertain where the change began, or even when we first became aware of it. Perhaps it was the intrusion of Morganna, the buxom exotic dancer for whom diamonds were a publicity-conscious girl's best friend. Billing herself as the Kissing Bandit of Baseball, she began a series of raids onto major-league fields in pursuit of a well-documented smooch with a ballplayer.

This is how values have changed. At the 1970 major-league All-Star Game in Cincinnati, she was apprehended as she at-

---

As a well-traveled columnist for Newsday *and* The Sporting News, *Joe Gergen has been where the action is. But he still awaits a kiss from Morganna.*

Cheek-to-cheek before Game 7 of NBA Finals.

tempted to cross the white line, removed from the field and bundled off to jail. At the 1988 Triple-A All-Star Game in Buffalo, she sashayed down the first-base line to home plate, planted a kiss on designated target, Benny Distefano of the Buffalo Bisons, and waltzed into the home-team dugout, where she was interviewed live by ESPN, the sports cable network. She proudly announced this was her first Triple-A foray after 21 successful major-league operations and even got in a plug for the Utica Blue Sox, a minor-league team which counts her as a part-owner. Yes, Morganna has become part of the establishment.

Perhaps that was inevitable, given the state of society. The 1988 baseball season was notable for the flood of stories and television debates on the Boston Red Sox' Wade Boggs and his adventures with former traveling partner, Margo Adams. That followed months of controversy revolving around the tiffs, real or imagined, between heavyweight boxing champion Mike Tyson and his recent bride, actress Robin Givens. Those disclosures followed the made-in-body-builders' heaven affair between Jets' defensive end Mark Gastineau and Brigitte Nielsen, the former Mrs. Rambo.

Yet, none of these celebrated entanglements did much more than increase the circulation of *People* magazine and provide another topic for Johnny Carson. Boggs continued to hit well over .300 for the Red Sox, Tyson demolished Michael Spinks in 91 seconds to retain his crown and, if Gastineau was not a dominant pass-rusher, his formidable skills had dissipated well before he encountered Sly Stallone'e ex-wife. Fans who argued that such reports had nothing to do with sports were technically correct.

They were staples of the entertainment business, where rumors, gossip and the occasional scandal fed the public appetite and insured the popularity of actors, singers, shows and movies. In its alignment with television and its reliance upon the income from that media source, sports had bought into what in Hollywood they call "the industry." One byproduct was the appearance of athletes on the covers of those supermarket scandal sheets. It was no longer possible to hide behind a fielder's glove.

Still, the reasoning went, boys will be boys. The field, the ring, the court were sanctuaries and would remain inviolate. There, men were men. At least, that's what many believed until that moment in the showcase of the NBA Finals when two of the most honored athletes in all the United States met at midcourt and exchanged kisses.

The crowd gasped. The nation blinked in disbelief. Dr. James Naismith performed a 360-degree helicoptor spin and slam dunk in his grave. These weren't old Russian generals plotting the

Morganna nailed George Brett at 1979 All-Star Game

elimination of a comrade. They were the elite of American sports, Earvin (Magic) Johnson and Isiah Thomas.

Not only did they do it once but they did it again and again at the outset of games between the defending champion Los Angeles Lakers and the Detroit Pistons. Johnson and Thomas, it so happened, were good friends. Make that the best of friends. In past years, in fact, Thomas would journey to the West Coast to stay with Johnson during the latter's almost annual involvement in the NBA Finals.

In 1988, however, the Pistons qualified for the first time since the franchise moved from Fort Wayne to Detroit three decades earlier. They defeated the Boston Celtics in the Eastern Conference championship round, setting the stage for the first primetime showdown between the two great point guards, stars of their respective teams. They celebrated in their own special way, with a kiss.

To understand the shock waves that set off, one has to appreciate the hard-line approach to sports typical of an earlier generation. For many, a handshake before an event would have been an excessive display of tenderness not in the best interests of a competitor. As a player, Frank Robinson made it a point not to acknowledge members of the other team before games, even those who had been former teammates or remained offseason friends. He was not alone in this practice.

Another who shared a contempt for the opposition was Bob Gibson, the great pitcher for the St. Louis Cardinals. In light of the Johnson-Thomas greetings, a newsman asked Robinson what would have happened had he planted a kiss on Gibson's cheek. "He would have knocked me down even quicker," Robinson said.

They didn't even set the established order. Before them, there was Early Wynn, the tough pitcher for the Cleveland Indians and Chicago White Sox, of whom it was said he would knock down his own mother in pursuit of a victory. "Yeah," he said in clarification, "but you got to remember that mother was a helluva hitter."

This, after all, was hardball. It wasn't much different in the NBA. Can you picture Bill Russell and Wilt Chamberlain kissing for the cameras before the center jump in a Boston-Philadelphia playoff game? NFL linemen routinely spit and cursed at each other both before and after the arrival of the plastic helmet. There were more than a few hockey players who would sooner have their faces carved by a stick than pucker up at the faceoff.

Indeed, a kiss by a gentleman was no compliment. Recall the low comedy of the George Foreman vs. Five extravaganza staged in Toronto in 1975, at a time when Big George was waiting for the rematch against Muhammad Ali that never developed. Among the five boxers Foreman pledged to knock out within three rounds on the same afternoon was Charley Polite, a warrior whose punches were tempered by mercy.

That is to say, Polite couldn't hurt a flyweight. He was the fourth opponent in the ring, after Foreman had stopped Alonzo Johnson, had knocked out Jerry Judge and had pummelled Terry Daniels (with a second from Daniels' corner engaging in a more heated battle with a second from Foreman's corner). During the introductions, Foreman glowered at Polite, who had lost more than twice as many fights as he had won during his career. Polite smiled and landed a kiss from short range.

"He was trying to psych me," Polite explained. "He was telling me he was going to knock me out in one round. He was getting closer and closer so I kissed him. When he gets mad, he loses control out there and he can't hit anything." Foreman did not hit Polite with his knockout punch. He became the only opponent not to suffer a knockdown.

"I thought," Foreman offered later, "maybe it was the kiss of death." Perhaps it was. He never again fought Ali, nor for the heavyweight title.

But by all accounts the ceremony between Johnson and Thomas was not meant to demean or target the opponent. It was a statement of affection and respect. Still, not even his teammates could imagine themselves in Isiah's position. "Before that," Dennis Rodman decided, "we'd have to get engaged."

By right, if there were any sport in which kissing were acceptable behavior, it should be tennis. Not only does it permit competition in mixed doubles, but its scoring system substitutes love for nothing.

In this era of tennis around the globe and jet-setting millionaires, however, there is no necessity and little opportunity to establish even surface friendships. If John McEnroe, Ivan Lendl, Boris Becker and Jimmy Connors share anything, it is their dislike for each other. With the exception of the Swedes, who are inclined to hang together like a college team, the men's tour is a collective of one-man corporations.

Perhaps because their struggle for equal acceptance required greater commitment and effort, the women remain closer. But that unity may not last another generation. In fact, the feeling may not survive the great personal rivalry of our times, Chris Evert vs. Martina Navratilova.

Although teenager Steffi Graf has pushed past both of them to attain top ranking, the duel of the two former queens still ener-

All-Star lineup at the Chris Evert-Andy Mill wedding in July at Boca Raton, Fla.: (from left) Martina Navratilova, Pam Shriver, Andy and Chris, Lynda Carter and Billie Jean King.

gizes the sport. And their mutual respect continues to resonate in the lives of both women. How fitting that Navratilova should be indirectly responsible for Evert's second marriage.

Evert was one of the first players to comfort Navratilova when the Czech teenager defected during the 1975 U.S. Open and their friendship has lasted through 78 meetings, including some of the most memorable battles in tennis history. When the younger Navratilova drew even in the series at the 1984 Wimbledon championships en route to taking charge, she said, "I wish we could stop now when no one could say which of us was the best." And she meant it.

Two months later, after suffering a difficult loss in the U.S. Open final, Evert recalled sharing a bagel with Navratilova before their match while the two sat in the clubhouse watching a marathon men's semifinal on television. "Of all the players," Evert said, "I probably feel more comfortable with her than with anyone else before a match."

Last winter, Navratilova invited Evert, who was divorced from English tennis player John Lloyd, to her house in Aspen for skiing. As fate would have it, Evert fell on the slopes. Along came Andy Mill, a former U.S. downhill champion. He picked up Evert, literally. The two now are one.

And yet none of this interaction has taken the edge off the rivalry. Navratilova and Evert staged another magnificent duel in the Wimbledon semifinals this past summer, only to have it end in Navratilova's favor on a call which Evert uncharacteristically disputed. If anything, the players' personal relationship has enriched the competition.

Certainly, that was the case in the decathlon showdown at the 1960 Olympic Games in Rome. The two major figures in the event were Rafer Johnson, an American, and Yang Chuan-kwang of Nationalist China. They were old friends as well as adversaries, having trained together under coach Ducky Drake at UCLA, where C.K. Yang was an undergraduate and Johnson a graduate student.

The event unfurled just as expected. Yang, smaller and quicker, won the first six running and jumping events. Yet, the larger, more muscular Johnson had swept the three weight events by such a large margin that he carried a 67-point lead into the final test of the gruelling two-day affair, the 1,500-meter race. Yang needed to defeat Johnson by 10 seconds or more to claim a gold medal.

They had been placed in the same heat by the luck of the draw. That was fortunate for Johnson, the dignified flag-bearer for the American team whose strategy was simply to stay with Yang no matter what the cost. "I could see him behind me at the turns," Yang said. "I could see his dark form and I knew he would never let go of me unless he collapsed."

Running under the lights of Olympic Stadium, Johnson stayed on Yang's right shoulder almost to the tape. They finished 1.2 seconds apart, allowing Johnson to be acclaimed champion, 8,392 to 8,334 points, both well above the previous Olympic record. They collapsed in each other's arms and staggered off the track together, still friends.

"I knew I had lost my chance as soon as I found out I was in Rafer's 1,500-meter heat," Yang said later. "If I had run alone, if Rafer had not run in the same heat with me, I would have won the gold medal." Johnson did not disagree. "I wanted that one real bad," he said. "But I never want to go through that again—ever."

So indelible was the sight of the two great athletes summoning every ounce of will in the final lap that many were hoping for a reprise in Los Angeles. When reports began circulating that Johnson had been chosen to light the Olympic flame at the Los Angeles Memorial Coliseum, signalling the start of the 1984 Games, newsmen speculated among themselves that it would be entirely fitting if the former marathon champion entered the stadium in a familiar position—on the outside shoulder of Yang, his great rival.

Perhaps that is the kind of relationship Johnson and Thomas, who led Big Ten teams to NCAA championships as sophomores two years apart, sought to express before an audience of millions. They certainly were not prepared to back down, to defer to the other once play got underway. In Game Four, which the Pistons won in impressive fashion to even the series, Thomas absorbed what he considered a cheap shot from Magic and shoved back. "Just a lovers' quarrel," decided Lakers' coach Pat Riley.

If the body contact between the two players occasionally resembled action more closely associated with ice, it was entirely appropriate. Of all the major team sports competing for popularity in North America, hockey is the most familiar and familial. With a smaller talent pool to draw from and with a less extensive system of development teams, it's not unusual for a player to discover he had just cross-checked a good friend, perhaps even his best man.

Rarely does he give it a second thought. No other sport offers such unusual examples of brotherly love. Phil Esposito beating his brother, Tony, with a goal. The Plagers bloodying each other's face. And the Sutters, all six of them, scrapping with anyone wearing a different uniform, no matter what the name on the back of his jersey.

The Sutters, the largest family contingent ever assembled in the National Hockey League, came by their aggressiveness on the farm in Viking, Alberta. They fought in the kitchen and they fought in the hayloft and they fought while awaiting the school bus every morning. "We'd have clean shirts on," recalled Duane Sutter, "we'd be all dressed up and everything, and by the time we got on the bus, the shirts would be ripped, the pants would be dirty and we'd have bloody noses."

They have had their moments in the NHL, most notably during a crucial late-season game in 1981 with the regular-season championship at stake. Brian, then the captain of the St. Louis Blues, took on Duane, a winger with the New York Islanders. They had to be separated by Clark Gillies. Duane felt badly afterward. "I'd rather go up in the hayloft and fight him," he said. "Or out in the parking lot. I certainly don't want to do it in front of other people." But Brian, now the Blues' coach, didn't seem to mind. As the eldest brother, he instigated most of the encounters in the hayloft. "And," he said, "I finished them."

But let anyone else take a run at a Sutter, and he might have to defend himself against two or even three. Paul Holmgren, now the coach of the Philadelphia Flyers, recalled a fight between Rich Sutter and Bill Stewart, Brian's teammate on the Blues. Within seconds, Rich's twin, Ron, also with the Flyers, joined in the skirmish. "Then I saw Brian go over to the fight," Holmgren said, "and I thought he was going to jump on Stewart, too." After all, blood is thicker than teamwork.

In the winter of 1980, en route to its destiny at Lake Placid, the U.S. Olympic squad played an exhibition against the Warroad Lakers in Warroad, Minn. What made the game notable was the presence of Dave Christian on the U.S. team and his father, Bill Christian, on the Warrod team. Bill and his brother, Roger, had been standouts on the 1960 Olympic team which had won the gold medal at Squaw Valley.

The father had coached the son through bantams. The two had played together before it was time for Dave to go off to college. But now, on this one memorable evening, they were on opposing sides and chanced to meet in a corner of the town rink. "He knocked the wind out of me," Bill Christian recalled. "I was glad to get off the ice without any broken bones."

To judge by the smile on his face, the check was tantamount to a kiss. And there was no man in Lake Placid prouder that the U.S. won the gold than the man who had taken part in the first miracle on ice 20 years earlier.

Johnson and Thomas weren't family but they felt a special bond both before and after their rugged series. That didn't prevent Johnson, frustrated by taking some hard fouls from the Pistons and his teammates' passive resistance to physical play, from slamming Thomas on his already injured back in Game Five. All this just one day after Isiah had become a father for the first time.

The basketball season ended in heroic fashion. Thomas scored 43 points in Game Six at the Forum but the Pistons couldn't finish off the Lakers. And then, with Thomas limited by a badly-sprained right ankle as well as a lower back condition, Los Angeles prevailed, 108-105, in Game Seven, becoming the first franchise in 19 years to repeat as NBA champion.

For his accomplishment, Johnson received a sizeable check, another treasured ring and a measure of satisfaction. With no shortage of adoring fans in Los Angeles, it was believed he may also have been in position to accept a kiss or two from the ladies. And if it wasn't love, it would have to do until the real thing came along again this season.

REMARKABLE! THE BLOOMING OF KNICK JACKSON

By FRED KERBER

The cab coming in from St. Albans, New York, last May 4 was still a good three hours and eight blocks away from game-time and courtside. The first round of the Eastern Conference playoffs were going as expected: the Celtics had beaten the Knicks rather handily in the first two games at the Boston Garden parquet slayground. Now in a few hours at Madison Square Garden in Manhattan, the Celtics could close out the Knicks' season and continue their own appointed rounds.

So Mark Jackson told the cabbie to pull over.

The Knicks' magnificent rookie point guard had tossed around in his head the predicament facing his team. For 82 games, they fought to make the playoffs and now they were on the verge of exiting without even bruising the Boston ego.

And although the results had been foreseen, predicted by virtually everyone, Jackson, whose electrifying regular season passes formed a Knick highlight film all by themselves, seethed inside. His first two playoff game efforts had been very rookie-like, not Rookie of the Year-like. Overmatched he was, some snickered. Can't handle the big boys, others sneered.

It didn't matter to the critics that the Celtics had concentrated heavily on stopping Jackson. They made adjustments, sought above all else to halt Jackson and the ball farther out. Veteran, let alone rookie, couldn't have a rollicking time against such a single-minded purpose.

So Jackson simmered. He decided tonight would be different. He also decided it was a nice night for a walk. About eight blocks' worth. "I just wanted to go for a walk to help get men-

---

Fred Kerber of the New York Daily News *saw more Knick games and practices last season than any other member of the media.*

Mark Jackson celebrates Rookie award with Rick Pitino.

tally prepared and psyched," Jackson said.

And part of the psyche job came from the dozens of New Yorkers who recognized the 6-3 basketball celebrity. As he hiked across town among commuters and fans, the high brow and the not so high brow, Jackson received high fives, pats on the back, gushing smiles and words of encouragement. Jackson was psyched. He was home, in his element. Mark Jackson, after all, is one of them.

"That was the best way to get prepared," he said. "All these people were psyched about the year. They were giving me credit, telling me to forget what happened [in the first two playoff games]. Anybody can be a good guy to you when things go well. I wasn't playing up to par, but all these people were coming up to me, sticking by me. It wasn't that I was playing BAD, but it just wasn't the way Mark Jackson can play."

And he went out and played the way Mark Jackson can play and did play all season. His outstanding rookie campaign was miniaturized in that game: 14 assists, five steals, seven rebounds, nine points, 46 minutes. On the negative side, there was the so-so shooting (4-of-14) that taunted him all year. But above all, there was victory.

The Knicks would bow out of the playoffs and the 1987-88 season in the following game but not before leaving warnings for others about what lies ahead. They had gotten their playoff berth, even managed a playoff game victory. Through it all, Mark Jackson was the central gear around whom all else meshed. It should stay that way for seasons to come.

"With Mark Jackson in the forefront," said Boston's outgoing coach, K.C. Jones, "they'll really kick some butt in the future."

As the Knicks trudged off the court after their elimination, Celtic point guard Dennis Johnson intercepted Jackson. Like goalies in hockey and catchers in baseball, basketball point guards have their own informal brotherhood.

"Mark is going to be a great guard, that's what I told him," D.J. said. "I also congratulated him on winning Rookie of the Year [the award hadn't been formally been given out]. He's the point guard of the future. He's got the skill and the charisma to succeed in New York."

New York is such a confounding, exasperating place. It can be Eden. It can be Hell. There is no middle ground. The demands are greater than any place else. Fail and expect no mercy. Dog-breath. Succeed and walk with the gods, M'Lord.

Jackson knew all this when the Knicks grabbed him on the first round with the 18th pick in the 1987 draft. He is a part of New York. He is Gotham's gift to itself. Jackson grew up there, went to elementary school (P.S. 136, I.S. 74) there, high school (Bishop Loughlin) there, college (St. John's) there. And now he plays in the pros there.

To Jackson, as a New Yorker might say, if you ain't foirst, you ain't nuthin'. He feels that way about everything. Consider one small incident on the road during his rookie season.

A popular eatery/saloon near Milwaukee's Mecca, has this mini basketball game. Small ball, small goal. The idea is to keep shooting four balls as quickly—and accurately—as possible within 30 seconds. Thirty is considered a quality score.

Mark defied the skeptics as he rose to unpredicted heights.

Two reporters were playing the game when Jackson walked in with inseparable friend and teammate, Johnny Newman. The players took a table. One of the reporters joked to Jackson that with his shooting, he'd lose in the game. Jackson, having never played the game, smiled, walked over and dropped in a quarter.

"I'm a dust you off," he said.

He lost his first game. In went another quarter.

"I'm a dust you off," he repeated.

The reporter went first and scored in the high 50s, the best total of the night.

"Guess I gotta get serious," Jackson said.

His score was 65.

"Told ya," he smiled.

It was a completely meaningless game, but Jackson couldn't stand the thought of losing, of being less than the best. He proved his point. Just like he did all season.

Jackson admittedly was stung by lasting until the 18th pick in the 1987 draft. Seven guards had been selected before him. As he sat in the Felt Forum listening to the names of many who would be first-year busts called before his, he vowed the drafters would regret not taking him higher.

"I'd be lying if I said I didn't think about that all season," said Jackson, who merely went out and passed for more assists (868, 10.6 avg.) than any rookie in NBA history while ranking third in the league in that category and sixth in steals (2.50 per as his 205 swipes made him only the third novice ever to get 200 steals).

"I used the fact that I was picked 18th to motivate me night in and night out," he said. "I really question how smart the critics were. I can say that now but I couldn't say it then."

One reason often cited for Jackson lasting until No. 18 was his absence from the post-collegiate season meat market all-star games. While other stars were displaying their ample talents, Jackson was back at St. John's completing the requirements for his communications degree. Some cynics even hinted Jackson deliberately ducked the all-star games to avoid being shown up.

"What would they see in me in a week that they didn't see in four years?" Jackson asked with irrefutable logic. "They always said I couldn't shoot, I couldn't play strong defense, that I was too slow. Always, I had to prove myself and I did. But it's like rumors on the street. Somebody says something about somebody else and that reputation sticks. Nobody seems to want to walk down to the corner to check it out for themselves."

Jackson spreads that message to kids throughout New York City. After his rookie season, he was in hot demand for appearances and speaking engagements. Some, he bypassed (does he really have to cut a ribbon at a supermarket opening?). But he accepted all offers to speak to kids. At the commencement ceremonies at Nathaniel Hawthorne High in Queens—where nine years earlier Jackson sat in the audience with a fresh, eager face —he told the kids:

"Life is all about making adjustments, about overcoming obstacles. Believe me, you can be anything you want to become in life. Along the way, there will always be people knocking you, telling you you're not good enough. It's your job to prove them wrong . . . No matter how hard I tried, critics always seemed to find something wrong with my game. But I didn't let it bother me. I just kept trying."

All the critics soon shut up regarding Jackson. Foot speed? Gee, it's not THAT important, is it? Where once they considered Jackson a turtle, they amended and said how he made up for all that with smarts. He went from being molasses to Einstein by midseason. Actually even before that.

And Jackson is court smart. He says he frames "a picture in my mind" when leading a fast break. Time and again last season, that picture was of Picasso quality as he made possible passes he couldn't possibly make. It's no coincidence that emerging monster Patrick Ewing had his finest pro season with Jackson around feeding the set-ups.

The ink was still drying on his first pro contract when Jackson laid claim to the starting reins. After a short look at Jackson, the Knicks slammed the broom on Rory Sparrow and Gerald Henderson. By the third game, Jackson was entrenched as a starter.

"It was so glaring to us right away," said Knick coach Rick Pitino. "It was so obvious that Mark made people around him better. When he saw how the plays were being run, how our fastbreak was being run, it was clear which way we should go."

And by season's end, there was no question of who was the best rookie. Jackson joined Willis Reed and Patrick Ewing as the only Knicks ever to win the Rookie of the Year award. It was a landslide, though inexplicably, not unanimous. Jackson's 10.6 assist average exceeded the all-time rookie norm of 9.6 established by Oscar Robertson. By comparison, Magic Johnson— who offered high praise indeed when he said of Jackson, "When I look at him, what I see is myself"—averaged 7.3 assists as a rookie while Isiah Thomas averaged 7.9.

All the numbers aside, the one element of Jackson's game that shone through like a beacon was his poise. From Day One, he made Perry Como seem like Don Knotts. Opponents saw it—"He has calm," Magic Johnson said, "and that's nice." Coaches sensed it—"He's no rookie. He's like a three-year veteran," Milwaukee's Del Harris said. Everyone talked about it—"A Mark Jackson just doesn't happen. Point guards usually evolve over a couple of years," Tom Chambers said.

The media noticed it right away. Ask him a question and, by gosh, the guy took his time, thought and then answered. No random babbling. Although he did have some stock lines ("Work hard, good things come from it"), Jackson was as deft handling the media as he was with a basketball.

The Knicks, sensing what Pitino called "talent, tremendous character and the willingness to work hard," gambled with the rookie, changed their plans and with them changed their fortunes because of Jackson, who really didn't change one iota.

Except for the obvious professional stature, Jackson is the same kid who grew up in a two-story brick home in a middle-class Queens neighborhood, following a move 16 years ago from Brooklyn. Yes, in New York, Mark Jackson is home. But "home" to this wunderkind is exactly what the word conjures up. Home is Mom Marie, Jackson's all-purpose guru and confidant. Home is Dad Harry, a Transit Authority worker who sacrificed so much to help Jackson attain the pros. Home is the childhood bedroom where he reads and writes poetry, listens to music, the same bedroom he still shares with younger brother Troy, another of the Jacksons' five children (Yeah, right, The Jackson Five).

"My parents are the reason I am where I am," said Jackson. "They have always been there. After school, after games. You get used to it and it's a great feeling. That's why I'm still home."

Jackson looked for a place of his own in all the typically upscale New York suburbs. Then he simply asked himself, "What am I doing? I have a home."

So it was back to sharing the bedroom with Troy, a Knicks' ballboy, and living by Mom and Dad's guidelines.

And "home" games takes on a literal meaning for Jackson. His entourage is always there. Family and friends form an ever-present cheering section built and forged with love. When things go bad, they are there for support—and some common-sense advice.

"Mark is his own worst critic," said bank worker Marie Jackson, with a look of "If I've told him once, I've told him a million times . . ." crossing her face. "What I try to tell him is not to be so hard on himself. Most people are satisfied with giving 100 percent. Mark gives 150 percent. But I tell him, 'You can't be 150 percent every day, don't be so hard on yourself.'"

A Mark of defense as Jackson returns to his old playground.

"He'll call home every day he's on the road," said Harry Jackson, whose playing was limited to what he called the "semi-pro, nothing special" ranks. "We hear about, read about the problems some athletes get into and naturally, as a parent, you're always worried. But we know Mark. We know that even though he'll call every day, he's strong enough to pull himself up by his own bootstraps."

It's one way of Jackson saying thanks to his parents. To Mom for the advice, to Dad for all the Knick games he took him to as a youngster. Harry Jackson always seemed to manage some better than average seats so Mark could get a closer glimpse of his idol, Walt Frazier. When Mark was old enough to attend games on his own, he went via bus and subway with friends and then waited endlessly by the players' entrance for a better glimpse, maybe a handshake and autograph.

"Walt Frazier was my idol," he recalled. "I said to myself, 'Someday, I'll step on the Garden floor and perform for all those people. I'll step into Walt Frazier's shoes.'"

It was, of course, a dream. But if you're going to dream, why not dream big? Now the big dream has been fulfilled.

And Jackson realized another fantasy last season when he met Frazier. All the times he waited outside the Garden never got him real close to his idol. But then following a basketball dinner last year, Jackson spotted Frazier hailing a cab. He offered a ride, Frazier accepted.

"I didn't want the ride to end," Jackson smiled, "so I drove about 15 miles an hour trying to make the ride last. He's probably thinking, 'What a jerk, he doesn't even know how to drive a car.'"

"In the beginning, when I saw him play, I'd make a note about something I thought I could help him on," Frazier said. "Then, about three games later, he was already doing it without me having a chance to tell him."

Comparisons to Frazier are inevitable for any Knick point guard. Frazier and Jackson, though, were dissimiliar in style. Considered a big guard in his time at 6-4, Frazier was able to back in on opponents for a quick turnaround. And one other area where, as rookies, they differed, was confidence. Jackson oozed the stuff. Not so Frazier.

"I lacked confidence when I first came into the league and was not a good shooter," Frazier said. "But my second season, my shooting started to come around."

Jackson had a rough time shooting as a rookie but never got flustered. His work ethic told him it would come. Don't forget that favorite slogan (the one he let loose on the media even more times than he passed for assists) was: "Work hard and good things come from it." So he vowed to work hard during the offseason.

And if a summer league liberally dotted with pros and former pros is any gauge, more good things are coming. At the City College of New York Summer League in Harlem, Jackson regularly scored in the 40s all during the hot months. Is New York going to see more of an offensive explosion in Jackson's second season?

"Nah," he said. "During the season, I'm a passer. In the summer, I'm a scorer."

Jackson averaged 13.6 points as his average steadily rose last season. His numbers might not reach those totals again because the Knicks feel they came up with a certified backup in the draft in Rod Strickland. Because the Knicks were without a quality backup point guard most of the season, Jackson averaged just a shade under 40 minutes a game. That's a pretty fair way to wind up in a coronary ward before your time.

But Strickland may make Jackson even better. Last year, there was no threat around and Jackson performed beyond all expectations. Now, there's an equally hungry kid yearning for playing time, someone to actually push the incumbent.

Jackson's first-year salary was roughly $225,000 (including incentives) and that figure will soar as he makes an even bigger mark with the Knicks, who earned their first playoff bid after three years of resounding failure.

"We learned what it takes to win," he said. "This is a young team with a great nucleus and we'll be a force in time to come."

The Flea-Market All-Star Teams

By JAN HUBBARD

ALL-NASTY

Say you've just driven through the lane. You knew who was on the other team. You knew there was a good chance you were going to feel an elbow, forearm, hip, or something else designed to flatten you. You look up and the transgressor is there smiling. You don't reach out for a hand to help you up. Once guys on this team put you down, you stay there.

F—Karl Malone
F—Rick Mahorn (Capt.)
C—Akeem Olajuwon
G—Bob Hansen
G—Michael Cooper

ALL-BIG MAC

These guys think using restraint means that for lunch they eat only four burgers, two orders of large fries, fried bread, fried salad, fried apple cobbler and, if all else fails, fried plates. They lose weight sometimes, but it usually finds a way to come back.

F—Antoine Carr
F—Wayman Tisdale
C—Mel Turpin (Capt.)
G—John Bagley
G—Pearl Washington

One of Turpin's nicknames is "Turp," which of course, rhymes with burp. Must be a message there somewhere.

All-Nasty Karl Malone: In top five in scoring, rebounding.

Flea-market connisseur Jan Hubbard covers the pros for the Dallas Morning News *and writes the "NBA Beat" for* The Sporting News.

ALL-UNIVERSE

When the subject is greatness, some NBA truths are self-evident: For instance, The All-Universe team is so good that only four players are needed. And they're obvious.

F—Larry Bird
C—Akeem Olajuwon
G-F—Magic Johnson (Capt.)
G—Michael Jordan

None need any explanation, but a note about the Magic Man, otherwise known as Johnson & Johnson. He is unquestionably the most accomplished point guard-power forward in history. This guy runs an offense better than anyone ever has, and in two of the Lakers' playoff series triumphs last season he guarded the center on defense.

ALL-SOBBING

When a foul is called, the only thing these guys lack is tears in their eyes. They may fall to the floor, jump up and down like a two-year-old who is protesting the loss of his favorite toy, or simply whine in some sort of creative, yet embarrassing manner. The usual response from fans is, "Grow up."

F—Charles Barkley
F—Mark Aguirre
C—Bill Laimbeer
G—Danny Ainge
G—Isiah Thomas
Coach—Doug Moe

Denver's Moe is calm until the first referee's whistle blows, then he starts running up and down the sidelines, waving his arms and jumping up and down like someone stole his favorite set of golf clubs. Calm down, Doug.

ALL-RIM RATTLING

We're not talking about the Darryl Dawkins Memorial Dunk Squad, also known as the "Chocolate Thunder Flyin', Robinzine

Denver's Doug Moe: Coach All-Sobbers.

Cryin', Teeth-Shakin', Glass Breakin', Rump Roastin', Bun Toastin', Wham, Bam, Glass Breaker I Am Jam," Unit.

We're referring to the gentlemen who approach the free-throw line with all the subtlety of an elephant in heat. Check these free-throw percentages from last season.

F—Dennis Rodman (Capt.), .535
F—Walter Berry, .600
C—Manute Bol, .531
G—Vinnie Johnson, .677
G—Pearl Washington, .698

Some players may have worse percentages, but few look worse at the free-throw line than our All-RR team, especially Rodman, who makes free-throw shooting look as difficult as brain surgery. Special mention must go, however, to Larry Smith, who played in only 20 games for Golden State last season because of injuries. Mr. Mean went to the free-throw line 27 times and made 11 for a singular .407 percentage. With Bol coming to Golden State this season, the newest organization in Oakland Coliseum will be Battered Rims.

ALL-AT&T

Players qualify for this team by originating their shots from different time zones. They are also hoping that the NBA eventually will approve a four-point shot from 35 feet and who knows? Maybe all that practice time they spent shooting from midcourt will eventually pay off.

F—Larry Bird
F—Chuck Person
C—Bill Laimbeer
G—Danny Ainge
G—Michael Adams (Capt.)

Adams attempted 379 three-pointers last season and Ainge attempted 357, but the most amazing statistic may be that Laimbeer, a center and the 10th-leading rebounder in the NBA, attempted 39 three-pointers. Of course, Bill gets most of his rebounds on defense. On offense, he's too busy jacking it up.

ALL-OVERRATED

Anyone else tired of hearing that Isiah Thomas is a Hall of Fame player? He has great skills, he's tough, he'll play with pain, but he's a sporadic shooter who overestimates his ability to control games and it seems like every time he shoots a lot, his team loses. Good? Yes. Great? Sometimes. Hall of Fame? Absolutely not. But then, he's joined on this team by pretty good company.

F—Tom Chambers
F—Rodney McCray
C—Kareem Abdul-Jabbar
G—Isiah Thomas (Capt.)
G—Sleepy Floyd

Kareem is, perhaps, the greatest player ever, but as the playoffs showed last season, now that he has passed 40 he is only minimally effective at the highest level. Has anyone done more for the reputations of Utah's Mark Eaton and Dallas' James Donaldson than Abdul-Jabbar, who was either outplayed or played to a standstill by both?

ALL-CEILING

A genuine concern among this group is that when jumping, there is serious fear of concussion from bumping heads on the rafters. As a man versed in the finest basketball cliches once said, these suckers can jump out of the gym.

F—Dominique Wilkins
F—Jerome Kersey
C—Ralph Sampson
G—Michael Jordan (Capt.)
G—Spud Webb

Sampson, of course, has the added advantage (disadvantage?) of being closer to the ceiling when he jumps since he is 7-4. But there is no height discrimination here. If a guy can hit the ceiling, he's on the team.

He may be 5-6, but Spud Webb makes All-Ceiling.

ALL-STAR WARS

No one can stop our All-Universe team, of course, but if we had to try to develop an exotic defensive system, these players would comprise our starters.

F—Kevin McHale
F—Sam Perkins
C—Mark Eaton
G—Michael Cooper (Capt.)
G—Bob Hansen

Special mention goes to the Detroit team consisting of Dennis Rodman, John Salley, Rick Mahorn, Isiah Thomas and Joe Dumars. That was an artistic defensive unit during last year's playoffs.

All-Star Wars Mark Eaton: Power on the boards.

ALL-PENICILLIN

No, these guys aren't sick, although their shot selection, at times, can make their coaches ill. Still, that's not the point. It's just that these guys have never met a shot they wouldn't take, no matter how diseased it was.

F—Dominique Wilkins (Capt.)
F—Mark Aguirre
C—Akeem Olajuwon
G—Isiah Thomas
G—Jeff Malone

O.K., not a bad lot. Olajuwon actually makes better than 50 percent of his, but then he never met a pass that he liked. One thing these guys have in common is a basic lack of understanding of three, common English basketball words. "GIVE IT UP."

ALL-SPLINTER

Or, we could call them the Princes of Darkness. Or, perhaps, the Huddle Ornaments. These were the guys begging to be taken by expansion teams. Talk about hidden. They played a combined 592 minutes last season.

F—Ron Moore
F—John Stroeder
C—Chuck Nevitt (Capt.)
G—Bill Wennington
G—Greg Dreiling

The sharp fans will know that all five of the above are centers, but their minutes were so minute that we had to find a place for them. Four pale in comparison to the incomparable Nevitt. Check these totals. Since 1982, he has been waived five times and signed to two 10-day contracts. In his five years, he has played respective totals of 64, 59, 126, 267 and 63 minutes. For the whole season. Stroeder was noticed and selected by Miami in the expansion draft. Congratulations, John. Sitting in Miami should be more fun than sitting in Milwaukee.

ALL-BUSINESS

Lakers' coach Pat Riley likes to talk about being focused. He'd like this team. When these guys take the floor, their are no histrionics and no diversions. They come to play the game. Seriously. Intently.

F—Alex English
F—Buck Williams (Capt.)
C—Brad Daugherty
G—Rolando Blackman
G—John Stockton
Coach—Pat Riley

What? No Bird or Magic? Relax, they are already in the All-Business Hall of Fame.

ALL-FUTURE ALL-STAR

They have not made the NBA All-Star team yet (of course, Danny Manning is a Clipper rookie), but they will, some as early as this year. And then they will make it next year, and the year after that and the year after that and maybe forever.

F—Roy Tarpley
F—Danny Manning
C—Kevin Duckworth
G—Ron Harper
G—John Stockton (Capt.)

Perhaps the only question mark is Duckworth, who went from anonymity to stardom in only his second season at Portland. It will be fascinating to see if he can keep it up, especially when David Robinson shows up in San Antonio. Who will be better?

ALL-THUD

The worst thing that happened to these guys occurred when television hooked up microphones to backboards. And then when our men shot, you kept hearing, "Thud, thud, thud."

F—Joe Barry Carroll
F—Reggie Williams (Capt.)
C—Mark Eaton
G—Trent Tucker
G—Glenn Rivers

Williams has played only one year, but he had a .356 shooting percentage, so we couldn't keep him off the team. Fortunately, Carroll played forward when he was traded to Houston, so we could fit him in. But before Carroll went to Italy in 1984, he had a career .499 shooting percentage. Since then he has shot .460. Suppose it was the pasta?

ALL-UNDERRATED

These guys are really good, and several of them may eventually be great. But you don't often hear them mentioned among the best. You'll be hearing more.

F—Otis Thorpe
F—Thurl Bailey
C—Dan Schayes
G—Joe Dumars (Capt.)
G—Terry Porter

Schayes, perhaps, is the surprise on this list. His development has been quiet and overshadowed by the presence of Denver teammates Alex English and Fat Lever. But he has become an accomplished offensive player whose best years are still ahead.

ALL-WORLD BASKETBALL LEAGUE

Know about this league? It's for players 6-4 and under. If there ever were any big bucks involved, someone should put this team together.

F—Mark Price, 6-1
F—Tyrone Bogues, 5-3
C—Spud Webb, 5-6 (Capt.)
G—Michael Adams, 5-10
G—John Stockton, 6-0

Good Luck
Miami & Charlotte!

By DAVID KAPLAN

Welcome to the NBA 1988-89 season of expansion as the Charlotte Hornets and Miami Heat try to answer that age-old expansionist question, "Can anyone here play this game?"

And judging by the history of newly assembled teams, and by the two rosters born from the scraps of 23 established NBA teams, the Hornets and Heat shouldn't expect miracles.

"I'd be very surprised if either team won 15 games," said Jim Spanarkel, who was the scoring leader of the 1980–81 expansionist Dallas Mavericks, who won exactly 15 games in their initial season. This year marks the introduction of the first expansion teams since the Mavericks.

Its entry mark not withstanding, Dallas is considered a model of successful expansion teams—sound management, stability, building through the draft, improved records in their first four years and now regularly packed houses.

But the road to NBA respectability is too often littered with the casualties of impatience. Witness the New Orleans Jazz, who were born in 1974-75 and died four years later before being reincarnated in Utah. The expansion Jazz built enormous fan interest immediately by trading for LSU legend Pete Maravich. But then they began a series of rash moves such as firing coach Scotty Robertson 15 games into the season and acquiring an over-the-hill Gail Goodrich from the Lakers for two No. 1 picks—one of whom turned out to be Magic Johnson.

"That trade just buried the franchise," said Hot Rod Hundley, who has broadcast Jazz games since their inception. "When we moved to Utah in 1980, the new management looked at the Jazz as an expansion team and built them back up patiently. No more panic."

Don't think the lesson hasn't been lost on Charlotte and

David Kaplan of the New York Daily News *is contributing editor of the Handbook.*

Record of NBA Coaches With Expansion Teams

The first-year record is in parentheses.

Johnny Kerr, Chicago, 1966-68, (33-48) . . . 62-101
Al Bianchi, Seattle, 1967-69, (23-59) . . . 53-111
Jack McMahon, San Diego, 1967-69, (15-67) . . . 61-129
Johnny Kerr, Phoenix, 1968-70, (16-66) . . . 31-89
Larry Costello, Milwaukee, 1968-76, (27-55) . . . 409-264
Dolph Schayes, Buffalo, 1970-71, (22-60) . . . 22-61
Rolland Todd, Portland, 1970-72, (29-53) . . . 41-97
Bill Fitch, Cleveland, 1970-79, (15-67) . . . 304–434
Scotty Robertson, New Orleans, 1974, (1-14) . . . 1-14
Elgin Baylor, New Orleans, 1974, (0-1) . . . 0-1
Bill van Breda Kolff, New Orleans, 1974-77, (22-44) . . . 74-100
Dick Motta, Dallas, 1980-87, (15-67) . . . 267-307

Miami executives. But as Al Bianchi, the Knick GM who has 32 years' experience as a player, coach, scout and general manager, notes, "No matter what anyone says in June, July and August, the attitude changes. For whatever reason, people lose that willpower to stick with the plan. I've seen it many times."

Like in Cleveland. Upon taking over the expansionist Cavaliers in 1970-71, coach Bill Fitch warned, "Just remember, the name is Fitch, not Houdini"—and he proved it when the club got off to an 3-37 start. But after Fitch helped the Cavs become an over-.500 team several years later, the success apparently became all too heady for new owner Ted Stepien. In his zeal for a championship, Stepien nearly destroyed the franchise by going through 40 players, six coaches and $11 million in salaries in 2½ years. In 1980, NBA commissioner Larry O'Brien took the unprecedented step of forbidding Stepien to engage in any more trades because the team—which would set an all-time losing mark of 24 straight defeats—was becoming an embarrassment to the league.

Enough of the horror stories. Charlotte and Miami can look with hope at the 1966-67 Chicago Bulls, who made the playoffs in their first year and whose 33 victories are the most ever for an expansion team. Or the Milwaukee Bucks, who entered the league in the 1968-69 season and won the championship three years later. Their master stroke? Winning a coin flip with fellow expansionist Phoenix in 1969 for the right to draft Lew Alcindor (a.k.a. Kareem-Abdul Jabbar) rather than Neal Walk. And then there's the tales of success in the Great Northwest. The Portland Trail Blazers, who began play in 1970-71, won the NBA title six seasons later, and the Seattle SuperSonics, who started in 1967-68, won in 1978-79.

But with today's watering-down of talent in the NBA, rapid success will unlikely occur in Charlotte and Miami. Especially since two more expansion teams, Minnesota and Orlando, join the league next season. The Heat and Hornets will serve up fringe players desperately trying to survive in the league and Walter Mitty-type tryouts in the relentless search to uncover talent. Spanarkel, now a Nets' broadcaster and a four-year survivor with the early Mavs, remembers the constant shuffle and newly signed teammates with taped names on their uniform. "There's nothing as insecure," he said, "as the insecurity of being on an expansion team."

And Bianchi, an assistant coach with the expansion Bulls and later the first-ever coach for the Sonics, recalls a tryout in Chicago that drew some 200 hopefuls from every walk of basketball experience. How to narrow the field? Johnny Kerr, the Bulls' coach, told Bianchi to get the aspirants "to count off by twos, and send all the twos home."

Charlotte and Miami will spend their first year laying the foundation until their future draft picks reap dividends. "We're all agreed, we're going to go young," said Miami director of personnel Stu Inman, who held a similar post with the expansionist Trail Blazers. "We're trying to find two or three vets who are character people who'll set the tone for this franchise. That's why guys like Scott Hastings and Jon Sundvold are more important to us as persons than they are basketball players."

That may be true, but how do you market patience where the sports fans have a sophisticated mentality?

"We're initially selling the great teams and players of the NBA," said Inman, whose sentiments are echoed by Billy Cunningham, who has had a storied career as player, coach, broadcaster and is now part-owner of the Heat.

"We're hoping that the fans get caught up in the progress of our young players, that they'll be fun to watch even though outmanned and overmatched," added Inman. "To tell it any other way would be deceitful."

1988 EXPANSION DRAFT

The Charlotte Hornets and Miami Heat selected 23 players in the NBA Expansion Draft last June.

In trades that followed the selections, Miami, after taking Darnell Valentine from the LA Clippers, traded the veteran guard to Cleveland for a second-round draft pick in either 1990 or 1992, and, after selecting Fred Roberts from Boston, traded the veteran forward to Milwaukee for a 1988 second-round draft pick. Charlotte, meanwhile, traded Mike Brown—its pick from Chicago—to Utah for forward Kelly Tripucka.

Charlotte subsequently traded Bernard Thompson, its selection from Phoenix, to Houston for Robert Reid.

The following are the players in order of selection:

MIAMI

1. Arvid Kramer (Dallas)
3. Billy Thompson (LA Lakers)
5. Fred Roberts (Boston)
7. Scott Hastings (Atlanta)
9. Jon Sundvold (San Antonio)
11. Kevin Williams (Seattle)
13. Hansi Gnad (Philadelphia)
15. Darnell Valentine (LA Clippers)
17. Dwayne Washington (New Jersey)
19. Andre Turner (Houston)
21. Conner Henry Sacramento)
23. John Stroeder (Milwaukee)

CHARLOTTE

2. Dell Curry (Cleveland)
4. Dave Hoppen (Golden State)
6. Tyrone Bogues (Washington)
8. Mike Brown (Chicago)
10. Rickey Green (Utah)
12. Michael Holton (Portland)
14. Michael Brooks (Denver)
16. Bernard Thompson (Phoenix)
18. Ralph Lewis (Detroit)
20. Clinton Wheeler (Indiana)
22. Sedric Toney (New York)

Who is he?
Billy Cunningham as a young 76er in the mid-60s. Now a part-owner of the Heat, he's involved with the building of a franchise. If only he could play again...

INSIDE THE NBA

By FRAN BLINEBURY and FRED KERBER

PREDICTED ORDER OF FINISH

ATLANTIC	CENTRAL	MIDWEST	PACIFIC
Boston	Detroit	Dallas	LA Lakers
New York	Chicago	Houston	Portland
Philadelphia	Atlanta	Utah	Seattle
New Jersey	Cleveland	Denver	LA Clippers
Washington	Indiana	San Antonio	Phoenix
Charlotte	Milwaukee	Miami	Sacramento
			Golden State

EASTERN CONFERENCE: Boston
WESTERN CONFERENCE: LA Lakers
CHAMPION: LA Lakers

There were guarantees. There were footprints of greatness. There were footnotes in history. There were shadows cast over an entire league.

And finally, after 19 years, there was a repeat. Back-to-back titles. The Los Angeles Lakers put their purple and gold stamp on the decade of the 1980s and permanently claimed it as their own with five championships.

Mission accomplished. Well done, Lakers.

But wait a minute. Unless our calendar has gone haywire, the 1980s aren't over yet. Magic Johnson will be coming back, James Worthy will still have his goggles in place, Byron Scott is

Fran Blinebury, a veteran follower of the pro hoops, is a sports columnist for the Houston Chronicle *and Fred Kerber covers the NBA for the* New York Daily News. *Kerber wrote the Eastern Conference, Blinebury the Western Conference and the introduction after consultation with his counterpart.*

becoming more of a big-time player and old Mount Baldy will once more be in there throwing in a few of those timely—and timeless—skyhooks. So maybe it's not time to say the king is dead.

Oh, times definitely are changing in the NBA and the established old-line powers can't expect to cakewalk through the regular season and the early rounds of the playoffs anymore. Just look at how hard the Lakers had to work last spring to sneak past Utah, Dallas and Detroit in successive seven-game series.

There are youthful contenders all over the place.

In the West, you would have to start out with Dallas, which made it to the Western Conference Finals for the first time in history. The only mistake the Mavs might be making is deciding to stand with a pat hand. You've got to like the size and the potential of the Utah Jazz and be wary of a Seattle club that has gone through a shake-up.

In the East, the Pistons have got to be kicking themselves for letting a title slip away that was within one minute of their grasp in Game 6. But they have also got to figure that they are taking this road to the championship one step at a time. The challenges will come from Atlanta, reinforced by the addition of Moses Malone, and from New York, where Patrick Ewing and Mark Jackson now have some rebounding help in the person of Charles Oakley. What Oakley's departure will mean to his good buddy Michael Jordan will have to be seen. And oh yes, there are those Boston Celtics, aging, infirmed and very vulnerable. Yes, that is just what they'd like you to think.

This is the dawning of a new age in the NBA. It is a league filled with parity and with new faces in the expansion cities of Charlotte and Miami.

But this is also a league of tradition. So just when you thought it was time to turn the page for a new chapter, don't be surprised if, in the end, not much has changed.

Make it one last hurrah for the Celtics and one more championship for the Lakers.

Three in a row? Yes. Remember, this is still the 1980s—their decade.

DALLAS MAVERICKS

TEAM DIRECTORY: Pres.: Donald Carter; Chief Oper. Off./ GM: Norm Sonju; VP Basketball Oper.: Rick Sund; Dir. Communications: Allen Stone; Dir. Media Services: Kevin Sullivan; Coach: John MacLeod; Asst. Coaches: Rich Adubato, Garfield Heard. Arena: Reunion Arena (17,007). Colors: Blue and green.

SCOUTING REPORT

SHOOTING: They say that good shooting is contagious. Well, if that's the case, you've got to wonder if it's possible for a shooting slump to rub off from player to player, too. Because it is certainly a curious phenomenon when one of the traditionally best-shooting teams in the NBA falls into the bottom half of the league without significant personnel changes. But that's what happened to the Mavericks last season as the club just seemed to lose much of its edge. That is, until playoff time, when the magic touch returned and they were able to advance to the Western Conference finals.

Still, shooting is not a problem in Big D. Not when you consider that a "slump" for big James Donaldson means him dropping to .558 on the year, actually the worst figure of his eight-year pro career. NBA Sixth Man of the Year Roy Tarpley is another who converts the high-percentage inside shot and has accurate range away from the basket. Toss in the old faithfuls like Mark Aguirre, Rolando Blackman, Brad Davis and the rest and this is a club that will beat you if given the open shot.

The biggest drop-offs last season were Derek Harper (.459) and Detlef Schrempf (.456) and you've got to figure they'll come back around.

PLAYMAKING: This is an area where you've got to think the Mavs should be as good in frontline talent as any team in the league by now. After all, Harper is in his fifth season and has been playoff-tested enough to be a capable offensive quarterback. But something happened to Harper last season. Some say he missed the constant prodding, challenging and driving of former coach Dick Motta. If that's the case, then coach John MacLeod is just going to have to break out a whip in practice this year. Harper has got to lead the way for this club to challenge for the title. Davis has been a decent backup, but is beginning to show his age and there is no one yet to take over the backup role.

DEFENSE: If you're looking for one area where this team has taken the necessary strides to be considered an honest-to-good-

Rolando Blackman, at 6-6, is one of NBA's best off-guards.

ness threat to the Lakers in the Western Conference, it's in defense. Since the addition of assistant coach Richie Adubato a couple of years back, the Mavs are no longer content to try to outscore their opponents. Adubato has got them jumping into the passing lanes, denying the ball inside and playing solid, all-around defense.

Of course, it hasn't hurt at all to have jumping-jack Tarpley blossom as a legitimate shot-blocking force in the middle. Blackman can take on the burden of checking any guard in the league. But the guy who makes or breaks them as a great defensive team is Donaldson. When the big fella is active in the middle, he can make Dallas very imposing. See his work last year in the playoffs

MAVERICK ROSTER

No.	Veteran	Pos.	Ht.	Wt.	Age	Yrs. Pro	College
24	Mark Aguirre	F	6-6	221	28	7	DePaul
4	Steve Alford	G	6-2	185	23	1	Indiana
33	Uwe Blab	C	7-1	251	26	3	Indiana
22	Rolando Blackman	G	6-6	200	29	7	Kansas State
15	Brad Davis	G	6-3	180	32	10	Maryland
40	James Donaldson	C	7-2	278	31	8	Washington State
21	Jim Farmer	G	6-4	203	24	1	Alabama
12	Derek Harper	G	6-4	206	27	5	Illinois
44	Sam Perkins	F-C	6-9	250	27	4	North Carolina
32	Detlef Schrempf	F	6-10	222	25	3	Washington
42	Roy Tarpley	C-F	7-0	247	23	2	Michigan
23	Bill Wennington	C	7-0	247	23	3	St. John's

Rd.	Top Rookies	Sel. No.	Pos.	Ht.	Wt.	College
2	Morlon Wiley	46	G	6-4	192	Long Beach State
2	Jose Vargas	49	F-C	6-10	228	Louisiana State
3	Jerry Johnson	70	G	5-11	165	Florida Southern

and then look at the films of the year before when he was injured and the Mavs were whipped in the first round.

REBOUNDING: You think of rebounds and you think of the bruising likes of the Celtics or the hustling Lakers or a team like Chicago when they had Charles Oakley up front. But you could win a lot of bar bets by telling people that last season the Mavs were the best rebounding club in the NBA. Quietly, efficiently, steadily. It's not so much that they have one awesome board man—and they do in Tarpley. They're blessed with a flock of people—Sam Perkins, Donaldson, Schrempf, even Aguirre when the mood strikes—who can go and get the ball off the glass. They are very underrated here.

OUTLOOK: For several seasons now, everybody's image of the Mavs has been that of a nice little team that can't quite cut it in the playoffs. Maybe last spring was a fluke, but until they fall flat on their faces, you've got to think their work, especially against the Lakers in the conference finals, served notice that Dallas has to be taken seriously. As long as they've got Tarpley, they'll be in every game. Dallas in the NBA Finals? Sounds improbable, but this could be the year.

MAVERICK PROFILES

ROLANDO BLACKMAN 29 6-6 200   Guard

Forget Mark Aguirre, this is the real team leader...Voted Mavs' captain the last four seasons running...Can do it all...Shoots from the perimeter, goes strong to the basket and will never give up on defense...One of the underrated guards in the NBA...Born Feb. 26, 1959, in Panama City, Panama... Was raised in Brooklyn, N.Y., where his first love was soccer...Took up basketball as a teen and was cut from his school team in seventh, eighth and ninth grades...Wonder what the coach would say now...Made his college mark at Kansas State and then made the U.S. Olympic team in 1980... Maybe it's good the U.S. boycotted Moscow that year, because this guy was not officially a U.S. citizen and could have cost his team a disqualification in the medal competition...A minor knee injury probably cost him his third straight spot on the Western Conference All-Star team...Was great in the 1987 game in Seattle and should have been named MVP...A class act all the way...Dallas made him the No. 9 pick overall in the 1981 draft, with the selection obtained from Denver in the Kiki Vandeweghe trade.

Year	Team	G	FG	FG Pct.	FT	FT Pct.	Reb.	Ast.	TP	Avg.
1981-82	Dallas	82	439	.513	212	.768	254	105	1091	13.3
1982-83	Dallas	75	513	.492	297	.780	293	185	1326	17.7
1983-84	Dallas	81	721	.546	372	.812	373	288	1815	22.4
1984-85	Dallas	81	625	.508	342	.828	300	289	1598	19.7
1985-86	Dallas	82	677	.514	404	.836	291	271	1762	21.5
1986-87	Dallas	80	626	.495	419	.884	278	266	1676	21.0
1987-88	Dallas	71	497	.473	331	.873	246	262	1325	18.7
	Totals	552	4098	.507	2377	.830	2035	1666	10593	19.2

MARK AGUIRRE 28 6-6 221   Forward

Feast or famine...A great scorer, but perhaps more trouble than he's worth...First-year coach John MacLeod did everything possible to smooth the path for him last season, but he still managed to pout and complain every so often...Wound up as the NBA's eighth-best scorer in the regular season, but was often on the bench down the stretch during some of team's biggest playoff wins...Pumped in 27 points in the fourth quarter of Game 4 vs. Houston to clinch that series...Born

Dec. 10, 1959, in Chicago . . . Is good buddies with Magic Johnson and Isiah Thomas, but lacks their charisma . . . Known as much for his pouty expressions as the quick release on his jumper . . . As a small forward, he's a great post-up player . . . The No. 1 pick in the 1981 draft, ahead of Isiah and Buck Williams . . . Always folded up in the big tournament games at DePaul . . . Frequently the object of trade talks, but is a personal favorite of owner Donald Carter.

Year	Team	G	FG	FG Pct.	FT	FT Pct.	Reb.	Ast.	TP	Avg.
1981-82	Dallas	51	381	.465	168	.680	249	164	955	18.7
1982-83	Dallas	81	767	.483	429	.728	508	332	1979	24.4
1983-84	Dallas	79	925	.524	465	.749	469	358	2330	29.5
1984-85	Dallas	80	794	.506	440	.759	477	249	2055	25.7
1985-86	Dallas	74	668	.503	318	.705	445	339	1670	22.6
1986-87	Dallas	80	787	.495	429	.770	427	254	2056	25.7
1987-88	Dallas	77	746	.475	388	.770	434	278	1932	25.1
	Totals	522	5068	.495	2637	.743	3009	1974	12977	24.9

JAMES DONALDSON 31 7-2 278   Center

Big James . . . The barometer . . . When he comes in and plays tough and aggressive, this club is tough to beat . . . Too often this gentle giant off the court does not want to throw his weight around in games . . . Gave aging Kareem Abdul-Jabbar all he could handle in the Western Conference finals in the games at Dallas . . . In Game 7, he sat on the bench for a long stretch of the second half and it may have cost the Mavs a chance of upsetting LA . . . Born Aug. 16, 1957, in Meachem, England . . . Was a clumsy kid and used to be embarrassed to even be seen in shorts . . . A project who began to blossom in college in Washington State . . . Seattle plucked him out of the fourth round in the 1979 draft . . . Shipped to San Diego in 1983 and became the missing link in the middle for Dallas in 1986 when traded from the Clippers for Kurt Nimphius . . . Started 81 of 82 games last season . . . Incredibly, his .558 shooting percentage was the second lowest of his eight-year career.

Year	Team	G	FG	FG Pct.	FT	FT Pct.	Reb.	Ast.	TP	Avg.
1980-81	Seattle	68	129	.542	101	.594	309	42	359	5.3
1981-82	Seattle	82	255	.609	151	.629	490	51	661	8.1
1982-83	Seattle	82	289	.583	150	.688	501	97	728	8.9
1983-84	San Diego	82	360	.596	249	.761	649	90	969	11.8
1984-85	L.A. Clippers	82	351	.637	227	.749	668	48	929	11.3
1985-86	LAC-Dal.	83	256	.558	204	.803	795	96	716	8.6
1986-87	Dallas	82	311	.586	267	.812	973	63	889	10.8
1987-88	Dallas	81	212	.558	147	.778	755	66	571	7.0
	Totals	642	2163	.588	1496	.737	5140	553	5822	9.1

DEREK HARPER 27 6-4 206   Guard

Took a step backward last season... He's one player who benefitted from the iron-fisted approach of former coach Dick Motta and he may have missed that daily driving under John MacLeod... You could count on his solid outside shot until he dropped to .459 last season ... Should actually be better at running the club... Had a big, big 34-point performance to beat the Lakers in Game 4 of the Western Conference finals ... Defense suffered last year, too. Dropped out of the top 10 in steals... Born Oct. 13, 1961, in New York City, but grew up in West Palm Beach, Fla.... Relatively unheralded coming out of college at Illinois, where he played with Phoenix' Eddie Johnson ... A tough competitor who will probably bear down and bounce back to have a good season.

Year	Team	G	FG	FG Pct.	FT	FT Pct.	Reb.	Ast.	TP	Avg.
1983-84	Dallas............	82	200	.443	66	.673	172	239	469	5.7
1984-85	Dallas............	82	329	.520	111	.721	199	360	790	9.6
1985-86	Dallas............	79	390	.534	171	.747	226	416	963	12.2
1986-87	Dallas............	77	497	.501	160	.684	199	609	1230	16.0
1987-88	Dallas............	82	536	.459	261	.759	246	634	1393	17.0
	Totals............	402	1952	.491	769	.726	1042	2258	4845	12.1

SAM PERKINS 27 6-9 250   Forward-Center

Silent Sam... What does he do that makes him so good?... Nobody seems able to name specifics, but he does all the little fundamental things on defense and in rebounding that help good teams win consistently... Has had to live down a rap that he is a "soft" player... Born June 14, 1961, in New York City... Grew up in Brooklyn under the auspices of Herb Crossman, who became his legal guardian... An All-American under Dean Smith at North Carolina... Critics always want to pick apart things about his game, but most teams would love to have him on their roster... Plays taller than he is with a 77-inch wingspan... Seems content to sit in the background on this team and let others grab all of the headlines and glory.

Year	Team	G	FG	FG Pct.	FT	FT Pct.	Reb.	Ast.	TP	Avg.
1984-85	Dallas............	82	347	.471	200	.820	605	135	903	11.0
1985-86	Dallas............	80	458	.503	307	.814	685	153	1234	15.4
1986-87	Dallas............	80	461	.482	245	.828	616	146	1186	14.8
1987-88	Dallas............	75	394	.450	273	.822	601	118	1066	14.2
	Totals............	317	1660	.477	1025	.821	2507	552	4389	13.8

BRAD DAVIS 32 6-3 180   Guard

The Last of the Mohicans... Actually, the last of the original Mavericks... This old dog is starting to wear down, but he can still come in for spot duty and give you a solid contribution ... Will hit the medium-range shot or toss in the occasional three-point bomb... Also not afraid to go into the lane... Was one of the Mavs' best players in the first two rounds of the playoffs... Tailed off in the Lakers' series... Born Dec. 17, 1955, in Rochester, Pa.... Played college ball under Lefty Driesell at Maryland... A first-round draft pick of the Lakers as an undergrad in 1977... Was cut and had to bounce around in the CBA before getting another chance... Was playing for the Anchorage Northern Knights when the first-year expansion team Mavs gave him a second chance at the big time... He's never looked back... Coming to the end of the line and any training camp now could be his last.

Year	Team	G	FG	FG Pct.	FT	FT Pct.	Reb.	Ast.	TP	Avg.
1977-78	Los Angeles.........	33	30	.417	22	.759	35	83	82	2.5
1978-79	L.A.-Ind............	27	31	.564	16	.696	17	52	78	2.9
1979-80	Ind.-Utah..........	18	35	.556	13	.813	17	50	83	4.6
1980-81	Dallas.............	56	230	.561	163	.799	151	385	626	11.2
1981-82	Dallas.............	82	397	.515	185	.804	226	509	993	12.1
1982-83	Dallas.............	79	359	.572	186	.845	198	565	915	11.6
1983-84	Dallas.............	81	345	.530	199	.836	187	561	896	11.1
1984-85	Dallas.............	82	310	.505	158	.888	193	581	825	10.1
1985-86	Dallas.............	82	267	.532	198	.868	146	467	764	9.3
1986-87	Dallas.............	82	199	.456	147	.860	114	373	577	7.0
1987-88	Dallas.............	75	208	.501	91	.843	102	303	537	7.2
	Totals.............	697	2411	.522	1378	.838	1386	3929	6376	9.1

ROY TARPLEY 23 7-0 247   Center-Forward

Sixth-man supreme... Won the NBA honor last season as the best man in the league off the bench... He went from being a bit player in the Dallas scenario to a fire-breathing dragon and one of the cogs of the future... Admitted a problem with alcohol and cocaine early in the season and entered a drug rehabilitation center... As soon as he got out, he made the most of his second chance... Finished seventh in the league in rebounding, incredible for a reserve... He was the biggest difference in the attack that allowed the Mavs to go so deep in the playoffs... Ferocious style... Goes for every loose ball and rebound... Has an outstanding outside shot for a big man ... Will only get better... Born Nov. 22, 1964, in Detroit...

Attended the University of Michigan, where his reputation was questionable . . . Dallas got him with the No. 7 pick in the 1986 draft . . . Dallas considered trading his rights along with Mark Aguirre to the Lakers two years ago for James Worthy . . . Dallas is happy that is one deal that was never made.

Year	Team	G	FG	FG Pct.	FT	FT Pct.	Reb.	Ast.	TP	Avg.
1986-87	Dallas.............	75	233	.467	94	.676	533	52	561	7.5
1987-88	Dallas.............	81	444	.500	205	.740	959	86	1093	13.5
	Totals.............	156	677	.488	299	.719	1492	138	1654	10.6

DETLEF SCHREMPF 25 6-10 222   Forward

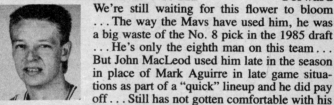

We're still waiting for this flower to bloom . . . The way the Mavs have used him, he was a big waste of the No. 8 pick in the 1985 draft . . . He's only the eighth man on this team . . . But John MacLeod used him late in the season in place of Mark Aguirre in late game situations as part of a "quick" lineup and he did pay off . . . Still has not gotten comfortable with his offense in the NBA . . . Born Jan. 21, 1963, in Leverkusen, West Germany . . . Is still a German citizen and played for his native country in the 1984 Olympic Games in Los Angeles . . . Played in all 82 regular-season games and started four . . . But missed the last four games of the LA playoff series with a bad ankle injury . . . A solid open-court player . . . At one time people compared him to Larry Bird . . . That obviously was inaccurate, but he should still be showing more.

Year	Team	G	FG	FG Pct.	FT	FT Pct.	Reb.	Ast.	TP	Avg.
1985-86	Dallas.............	64	142	.451	110	.724	198	88	397	6.2
1986-87	Dallas.............	81	265	.472	193	.742	303	161	756	9.3
1987-88	Dallas.............	82	246	.456	201	.756	279	159	698	8.5
	Totals.............	227	653	.461	504	.743	780	408	1851	8.2

BILL WENNINGTON 23 7-0 247   Center

A great cheerleader . . . Has excellent technique waving his towel from the bench . . . Now you know why we don't go to Canada to look for more basketball players . . . Now you also know why Canada didn't win a medal in the Olympics with this guy as its 1984 star . . . Born Dec. 26, 1964, in Montreal . . . Appeared in just 30 games for a total of 125 minutes all of last season . . . Can't rebound, jump, shoot or play defense . . . Other than that, he's got all the tools . . . Became a kind of cult figure in college at St. John's... On that basis, Dallas foolishly made him the No. 16 pick in the 1985 college draft... Mavs left him unprotected in the expansion draft.

Year	Team	G	FG	FG Pct.	FT	FT Pct.	Reb.	Ast.	TP	Avg.
1985-86	Dallas.............	56	72	.471	45	.726	132	21	189	3.4
1986-87	Dallas.............	58	56	.424	45	.750	129	24	157	2.7
1987-88	Dallas.............	30	25	.510	12	.632	39	4	63	2.1
	Totals.............	144	153	.458	102	.723	300	49	409	2.8

UWE BLAB 26 7-1 251 Center

They say he's a long-term project... At the rate he's progressing, he'll be ready to contribute in the league right about the time he qualifies for Social Security... A matching bookend of uselessness for the last two years with Bill Wennington on the Mavericks' bench... Born March 26, 1962, in Munich, West Germany... Arrived in U.S. to attend high school as part of an international exchange program... Bobby Knight somehow milked quality minutes from him at Indiana... If Bobby got a look at him now, he'd probably throw one of those famous folding chairs in his direction... Was left available for the expansion draft... Taken originally by the Mavs with the No. 17 pick in 1985, one spot after Bill Wennington.

Year	Team	G	FG	FG Pct.	FT	FT Pct.	Reb.	Ast.	TP	Avg.
1985-86	Dallas.............	48	44	.468	36	.537	91	17	124	2.6
1986-87	Dallas.............	30	20	.392	13	.464	36	13	53	1.8
1987-88	Dallas.............	73	58	.439	46	.708	134	35	162	2.2
	Totals.............	151	122	.440	95	.594	261	65	339	2.2

JIM FARMER 24 6-4 203 Guard

They've got hope for him in the future... Hard to say why, since he got into only 30 games and played just 157 minutes... They like his smarts and fundamentals and they will eventually need somebody to replace Brad Davis in a reserve role... Mavs liked him so much that they decided to protect him in the expansion draft... Nothing flashy, just a solid performer... Born Sept. 23, 1964, in Dothan, Ala.... Stayed at home to attend the University of Alabama... Jumped up in the eyes of the pro scouts with strong showing at the Aloha Classic.

Year	Team	G	FG	FG Pct.	FT	FT Pct.	Reb.	Ast.	TP	Avg.
1987-88	Dallas.............	30	26	.377	9	.900	18	16	61	2.0

STEVE ALFORD 23 6-2 185   Guard

Quite a change from Indiana days, when he virtually became Mr. College Basketball under Bobby Knight... He was mad at the Indiana Pacers for not drafting him... Then said he had a hit-list of teams and people he was going to pay back in the pros for passing him by ... Well, everybody's still sleeping soundly, because the hit-man played less than 200 minutes... In fact, the Mavs left him unprotected in the expansion draft and kept Jim Farmer... Born Nov. 23, 1964, in Franklin, Ind.... Named Indiana Mr. Basketball in 1983... One of the boyish heroes for the U.S. team in the 1984 Olympics... Now he's faced with reality. This is a different and tougher league and he just can't cut it as a star anymore.

Year	Team	G	FG	FG Pct.	FT	FT Pct.	Reb.	Ast.	TP	Avg.
1987-88	Dallas............	28	21	.382	16	.941	23	23	59	2.1

TOP ROOKIE

MORLON WILEY 22 6-4 192   Guard

All-PCAA during senior year at Long Beach State... Was a big scorer on a team that had its first winning season in six years... Played primarily as an off-guard in college, but scouts believe he will have to make it in the NBA as a point guard... Born Sept. 24, 1966... Has been compared to former San Antonio guard Johnny Moore... That means he'll have to work hard, but could make it... Dallas traded its first-round pick and made this guy its top selection in the No. 46 spot overall.

COACH JOHN MacLEOD: If only he talked as flashily as he

dressed... This guy looks like he stepped off the cover of Gentlemen's Quarterly, but is about as dull as a potted plant... The non-controversial personality was a welcome change after the volatile Dick Motta and he took the team to new limits in the Western Conference finals... Made the offense more balanced and cut down the individual roles of Mark Aguirre and Rolando Blackman... At times players were unhappy with the system, but nobody could argue with the results... Born Oct. 3, 1937, in New Albany, Ind.... Started out in the high-school ranks before jumping to Oklahoma and then the Phoenix Suns . . . Took Phoenix to NBA Finals in 1976 and usually had winning teams there . . . Just wore out his welcome and it was time to move on . . . He'll never be controversial or win a Mr. Personality Award, but he does get the job done . . . NBA record is 632-572.

GREATEST THREE-POINT SHOOTER

You might as well close your eyes and take a stab with your finger at any number of names on the Mavericks' roster. The problem isn't with a dearth of candidates, but with the large number of them.

In the early days of the franchise, the obvious nod belonged to the scrappy Brad Davis, who cocked his arm and let fly with threes like he was launching a rocket. Then Derek Harper came aboard and it quickly became obvious that this so-called defensive specialist could dial long range, too.

A year ago, Detlef Schrempf arrived in Dallas and made his mark, even reaching the finals of the NBA three-point Shootout before losing to Larry Bird. But last season Mark Aguirre got into the act and hit 50 three-pointers. So how can you pick just one? If we must, we'll take the guy who would probably get the call in the clutch—Harper.

ALL-TIME MAVERICK LEADERS

SEASON

Points: Mark Aguirre, 2,330, 1983-84
Assists: Derek Harper, 634, 1987-88
Rebounds: James Donaldson, 973, 1986-87

GAME

Points: Mark Aguirre, 49 vs. Philadelphia, 1/28/85
Assists: Brad Davis, 17 vs. Cleveland, 3/16/85 (OT)
Rebounds: Roy Tarpley, 24 vs. New York, 3/22/88

CAREER

Points: Mark Aguirre, 12,977, 1981-88
Assists: Brad Davis, 3,744, 1980-88
Rebounds: Mark Aguirre, 3,009, 1981-88

DENVER NUGGETS

TEAM DIRECTORY: Owner: Sidney Shlenker; Pres.-GM: Pete Babcock; Asst. to Pres.: Dan Issel; Dir. Pub. Rel.: Bill Young; Coach: Doug Moe; Asst. Coaches: Allan Bristow, Doug Moe Jr. Arena: McNichols Sports Arena (17,022). Colors: White, blue, green, yellow, red, purple and orange.

Do-it-all Fat Lever is gem of a Nugget.

SCOUTING REPORT

SHOOTING: Nobody has ever accused coach Doug Moe of marching in step with the rest of the world. So while the emphasis everywhere else is on quality, leave it to Moe to lean more on quantity to get his team to the top of the heap. You see, it doesn't really matter if you can't make half your shots as long as your club is getting off 15 to 20 more attempts at the basket per game. That's the name of the game for Denver, which beats you with a non-stop barrage of shots.

Only Danny Schayes hit at a .500 clip last season, but it didn't stop Denver from winning the Midwest Division title. Now they've added free-agent signee Walter Davis from Phoenix, who'll help some. Don't expect the Nuggets' numbers to be much higher this time around. But don't make the same mistake and write them off again.

PLAYMAKING: Another summer and another offseason of listening to Fat Lever trade rumors. What is it with this guy? He spends most of the season carrying this club on his back with tons of points and assists and rebounds, then is left out like stale bread when the playoffs are over. This time there are ignorant critics questioning his guts because he missed the last three playoff games while injured.

You might not put him on the level of Magic Johnson—who would you put at that level?—but Lever is one of the best point guards in the league and actually the only real one that the Nuggets have. Former No. 1 pick Maurice Martin has yet to exhibit enough to run the show and nobody else here— including Michael Adams—seems to have the size.

DEFENSE: Only six other NBA clubs allowed their opponents to shoot at a higher percentage than the Nuggets. All six of those clubs finished with losing records, while the Nuggets won the Midwest Division title over the much more talented Dallas Mavericks. How do you explain it? Look in the turnover category, where the Nuggets forced more than any club except the full-court pressing New York Knicks.

The Nuggets don't have an intimidating presence in the middle, so they get the job done with a bunch of scrappy bees who buzz around the perimeter and create havoc. The most hustling one of all is Bill Hanzlik, who always seems to be stepping into a passing lane to cut off an opponent's feed inside. The Nuggets are more of a bother than ants at a picnic and just as effective at getting the job done.

NUGGET ROSTER

No.	Veteran	Pos.	Ht.	Wt.	Age	Yrs. Pro	College
14	Michael Adams	G	5-11	165	25	3	Boston College
42	Wayne Cooper	C	6-10	220	32	10	New Orleans
6	Walter Davis	G	6-6	200	34	11	North Carolina
2	Alex English	F	6-7	190	34	12	South Carolina
24	Bill Hanzlik	G-F-C	6-7	200	30	8	Notre Dame
12	Lafayette Lever	G	6-3	175	28	6	Arizona State
11	Maurice Martin	G	6-6	200	24	2	St. Joseph's (Pa.)
33	Calvin Natt	F	6-6	220	31	9	NE Louisiana
41	Blair Rasmussen	C	7-0	250	25	3	Oregon
34	Danny Schayes	C	6-11	260	29	7	Syracuse
30	Jay Vincent	F	6-7	220	29	7	Michigan State

Rd.	Top Rookies	Sel. No.	Pos.	Ht.	Wt.	College
1	Jerome Lane	23	F	6-6	232	Pittsburgh
2	Todd Mitchell	43	F	6-7	215	Purdue
3	Dwight Boyd	66	G	6-4	195	Memphis State

REBOUNDING: Here it is, another season where their best board man is a 6-3 guard with a build that nobody will ever confuse with Arnold Schwarzenegger. Lever just has a knack for getting inside and getting the ball off the glass and it's a good thing, because the Nuggets might have starved for rebounds the last few years without him.

If Calvin Natt can make a successful comeback from two years of injuries, it will give them some muscle. Otherwise, they'll be counting on rookie Jerome Lane, a 6-6 rebounding machine from Pittsburgh, to help out right away.

OUTLOOK: How do you even begin to try to figure this team out? You look at the individual parts and the club doesn't look impressive. But somehow, year after year, Moe gets the most out of his talent. There has got to be something to that old axiom about keeping your players happy. Moe seems to do that better than any coach in the league and is usually rewarded with a club that puts out from October to April. Once again, they don't look like much. But if they get any help at all from rookie Lane, they'll probably wind up back in the middle of the race again.

NUGGET PROFILES

ALEX ENGLISH 34 6-7 190   Forward

Aging so gracefully, along with that gorgeous jump shot . . . Scoring average was his lowest since 1980-81, but that was more a result of overall team balance . . . Will still hit that leaning, off-balance hoop in traffic when you need it late in the game . . . Ranks 10th on the NBA all-time scoring list with 21,242 points . . . Poetry in motion on the court and a published poet off it . . . Also starred in an anti-nuclear film *The Amazing Grace and Chuck*. Played a member of the Boston Celtics . . . Born Jan. 5, 1954, in Columbia, S.C. . . . Wasn't drafted until the second round by Milwaukee in 1976 and Don Nelson made a rare mistake by not keeping him . . . Bounced to Indiana for a 1½ years and did not become a superstar until arriving in the Rockies in 1980 . . . Came in trade for George McGinnis . . . Played his college ball at South Carolina . . . Doesn't get the lion's share of publicity, but is well-compensated at $1.5 million.

Year	Team	G	FG	FG Pct.	FT	FT Pct.	Reb.	Ast.	TP	Avg.
1976-77	Milwaukee	60	132	.477	46	.767	168	25	310	5.2
1977-78	Milwaukee	82	343	.542	104	.727	395	129	790	9.6
1978-79	Indiana	81	563	.511	173	.752	655	271	1299	16.0
1979-80	Ind.-Den.	78	553	.501	210	.789	605	224	1318	16.9
1980-81	Denver	81	768	.494	390	.850	646	290	1929	23.8
1981-82	Denver	82	855	.551	372	.840	558	433	2082	25.4
1982-83	Denver	82	959	.516	406	.829	601	397	2326	28.4
1983-84	Denver	82	907	.529	352	.824	464	406	2167	26.4
1984-85	Denver	81	939	.518	383	.829	458	344	2262	27.9
1985-86	Denver	81	951	.504	511	.862	405	320	2414	29.8
1986-87	Denver	82	965	.503	411	.844	344	422	2345	28.6
1987-88	Denver	80	843	.495	314	.828	373	377	2000	25.0
	Totals	952	8778	.512	3672	.827	5672	3638	21242	22.3

LAFAYETTE LEVER 28 6-3 175   Guard

The mini-dynamo . . . For a fella who is not very big, he did so many big things for the Nuggets . . . Their second-leading scorer, top rebounder and assist man and also led the club in steals . . . After a start to his career that did not raise eyebrows, he's exploded into an all-around threat . . . Born Aug. 18, 1960, in Pine Bluff, Ark. . . . Raised in Tucson, Ariz. . . . Played at Arizona State on same team with Byron Scott, Kurt Nimphius, Sam Williams and Alton Lister. All five made it to the NBA . . . Acquired nickname "Fat" as a child, because his younger brothers and sisters could not pronounce his full name ... Missed the last three games of Denver's second-round playoff loss to Dallas with a knee injury and took some criticism for it. That was ridiculous, because he's a gamer ... Taken as the 11th pick in the 1982 draft by Portland ... Came to Denver with Calvin Natt, Wayne Cooper and two draft picks for Kiki Vandeweghe in 1984 ... Earns $457,000.

Year	Team	G	FG	FG Pct.	FT	FT Pct.	Reb.	Ast.	TP	Avg.
1982-83	Portland	81	256	.431	116	.730	225	426	633	7.8
1983-84	Portland	81	313	.447	159	.743	218	372	788	9.7
1984-85	Denver	82	424	.430	197	.770	411	613	1051	12.8
1985-86	Denver	78	468	.441	132	.725	420	584	1080	13.8
1986-87	Denver	82	643	.469	244	.782	729	654	1552	18.9
1987-88	Denver	82	643	.473	248	.785	665	639	1546	18.9
	Totals	486	2747	.452	1096	.762	2668	3288	6650	13.7

WALTER DAVIS 34 6-6 200   Guard

Near end of the line ... Announced last year that this would be his final season in the NBA, but his ailing back improved and he signed two-year contract with Nuggets as unrestricted free agent ... Plans to start a drug rehabilitation program in the Phoenix area ... His way of giving back to a city that helped him through some tough times ... Has been been in rehab twice in the last three years for substance abuse ... When he's healthy, he's one of the quickest and most dangerous off-guards in the league ... Nicknamed "Greyhound" because of his pure speed ... Also an excellent leaper ... All-time leading scorer in Suns' history ... Played entire career in Phoenix after being taken as the No. 5 pick overall in the 1977 draft ... Born Sept. 9, 1954, in Pineville, N.C. ... Starred for Dean Smith at North Carolina and was a member of 1976 U.S. Olympic team ... Had his problems, but overall is a class act.

Year	Team	G	FG	FG Pct.	FT	FT Pct.	Reb.	Ast.	TP	Avg.
1977-78	Phoenix	81	786	.526	387	.830	484	273	1959	24.2
1978-79	Phoenix	79	764	.561	340	.831	373	339	1868	23.6
1979-80	Phoenix	75	657	.563	299	.819	272	337	1613	21.5
1980-81	Phoenix	78	593	.539	209	.836	200	302	1402	18.0
1981-82	Phoenix	55	350	.523	91	.820	103	162	794	14.4
1982-83	Phoenix	80	665	.516	184	.818	197	397	1521	19.0
1983-84	Phoenix	78	652	.512	233	.863	202	429	1557	20.0
1984-85	Phoenix	23	139	.450	64	.877	35	98	345	15.0
1985-86	Phoenix	70	624	.485	257	.843	203	361	1523	21.8
1986-87	Phoenix	79	779	.514	288	.862	244	364	1867	23.6
1987-88	Phoenix	68	488	.473	205	.887	159	278	1217	17.9
	Totals	766	6497	.520	2557	.841	2472	3340	15666	20.5

MICHAEL ADAMS 25 5-11 165   Guard

The Mighty Mite . . . You see him trot onto the floor and think he's a kid who got lost on the way to a junior-high game . . . But the little man was a big hit, nailing 139 three-pointers —including a league record of at least one in 43 straight games—to provide the Nuggets with a big spark . . . You couldn't teach anybody to shoot the ball with uglier form, but he gets results . . . Can also be a pest on defense with his waterbug speed . . . Born Jan. 19, 1963, in Hartford, Conn. . . . Developed a cult following at Boston College . . . A third-round pick of Sacramento in 1985 . . . Hung on in the CBA and USBL until he got his chance under Doug Moe in Denver . . . Came with Jay Vincent in the trade for Mark Alarie and Darrell Walker.

Year	Team	G	FG	FG Pct.	FT	FT Pct.	Reb.	Ast.	TP	Avg.
1985-86	Sacramento	18	16	.364	8	.667	6	22	40	2.2
1986-87	Washington	63	160	.407	105	.847	123	244	453	7.2
1987-88	Denver	82	416	.449	166	.834	223	503	1137	13.9
	Totals	163	592	.434	279	.833	352	769	1630	10.0

DANNY SCHAYES 29 6-11 260   Center

To think they ran this guy right out of Utah . . . Called him a stiff and forced the Jazz to trade him for Rich Kelley . . . He's getting the last laugh . . . Gets better and tougher every year . . . Without his strong inside play, the Nuggets wouldn't have won the Midwest title last year in the absence of Calvin Natt and Wayne Cooper . . . Solid perimeter shooter who is really learning to throw his weight around . . . Born May 10, 1959, in Syracuse, N.Y. . . . Son of NBA Hall of Famer Dolph, was born while dad was still playing for the old Syracuse Nats . . . First-round draft choice of Utah in 1981 . . . Quickly fell out of favor with the local fans . . . Earned $425,000 last season, but became a free agent and last summer signed a contract full of nuggets— $9 million for six years.

Year	Team	G	FG	FG Pct.	FT	FT Pct.	Reb.	Ast.	TP	Avg.
1981-82	Utah	82	252	.481	140	.757	427	146	644	7.9
1982-83	Utah-Den	82	342	.457	228	.773	635	205	912	11.1
1983-84	Denver	82	183	.493	215	.790	433	91	581	7.1
1984-85	Denver	56	60	.465	79	.814	144	38	199	3.6
1985-86	Denver	80	221	.502	216	.777	439	79	658	8.2
1986-87	Denver	76	210	.519	229	.779	380	85	649	8.5
1987-88	Denver	81	361	.540	407	.836	662	106	1129	13.9
	Totals	539	1629	.496	1514	.794	3120	750	4772	8.9

JAY VINCENT 29 6-7 220   Forward

Instant offense . . . Blossomed again as an off-the-bench scorer after having a bad previous year in Washington . . . Bullets traded Vincent and Michael Adams to Denver for Darrell Walker and Mark Alarie . . . He played a big role as a reserve in the drive to the Midwest Division title . . . But a bad back forced him to miss the last three games of the playoff series with Dallas and it proved costly to the Nuggets . . . Born July 10, 1959, in Kalamazoo, Mich . . . Nicknamed "Big Daddy" and "Vacation" . . . A college teammate of Magic Johnson in high school in Lansing, Mich., and again in college at Michigan State . . . A steal on the second-round of the 1981 draft by Dallas . . . A frustrated backup to Mark Aguirre with the Mavs for five seasons . . . He's a businessman in high-tops, always has a deal cooking . . . Brother Sam plays in the backcourt with Michael Jordan in Chicago . . . Pulls down $415,000 a year.

Year	Team	G	FG	FG Pct.	FT	FT Pct.	Reb.	Ast.	TP	Avg.
1981-82	Dallas.	81	719	.497	293	.716	565	176	1732	21.4
1982-83	Dallas.	81	622	.489	269	.784	592	212	1513	18.7
1983-84	Dallas.	61	252	.435	168	.781	247	114	672	11.0
1984-85	Dallas.	79	545	.479	351	.836	704	169	1441	18.2
1985-86	Dallas.	80	442	.481	222	.810	368	180	1106	13.8
1986-87	Washington.	51	274	.447	130	.769	210	85	678	13.3
1987-88	Denver.	73	446	.466	231	.805	309	143	1124	15.4
	Totals.	506	3300	.476	1664	.786	2995	1079	8266	16.3

BILL HANZLIK 30 6-7 200   Guard-Forward-Center

The whipping boy . . . The butt of all Doug Moe's jokes . . . He's the Nugget who was most often criticized by the coach, but also the Nugget who Moe used in so many different ways . . . There is nothing pretty about his game, it's just effective . . . With a wiry body and a gritty resolve he's been able to play every position on the court in a valuable utility role. Yes, he even plays center at times . . . Born Dec. 6, 1957, in Middletown, Ohio . . . He was probably the last guy out of the Notre Dame stable that you'd have expected to have a long career . . . Seattle took him with the No. 20 pick in the 1982 draft . . . It wasn't until he was traded to Denver in 1982 (with a No. 1 draft choice for David Thompson) that he began to bloom . . . An Olympian in 1980 . . . Earns $366,666 a year . . . If you can't find him, look down on the floor where he'll probably be chasing a loose ball... Hit the driving shot to beat Dallas in Game 3 of Western Conference Semifinals.

Year	Team	G	FG	FG Pct.	FT	FT Pct.	Reb.	Ast.	TP	Avg.
1980-81	Seattle	74	138	.478	119	.793	153	111	396	5.4
1981-82	Seattle	81	167	.468	138	.784	266	183	472	5.8
1982-83	Denver	82	187	.428	125	.781	236	268	500	6.1
1983-84	Denver	80	132	.431	167	.807	205	252	434	5.4
1984-85	Denver	80	220	.421	180	.756	207	210	621	7.8
1985-86	Denver	79	331	.447	318	.785	264	316	988	12.5
1986-87	Denver	73	307	.412	316	.786	256	280	952	13.0
1987-88	Denver	77	109	.380	129	.791	171	166	350	4.5
	Totals	626	1591	.432	1492	.785	1758	1786	4713	7.5

BLAIR RASMUSSEN 25 7-0 250　　　　Center

What do you do with a 7-footer who plays as if he's allergic to the lane area?... Send him to Doug Moe's motion offense in Denver and let him shoot 18-footers... Really needs to add more of an inside presence to his game, but has fit in nicely here hitting the perimeter shot... A good shooter for a big man... Improved in each of his first three pro seasons ... Born Nov. 13, 1952, in Auburn, Ore.... An All-Pac 10 perfomer at Oregon who shot up in the draft ratings with a good showing at the Aloha Classic... At first the Nuggets were worried that they wasted a pick when they made him the No. 15 choice in 1985... A player who fits the system... Still gets chewed out a lot by the coach.

Year	Team	G	FG	FG Pct.	FT	FT Pct.	Reb.	Ast.	TP	Avg.
1985-86	Denver	48	61	.407	31	.795	97	16	153	3.2
1986-87	Denver	74	268	.470	169	.732	465	60	705	9.5
1987-88	Denver	79	435	.492	132	.776	437	78	1002	12.7
	Totals	201	764	.476	332	.755	999	154	1860	9.3

WAYNE COOPER 32 6-10 220　　　　Center

Another injury-plagued season... Chronic back problems forced him to miss 37 games and was used as just a bit player the rest of the time... He hasn't shown much in the last two seasons after earning a salary increase to $650,000... Has a decent outside shot, but is most effective when using his skills as a shot-blocker... Born Sept. 16, 1956, in Milan, Ga.... Low-profile player at New Orleans U.... Golden State was smart enough to tab him in the second round in 1978 and, as usual, the Warriors were dumb enough to let him get away...

Bounced around to Utah and Dallas and Portland before finding a Mile High home in Denver . . . Played under former coaching legend Butch van Breda Kolff in college . . . Desire is the biggest question about him now.

Year	Team	G	FG	FG Pct.	FT	FT Pct.	Reb.	Ast.	TP	Avg.
1978-79	Golden State........	65	128	.437	41	.672	280	21	297	4.6
1979-80	Golden State........	79	367	.489	136	.751	507	42	871	11.0
1980-81	Utah...............	71	213	.452	62	.689	440	52	489	6.9
1981-82	Dallas.............	76	281	.420	119	.744	550	115	682	9.0
1982-83	Portland...........	80	320	.443	135	.685	611	116	775	9.7
1983-84	Portland...........	81	304	.459	185	.804	476	76	793	9.8
1984-85	Denver.............	80	404	.472	161	.685	631	86	969	12.1
1985-86	Denver.............	78	422	.466	174	.795	610	81	1021	13.1
1986-87	Denver.............	69	235	.448	79	.725	473	68	549	8.0
1987-88	Denver.............	45	118	.437	50	.746	270	30	286	6.4
	Totals.....:......	724	2792	.456	1142	.737	4848	687	6732	9.3

CALVIN NATT 31 6-6 220   Forward

The wheels are falling off . . . Two seasons ago he missed 81 games with a torn Achilles tendon and last season he missed 55 games with a bad left knee that eventually required surgery . . . Tough guy won't give up, though, and says he's coming back . . . Powerful inside player despite lack of height . . . A scrapper, a hustler . . . Says he loves to see the blood and feel the pain from diving after loose balls . . . Whatever turns you on . . . Born Jan. 8, 1957, in Bastrop, La. . . . The son of a Baptist minister . . . Brother Kenny was briefly in the NBA and is now making a career out of the CBA . . . He's come a long way from tiny Northeastern Louisiana . . . Traded to Denver in 1984 as part of the package of Fat Lever, Wayne Cooper and two draft choices that Nuggets sent to Portland for Kiki Vandeweghe . . . Everybody should play as hard as this guy . . . Earns all of his $808,000 a year.

Year	Team	G	FG	FG Pct.	FT	FT Pct.	Reb.	Ast.	TP	Avg.
1979-80	N.J.-Port...........	78	622	.479	306	.730	691	169	1553	19.9
1980-81	Portland...........	74	395	.497	200	.707	431	159	994	13.4
1981-82	Portland...........	75	515	.576	294	.750	613	150	1326	17.7
1982-83	Portland...........	80	644	.543	339	.792	599	171	1630	20.4
1983-84	Portland...........	79	500	.583	275	.797	476	179	1277	16.2
1984-85	Denver.............	78	685	.546	447	.793	610	238	1817	23.3
1985-86	Denver.............	69	469	.504	278	.801	436	164	1218	17.7
1986-87	Denver.............	1	4	.400	2	1.000	5	2	10	10.0
1987-88	Denver.............	27	102	.490	54	.740	96	47	258	9.6
	Totals.............	561	3936	.530	2195	.769	3957	1279	10083	18.0

Alex English should hit 23,000-point mark this season.

TOP ROOKIE

JEROME LANE 21 6-6 232   **Forward**
Lacks height, but seems to have the desire and aggressiveness to
still be a rebounding force ... The smallest player in 26 years to

lead the NCAA Division I in rebounding . . . Born Dec. 4, 1966 . . . Denver made him its No. 1 pick out of the 23rd slot . . . Will need to develop his virtually non-existent outside game in order to make a big impression as a pro . . . An early-entry into the draft, having left Pittsburgh after his junior season . . . Will likely get a chance to inherit the enforcer job that used to belong to the ailing and aging Calvin Natt.

COACH DOUG MOE: The 1987-88 Coach of the Year . . . So what's next, Robin Williams as president or Cher as the first lady? . . . It's amazing that after all these years of having his talents undervalued, the man with the horse laugh and the great sense of humor was recognized . . . Of course, all he did was take a middle-of-the-pack team that played much of the year without Calvin Natt and won the Midwest Division title with a 53-29 record . . . His practices are short and so is his temper during games, but he gets the most out of his talent . . . Runs the motion offense that players and fans love . . . Born Sept. 21, 1938, in New York City . . . "On the streets of New York is where I learned how to curse," he said. "But I've gotten worse as I've gotten older." . . . Never takes himself or the game too seriously . . . Played under Dean Smith at North Carolina. Now calls his old boss "El Deano." . . . "Doug is the only player," says Smith, "who quit smoking when he came to college." . . . Spent five years playing in the old ABA . . . Started coaching career with San Antonio . . . When Spurs fired him, it was the Nuggets who benefited . . . Has finished his seventh full season in the Rockies . . . One of highest-paid coaches in the NBA . . . Has 522-415 record.

GREATEST THREE-POINT SHOOTER

It wasn't very long ago when this little guy was unsure whether he belonged in the NBA. But finally, in his third year of trying, Michael Adams has become one of the league's most potent weapons from long range. The 5-11 mighty mite out of Boston College spent part of one season in Sacramento and then all of his second with Washington. But it wasn't until a trade prior to the 1987-88 season that sent him and Jay Vincent from the Bullets to the Nuggets for Darrell Walker and Mark Alarie that he found his niche.

Feeling at home in coach Doug Moe's motion offense, Adams became Denver's version of an air-to-ground missile, drilling more than 135 threes and hitting at better than a .333 clip. In fact, he hit threes in the last 43 straight games of the season to set an NBA record. Along with Mike Evans, Michael Adams has made the Nuggets a threat to score from anywhere but the locker room. Now, at last, he belongs.

ALL-TIME NUGGET LEADERS

SEASON

Points: Spencer Haywood, 2,519, 1969-70
Assists: Lafayette Lever, 664, 1986-87
Rebounds: Spencer Haywood, 1,637, 1969-70

GAME

Points: David Thompson, 73 vs. Detroit, 4/9/78
Assists: Larry Brown, 23 vs. Pittsburgh, 2/20/72
Rebounds: Spencer Haywood, 31 vs. Kentucky, 11/13/69

CAREER

Points: Alex English, 18,307, 1979-88
Assists: Alex English, 3,071, 1979-88
Rebounds: Dan Issel, 6,630, 1975-85

GOLDEN STATE WARRIORS

TEAM DIRECTORY: Owner: Jim Fitzgerald; Pres.: Daniel Finnane; Dir. Player Personnel: Jack McMahon; GM-Coach: Don Nelson; Asst. Coaches: Garry St. Jean, Ed Gregory; Dir. Pub. Rel.: Cheri White. Arena: Oakland Coliseum (15,025). Colors: Gold and blue.

Warriors are rebuilt around a tower named Sampson.

SCOUTING REPORT

SHOOTING: You've got to wonder whether the Warriors could drop a basketball off the Golden Gate Bridge and be successful in hitting San Francisco Bay. Yes, the best place to stand if you don't want to get hit with a Warrior shot is right on the rim. Once again, they looked like the Gang That Couldn't Shoot Straight.

Only the LA Clippers—and they hardly qualify as a pro team —shot worse than Golden State's .468 percentage in the West last season. The figures should come up if the Warriors can benefit from a healthy season out of Ralph Sampson and get productive minutes from rookie sharpshooter Mitch Richmond. Chris Mullin is finally settling down and performing steadily. All in all, things should be looking better here. They couldn't get much worse.

PLAYMAKING: A year ago, they had a shooting guard in Sleepy Floyd running the offense to start the season. It was a tenuous situation at best. Now that Floyd is gone, new coach (and GM) Don Nelson will be relying heavily on Winston Garland and Otis Smith, a couple of unknown and unheralded types, to run the show. With all of the new faces that have come here in the last year and all of the turmoil surrounding the team, it will be imperative for one of that pair to seize control of the reins and assert himself as the leader of the offense. Otherwise, it could be another very long season.

DEFENSE: By the end of last season, the only thing easier than finding an empty seat at the Oakland Coliseum was scoring a basket on the Warriors. This was the NBA's version of Layups 'R Us. Everybody was able to take the ball inside on the Warriors. Nelson could see that from the sidelines, where he was acting as GM, and that's one of the reasons he went out and acquired 7-6 Manute Bol from Washington. Bol will, along with 7-4 Ralph Sampson, at least give the Warriors the tallest front line in the league.

The question is whether that combination—neither is an incredible hulk—can stop people from driving the lane. Nelson's forte in Milwaukee was coaching defense and he's going to have to use those skills to the utmost here.

REBOUNDING: One look at last year's numbers on the Boston Celtics will tell you that you don't have to get the most rebounds in order to be a consistent winner. But for a young and very disorganized team like the Warriors, this is where the job of pull-

WARRIOR ROSTER

No.	Veteran	Pos.	Ht.	Wt.	Age	Yrs. Pro	College
10	Manute Bol	C	7-6	225	26	3	Bridgeport
12	Winston Garland	G	6-2	170	23	1	SW Missouri State
32	Tellis Frank	F	6-10	240	23	1	Western Kentucky
11	Steve Harris	G	6-5	195	25	3	Tulsa
22	Rod Higgins	F	6-7	210	28	6	Fresno State
30	Ben McDonald	F	6-8	210	26	3	Cal-Irvine
17	Chris Mullin	G	6-7	220	25	3	St. John's
50	Ralph Sampson	C	7-4	230	28	5	Virginia
13	Larry Smith	F	6-8	225	30	8	Alcorn State
18	Otis Smith	G	6-5	210	24	2	Jacksonville
20	Terry Teagle	G	6-5	195	28	6	Baylor
4	Tony White	G	6-2	170	23	1	Tennessee
33	Jerome Whitehead	C	6-10	240	32	10	Marquette

Rd.	Top Rookies	Sel. No.	Pos.	Ht.	Wt.	College
1	Mitch Richmond	5	G	6-5	215	Kansas State
2	Keith Smart	41	G	6-2	175	Indiana

ing it all together begins. A healthy Sampson was worth nearly 11 rebounds a game for the first four years of his career in Houston. But if he can't return as a main force on the boards, the Warriors will be in trouble.

They also need a return to health—and form—of power forward Larry Smith. They need jump-shooter Tellis Frank to get inside the paint and they'll need some crashing by Richmond, who had a penchant for rebounding in college.

OUTLOOK: A year ago, they were coming off their first playoff appearance in the decade and looked like they had finally turned the corner. But GM Nelson decided he didn't like the picture, so he gutted the entire team and is now starting over with himself as coach. Nelson is putting his reputation on the line here and it may be a couple of more years before we see if he survives with it intact. The playoffs—even though eight of 13 teams qualify—are likely out of the question and just a return to semi-respectability would be an achievement.

GOLDEN STATE PROFILES

RALPH SAMPSON 28 7-4 230   Center

Starting over . . . After four-plus years on a roller-coaster in Houston, he was shipped to the Warriors with Steve Harris on Dec. 12, 1987, for Sleepy Floyd and Joe Barry Carroll . . . One of the biggest blockbusters in NBA history, the trade was prompted by his personality clashes with Rockets' coach Bill Fitch . . . Played in just 19 games with Warriors before going on injured list with knee surgery for the second straight season . . . Born July 7, 1960, in Harrisonburg, Va. . . . Has always played under the burden of extremely high expectations . . . His statistics say he is an all-star, but critics don't buy it . . . Rap is that he has never won a title in college (Virginia) or the NBA . . . Working under a new contract that paid $1.74 million last season . . . He'll be back where he belongs—in the middle—at Golden State, instead of out on the wing when he played with Akeem Olajuwon . . . Being away from Fitch will help most of all . . . He is a quality player and time will prove that . . . The No. 1 pick in the 1983 draft.

Year	Team	G	FG	FG Pct.	FT	FT Pct.	Reb.	Ast.	TP	Avg.
1983-84	Houston	82	716	.523	287	.661	913	163	1720	21.0
1984-85	Houston	82	753	.502	303	.676	853	224	1809	22.1
1985-86	Houston	79	624	.488	241	.641	879	283	1491	18.9
1986-87	Houston	43	277	.489	118	.624	372	120	672	15.6
1987-88	Hou.-G.S.	48	299	.438	149	.760	462	122	749	15.6
	Totals	334	2669	.495	1098	.668	3479	912	6441	19.3

CHRIS MULLIN 25 6-7 220   Guard

Fallen angel . . . Three years ago he was the College Player of the Year and everybody's idea of the All-American boy . . . In pros he has suffered through one contract holdout and last season entered a rehab center for an alcohol problem . . . Returned just before midseason and Warriors still have bright hopes for his future . . . Born July 30, 1963, in Brooklyn, N.Y. . . . A true gym rat . . . A real slice of the Big Apple . . . Starred at St. John's . . . The No. 7 pick in the 1985 draft . . . Earned a guaranteed $800,000 last season . . . Possesses virtually no pure speed, so has to get the job done with his smarts . . . Curiously, Warriors drafted him as a long-range bomber . . . His forte is the mid-range shot . . . Could still turn out to be a key piece in a blossoming program . . . Might have worst haircut in the NBA.

Year	Team	G	FG	FG Pct.	FT	FT Pct.	Reb.	Ast.	TP	Avg.
1985-86	Golden State........	55	287	.463	189	.896	115	105	768	14.0
1986-87	Golden State........	82	477	.514	269	.825	181	261	1242	15.1
1987-88	Golden State........	60	470	.508	239	.885	205	290	1213	20.2
	Totals............	197	1234	.499	697	.864	501	656	3223	16.4

TERRY TEAGLE 28 6-5 195   Guard

Tough to figure . . . He's an NBA seesaw, up and down . . . It looked like he had found a home in the Bay Area, but then fell out of favor with departed coach George Karl . . . Asked to be traded, but may get another chance here under new boss Don Nelson . . . Has good range on the outside shot, but tends to play well only in streaks . . . Excellent leaper . . . A good rebounder . . . Born April 10, 1960, in Broaddus, Tex. . . . Was a first-round draft choice by Houston in 1982 . . . Flopped there and went to Detroit before signing on as a free agent with Warriors in 1985 . . . Became the Southwest Conference's all-time leading scorer while at Baylor . . . Earns $350,000.

Year	Team	G	FG	FG Pct.	FT	FT Pct.	Reb.	Ast.	TP	Avg.
1982-83	Houston............	73	332	.428	87	.696	194	150	761	10.4
1983-84	Houston............	68	148	.470	37	.841	78	63	340	5.0
1984-85	Det.-G.S...........	21	74	.540	25	.714	43	14	175	8.3
1985-86	Golden State........	82	475	.496	211	.796	235	115	1165	14.2
1986-87	Golden State........	82	370	.458	182	.778	175	105	922	11.2
1987-88	Golden State........	47	248	.454	97	.802	81	61	594	12.6
	Totals............	373	1647	.465	639	.775	806	508	3957	10.6

WINSTON GARLAND 23 6-2 170   Guard

The human yo-yo . . . Warriors kept him on a string and he came right back . . . Signed as a free agent in the early part of last season . . . Played a handful of games, was cut, then re-signed about a week later . . . If he continues to work hard, the Warriors may have turned up a full-time point guard . . . Wound up starting 58 of 63 games in which he played . . . Quick and a good passer . . . Showed lots of promise . . . Born Dec. 19, 1964, in Gary, Ind. . . . Originally a second-round pick of Milwaukee in 1987 draft . . . Couldn't cut it with the Bucks . . .

Attended Southwest Missouri State... Playing for the NBA minimum $75,000 and that makes him a steal.

Year	Team	G	FG	FG Pct.	FT	FT Pct.	Reb.	Ast.	TP	Avg.
1987-88	Golden State........	67	340	.439	138	.879	227	429	831	12.4

LARRY SMITH 30 6-8 235   Forward

The Last of the Mohicans... This guy went on the injured list at the start of last season and when he came back all of his former teammates were gone... Well, almost all... Was saddened that management decided to take apart the club that made the playoffs the previous season... Returned to play in 20 games ... Born Jan. 18, 1958, in Rolling Fork, Miss.... Nicknamed Mr. Mean and you wouldn't have to ask why if he came over your back to grab an offensive rebound... One of the unheralded stars in the league... A workaholic who has an offensive range of only about three feet... Incredibly, the Warriors got him on the second round of the 1980 draft out of tiny Alcorn State... He'll still give you an honest days work and is worth every penny of his $600,000 salary.

Year	Team	G	FG	FG Pct.	FT	FT Pct.	Reb.	Ast.	TP	Avg.
1980-81	Golden State........	82	304	.512	177	.588	994	93	785	9.6
1981-82	Golden State........	74	220	.534	88	.553	813	83	528	7.1
1982-83	Golden State........	49	180	.588	53	.535	485	46	413	8.4
1983-84	Golden State........	75	244	.560	94	.560	672	72	582	7.8
1984-85	Golden State........	80	366	.530	155	.605	869	96	887	11.1
1985-86	Golden State........	77	314	.536	112	.493	856	95	740	9.6
1986-87	Golden State........	80	297	.546	113	.574	917	95	707	8.8
1987-88	Golden State........	20	58	.472	11	.407	182	25	127	6.4
	Totals.............	537	1983	.537	803	.560	5788	605	4769	8.9

MANUTE BOL 26 7-6 225   Center

World's tallest stickball bat... Traded to Warriors last summer for Dave Feitl... Paired with Ralph Sampson and you've got the tallest front court duo in history... "Manute is the greatest shot-blocker I've ever seen," said coach Don Nelson... And perhaps worst offensively skilled player... Nice guy, except around lions in native Sudan, where he once killed one with a spear... Has 907 blocks in 4,778 minutes. That's one every 5.3 minutes, or 9 per 48... Alters dozens more with superb timing and surprising grace for his ultra-gangling size... Could bust out and average four points a game if he gets proper minutes... More blocks than points each year... Has played just four years of basketball: one at University of Bridgeport, three in NBA... Born Oct. 16, 1962, in Gongrial, Sudan ... Another of Bullet GM Bob Ferry's unorthodox picks as 31st selection in 1985 draft... Will get $400,000 this season.

Year	Team	G	FG	FG Pct.	FT	FT Pct.	Reb.	Ast.	TP	Avg.
1985-86	Washington.........	80	128	.460	42	.488	477	23	298	3.7
1986-87	Washington.........	82	103	.446	45	.672	362	11	251	3.1
1987-88	Washington.........	77	75	.455	26	.531	275	13	176	2.3
	Totals.............	239	306	.454	113	.559	1114	47	725	3.0

ROD HIGGINS 28 6-7 210   Forward

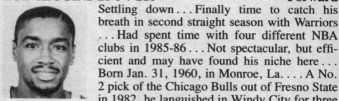

Settling down... Finally time to catch his breath in second straight season with Warriors ... Had spent time with four different NBA clubs in 1985-86... Not spectacular, but efficient and may have found his niche here... Born Jan. 31, 1960, in Monroe, La.... A No. 2 pick of the Chicago Bulls out of Fresno State in 1982, he languished in Windy City for three years... Solid defensive player who could blossom under new coach Don Nelson... Top percentage shooter on Warriors last season... He's a hard worker who makes the most of his extra long arms... Worth the price at $150,000.

Year	Team	G	FG	FG Pct.	FT	FT Pct.	Reb.	Ast.	TP	Avg.
1982-83	Chicago............	82	313	.448	209	.792	366	175	848	10.3
1983-84	Chicago............	78	193	.447	113	.724	206	116	500	6.4
1984-85	Chicago............	68	119	.441	60	.667	147	73	308	4.5
1985-86	Sea.-S.A.-N.J.-Chi...	30	39	.368	19	.704	51	24	98	3.3
1986-87	Golden State........	73	214	.519	200	.833	237	96	631	8.6
1987-88	Golden State........	68	381	.526	273	.848	293	188	1054	15.5
	Totals.............	399	1259	.476	874	.795	1300	672	3439	8.6

TELLIS FRANK 23 6-10 240   Forward

Very soft for a big man... The word coming out of college was that he was a small forward in a power forward's body and his rookie season did nothing to change that opinion... Likes to shoot from the outside but does not have a high percentage... Born April 26, 1965, in Gary, Ind.... A late bloomer who did not play much in his first two years at Western Kentucky... Warriors made him the No. 14 pick in the 1987 draft... The potential seems to be there... Remember, coach Don Nelson made decent NBA players out of Randy Breuer and Alton Lister, so there is still hope.

Year	Team	G	FG	FG Pct.	FT	FT Pct.	Reb.	Ast.	TP	Avg.
1987-88	Golden State........	78	242	.428	150	.725	330	111	634	8.1

JEROME WHITEHEAD 32 6-10 240   Center

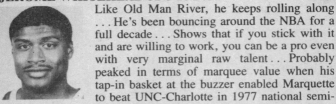

Like Old Man River, he keeps rolling along ... He's been bouncing around the NBA for a full decade ... Shows that if you stick with it and are willing to work, you can be a pro even with very marginal raw talent ... Probably peaked in terms of marquee value when his tap-in basket at the buzzer enabled Marquette to beat UNC-Charlotte in 1977 national semifinals and sent Al McGuire on way to his only NCAA title ... Born Sept. 30, 1956, in Waukegan, Ill. ... Second-round pick of Buffalo Braves in 1978 ... The son of a minister ... Devout in his work ethic and has kept his career alive through six stops with five different teams ... Has played at Golden State for last four seasons ... Longevity is main reason for his $400,000 salary ... Wears goggles like Kareem Abdul-Jabbar, but that's where similarity ends.

Year	Team	G	FG	FG Pct.	FT	FT Pct.	Reb.	Ast.	TP	Avg.
1978-79	San Diego...........	31	15	.441	8	.444	50	7	38	1.2
1979-80	S.D.-Utah........	50	58	.509	10	.286	167	24	126	2.5
1980-81	Dal.-Clev.-S.D.......	48	83	.461	28	.500	214	26	194	4.0
1981-82	San Diego...........	72	406	.559	184	.763	664	102	996	13.8
1982-83	San Diego...........	46	164	.536	72	.828	261	42	400	8.7
1983-84	San Diego...........	70	144	.490	88	.822	245	19	376	5.4
1984-85	Golden State........	79	421	.510	184	.783	622	53	1026	13.0
1985-86	Golden State........	81	126	.429	60	.619	328	19	312	3.9
1986-87	Golden State........	73	147	.450	79	.699	262	24	373	5.1
1987-88	Golden State........	72	174	.483	59	.720	321	39	407	5.7
	Totals.............	622	1738	.502	772	.721	3134	355	4248	6.8

BEN McDONALD 26 6-8 225   Forward

Classic journeyman ... Works and hustles and earns his paycheck ... Will never be a big-name star, but could be a role player on decent team ... Born July 20, 1962, in Torrance, Cal. ... Not much of an offensive threat ... Forte is defense, which earned him reputation at Cal-Irvine ... Picked by Cleveland on third round of 1984 draft ... Didn't make Cavs' roster until 1985-86 and was given a shot by former coach

George Karl in the Bay Area . . . Not your average NBA player with hobbies like drawing, painting, caligraphy and golf.

Year	Team	G	FG	FG Pct.	FT	FT Pct.	Reb.	Ast.	TP	Avg.
1985-86	Cleveland	21	28	.483	5	.625	38	9	61	2.9
1986-87	Golden State	63	164	.456	24	.632	183	84	353	5.6
1987-88	Golden State	81	258	.467	87	.784	335	138	612	7.6
	Totals	165	450	.464	116	.739	556	231	1026	6.2

STEVE HARRIS 25 6-5 195   Guard

A puzzle . . . Seems to have what it takes in terms of shooting ability to make it in this league . . . But nobody has been able to find the button to switch him on . . . Born Oct. 15, 1963, in Kansas City, Mo. . . . The all-time leading scorer at Tulsa under then-coach Nolan Richardson . . . Excellent foul shooter and good touch from mid-range when he's on . . . But he's still afraid to venture into the middle . . . Houston made him No. 19 pick in the 1985 draft . . . Went one spot behind Joe Dumars. What a difference one spot can make . . . Will go down in history as a trivia answer. He was the fourth leg in the big trade last December involving Ralph Sampson, Sleepy Floyd and Joe Barry Carroll.

Year	Team	G	FG	FG Pct.	FT	FT Pct.	Reb.	Ast.	TP	Avg.
1985-86	Houston	57	103	.442	50	.926	57	50	257	4.5
1986-87	Houston	74	251	.419	111	.854	170	100	613	8.3
1987-88	Hou.-G.S.	58	223	.458	89	.788	126	87	535	9.2
	Totals	189	577	.437	250	.842	353	237	1405	7.4

TONY WHITE 23 6-2 170   Guard

Longshot . . . If the Warriors hadn't decided to dismantle their team in the middle of the season, he might not be in the league . . . Born Feb. 15, 1965, in Charlotte, N.C. . . . Made himself a reputation as a decent player at Tennessee and was plucked by Chicago on the second round (No. 33 overall) of the 1987 draft . . . Couldn't crack the lineup of the young and charging Bulls . . . Was waived, was picked up by the Knicks but was soon waived, and signed on with Golden State on Dec. 15 . . . Reputation says he's a better shooter than his .446 of last season . . . He'll be hard-pressed to hang onto a job for another year.

Year	Team	G	FG	FG Pct.	FT	FT Pct.	Reb.	Ast.	TP	Avg.
1987-88	Chi.-N.Y.-G.S.	49	111	.446	39	.722	31	59	261	5.3

OTIS SMITH 24 6-5 210   Guard

Second-chance man... Denver thought he had ability but he never showed it outside of summer camps... Drafted on second round in 1986 by the Nuggets... Spent most of his rookie season on the injured list with knee problems... Cut by Nuggets and signed as free agent by the Warriors... Quickly impressed and now may have found a home...
Former coach George Karl said he will become a big-time star... Has outstanding leaping ability and took part in 1988 NBA Slam Dunk Contest... Born Jan. 30, 1964, in Jacksonville, Fla.... Hometown boy was four-time All-Sun Belt Conference performer at Jacksonville... If he blossoms, the Warriors will have found a gem at a flea-market price.

Year	Team	G	FG	FG Pct.	FT	FT Pct.	Reb.	Ast.	TP	Avg.
1986-87	Denver.............	28	33	.418	12	.571	34	22	78	2.8
1987-88	Den.-G.S..........	72	325	.491	178	.777	247	155	841	11.7
	Totals.............	100	358	.483	190	.760	281	177	919	9.2

TOP ROOKIE

MITCH RICHMOND 23 6-5 215   Guard

Very physical player and a great scorer... Shooting range is up to 25 feet... Also can play solid defense... The only questions are about his ball-handling... A second-team All-American at Kansas State... Born June 30, 1965... Began college career at Moberly JC in Kansas... Played on the U.S. team in the 1987 World Championships... Gets his shot off anywhere... The first guard taken in the 1988 draft... Plucked by Golden State as No. 5 overall... Will get a chance to step right in and play under Don Nelson.

COACH DON NELSON: You always knew it would happen, but you didn't know when... After spending one season in the front office as the GM, Nellie returns to the sidelines as head coach at the request of team owner Jim Fitzgerald... Replaces George Karl, who resigned late last season... Spent last season gutting a team that had made the playoffs the year before with a 42-40 record... Engineered the blockbuster trade that sent Joe Barry Carroll and Sleepy Floyd to Houston for

Ralph Sampson and Steve Harris...Also shipped out Chris Washburn to Atlanta...Spent 10 seasons as coach of the Milwaukee Bucks and led them to seven straight division titles and six straight years of more than 50 wins...Born May 15, 1940, in Muskegon, Mich....Played on five NBA title teams during career with Boston, but is still looking for first crown as coach ...An excellent game coach who gets the most out of his talent ...He'll have to in this tough assignment...Career coaching record is 540-346.

GREATEST THREE-POINT SHOOTER

They used to call him "Sonar". That was because of the way Joey Hassett could zero in on the basket from the farthest distances. He played just six seasons in the NBA, but made his mark by making the most of the relatively new three-point rule. In the first year it was introduced, Hassett bombed in 35 percent, thus assuring him a spot on rosters around the league for a couple of years. You might call him a one-trick pony, since the long-range missiles were really the only weapon in his arsenal.

He first started pumping them in for Seattle on the Sonics' championship team in 1979. Then he went to Indiana and Dallas before arriving in Golden State in 1981, where he spent 2½ seasons. Of course, Rick Barry, in his prime was probably at least as good an outside shot. But the three-point rule wasn't in effect for Barry in Golden State, so the honors must go to Hassett.

ALL-TIME WARRIOR LEADERS

SEASON

Points: Wilt Chamberlain, 4,029, 1961-62
Assists: Eric Floyd, 848, 1986-87
Rebounds: Wilt Chamberlain, 2,149, 1960-61

GAME

Points: Wilt Chamberlain, 100 vs. New York, 3/2/62
Assists: Guy Rodgers, 28 vs. St. Louis, 3/14/63
Rebounds: Wilt Chamberlain, 55 vs. Boston, 11/24/60

CAREER

Points: Wilt Chamberlain, 17,783, 1959-65
Assists: Guy Rodgers, 4,845, 1958-70
Rebounds: Nate Thurmond, 12,771, 1963-74

HOUSTON ROCKETS

TEAM DIRECTORY: Chairman: Charlie Thomas; Pres./GM: Ray Patterson; Dir. Pub. Rel.: Jay Goldberg; Coach: Don Chaney; Asst. Coaches: Carroll Dawson, Rudy Tomjanovich. Arena: The Summit (16,611). Colors: Red and gold.

SCOUTING REPORT

SHOOTING: Just about all you need to know about the Rockets' shooting ability was summed up by the final shot of Game 3 in their first-round playoff series with Dallas. Down by a point, Akeem Olajuwon had an open 15-footer from the foul line—and missed. The irony of that is Olajuwon was one of only two Houston players to connect at a 50-percent clip for the season.

This team that used to live on a steady diet of layups and dunks became unraveled and unglued as jump shooters couldn't hit jump shots and Olajuwon couldn't make every shot of the game, especially with three defenders hanging on him. Things should improve somewhat this time around.

First off, there is rookie hotshot Derrick Chievous, who has been talking up his outside game over the summer. Secondly, Sleepy Floyd, who came from Golden State in the trade for Ralph Sampson, should be able to play with a looser attitude now that coach Bill Fitch isn't around anymore to cramp his style. Also, the Rockets hope newly signed designated shooter Mike Woodson, who was a Clipper free agent, will provide a boost. Still, it's going to take a return to the days of the running game to make the rest of them look like top guns.

PLAYMAKING: Is this beginning to sound like a broken record or what? It certainly seems like the Rockets have been in need of a classic point guard ever since they moved to Houston 20 years ago. The only time that gap has been filled was when John Lucas was in town.

They brought in Floyd from the Warriors last season and said he was the answer. In truth, Floyd is just a two-guard and a creator in point guard's clothing.

The old standby here is to fall back on the talents of Allen Leavell. But that talent always was marginal and uncontrollable. If they don't get a real quarterback or Floyd doesn't step forward and take control, the Rockets will be in for another season of frustration.

Akeem the Dream is best all-around center in the game.

DEFENSE: Houston likes to point out that its opponents' field-goal percentage was second lowest in the NBA last season. Just goes to show that you can make statistics say just about anything you want. The opposition's scoring average dropped late in the season, but a lot of that was due to the slow pace the Rockets played. Floyd has never been much of a defender and Chievous is an untested rookie.

They do have All-Defensive team members Olajuwon and Rodney McCray. And journeyman swingman Bernard Thompson, who came from expansion Charlotte in the Robert Reid trade, can play defense, if nothing else. But the overall team concept badly misses the shot-blocking ability and intimidation

ROCKET ROSTER

No.	Veteran	Pos.	Ht.	Wt.	Age	Yrs. Pro	College
2	Joe Barry Carroll	C	7-0	255	30	7	Purdue
7	Lester Conner	G	6-4	188	29	5	Oregon State
11	Eric Floyd	G	6-4	178	28	6	Georgetown
1	Buck Johnson	F	6-7	190	24	2	Alabama
30	Allen Leavell	G	6-2	190	31	9	Oklahoma City
18	Cedric Maxwell	F	6-8	215	32	11	NC-Charlotte
22	Rodney McCray	F	6-8	235	27	5	Louisville
34	Akeem Olajuwon	C	7-0	250	25	4	Houston
43	Jim Petersen	F-C	6-10	236	26	4	Minnesota
10	Purvis Short	F-G	6-7	217	31	10	Jackson State
—	Bernard Thompson	G	6-6	208	26	4	Fresno State
42	Mike Woodson	G	6-5	198	30	8	Indiana

Rd.	Top Rookies	Sel. No.	Pos.	Ht.	Wt.	College
1	Derrick Chievous	16	F	6-7	195	Missouri

factor of Sampson. Joe Barry Carroll can't and doesn't want to exert himself at this end of the floor. New coach Don Chaney says he'll use full-court pressure. Why not? They definitely need something to recapture the spark.

REBOUNDING: The second-best club in the league last season at taking the ball off the glass. That number is slightly deceiving, since they depend so heavily on Olajuwon to do half of the board work by himself. Carroll, despite all the ballyhoo at the time of the trade, could not replace Sampson on the boards. McCray must bounce back from a season in which his aggressiveness in this area slipped badly. Jim Petersen is up and down and must give more support to Olajuwon every night.

OUTLOOK: Remember the Team of the '90s? Yes, that was supposed to be the Rockets. But the wheels fell off this little dynasty that couldn't and now they are stuck back in the middle of the pack, seemingly with everybody else in the NBA.

They will go as far as Olajuwon can carry them. Of course, when the playoffs roll around, Olajuwon will again have to carry that load against double- and triple-teams. They could contend for the Midwest title, but will likely finish in a runnerup spot. And there is no reason to take them very seriously as real contenders in the playoffs.

ROCKET PROFILES

AKEEM OLAJUWON 25 7-0 250 Guard

The Dream... Seems too good to be true... The most feared single force in the game today, bar none... That includes Bird and Magic... Can singlehandedly take control of a game and dominate it... Problem last season was that too often he had to dominate and do everything in order for the Rockets to win... After Ralph Sampson was traded, defenses were able to triple-team him... Led the NBA 20-20 club with six games in which he scored more than 20 points and pulled down more than 20 rebounds... Born Jan. 23, 1963, in Lagos, Nigeria... Just began to play the game 10 years ago... It's an incredible story... Walked on at University of Houston and soon took Cougars on three straight trips to the Final Four... Left school early... Rockets won coin flip and made him No. 1 pick in 1984... An all-star every year in league, a Western Conference starter for two years running... Working under a long-term contract that paid him $1.452 million last season... A bull on the inside and a light touch on the jumper... Can do it all... Ranked in top 10 in blocked shots, steals and scoring.

Year	Team	G	FG	FG Pct.	FT	FT Pct.	Reb.	Ast.	TP	Avg.
1984-85	Houston	82	677	.538	338	.613	974	111	1692	20.6
1985-86	Houston	68	625	.526	347	.645	781	137	1597	23.5
1986-87	Houston	75	677	.508	400	.702	858	220	1755	23.4
1987-88	Houston	79	712	.514	381	.695	959	163	1805	22.8
	Totals	304	2691	.521	1466	.664	3572	631	6849	22.5

ERIC (SLEEPY) FLOYD 28 6-4 178 Guard

Sleepy or Bashful?.... Something happened to this wonderfully creative one-on-one player after he arrived on the scene in Houston from Golden State... Some criticized him, but the blame probably lies with Bill Fitch's unimaginative offense that stifled his ability... Was ripped by Akeem Olajuwon for not being a true point guard... Born March 6, 1960, in Gastonia, N.C.... Carved out a nice reputation at Georgetown while playing under John Thompson... Led Hoyas in scoring four straight seasons... A disappointment in New Jersey after being selected on first round in 1982 . . . Golden State obtained him for Micheal Ray Richardson . . . Set an NBA playoff record with 29 points in fourth quarter of Game 4 of 1987 series vs. Lakers; had 51 points in the game . . . While that performance enhanced his image with public, then-coach George Karl said it was worst thing that could have happened . . . Made him more selfish . . . Came to Houston with Joe Barry Carroll in blockbuster trade for Ralph Sampson and Steve Harris on Dec. 12, 1987 . . . Jury is still out.

Year	Team	G	FG	FG Pct.	FT	FT Pct.	Reb.	Ast.	TP	Avg.
1982-83	N.J.-G.S.	76	226	.429	150	.833	137	138	612	8.1
1983-84	Golden State	77	484	.463	315	.816	271	269	1291	16.8
1984-85	Golden State	82	610	.445	336	.810	202	406	1598	19.5
1985-86	Golden State	82	510	.506	351	.796	297	746	1410	17.2
1986-87	Golden State	82	503	.488	462	.860	268	848	1541	18.8
1987-88	G.S.-Hou	77	420	.433	301	.850	296	544	1155	15.0
	Totals	476	2753	.463	1915	.828	1471	2951	7607	16.0

RODNEY McCRAY 27 6-8 235   Forward

It's obviously time to admit the big, big mistake . . . Rockets made him the No. 3 pick in the 1983 draft when they could have taken Clyde Drexler . . . Steady and solid defender and passer . . . Just doesn't have the offensive skills to justify starting at small forward on a contending team . . . Was badly exposed by Dallas in first-round playoff loss . . . Mark Aguirre burned him for most of 25 points in a single quarter in the clinching game . . . No outside shot . . . Born Aug. 29, 1961, in Mt. Vernon, N.Y. . . . Started as a freshman at Louisville when brother Scooter went down with an injury and helped Cards win NCAA title in 1980 . . . After becoming free agent, signed with Rockets for $925,000 last season. . . . Didn't play up to the dollar value of his contract. . . . Has got to produce or will go from being on the All-Underrated to the All-Overrated team.

Year	Team	G	FG	FG Pct.	FT	FT Pct.	Reb.	Ast.	TP	Avg.
1983-84	Houston	79	335	.499	182	.731	450	176	853	10.8
1984-85	Houston	82	476	.535	231	.738	539	355	1183	14.4
1985-86	Houston	82	338	.537	171	.770	520	292	847	10.3
1986-87	Houston	81	474	.552	306	.779	578	434	1170	14.4
1987-88	Houston	81	359	.481	288	.785	631	264	1006	12.4
	Totals	405	1940	.522	1178	.763	2718	1521	5059	12.5

JOE BARRY CARROLL 30 7-0 255   Center

A prolific promulgator of polysyllabic palaver . . . In other words, he likes to use big words . . . Fancies himself as a real intellectual . . . It would be nicer if he just worked harder at playing basketball . . . Long regarded as one of the game's great underachievers . . . Golden State finally tired of his act and shipped him to Houston with Sleepy Floyd on Dec. 12, 1987, for Ralph Sampson and Steve Harris . . . As usual, showed flashes of potential with Rockets . . . Let them down badly in the playoffs . . . Used to be called Joe Barely Cares . . . Maybe it should be changed to Joe Barely Can . . . Born July 24, 1958, in Pine Bluff, Ark. . . . Grew up in Denver . . . All-American at Purdue . . . Taken No. 2 in 1980 draft by Warriors . . . Golden State also could have drafted Kevin McHale . . . Pulled down $1,325,000 last season, but please, don't say he earned it.

Year	Team	G	FG	FG Pct.	FT	FT Pct.	Reb.	Ast.	TP	Avg.
1980-81	Golden State........	82	616	.491	315	.716	759	117	1547	18.9
1981-82	Golden State........	76	527	.519	235	.728	633	64	1289	17.0
1982-83	Golden State........	79	785	.513	337	.719	688	169	1907	24.1
1983-84	Golden State........	80	663	.477	313	.723	636	198	1639	20.5
1985-86	Golden State........	79	650	.463	377	.752	670	176	1677	21.2
1986-87	Golden State........	81	690	.472	340	.787	589	214	1720	21.2
1987-88	G.S.-Hou...........	77	402	.435	172	.764	489	113	976	12.7
	Totals.............	554	4333	.483	2089	.740	4464	1051	10755	19.4

PURVIS SHORT 31 6-7 217   Forward-Guard

He may be short, but he's never shy . . . This guy would shoot if he had a blindfold over his face . . . Supposed to give Houston the outside shot it needed to balance Akeem Olajuwon . . . He tailed off badly after spraining an ankle late in season and was horrible in playoff loss to Dallas . . . Some teammates say he's just a one-dimensional gunner . . . Yet that rainbow jumper sure looks pretty kissing the ceiling and swishing through the net when he's on . . . Houston used him primarily as a reserve in the backcourt last season . . . Born July 2, 1957, in Hattiesburg, Miss. . . . Played at Jackson State and was first-round choice of Golden State in 1978 . . . Played nine seasons in Bay Area before preseason trade brought him to Texas in exchange for

Dave Feitl and a first-round draft choice . . . Earned $425,000 last season . . . Quiet, unassuming . . . Poor defensive player.

Year	Team	G	FG	FG Pct.	FT	FT Pct.	Reb.	Ast.	TP	Avg.
1978-79	Golden State	75	369	.479	57	.671	347	97	795	10.6
1979-80	Golden State	62	461	.503	134	.812	316	123	1056	17.0
1980-81	Golden State	79	549	.475	168	.820	391	249	1269	16.1
1981-82	Golden State	76	456	.488	177	.801	266	209	1095	14.4
1982-83	Golden State	67	589	.487	255	.828	354	228	1437	21.4
1983-84	Golden State	79	714	.473	353	.793	438	246	1803	22.8
1984-85	Golden State	78	819	.460	501	.817	398	234	2186	28.0
1985-86	Golden State	64	633	.482	351	.865	329	237	1632	25.5
1986-87	Golden State	34	240	.479	137	.856	137	86	621	18.3
1987-88	Houston	81	474	.481	206	.858	222	162	1159	14.3
	Totals	695	5304	.479	2339	.821	3198	1871	13053	18.8

Rockets hope for Sleepy Floyd revival under new coach.

JIM PETERSEN 26 6-10 236   Forward-Center

Like a guy who's been locked out of his house without any clothes, boy, was he exposed... Pushed into a starting role after Houston traded Ralph Sampson to Golden State.... It was clear he is not cut out for 30-35 minutes a night... Will do well in reserve role, banging the boards, hitting the follow shots... Has decent range on the medium-range jumper ... Quick with a quote, has become a media favorite... Born Feb. 22, 1962, in Minneapolis... Followed Mychal Thompson and Kevin McHale at the University of Minnesota, but doesn't have their talent... Houston made an excellent third-round choice in 1984, but he must be used properly to become an asset.

Year	Team	G	FG	FG Pct.	FT	FT Pct.	Reb.	Ast.	TP	Avg.
1984-85	Houston...........	60	70	.486	50	.758	147	29	190	3.2
1985-86	Houston...........	82	196	.477	113	.706	396	85	505	6.2
1986-87	Houston...........	82	386	.511	152	.727	557	127	924	11.3
1987-88	Houston...........	69	249	.510	114	.745	436	106	613	8.9
	Totals...........	293	901	.501	429	.730	1536	347	2232	7.6

ALLEN LEAVELL 31 6-2 190   Guard

Like a bad cold, he keeps coming back... As long as he is a starter or a significant performer, then you know his club cannot contend for a championship... Quick and fast, but too wild and erratic... One of the worst ball-handlers you'll ever see... Always leaving the ball behind on the dribble... Can be a very streaky shooter who has decent range on the three-pointer... A childhood disease locked his elbow and gave him very strange-looking jump shot.... Born May 27, 1957, in Muncie, Ind.... Rockets made him a fifth-round (104th overall) draft choice in 1979 and just love to keep him around ... Why not? He played for $250,000 last year, over $100,000 less than he was earning four years ago.

Year	Team	G	FG	FG Pct.	FT	FT Pct.	Reb.	Ast.	TP	Avg.
1979-80	Houston...........	77	330	.503	180	.814	184	417	843	10.9
1980-81	Houston...........	79	258	.471	124	.832	134	384	642	8.1
1981-82	Houston...........	79	370	.467	115	.852	168	457	864	10.9
1982-83	Houston...........	79	439	.415	247	.832	195	530	1167	14.8
1983-84	Houston...........	82	349	.477	238	.832	117	459	947	11.5
1984-85	Houston...........	42	88	.421	44	772	37	102	228	5.4
1985-86	Houston...........	74	212	.463	135	.854	67	234	583	7.9
1986-87	Houston...........	53	147	.411	100	.840	61	224	412	7.8
1987-88	Houston...........	80	291	.437	218	.869	148	405	819	10.2
	Totals...........	645	2484	.453	1401	.837	1111	3212	6505	10.1

MIKE WOODSON 30 6-5 198   Guard

A former deadeye... This fella was a good percentage shooter from the outside before slumping the past two seasons in LA... He loves to sling them up... Just ask the Houston Rockets, who were victim of his best day ever (22-for-24) when he played for KC Kings back in 1983... Born March 24, 1958, in Indianapolis... Give him a medal for surviving Bobby Knight at Indiana... Calls being named Big 10 MVP in 1979 his greatest achievement... Taken No. 12 in the 1980 draft by the Knicks... Doesn't stay in one place long... He's had stops in NJ, KC and Sacramento before coming to the Clippers with Larry Drew in a deal for Derek Smith, Franklin Edwards and Junior Bridgeman in 1986... Won't stop anybody with his defense... People won't notice the lack of "D" though if he regains his shooting touch with the Rockets, with whom he signed in July as a Clipper free agent.

Year	Team	G	FG	FG Pct.	FT	FT Pct.	Reb.	Ast.	TP	Avg.
1980-81	New York...........	81	165	.442	49	.766	97	75	380	4.7
1981-82	N.J.-K.C..........	83	538	.503	221	.773	247	222	1304	15.7
1982-83	Kansas City........	81	584	.506	298	.790	248	254	1473	18.2
1983-84	Kansas City.........	71	389	.477	247	.818	175	175	1027	14.5
1984-85	Kansas City.........	78	530	.496	264	.800	198	143	1329	17.0
1985-86	Sacramento.........	81	510	.475	242	.837	226	197	1264	15.6
1986-87	L.A. Clippers........	74	494	.437	240	.828	162	196	1262	17.1
1987-88	L.A. Clippers........	80	562	.445	296	.868	190	273	1438	18.0
	Totals.............	629	3772	.475	1857	.815	1543	1535	9477	15.1

BERNARD THOMPSON 26 6-6 208   Guard

On the bubble... He'll be one of those guys who is always fighting for a job in training camp and always hanging onto his career by the end of each season... Was eighth player selected by Charlotte in expansion draft, but was traded in July for Houston's Robert Reid... Hard to believe he was actually a first-round draft choice in 1984... Portland took him with the No. 19 pick... Traded to Phoenix the following season and never averaged nine points in three seasons with the Suns... Born Aug. 30, 1962, in Phoenix... Developed reputation as a defensive specialist at Fresno State... A criminology major who wants to become a probation officer... So far his career has been a case of arrested development.

Year	Team	G	FG	FG Pct.	FT	FT Pct.	Reb.	Ast.	TP	Avg.
1984-85	Portland............	59	79	.373	39	.765	76	52	197	3.3
1985-86	Phoenix............	61	195	.489	127	.809	141	132	517	8.5
1986-87	Phoenix............	24	42	.400	27	.818	31	18	111	4.6
1987-88	Phoenix............	37	74	.465	43	.717	76	51	191	5.2
	Totals.............	181	390	.446	236	.784	324	253	1016	5.6

CEDRIC MAXWELL 32 6-8 215   Forward

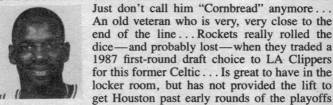

Just don't call him "Cornbread" anymore... An old veteran who is very, very close to the end of the line... Rockets really rolled the dice—and probably lost—when they traded a 1987 first-round draft choice to LA Clippers for this former Celtic... Is great to have in the locker room, but has not provided the lift to get Houston past early rounds of the playoffs ... Played for UNC-Charlotte and was a first-round pick of the Celtics in 1977... Was MVP of the NBA finals when Boston beat Houston in 1981... Played key role on 1984 Celtic title win over the Lakers... Gangly... Great inside moves... One of the best big-game players of all time... It will be a shame to see him leave the league.

Year	Team	G	FG	FG Pct.	FT	FT Pct.	Reb.	Ast.	TP	Avg.
1977-78	Boston.............	72	170	.538	188	.752	379	68	528	7.3
1978-79	Boston.............	80	472	.584	574	.802	791	228	1518	19.0
1979-80	Boston.............	80	457	.609	436	.787	704	199	1350	16.9
1980-81	Boston.............	81	441	.588	352	.782	525	219	1234	15.2
1981-82	Boston.............	78	397	.548	357	.747	499	183	1151	14.8
1982-83	Boston.............	79	331	.499	280	.812	422	186	942	11.9
1983-84	Boston.............	80	317	.532	320	.753	461	205	955	11.9
1984-85	Boston.............	57	201	.533	231	.831	242	102	633	11.1
1985-86	L.A. Clippers........	76	314	.475	447	.795	624	215	1075	14.1
1986-87	LAC-Hou............	81	253	.530	303	.775	435	197	809	10.0
1987-88	Houston............	71	80	.468	110	.769	179	60	270	3.8
	Totals.............	835	3433	.546	3598	.784	5261	1862	10465	12.5

BUCK JOHNSON 24 6-7 190   Forward

Still a mystery... After two seasons, he hasn't been given enough time consistently or a definite role to decide if he can really make it... Has a willowy body that is deceptively strong and gets off shots in traffic despite lack of great height... Does not handle the ball well enough to move into the backcourt... Born Jan. 3, 1964, in Birmingham, Ala....

Hometown boy led University of Alabama to four straight NCAA appearances . . . Played a lot in the middle in college . . . Possibly could be a force in a running game as a pro . . . Rockets called him a young Alex English. . . . That's going too far right now . . . But it's far too early to give up on him . . . Real name is Alphonso Jr.

Year	Team	G	FG	FG Pct.	FT	FT Pct.	Reb.	Ast.	TP	Avg.
1986-87	Houston	60	94	.468	40	.690	88	40	228	3.8
1987-88	Houston	70	155	.520	67	.736	168	49	378	5.4
	Totals	130	249	.499	107	.718	256	89	606	4.7

LESTER CONNER 29 6-4 188 Guard

Mr. Garbage Time . . . Signed by the Rockets last season as a free agent, he rarely played except when games were out of reach . . . Funny, friendly . . . One of the nicest guys you'll ever meet . . . But whoever told him he could play NBA basketball? . . . Has long arms that make him a good defender . . . But you wouldn't want him taking a 10-foot open jumper with your life on the line . . . Born Sept. 17, 1959, in Memphis, Tenn. . . . Grew up in Oakland as a Warrior fan . . . Drafted by the Warriors on the first round in 1982 . . . Had one decent season, 1983-84 . . . As long as he's in NBA, he'll be riding the end of the bench.

Year	Team	G	FG	FG Pct.	FT	FT Pct.	Reb.	Ast.	TP	Avg.
1982-83	Golden State	75	145	.479	79	.699	221	253	369	4.9
1983-84	Golden State	82	360	.493	186	.718	305	401	907	11.1
1984-85	Golden State	79	246	.451	144	.750	246	369	640	8.1
1985-86	Golden State	36	51	.375	40	.741	62	43	144	4.0
1987-88	Houston	52	50	.463	32	.780	38	59	132	2.5
	Totals	324	852	.467	481	.730	872	1125	2192	6.8

TOP ROOKIE

DERRICK CHIEVOUS 21 6-7 195 Forward

A big-time scorer who may have to make the switch to guard in the NBA . . . Great range on his outside shot and also possesses an excellent first step on drives to the hoop . . . Born July 3, 1967 . . . Second-team All-American in senior year at Missouri . . . Tremendous leaping ability . . . Finished career as the Tigers' all-time leading scorer . . . The rap is that he often plays out of control . . . But he's fearless and is willing to take the big shot late in a game . . . A worthwhile pick by the Rockets at No. 16 on the first round.

COACH DON CHANEY: Getting a second chance . . . Actually, this may be his real first chance at the NBA, since he was in charge of the LA Clippers and they hardly qualify as a pro team . . . Strengths are said to be his ability to communicate and get the players to play for him . . . That will be a welcome change in Houston after the five-year reign of terror under Bill Fitch . . . There are scars to be healed, players who must be taught to play together . . . The emphasis nowadays with the Rockets will be developing a sense of family . . . Also have to rebuild a team that just three years ago played in the NBA Finals and then was taken apart . . . Has spent the last two seasons as an assistant under Mike Fratello with the Atlanta Hawks . . . Born March 22, 1946, in Baton Rouge, La. . . . Starred in college at the University of Houston . . . Played on the same team with Elvin Hayes that defeated Lew Alcindor and UCLA in the celebrated showdown in the Astrodome 20 years ago . . . Nicknamed "Duck" . . . He's got a team on his hands that nearly "quacked up" last year, getting bounced out of the playoffs in the first round by Dallas . . . Challenge will be to get All-NBA center Akeem Olajuwon to channel some of his great talents into more of a team concept . . . Clipper record was 53-142.

GREATEST THREE-POINT SHOOTER

He finished his career ranked in the top 20 NBA scorers of all time. But there is no telling how many points Rick Barry would have scored if the three-point rule was in effect all through his NBA career. Barry benefited for only the last two years of his playing days, both of those with the Rockets, but he made the most of it.

He hit eight of 12 three-pointers on Feb. 9, 1980, an incredible feat of long-distance accuracy that still stands today as the single-game NBA record. Barry also still holds the Rockets' club record for season percentage with a mark of .330.

Houston has had others who have launched the bomb, most

notably John Lucas, who used it at crucial times as a devastating weapon. Mike Dunleavy made his share and Allen Leavell still likes to fire away, though he doesn't make many. But the standard by which we can still judge them all is Rick Barry. He just came along a little too early.

ALL-TIME ROCKET LEADERS

SEASON

Points: Moses Malone, 2,520, 1980-81
Assists: John Lucas, 768, 1977-78
Rebounds: Moses Malone, 1,444, 1978-79

GAME

Points: Calvin Murphy, 57 vs. New Jersey, 3/18/78
Assists: Art Williams, 22 vs. San Francisco, 2/14/70
          Art Williams, 22 vs. Phoenix, 12/28/68
Rebounds: Moses Malone, 37 vs. New Orleans, 2/9/79

CAREER

Points: Calvin Murphy, 17,949, 1970-83
Assists: Calvin Murphy, 4,402, 1970-83
Rebounds: Elvin Hayes, 6,974, 1968-72, 1981-84

LOS ANGELES CLIPPERS

TEAM DIRECTORY: Owner Donald T. Sterling: Pres.: Alan I. Rothenberg; Exec. VP/GM: Elgin Baylor; Exec. VP/Bus. Oper.: Andy Roeser; Dir. Pub. Rel.: Jack Gallagher; Coach: Gene Shue; Asst. Coach: Don Casey. Arena: Los Angeles Sports Arena (15,371). Colors: Red, white and blue.

Will top pick Danny Manning be Clipper savior?

SCOUTING REPORT

SHOOTING: You always hear these visionaries of the future talking about raising the basket to make the game more fun. Well, in the Clippers' case, you could put the fun back in the game by making the basket bigger. And maybe a little lower, too. You've got to wonder if anybody here could shoot 50 percent while sitting on the back of the rim.

Things should improve with the addition of a talented rookie crop of Danny Manning, Charles Smith and Gary Grant. But we said that last year with Reggie Williams, Joe Wolf and Ken Norman, too.

Look at poor Reggie, the former Georgetown star. He spent most of the year plagued by injuries and managed to shoot only .356 when he was in the lineup. Eventually, though, this has got to turn around. Now with Manning leading the way, the Clippers have someone they can count on for offense and maybe he can take them out of the depths of their despair.

PLAYMAKING: If only Norm Nixon would stop playing softball in the summer or taking part in training camp. The slick veteran has not played, due to injuries, in two years and he's also getting up in age. That's certainly one of the reasons the Clippers went for Grant, known as "The General" at Michigan, with the third of their first-round draft picks. They feel so good, they went and traded away Darnell Valentine.

It may be too early for them to feel cocky and it may be a risk to throw Grant right to the wolves as a rookie. But why not? This franchise is at rock bottom and has to start somewhere. Besides, if there is that much trouble running the show, then Manning can just shift into the backcourt and play point guard, too. Can't he?

DEFENSE: You know what they always say—the heart of any defense starts in the middle. And that's why you've got to be so worried about the Clippers, because they've got Benoit Benjamin in the middle and he's already shown that he doesn't have any heart. This big clod could make the difference in the Clips being just a talented kindergarten class that doesn't live up to its ability or a team that actually creeps into the playoffs.

Smith, the rookie, said it best: "We've got to find a way to get Benoit motivated." Good luck. The rest of the picture here is really shaping up. Manning can guard forwards; Norman came on strong at the end of last year. Grant was a proven defensive stopper in college and Williams, despite his rookie problems, can

CLIPPER ROSTER

No.	Veteran	Pos.	Ht.	Wt.	Age	Yrs. Pro	College
00	Benoit Benjamin	C	7-0	245	23	3	Creighton
15	Steve Burtt	G	6-2	185	25	2	Iona
20	Quintin Dailey	G	6-3	190	27	6	San Francisco
22	Larry Drew	G	6-2	190	30	8	Missouri
32	Greg Kite	C	6-11	255	27	5	Brigham Young
10	Norm Nixon	G	6-2	175	33	11	Duquesne
33	Ken Norman	F	6-8	215	24	1	Illinois
31	Eric White	F	6-8	210	22	1	Pepperdine
34	Reggie Williams	G-F	6-7	180	24	1	Georgetown
24	Joe Wolf	C-F	6-11	230	23	1	North Carolina

Rd.	Top Rookies	Sel. No.	Pos.	Ht.	Wt.	College
1	Danny Manning	1	F	6-10	230	Kansas
1	Charles Smith	3	F	6-10	230	Pittsburgh
1	Gary Grant	15	G	6-2	195	Michigan
2	Tom Garrick	45	G	6-1	197	Rhode Island
3	Robert Lock	51	F-C	6-10	235	Kentucky

play this end of the floor. It all comes down to Benoit. Which means this might be where it all comes down.

REBOUNDING: You've at least got to like the guts of any team that staggers in with the worst record in the league, then goes out and trades away the NBA's leading rebounder, Michael Cage. What the Clippers are saying is they think they've got enough big, fresh and active bodies to go to the glass and get the ball. You know what? They might be right.

OUTLOOK: They came up with Manning in the lottery and claimed two other quality rookies in Smith and Grant on the first round of the draft. That was a big enough bonanza to rid coach Gene Shue of a few gray hairs, if he wasn't already using shoe polish on his head. This is about the millionth time we've said this, but the Clips would seem to finally have acquired enough young talent to turn things around and start heading in the right direction.

But then again, knowing the Clips, we won't expect to see them in the playoffs until they actually get there. Nevertheless, don't be surprised if in a couple of years, Jack Nicholson becomes a regular at the Sports Arena rather than the Forum.

CLIPPER PROFILES

NORM NIXON 33 6-2 175   Guard

Will he ever be healthy again?... He's missed the last two full seasons with severe knee injuries that required surgery... Injured two years ago in a summer softball game... Last season he went down on the last practice of training camp... Now getting up in years to be returning from such a long layoff... Born Oct. 11, 1955, in Macon, Ga.... His shooting percentage has never been exceptionally high, but he'll take and make the big shots... Trademark is that lean-to-one-side jumper... Good ball-handler who can run the break... Played at Duquesne and was a first-round pick of the Lakers in 1977, but taken after Brad Davis... Played on champion Laker teams in 1980 and 1982... Shipped to SD Clippers in 1983 for Swen Nater and the rights to Byron Scott... Wife is actress Debbie Allen... He's slick and he's cool.

Year	Team	G	FG	FG Pct.	FT	FT Pct.	Reb.	Ast.	TP	Avg.
1977-78	Los Angeles	81	496	.497	115	.714	239	553	1107	13.7
1978-79	Los Angeles	82	623	.542	158	.775	231	737	1404	17.1
1979-80	Los Angeles	82	624	.516	197	.779	229	642	1446	17.6
1980-81	Los Angeles	79	576	.476	196	.778	232	696	1350	17.1
1981-82	Los Angeles	82	628	.493	181	.808	176	652	1440	17.6
1982-83	Los Angeles	79	533	.475	125	.744	205	566	1191	15.1
1983-84	San Diego	82	587	.462	206	.760	203	914	1391	17.0
1984-85	L.A. Clippers	81	596	.465	170	.780	218	711	1395	17.2
1985-86	L.A. Clippers	67	403	.438	131	.809	180	576	979	14.6
1986-87	L.A. Clippers					Injured				
1987-88	L.A. Clippers					Injured				
	Totals	715	5066	.485	1479	.773	1913	6047	11703	16.4

REGGIE WILLIAMS 24 6-7 180   Guard-Forward

Hardly an auspicious debut... Spent majority of the season on the injured list... Took part in just 35 games... Was out for much of the first half with a strained left knee, then went back to the sidelines on March 19 with a strained right knee... The question is whether playing with a bad team like the Clippers dragged him down... Shot just 35 percent from the field when he was healthy... Born March 5, 1964, in Baltimore... A tenacious defender and solid scorer in four years at Georgetown under John Thompson . . . Big East Player of the Year in 1987 . . . Fourth player selected in the 1987 draft . . . Don't give up on him after one bad year . . . All indications are that he can be a star.

Year	Team	G	FG	FG Pct.	FT	FT Pct.	Reb.	Ast.	TP	Avg.
1987-88	L.A. Clippers	35	152	.356	48	.727	118	58	365	10.4

BENOIT BENJAMIN 23 7-0 245   Center

Sometimes you get the feeling that you'd be better off with the Statue of Liberty playing center . . . A classic case of a young guy squandering a potentially great career . . . At this point you can't even compare him to Darryl Dawkins, he's been that disappointing . . . Has all of the tools, but none of the discipline . . . A healthy dose of common sense wouldn't hurt either . . . Born Nov. 22, 1964, in Monroe, La. . . . Made a big splash at Creighton, while playing for former Knick great Willis Reed . . . Even Reed didn't think he was ready for the NBA, but the Clippers still made him the No. 3 pick in the 1985 draft . . . They've been regretting it ever since . . . Real first name is Lenard . . . He'll be around for years because he's tall, but will make a career out of getting coaches fired.

Year	Team	G	FG	FG Pct.	FT	FT Pct.	Reb.	Ast.	TP	Avg.
1985-86	L.A. Clippers	79	324	.490	229	.746	600	79	878	11.1
1986-87	L.A. Clippers	72	320	.449	188	.715	586	135	828	11.5
1987-88	L.A. Clippers	66	340	.491	180	.706	530	172	860	13.0
	Totals	217	984	.476	597	.724	1716	386	2566	11.8

QUINTIN DAILEY 27 6-3 190   Guard

Another reclamation project . . . The Q . . . Formerly known as San Quintin in some circles due to his run-ins with the law and two trips to a drug rehab center . . . Showed signs of straightening out last season and finished on a high note . . . Averaged 15.5 points while playing just 18.9 minutes a game during the month of February and provided a real spark off the bench . . . Born Jan. 22, 1961, in Baltimore . . . Starred at the University of San Francisco . . . Chicago made him No. 7 overall pick in the 1982 draft and he was nothing but a bad character there for four seasons . . . Clippers signed him as a free agent on Dec. 12, 1986... It could still pay off... Has good range and is a player—if he keeps his head on straight.

Year	Team	G	FG	FG Pct.	FT	FT Pct.	Reb.	Ast.	TP	Avg.
1982-83	Chicago............	76	470	.466	206	.730	260	280	1151	15.1
1983-84	Chicago............	82	583	.474	321	.811	235	254	1491	18.2
1984-85	Chicago............	79	525	.473	205	.817	208	191	1262	16.0
1985-86	Chicago............	35	203	.432	163	.823	68	67	569	16.3
1986-87	L.A. Clippers........	49	200	.407	119	.768	83	79	520	10.6
1987-88	L.A. Clippers........	67	328	.434	243	.776	154	109	901	13.4
	Totals.............	388	2309	.456	1257	.788	1008	980	5894	15.2

LARRY DREW 30 6-2 190   Guard

Living in the past... More accurately, living off one great season... He's parlayed the 1982-83 campaign when he played for the KC Kings into a $600,000 a year contract and hasn't been worth much more than a plugged nickel ever since... He's got the speed... But his shooting is sporadic and his defense is nonexistent... Born April 2, 1958, in Kansas City, Kan... Taken as the No. 17 pick in the 1980 draft by Detroit... Shipped to KC in 1981 for a pair of second-round draft choices... Moved west with the Kings for one season and then was traded south with Mike Woodson for Derek Smith, Franklin Edwards and Junior Bridgeman—a deal that benefited neither team.

Year	Team	G	FG	FG Pct.	FT	FT Pct.	Reb.	Ast.	TP	Avg.
1980-81	Detroit.............	76	197	.407	106	.797	120	249	504	6.6
1981-82	Kansas City.........	81	358	.473	150	.794	149	419	874	10.8
1982-83	Kansas City.........	75	599	.492	310	.820	207	610	1510	20.1
1983-84	Kansas City.........	73	474	.462	243	.776	146	558	1194	16.4
1984-85	Kansas City.........	72	457	.501	154	.794	164	484	1075	14.9
1985-86	Sacramento.........	75	376	.485	128	.795	125	338	890	11.9
1986-87	L.A. Clippers........	60	295	.432	139	.837	103	326	741	12.4
1987-88	L.A. Clippers........	74	328	.456	83	.769	119	383	765	10.3
	Totals.............	586	3084	.469	1313	.800	1133	3367	7553	12.9

KEN NORMAN 24 6-8 215   Forward

A late bloomer... Maybe he needed to gain confidence against the pros or maybe he just had to get his feet wet... But after a disappointing start, he was making consistent contributions by the end of the season... One of three first-round draft choices by the Clippers in 1987 and the only one who stayed healthy for the whole year... Born Sept. 5, 1964, in

LOS ANGELES LAKERS

TEAM DIRECTORY: Owner: Jerry Buss; Pres.: Bill Sharman; GM: Jerry West; Dir. Pub. Rel.: Josh Rosenfeld; Coach: Pat Riley; Asst. Coaches: Bill Bertka, Randy Pfund. Arena: The Forum (17,505). Colors: Royal purple and gold.

SCOUTING REPORT

SHOOTING: If they ever decided to pool their vast resources and open a franchise business, it will be called "Hoops 'R Us."

James Worthy's MVP heroics keyed championship repeat.

The most basic part of this game is putting the ball into the basket and these guys do it about as well as any team in the league. Hey, do you think that has something to do with their winning back-to-back championships? Funny thing is their main man, Magic Johnson, is the only member of the frontline stars not to shoot better than 50 percent last season. No matter, he slumped off to a mere .492.

The rest were right there in top form—Kareem Abdul-Jabbar (.532), James Worthy (.531), Byron Scott (.527), Mychal Thompson (.512) and A.C. Green (.503). The only one to have a major shooting slump was Michael Cooper (in the playoffs), but he snapped out just in time to get fitted for another championship ring. And now the Lakers have added Net free agent Orlando Woolridge for added depth in the frontcourt.

PLAYMAKING: He is the yardstick, the barometer, whatever you want to use to measure the best point guards who ever played the game. It may sound like heresy, but Magic has been around long enough now and won enough championships to finally be considered better even than the immortal Oscar Robertson. As long as those creaky knees, wracked with tendinitis, hold up, and as long as his interest in the game remains at a fever pitch, the offense is in good hands.

But he can't run the show forever. Coach Pat Riley has talked of shifting him to forward so he'll take less of a beating. Perhaps that's why the Lakers went out and drafted Notre Dame's David Rivers in the first round of the draft. Many are skeptical of Rivers' size and his ability as a true point guard. But who better to gamble than the Lakers? After all, they still have Magic.

DEFENSE: Yes sir, they play that here, too. But mostly only when it's really necessary, because all of those glitzy legs are getting up there in years. Kareem no longer intimidates anybody coming into the middle. Yet the Lakers, led by Magic, are still capable of keeping the heat on out around the perimeter and using their 1-3-1 trap in spots to be very effective in the big games.

The biggest problem these days is that their aging lineup has made them vulnerable to what used to be their own most formidable weapon—the fastbreak. If you can get the ball off the boards and down the floor, it's possible to run on the Lakers and score with relative ease.

REBOUNDING: No rebounds, no rings. That was Riley's slogan from a few years back to spur his team on to one of its five championships in the 1980s. Well, they don't rebound as fero-

LAKER ROSTER

No.	Veteran	Pos.	Ht.	Wt.	Age	Yrs. Pro	College
33	Kareem Abdul-Jabbar	C	7-2	267	41	19	UCLA
19	Tony Campbell	G	6-7	215	26	4	Ohio State
21	Michael Cooper	G	6-7	176	32	10	New Mexico
45	A.C. Green	F	6-9	224	25	3	Oregon State
32	Magic Johnson	G	6-9	220	29	9	Michigan State
3	Jeff Lamp	G-F	6-6	205	29	5	Virginia
1	Wes Matthews	G	6-1	170	29	8	Wisconsin
4	Byron Scott	G	6-4	193	27	5	Arizona State
52	Mike Smrek	C	7-0	263	26	3	Canisius
43	Mychal Thompson	C	6-10	235	33	10	Minnesota
12	Milt Wagner	G	6-5	185	25	1	Louisville
0	Orlando Woolridge	F	6-9	215	28	7	Notre Dame
42	James Worthy	F	6-9	225	27	6	North Carolina

Rd.	Top Rookies	Sel. No.	Pos.	Ht.	Wt.	College
1	David Rivers	25	G	6-0	180	Notre Dame

ciously anymore, but they are still adding rings to their fingers. Abdul-Jabbar is virtually non-existent on the glass these days and the real dirty work has to be done by Worthy and Magic and Thompson and Green. Kurt Rambis now has a new lease in Charlotte.

Green could and should be the big board man in the Lakers' future. Last season he was up and down, but he'll have to be consistent on the glass in order for them to maintain their level this time around.

OUTLOOK: Is it time for them to slip over the hill down in the mass of mediocrity that lives in the middle of the NBA? Well, you've got to think those same worn old legs can't carry them forever. Kareem is a liability, Worthy had bad wheels and Magic and Cooper have a lot of miles on them. One solution may be to shift Magic to forward and let Rivers run the offense and take even more advantage of the offensive skills of young horses like Green and Scott.

Despite the playoff struggles against Dallas and Utah last spring, there is no monstrous threat to LA in the Western Conference out there. So they're getting old. So they're getting tired. But when the Finals roll around again, don't be too surprised if the Lakers find a way to get back in there one more time.

LAKER PROFILES

EARVIN (MAGIC) JOHNSON 29 6-9 220   Guard

A winner . . . That's the best way to describe this guy who can do it all . . . People try to pick apart little things in his game, but all he does is win . . . Through nine pro seasons, he's won five NBA titles and been in the Finals seven times . . . The undisputed leader of the Lakers, who dragged them through three straight seven-game playoff series en route to the title over Detroit . . . Should have been the MVP of the Finals . . . Starts the break, finishes the break, shoots, passes, rebounds and inspires . . . Born Aug. 14, 1959, in Lansing, Mich. . . . Won a state title in high school, led Michigan State to the NCAA title in 1979 and took Lakers to NBA crown in rookie season . . . Missed 10 games late in the season with a severe groin injury, but came back and hobbled down the stretch . . . Makes $2.5 million a year and worth every cent . . . There is Magic and there is Larry Bird and nobody else is in their class.

Year	Team	G	FG	FG Pct.	FT	FT Pct.	Reb.	Ast.	TP	Avg.
1979-80	Los Angeles.	77	503	.530	374	.810	596	563	1387	18.0
1980-81	Los Angeles.	37	312	.532	171	.760	320	317	798	21.6
1981-82	Los Angeles.	78	556	.537	329	.760	751	743	1447	18.6
1982-83	Los Angeles.	79	511	.548	304	.800	683	829	1326	16.8
1983-84	Los Angeles.	67	441	.565	290	.810	491	875	1178	17.6
1984-85	L.A. Lakers.	77	504	.561	391	.843	476	968	1406	18.3
1985-86	L.A. Lakers.	72	483	.526	378	.871	426	907	1354	18.8
1986-87	L.A. Lakers.	80	683	.522	535	.848	504	977	1909	23.9
1987-88	L.A. Lakers.	72	490	.492	417	.853	449	858	1408	19.6
	Totals.	639	4483	.533	3189	.823	4696	7037	12213	19.1

JAMES WORTHY 27 6-9 225   Forward

The Laker barometer . . . When he's on top of this game, the club is just about unbeatable. When he struggles, they all struggle . . . Makes that much of a difference . . . Finals MVP, he was brilliant with 36 points and a triple-double in the Game 7 win over Detroit that gave the Lakers another championship . . . Was virtually unstoppable at home in the Forum in the series . . . Not particularly impressive in the regular season due to chronic tendinitis in both knees . . . Was unable to practice for most of the year . . . That caused his numbers to dip . . . They are worried about his health in the future . . . Born Feb. 27, 1961, in Gastonia, N.C. . . . Played with Michael Jordan on the North Carolina team that gave Dean Smith his only NCAA title . . .

When fit, has an incredible first step to the hoop...Strong moves and can be a good offensive rebounder...Has adopted the Kareem Abdul-Jabbar sky goggles on the floor...Came to LA as the No. 1 pick overall in the 1982 draft, obtained from Cleveland for Don Ford...Earned $1.1 million last season.

Year	Team	G	FG	FG Pct.	FT	FT Pct.	Reb.	Ast.	TP	Avg.
1982-83	Los Angeles.........	77	447	.579	138	.624	399	132	1033	13.4
1983-84	Los Angeles.........	82	495	.556	195	.759	515	207	1185	14.5
1984-85	L.A. Lakers.........	80	610	.572	190	.776	511	201	1410	17.6
1985-86	L.A. Lakers.........	75	629	.579	242	.771	387	201	1560	20.0
1986-87	L.A. Lakers.........	82	651	.539	292	.751	466	226	1594	19.4
1987-88	L.A. Lakers.........	75	617	.531	242	.796	374	209	1478	19.7
	Totals.............	471	3449	.558	1299	.751	2652	1176	8200	17.4

BYRON SCOTT 27 6-4 193　　　　　　　　Guard

Hard to read...Has long had the reputation of just being along for the ride in big games...But he led the Lakers in scoring during the regular season and critics eased up...Then he was up and down again in the playoffs and you still wonder...When he's got his game going, can be a devastating weapon from the perimeter...Good three-point range...Born March 28, 1961, in Ogden, Utah, but grew up in Inglewood, Cal., just down the street from the Forum...Starred for three years at Arizona State...Left school early and was top pick of the San Diego Clippers...Lakers got him and Swen Nater for Norm Nixon and Eddie Jordan before his rookie year began...New contract will pay him more than $1 million a year, but he really hasn't proven that he's worth it.

Year	Team	G	FG	FG Pct.	FT	FT Pct.	Reb.	Ast.	TP	Avg.
1983-84	Los Angeles.........	74	334	.484	112	.806	164	177	788	10.6
1984-85	L.A. Lakers.........	81	541	.539	187	.820	210	244	1295	16.0
1985-86	L.A. Lakers.........	76	507	.513	138	.784	189	164	1174	15.4
1986-87	L.A. Lakers.........	82	554	.489	224	.892	286	281	1397	17.0
1987-88	L.A. Lakers.........	81	710	.527	272	.858	333	335	1754	21.7
	Totals.............	394	2646	.512	933	.840	1182	1201	6408	16.3

KAREEM ABDUL-JABBAR 41 7-2 267　　　　Center

Yoda...He looks like a tall version of that Star Wars character with his shaved head nowadays...Way past his prime and should be watching the playoffs from home on TV...Playing now for the money—$3 million a year—having been swindled out of a fortune by a former agent...Can't perform consistently any more...He was the reason that teams like Utah and Dallas with Mark Eaton and James Donaldson were able to take the Lakers to the limit in the playoffs . . . Scored only four points in the Game 7 clincher over Detroit . . . But his two free throws in the final seconds provided the margin of victory in Game 6 . . . He's won six MVP awards and six NBA titles in his 19-year career . . . The all time leading scorer, holds almost every longevity record you can think of . . . Born April 16, 1947, in New York as Lewis Ferdinand Alcindor . . . No. 1 draft choice of Milwaukee in 1969, led the Bucks to the title in 1971 . . . Traded to LA in 1975 with Walt Wesley for Elmore Smith, Brian Winters, David Meyers and Junior Bridgeman . . . Says this is his final season . . . Has said that before.

Year	Team	G	FG	FG Pct.	FT	FT Pct.	Reb.	Ast.	TP	Avg.
1969-70	Milwaukee	82	938	.518	485	.653	1190	337	2361	28.8
1970-71	Milwaukee	82	1063	.577	470	.690	1311	272	2596	31.7
1971-72	Milwaukee	81	1159	.574	504	.689	1346	370	2822	34.8
1972-73	Milwaukee	76	982	.554	328	.713	1224	379	2292	30.2
1973-74	Milwaukee	81	948	.539	295	.702	1178	386	2191	27.0
1974-75	Milwaukee	65	812	.513	325	.763	912	264	1949	30.0
1975-76	Los Angeles	82	914	.529	447	.703	1383	413	2275	27.7
1976-77	Los Angeles	82	888	.579	376	.701	1091	319	2152	26.2
1977-78	Los Angeles	62	663	.550	274	.783	801	269	1600	25.8
1978-79	Los Angeles	80	777	.577	349	.736	1025	431	1903	23.8
1979-80	Los Angeles	82	835	.604	364	.765	886	371	2034	24.8
1980-81	Los Angeles	80	836	.574	423	.766	821	272	2095	26.2
1981-82	Los Angeles	76	753	.579	312	.706	659	225	1818	23.9
1982-83	Los Angeles	79	722	.588	278	.749	592	200	1722	21.8
1983-84	Los Angeles	80	716	.578	285	.723	587	211	1717	21.5
1984-85	L.A. Lakers	79	723	.599	289	.732	622	249	1735	22.0
1985-86	L.A. Lakers	79	755	.564	336	.765	478	280	1846	23.4
1986-87	L.A. Lakers	78	560	.564	245	.714	523	203	1366	17.5
1987-88	L.A. Lakers	80	480	.532	205	.762	478	135	1165	14.6
	Totals	1486	15524	.561	6590	.721	17106	5586	37639	25.3

A.C. GREEN 25 6-9 224 Forward

Those initials could mean "Always Crashing," because that's what he does on the boards . . . Actually the initials don't stand for anything. His real name is just A.C. . . . The Lakers think he is a star of the future with the ability to run, power inside and even shoot from the wings . . . Inconsistency has held him back . . . Started the first three quarters of the season, until coach Pat Riley benched him in favor of Kurt Rambis . . . Came back to start in the playoffs and his work inside did pay off in several big Laker wins . . . Must get better on defense though . . . Born Oct. 10, 1963, in Portland, Ore. . . . A quiet star at Oregon State . . . Lakers got a steal on the 23rd pick in the 1985 draft . . . Strong religious beliefs . . . Says he wants to be a minister when playing career is through...That shouldn't be for a long time...Earned $218,000 last season.

Year	Team	G	FG	FG Pct.	FT	FT Pct.	Reb.	Ast.	TP	Avg.
1985-86	L.A. Lakers	82	209	.539	102	.611	381	54	521	6.4
1986-87	L.A. Lakers	79	316	.538	220	.780	615	84	852	10.8
1987-88	L.A. Lakers	82	322	.503	293	.773	710	93	937	11.4
	Totals	243	847	.524	615	.743	1706	231	2310	9.5

MICHAEL COOPER 32 6-7 176   Guard

A tough season...Everything was fine until he crashed into the scorer's table and injured his foot in a February game at Dallas... Was then in and out of the lineup—missing 21 games—and never regained his form... Suffered through a miserable slump in the playoffs...Made just three of his first 27 shots in the Finals vs. Detroit before coming alive with a decent performance in Game 7...He's getting up there in age and can't quite do the high-flying act of old anymore...Born April 15, 1956, in Los Angeles...Another Laker steal in the draft...They got him from the 60th position in the 1978 draft out of New Mexico...Has been a vital part of five championship teams in the 1980s...Excellent three-point threat, usually...One of the best defenders in the league...Larry Bird says he's the toughest to play against...Earns $676,000.

Year	Team	G	FG	FG Pct.	FT	FT Pct.	Reb.	Ast.	TP	Avg.
1978-79	Los Angeles	3	3	.500	0	.000	0	0	6	2.0
1979-80	Los Angeles	82	303	.524	111	.776	229	221	722	8.8
1980-81	Los Angeles	81	321	.491	117	.785	336	232	763	9.4
1981-82	Los Angeles	76	383	.517	139	.813	269	230	907	11.9
1982-83	Los Angeles	82	266	.535	102	.785	274	315	639	7.8
1983-84	Los Angeles	82	273	.497	155	.838	262	482	739	9.0
1984-85	L.A. Lakers	82	276	.465	115	.865	255	429	702	8.6
1985-86	L.A. Lakers	82	274	.452	147	.865	244	466	758	9.2
1986-87	L.A. Lakers	82	322	.438	126	.851	254	373	859	10.5
1987-88	L.A. Lakers	61	189	.392	97	.858	228	289	532	8.7
	Totals	713	2610	.480	1109	.826	2351	3137	6627	9.3

MYCHAL THOMPSON 33 6-10 235   Center

Two years in LA, two rings...What more could a veteran player want...Wasn't as much of an aid in the drive for the title last year as his game fell off during the playoffs ...Able to spell the aging Kareem Abdul-Jabbar for long stretches...They want him to rebound and score the inside points...Shaky on the medium-range shot...A perennial member of the All-Interview team... Always quick with a joke or a great line... Born Jan. 30, 1955, in Nassau, Bahamas... Says he'll return one day to be prime minister... Made a reputation in college at Minnesota, then drafted on the first round by Portland in 1978... The first foreign-born player to be a No. 1 pick overall in the NBA... A fixture with the Blazers until 1986 when he was shipped to San Antonio for Larry Krystkowiak and Steve Johnson... Didn't play a full season in Texas before Lakers got him in a steal, sending Frank Brickowski, Petur Gudmundsson and a pair of draft picks to the Spurs... Pulls down $712,000 a year.

Year	Team	G	FG	FG Pct.	FT	FT Pct.	Reb.	Ast.	TP	Avg.
1978-79	Portland..........	73	460	.490	154	.572	604	176	1074	14.7
1979-80	Portland..........					Injured				
1980-81	Portland..........	79	569	.494	207	.641	686	284	1345	17.0
1981-82	Portland..........	79	681	.523	280	.628	921	319	1642	20.8
1982-83	Portland..........	80	505	.489	249	.621	753	380	1259	15.7
1983-84	Portland..........	79	487	.524	266	.667	688	308	1240	15.7
1984-85	Portland..........	79	572	.515	307	.684	618	205	1451	18.4
1985-86	Portland..........	82	503	.498	198	.641	608	176	1204	14.7
1986-87	S.A.-LAL..........	82	359	.450	219	.737	412	115	938	11.4
1987-88	L.A. Lakers........	80	370	.512	185	.634	489	66	925	11.6
	Totals.............	713	4506	.501	2065	.648	5779	2029	11078	15.5

TONY CAMPBELL 26 6-7 215   Guard

Blumpy... That's what the Lakers call him ... He's loaded with offensive potential and if he improves defensively could find himself a permanent home in the Forum... He's taken the roundabout route to LA... Taken by Detroit with the No. 20 pick in 1984... Rode the Pistons' bench for three seasons... Hooked on briefly with Chicago last season and then signed as a free agent by the Lakers... Born May 7, 1962, in Teaneck, N.J.... Played at Ohio State, where he was a big-time scorer for his last three seasons... One of those guys who could eventually be paid off for his perseverance.

Year	Team	G	FG	FG Pct.	FT	FT Pct.	Reb.	Ast.	TP	Avg.
1984-85	Detroit............	56	130	.496	56	.800	89	24	316	5.6
1985-86	Detroit............	82	294	.484	58	.795	236	45	648	7.9
1986-87	Detroit............	40	57	.393	24	.615	58	19	138	3.5
1987-88	L.A. Lakers........	13	57	.564	28	.718	27	15	143	11.0
	Totals.............	191	538	.482	166	.751	410	103	1245	6.5

WES MATTHEWS 29 6-1 170   Guard

If there's a luckier man alive, he hasn't been discovered yet . . . After six years of a pro career that had him distinguished only as a troublemaker, he's latched on in LA and collected two championship rings . . . Got to play meaningful minutes only when Magic Johnson and Michael Cooper were seriously injured . . . Has speed, but is also very erratic as both a ballhandler and a shooter . . . Born Aug. 24, 1959, in Sarasota, Fla. . . . Run off the college team at Wisconsin . . . A first-round pick (14th overall) of Washington in 1980 . . . Has bounced all around . . . Played for Bullets, Atlanta (twice), Philadelphia, Chicago and San Antonio before the Lakers signed him for the 1987 stretch run.

Year	Team	G	FG	FG Pct.	FT	FT Pct.	Reb.	Ast.	TP	Avg.
1980-81	Wash.-Atl.	79	385	.494	202	.802	139	411	977	12.4
1981-82	Atlanta.	47	131	.440	60	.759	58	139	324	6.9
1982-83	Atlanta.	64	171	.403	86	.768	91	249	442	6.9
1983-84	Atl.-Phil.	20	61	.466	27	.750	27	83	150	7.5
1984-85	Chicago.	78	191	.495	59	.694	67	354	443	5.7
1985-86	San Antonio.	75	320	.531	173	.820	131	476	817	10.9
1986-87	L.A. Lakers.	50	89	.476	29	.806	47	100	208	4.2
1987-88	L.A. Lakers.	51	114	.460	54	.831	66	138	289	5.7
	Totals.	464	1462	.478	690	.788	626	1950	3650	7.9

MIKE SMREK 26 7-0 263   Center

That's Smrek as in wreck . . . There have been a lot of jokes made about this big, tall building that is virtually cemented to the ground . . . But the Lakers are not laughing and believe that he can make a significant contribution after Kareem Abdul-Jabbar retires . . . Born Aug. 31, 1962, in Welland, Ont. . . . Became a cult figure among the hoop scouts at Canisius College in Buffalo . . . Drafted on the second round by Portland in 1985 and then traded right away to Chicago . . . Signed on as a free agent by the Lakers in 1986 and has picked up two championship rings . . . So who's laughing and making jokes now?

Year	Team	G	FG	FG Pct.	FT	FT Pct.	Reb.	Ast.	TP	Avg.
1985-86	Chicago.	38	46	.377	16	.552	110	19	108	2.8
1986-87	L.A. Lakers.	35	30	.500	16	.640	37	5	76	2.2
1987-88	L.A. Lakers.	48	44	.427	44	.667	85	8	132	2.8
	Totals.	121	120	.421	76	.633	232	32	316	2.6

ORLANDO WOOLRIDGE 28 6-9 215   Forward

Another chance for "O"... Suspended as a Net last February because of drug-related problems, he signed a multiyear Laker contract in August estimated at $500,000 a year ... He averaged 16.4 points in 19 games last season, missing games because of injuries before voluntarily entering a drug treatment center... Lakers didn't have to compensate Nets because the seven-year veteran was free agent under new collective bargaining agreement... In 1986-87 he was the first Net forward to average 20 points since Bernard King did it in 1978-79... Bulls drafted him sixth overall in 1981 after brilliant career at Notre Dame... Born Dec. 16, 1959, in Mansfield, La. ... Is a cousin of Willis Reed.

Year	Team	G	FG	FG Pct.	FT	FT Pct.	Reb.	Ast.	TP	Avg.
1981-82	Chicago	75	202	.513	144	.699	227	81	548	7.3
1982-83	Chicago	57	361	.580	217	.638	298	97	939	16.5
1983-84	Chicago	75	570	.525	303	.715	369	136	1444	19.3
1984-85	Chicago	77	679	.554	409	.785	435	135	1767	22.9
1985-86	Chicago	70	540	.495	364	.788	350	213	1448	20.7
1986-87	New Jersey	75	556	.521	438	.777	367	261	1551	20.7
1987-88	New Jersey	19	110	.445	92	.708	91	71	312	16.4
	Totals	448	3018	.527	1967	.743	2137	994	8009	17.9

MILT WAGNER 25 6-5 185   Guard

He's got one more championship ring than most of us... Deep reserve, he went along for the ride on the bench as the Lakers defended their title... Used mainly as a warm body in practice... Has not been able to achieve the attention he enjoyed at Louisville, where he was a backcourt cog in the Denny Crum machine that won the 1986 NCAA title... Drafted on second round (35th overall) of '86 draft by Dallas. He went 16 spots behind Louisville teammate Billy Thompson, who was with him on Lakers last season... Was cut by Mavs in training camp and signed as free agent by LA... Rarely got into games except in blow-out situations... Will be fighting to hang on to job... Born Feb. 20, 1963, in Camden, N.J.

Year	Team	G	FG	FG Pct.	FT	FT Pct.	Reb.	Ast.	TP	Avg.
1987-88	L.A. Lakers	40	62	.422	26	.897	28	61	152	3.8

TOP ROOKIE

DAVID RIVERS 23 6-0 180　　　　　　　　　　　**Guard**
Having starred at Notre Dame for four years, he's a well-known
name . . . The question is whether he is a true point guard . . .
Born Jan. 20, 1965, in Jersey City, N.J. . . . Led the Irish in scoring in every season of his college career . . . Also holds school
records for career assists and steals . . . Made a courageous comeback from a near-fatal auto accident a couple of years ago . . . The
world champs made him the final pick on the first round . . . A
good gamble for them.

COACH PAT RILEY: A winner—guaranteed! . . . It was the
boss man who gave the Lakers 1987-88 season
its theme and its drive by guaranteeing that
they would repeat as champs . . . They did it,
becoming the first NBA team in 19 seasons to
win two in a row . . . Riley has now won four
championships since taking over the reins in
1981 . . . Also the only coach in league history
to guide his team to four straight 60-win
seasons . . . Are all those numbers enough to get people to stop
talking about his custom-made suits and mousse-styled hair?
Probably not . . . But underneath it all, this guy can do everything
you want a great coach to do . . . Born March 20, 1945, in Rome,
N.Y. . . . Says he was a "punk" when he grew up . . . Big-time star
at Kentucky . . . Drafted No. 1 by the expansion club San Diego
Rockets in 1967 . . . Bounced to the Lakers and Phoenix in a mediocre playing career . . . Was working as a radio-TV commentator when head coach Jack McKinney was hurt in a bicycle
accident and was hired as an assistant to Paul Westhead . . . When
Westhead was bounced a year later, he became the main man . . .
The rest is history . . . Guaranteed . . . His seven-year regular-season winning percentage .727 (413-150) is best in NBA history.

GREATEST THREE-POINT SHOOTER

When Pat Riley first became coach of the Lakers, he did not
like the three-point shot at all and that reflected in the small

number his team attempted. Now Riley has had a change of heart. For good reason, too. The Lakers are one of the best at shooting threes, thanks to two of the best in Michael Cooper and Byron Scott. It depends on what you prefer when it comes to making a choice.

Scott makes a slightly better percentage, but Cooper's bombs have a tendency to come at just the right time in the biggest of games. Cooper uses more of a set-shot form and hammered in an NBA-playoff-record six in Game 2 of the 1987 finals vs. Boston. But Scott, more of a jump-shooter, holds the club record in percentage, making .436 in the 1986-87 season.

So is it Scott over Cooper or Cooper over Scott? If you're Pat Riley, it doesn't matter because usually you're right no matter what the choice.

ALL-TIME LAKER LEADERS

SEASON

Points: Elgin Baylor, 2,538, 1960-61
Assists: Earvin (Magic) Johnson, 977, 1986-87
Rebounds: Wilt Chamberlain, 1,712, 1968-69

GAME

Points: Elgin Baylor, 71 vs. New York, 11/15/60
Assists: Jerry West, 23 vs. Philadelphia, 2/1/67
Earvin (Magic) Johnson, 23 vs. Seattle, 2/21/84
Rebounds: Wilt Chamberlain, 42 vs. Boston, 3/7/69

CAREER

Points: Jerry West, 25,192, 1960-74
Assists: Earvin (Magic) Johnson, 7,037, 1980-88
Rebounds: Elgin Baylor, 11,463, 1958-72

SUN ROSTER

No.	Veteran	Pos.	Ht.	Wt.	Age	Yrs. Pro	College
24	Tom Chambers	F	6-10	230	29	7	Utah
23	Tyrone Corbin	F	6-6	222	25	3	DePaul
12	Winston Crite	F	6-7	233	23	1	Texas A&M
44	Kenny Gattison	F	6-8	252	24	2	Old Dominion
35	Armon Gilliam	F	6-9	245	24	1	Nevada-Las Vegas
25	Craig Hodges	G	6-3	190	24	6	Cal-Long Beach
14	Jeff Hornacek	G	6-3	190	25	2	Iowa State
8	Eddie Johnson	F	6-7	210	29	7	Illinois
11	Kevin Johnson	G	6-1	180	22	1	California
53	Ron Moore	F-C	6-10	260	26	1	West Va. State
41	Mark West	C	6-10	225	27	5	Old Dominion

Rd.	Top Rookies	Sel. No.	Pos.	Ht.	Wt.	College
1	Tim Perry	7	F	6-9	200	Temple
1	Dan Majerle	14	F	6-6	215	Central Michigan
2	Andrew Lang	28	C-F	6-11	245	Arkansas
2	Dean Garrett	38	F	6-9	220	Indiana
2	Steve Kerr	50	G	6-3	175	Arizona
3	Rodney Johns	55	G	6-2	205	Grand Canyon

OUTLOOK: They've done such a complete job of house-cleaning—from star players to the head coach—that this club is just slightly better right now than an expansion team. They are trusting Fitzsimmons to come in and lay a new foundation and the little guy has the ability and the track record. This is a definite youth movement and they'll need solid contributions from Gilliam and Perry and Johnson to make any waves this season.

Give them a year to work together under Fitzsimmons, another productive draft that produces a big man and by the 1989-90 season they might be ready to get back into the playoff race.

SUN PROFILES

ARMON GILLIAM 24 6-9 245   Forward

The Hammer... Also the man around whom the Suns are rebuilding their franchise... This guy is a stud... UNLV coach Jerry Tarkanian called him the best forward he has ever coached... Suns lost the 1987 NBA Draft Lottery and the rights to David Robinson and had to settle for him with the No. 2 pick... Not quite as big a drop-off as losing the 1968 coin flip to Milwaukee. Back then they lost Lew Alcindor and took Neal Walk...He's strong, has a powerful body...Was Suns' second-leading rebounder despite missing 27 games with a fractured toe on his left foot...Born May 28, 1968, in Pittsburgh...Has a much better touch on his short jumper than you'd expect from a big man...He'll be a fixture in the lineup for years and years...Highest-paid player on the team at $700,000.

Year	Team	G	FG	FG Pct.	FT	FT Pct.	Reb.	Ast.	TP	Avg.
1987-88	Phoenix............	55	342	.475	131	.679	434	72	815	14.8

JEFF HORNACEK 25 6-3 190   Guard

A baby-faced tough guy...Mixed it up on two different occasions last year with Houston's Sleepy Floyd and did not back down at all...Surprisingly hard-nosed player who started 49 games for the Suns last season... Not a great passer, but will play defense and had over 100 steals...Born May 3, 1963, in Elmhurst, Ill....Had a fine college career at Iowa State and was picked on the second round (46th overall) of the 1986 draft...Well worth the price at $94,000 last season... Good range from the outside...A definite three-point threat... Brother Jay is a minor-leaguer in the LA Dodgers' organization.

Year	Team	G	FG	FG Pct.	FT	FT Pct.	Reb.	Ast.	TP	Avg.
1986-87	Phoenix............	80	159	.454	94	.777	184	361	424	5.3
1987-88	Phoenix............	82	306	.506	152	.822	262	540	781	9.5
	Totals............	162	465	.487	246	.804	446	901	1205	7.4

TOM CHAMBERS 29 6-10 230   Forward

Can drive you crazy with selfish one-on-one tendencies or into esctasy when he uses his talent to work in framework of the team...An angel with a dirty face...He looks like a choirboy, but would hit you in the face with an elbow if it meant getting a rebound...An excellent outside shooter for a big man... Sometimes he takes that shot too much...After making $950,000 last season at Seattle, he became one of the first of the big-name free agents under the new NBA collective bargaining agreement and signed a five-year multimillion-deal with the Suns...Born June 21, 1959, in Ogden, Utah...Played in college at Utah and became No. 8 pick overall in 1981 draft by San Diego Clippers...Traded to Seattle in 1983 with Al Wood for James Donaldson, Greg Kelser and

Mark Radford... Was the MVP of the 1987 All-Star Game played in Seattle.

Year	Team	G	FG	FG Pct.	FT	FT Pct.	Reb.	Ast.	TP	Avg.
1981-82	San Diego	81	554	.525	284	.620	561	146	1392	17.2
1982-83	San Diego	79	519	.472	353	.723	519	192	1391	17.6
1983-84	Seattle	82	554	.499	375	.800	532	133	1483	18.1
1984-85	Seattle	81	629	.483	475	.832	579	209	1739	21.5
1985-86	Seattle	66	432	.466	346	.836	431	132	1223	18.5
1986-87	Seattle	82	660	.456	535	.849	545	245	1909	23.3
1987-88	Seattle	82	611	.448	419	.807	490	212	1674	20.4
	Totals	553	3959	.477	2787	.785	3657	1269	10811	19.5

CRAIG HODGES 28 6-3 190   Guard

Has a slight build, but a very solid game... Blossomed for three seasons in Milwaukee under Don Nelson... Lost his job and his role to John Lucas when Del Harris took over the Bucks' reins... Dealt to Phoenix during a flurry of Suns' activity just ahead of the trading deadline. Suns gave up Jay Humphries for this guy and a second-round draft pick... Could turn out to be a steal for Phoenix if he's given the chance ...A long-range bomber who has taken part in the NBA Three-Point Shootout the last three years... Born June 27, 1960, in Park Forest, Ill.... Out of Cal State-Long Beach... Drafted in the third round (48th overall) by the LA Clippers in 1982. Of course, the Clippers mistakenly let him get away.

Year	Team	G	FG	FG Pct.	FT	FT Pct.	Reb.	Ast.	TP	Avg.
1982-83	San Diego	76	318	.452	94	.723	122	275	750	9.9
1983-84	San Diego	76	258	.450	66	.750	86	116	592	7.8
1984-85	Milwaukee	82	359	.490	106	.815	186	349	871	10.6
1985-86	Milwaukee	66	284	.500	75	.872	117	229	716	10.8
1986-87	Milwaukee	78	315	.462	131	.891	140	240	846	10.8
1987-88	Mil.-Phoe.	66	242	.463	59	.831	78	153	629	9.5
	Totals	444	1776	.469	531	.814	729	1362	4404	9.9

EDDIE JOHNSON 29 6-7 210   Forward

Always overlooked... Never attained star status, but has been a steady contributor throughout his seven-year pro career... Spent first six with the Kings' franchise in Kansas City and Sacramento... Came to the Valley of the Sun in summer 1987 Trade of the Eddies —Johnson for Ed Pinckney... Has been both a starter and a reserve... Born May 1, 1959, in Chicago... Played on same high-school team as Mark Aguirre and went to Illinois with Derek Harper... He's never been known as a very good defensive player, but is willing to duck inside with the big guys and fight for rebounds . . . Good range on the outside shot . . . Does offseason work with charities and donated $30 for every 20-point game to Big Brothers/Big Sisters in the Phoenix area.

Year	Team	G	FG	FG Pct.	FT	FT Pct.	Reb.	Ast.	TP	Avg.
1981-82	Kansas City	74	295	.459	99	.664	322	109	690	9.3
1982-83	Kansas City	82	677	.494	247	.779	501	216	1621	19.8
1983-84	Kansas City	82	753	.485	268	.810	455	296	1794	21.9
1984-85	Kansas City	82	769	.491	325	.871	407	273	1876	22.9
1985-86	Sacramento	82	623	.475	280	.816	419	214	1530	18.7
1986-87	Sacramento	81	606	.463	267	.829	353	251	1516	18.7
1987-88	Phoenix	73	533	.480	204	.850	318	180	1294	17.7
	Totals	556	4256	.480	1690	.814	2775	1539	10321	18.6

KEVIN JOHNSON 22 6-1 180   Guard

Lightning quick . . . A solid playmaker . . . Was a bit of a surprise as the No. 7 pick overall in the 1987 draft by Cleveland . . . Cavs had yearned for playmaker Kenny Smith, but he was grabbed up one spot ahead by Sacramento . . . Coach Lenny Wilkens defended the pick and gave this guy a lot of playing time . . . Born March 4, 1966, in Sacramento, Cal. . . . Starred at California . . . A very good shooter with three-point range . . . Was part of big deal with Mark West and Tyrone Corbin who came west in exchange for Larry Nance and Mike Sanders just ahead of the Feb. 25 trading deadline last season . . . Was a shortstop briefly in Oakland A's system.

Year	Team	G	FG	FG Pct.	FT	FT Pct.	Reb.	Ast.	TP	Avg.
1987-88	Cle.-Phoe	80	275	.461	177	.839	191	437	732	9.2

MARK WEST 27 6-10 225   Center

Forget having any talent, don't you just wish you were big like this guy? . . . Has parlayed his size into a five-year NBA career and he'll likely hang around for a few more . . . Has already played for four different teams . . . Originally drafted on second round by Dallas in 1983 out of Old Dominion . . . Born Nov. 5, 1960, in Petersburg, Va., hometown of Moses Malone . . . Very limited shooting range . . . Barely makes a higher percentage from foul line than on field goals . . . Went from Dallas to Milwaukee to Cleveland . . . Was traded to Phoenix in big deal with Kevin Johnson, Tyrone Corbin and three draft choices for Larry Nance, Mike Sanders and No. 1 pick.

Year	Team	G	FG	FG Pct.	FT	FT Pct.	Reb.	Ast.	TP	Avg.
1983-84	Dallas	34	15	.357	7	.318	46	13	37	1.1
1984-85	Mil.-Clev.	66	106	.546	43	.494	251	15	255	3.9
1985-86	Cleveland	67	113	.541	54	.524	322	20	280	4.2
1986-87	Cleveland	78	209	.543	89	.514	339	41	507	6.5
1987-88	Clev. Phoe.	83	316	.551	170	.596	523	74	802	9.7
	Totals	328	759	.541	363	.542	1481	163	1881	5.7

WINSTON CRITE 23 6-7 233   Forward

Defensive specialist... Shot-blocker who swatted down over 200 in his college career at Texas A&M... An outstanding leaper... Nicknamed "Air Crite"... Has not shown much scoring ability in the NBA... Played in just 29 games and spent much of his rookie season on the injured list... He's never going to be anything flashy, but could eventually fill the bill as a role player... Born June 20, 1965, in Bakersfield, Cal.... Has a football player's body and played that sport in high school... Suns made him a third-round (No. 53 overall) draft choice in 1987.

Year	Team	G	FG	FG Pct.	FT	FT Pct.	Reb.	Ast.	TP	Avg.
1987-88	Phoenix	29	34	.500	19	.760	64	15	87	3.0

TYRONE CORBIN 25 6-6 222   Forward

Have suitcase will travel... Has already made three stops in three NBA seasons... Extra baggage in the deal that sent Mark West and Kevin Johnson to Phoenix for Larry Nance and Mike Sanders... Has a good body and is an excellent leaper... Just doesn't have great scoring ability or the overall talent to do anything but hang around on the bench forever... Born Dec. 12, 1962, in Columbia, S.C.... Starred at DePaul, where he became the best rebounder in Blue Demon history... Drafted on second round by San Antonio in 1985... Was cut by Spurs, re-signed, then cut again... Is preparing for life after basketball—which could come soon—by studying real estate and financial planning.

Year	Team	G	FG	FG Pct.	FT	FT Pct.	Reb.	Ast.	TP	Avg.
1985-86	San Antonio	16	27	.422	10	.714	25	11	64	4.0
1986-87	S.A.-Clev.	63	156	.409	91	.734	215	97	404	6.4
1987-88	Clev.-Phoe.	84	257	.490	110	.797	350	115	625	7.4
	Totals	163	440	.454	211	.764	590	223	1093	6.7

TOP ROOKIES

TIM PERRY 23 6-9 200   **Forward**
Late bloomer . . . A walk-on player as a freshman at Temple . . .
Developed steadily to become the highest-drafted Owl in school
history . . . Phoenix gobbled him up with the No. 7 pick overall in
the draft . . . Born June 4, 1965, in Freehold, N.J. . . . Has great
quickness and leaping ability . . . A real shot-blocking force in the
middle . . . Many of the questions about his game were answered
in the postseason all-star tournaments when he demonstrated outstanding offensive skills.

DAN MAJERLE 23 6-6 215   **Forward**
Strong inside force earned him the nickname "Thunder." . . . An
incredible hulk who uses the most of his bulk to score and
rebound . . . A solid defensive player out of Central Michigan . . .
The second of the Suns' two first-round picks, taken in the No.
14 spot overall . . . Born Sept. 9, 1965, in Traverse City, Mich.
. . . Scouts think he could be the sleeper of the draft . . . Jumped
up in the ratings by winning the MVP award at the Portsmouth
(Va.) Invitational.

COACH COTTON FITZSIMMONS: The return of the little
man . . . He's back in charge of the Suns,
where he began his pro coaching career in
1970 . . . His 97-67 record (.591) in two seasons still stands as highest career winning percentage in club history . . . Well traveled
. . . Also did stints on the bench at Atlanta,
Buffalo, Kansas City and San Antonio . . .
Was fired two years ago as coach of the Spurs
. . . Spent last two seasons in Phoenix area and was director of
player personnel for the Suns last year . . . Born Oct. 7, 1931, in
Hannibal, Mo. . . . You can't exactly picture him taking a lazy raft
trip down the Mississippi with Tom Sawyer and Huck Finn . . .
He's wound too tight for that . . . A little guy who is a hard driver
. . . Emphasizes defense . . . Known for getting the most out of
teams without much talent . . . Would seem to fit the bill here . . .
Will coach until organization decides that former star Paul Westphal is ready . . . Then he'll go back upstairs . . . Overall record is
553-587.

GREATEST THREE-POINT SHOOTER

The Suns are one of those teams who have not had a designated bomber since the inception of the three-point shot. That is, not until the last fourth of last season when they acquired Craig Hodges from Milwaukee.

This skinny little guy who looks like he doesn't have enough muscle to reach the rim from the three-point line wound up as the NBA leader in bombs-away percentage, hitting better than 49 percent. In fact, Hodges is an NBA oddity—his percentage actually drops lower the closer in he moves to the basket.

This is a club that has had the likes of Paul Westphal and Walter Davis. But until Hodges came aboard, the three-pointer was more exotica than an everyday part of their diet. Craig Hodges is king of the Phoenix bombers. Just don't give him a layup. He'd be too close and might miss it.

ALL-TIME SUN LEADERS

SEASON

Points: Charlie Scott, 2,048, 1972-73
Assists: Jay Humphries, 632, 1986-87
Rebounds: Paul Silas, 1,015, 1970-71

GAME

Points: Paul Westphal, 49 vs. Detroit, 2/21/80
Assists: Gail Goodrich, 19 vs. Philadelphia, 10/22/69
Rebounds: Paul Silas, 27 vs. Cincinnati, 1/18/71

CAREER

Points: Walter Davis, 15,666, 1977-88
Assists: Alvan Adams, 4,012, 1975-88
Rebounds: Alvan Adams, 6,937, 1975-88

PORTLAND TRAIL BLAZERS

TEAM DIRECTORY: Chairman: Paul Allen; Pres.: Harry Glickman; Dir. Pub. Rel.: John Lashway; Coach: Mike Schuler; Asst. Coaches: Rick Adelman, Maurice Lucas, Jack Schalow, John Wetzel. Arena: Memorial Coliseum (12,666). Colors. Red, black and white.

SCOUTING REPORT

SHOOTING: They're like Miss America. They look pretty, they're nice and they score a lot of points based on those attributes. But they'll never be taken seriously as a contender—and probably never get past the first round of the playoffs—until they learn to translate that offensive proficiency into other areas of the game. Don't worry about scorers, though. Like Jimmy Durante and his jokes, they've got a million of 'em.

Clyde Drexler has turned into one of the unstoppable forces in the game, having supplemented his transition game and drives to the hoop with a jump shot that now can be counted on. A healthy Kiki Vandeweghe will shoot an apple off your head from 20 feet. And now they've got former blob Kevin Duckworth, who has done an incredible turnabout in such a short time, to score for them in the middle. Also, the Blazers get good inside offense from the underrated Jerome Kersey and should receive an added boost from rookie forward Mark Bryant out of Seton Hall.

PLAYMAKING: He'll probably never make the All-Star team or get one of those big endorsement contracts. But Terry Porter quietly goes about running the offense as well as any non-Magic guard in the Western Conference. His shooting is still a bit suspect, but he spreads the ball around on the break and is usually in full control of the offense. Portland probably could use some backup help at this position, since Porter can't play all 48 minutes.

DEFENSE: Ah yes, you do have to play this game at the other end of the court and that's where the Blazers have been woefully inadequate the past couple of seasons. Before the geniuses around the league vote Mike Schuler as Coach of the Year again, why doesn't somebody ask him when he plans to install a defense?

Drexler gets attention for his steals and Porter will jump inside your uniform to take the ball away. But the rest of this crew is

Clyde Drexler (27.0 ppg) is devastating open-court player.

afraid to get its hands dirty. Vandeweghe just waves as his man goes by, Caldwell Jones is ancient and for all of the hullabaloo about Duckworth, who has he stopped? Maybe the rookie Bryant, a tough guy from the Big East, can give them some defensive guts. Goodness knows, they need it.

TRAIL BLAZER ROSTER

No.	Veteran	Pos.	Ht.	Wt.	Age	Yrs. Pro	College
10	Richard Anderson	F	6-10	240	27	4	Cal-Santa Barbara
31	Sam Bowie	C	7-2	237	27	4	Kentucky
22	Clyde Drexler	G	6-7	215	26	5	Houston
00	Kevin Duckworth	C	7-0	280	24	2	Eastern Illinois
27	Caldwell Jones	C	6-11	225	38	15	Albany State (Ga.)
8	Charles Jones	F	6-8	215	26	3	Louisville
25	Jerome Kersey	F	6-7	222	26	4	Longwood
33	Steve Johnson	F-C	6-10	235	30	7	Oregon State
34	Ronnie Murphy	G	6-5	235	24	1	Jacksonville
30	Terry Porter	G	6-3	195	25	3	Wisc.-Stevens Point
14	Jerry Sichting	G	6-1	175	31	8	Purdue
55	Kiki Vandeweghe	F	6-8	220	30	8	UCLA

Rd.	Top Rookies	Sel. No.	Pos.	Ht.	Wt.	College
1	Mark Bryant	21	F	6-9	245	Seton Hall
2	Rolando Ferreira	26	C	7-1	240	Houston
3	Anthony Mason	53	F	6-7	215	Tennessee State
3	Craig Neal	71	G	6-5	175	Georgia Tech

REBOUNDING: They made big strides in this area last season, moving up to the No. 3 ranking in the league, behind only Dallas and Houston. That's why a lot of people thought they were really ready to make some waves in the playoffs. So what happens? They run into Utah, one of the biggest teams in the league, in the first round and get bounced.

Duckworth is just all right in the middle, while Kersey does most of the dirty work and Steve Johnson and Vandeweghe rebound like it's against their religion. It says something when they need a guard like Drexler to crash the boards for 533 rebounds. Bryant could help the most here and that's why they drafted him.

OUTLOOK: Sure, you keep coming around touting the great regular-season records that the Blazers keep putting together and we'll keep asking you who cares? It's the playoffs that count in the NBA and until this team develops a backbone in terms of rebounding and playing defense, Portland will always be nothing more than first-round elimination fodder. Late in the season, teams try to jockey in the standings in hope of meeting Portland in the first round. That's the ultimate insult. It's also the hard truth.

TRAIL BLAZER PROFILES

CLYDE DREXLER 26 6-7 215   Guard

Clyde the Glide... Everybody knows the nickname... But it doesn't fully describe anymore the all-around player that he's become ... In addition to the soaring slam dunks, he's added a good outside shot and has always been an excellent defender... Finished sixth in the NBA in scoring and fifth in steals last season ... Born June 22, 1962, in New Orleans, but was raised in Houston... An underrated prep player who blossomed fast at the University of Houston and became leader of the Phi Slama Jama gang which went to 1983 NCAA title game... Taken by the Blazers with the No. 13 pick in the 1983 draft and has grown into a much better player than many skeptics believed ... A perennial all-star now... If he ever gets to play with a legitimate NBA center—or a healthy Sam Bowie—he could lead his team to great heights... Does a great deal of work with kids in anti-drug programs... An absolute steal at $350,000 last season.

Year	Team	G	FG	FG Pct.	FT	FT Pct.	Reb.	Ast.	TP	Avg.
1983-84	Portland...........	82	252	.451	123	.728	235	153	628	7.7
1984-85	Portland...........	80	573	.494	223	.759	476	441	1377	17.2
1985-86	Portland...........	75	542	.475	293	.769	421	600	1389	18.5
1986-87	Portland...........	82	707	.502	357	.760	518	566	1782	21.7
1987-88	Portland...........	81	849	.506	476	.811	533	467	2185	27.0
	Totals.............	400	2923	.491	1472	.774	2183	2227	7361	18.4

KEVIN DUCKWORTH 24 7-0 280   Center

How much is a duck worth?... A lot more than he was a year earlier... Ran away with the Most Improved Player Award as this former fat boy slimmed down, toughened up and embarrassed a lot of clubs that passed him by in the 1986 draft... With Sam Bowie injured and out for the season, he stepped in and gave the Blazers a solid presence in the middle... Born April 1, 1964, in Dolton, Ill.... San Antonio made him a second-round pick in '86 and quickly traded him to Portland for Walter Berry. Many thought Portland had been duped... Now it's the Spurs who may have been taken... Played at Eastern Illinois... Grew up as a Chicago Bears' fans and could probably be an NFL lineman.... Nicknamed "The

Freezer" and "Sir Duck"... A nice success story... And a bargain at $175,000.

Year	Team	G	FG	FG Pct.	FT	FT Pct.	Reb.	Ast.	TP	Avg.
1986-87	S.A.-Port.	65	130	.476	92	.687	223	29	352	5.4
1987-88	Portland	78	450	.496	331	.770	576	66	1231	15.8
	Totals	143	580	.492	423	.750	799	95	1583	11.1

JEROME KERSEY 26 6-7 222   Forward

One of these days he might leap right through the ceiling... A quiet, not very flashy guy who is known by the real hoop junkies as one of the best dunkers in the game... Has quietly come out of nowhere to make himself into a power forward many teams would love to have... Was the runnerup to Michael Jordan in the 1987 NBA Slam Dunk Contest... Born June 26, 1962, in Clarksville, Va.... Blazers scooped up a diamond in the rough on the second round (46th overall) of the 1984 draft... Played college ball at tiny Longwood (Va.)... Started slowly, but hard work has expanded his game... Can now hit the perimeter jumper as well as go to the basket strong... Earns $190,000... What this guy needs is a good publicist.

Year	Team	G	FG	FG Pct.	FT	FT Pct.	Reb.	Ast.	TP	Avg.
1984-85	Portland	77	178	.478	117	.646	206	63	473	6.1
1985-86	Portland	79	258	.549	156	.681	293	83	672	8.5
1986-87	Portland	82	373	.509	262	.720	496	194	1009	12.3
1987-88	Portland	79	611	.499	291	.735	657	243	1516	19.2
	Totals	317	1420	.507	826	.706	1652	583	3670	11.6

KIKI VANDEWEGHE 30 6-8 220   Forward

The scoring machine finally blew a gasket... He spent 45 games last season on the bench with a back injury and was really no help when he returned for the playoffs... That jumper that used to be a thing of beauty clanked off the rim like a sour note when it was needed... Doesn't play defense, doesn't rebound and doesn't pass... So when his shot is off, it makes him virutally useless... Born Aug. 1, 1958, in Weisbaden, West Germany into a rather distinguished family... Father is former Knicks' great Ernie Vandeweghe, mother a former Miss America and sister was on the U.S. Olympic volleyball team in 1976... Has done work during the last several off-seasons as a television commentator and probably has a future career in that field... Took UCLA to the 1980 NCAA title game

... The top pick of Dallas expansion club ... Would not sign and was traded to Denver ... Shipped to Portland in 5-for-1 deal that sent Wayne Cooper, Calvin Natt, Fat Lever and pair of draft picks to Denver ... Is best friends with teammate Clyde Drexler ... Collects antique cars as a hobby ... His $961,000 salary had him the center of many trade rumors during the offseason.

Year	Team	G	FG	FG Pct.	FT	FT Pct.	Reb.	Ast.	TP	Avg.
1980-81	Denver............	51	229	.426	130	.818	270	94	588	11.5
1981-82	Denver............	82	706	.560	347	.857	461	247	1760	21.5
1982-83	Denver............	82	841	.547	489	.875	437	203	2186	26.7
1983-84	Denver............	78	895	.558	494	.852	373	238	2295	29.4
1984-85	Portland...........	72	618	.534	369	.896	228	106	1616	22.4
1985-86	Portland...........	79	719	.540	523	.869	216	187	1962	24.8
1986-87	Portland...........	79	808	.523	467	.886	251	220	2122	26.9
1987-88	Portland...........	37	283	.508	159	.878	109	71	747	20.2
	Totals............	560	5099	.535	2978	.869	2345	1366	13276	23.7

STEVE JOHNSON 30 6-10 235   Forward-Center

You'd be safe letting him try to shoot an apple off your head ... One of the top marksmen in the league in this decade ... His .529 shooting percentage last season was the lowest of his career ... It only dropped that far because he suffered from bone spurs on both ankles and also underwent thumb surgery ... The injuries forced him to miss 39 regular-season games and the first-round playoff loss to Utah ... Born Nov. 3, 1957, in San Bernardino, Cal.... Has lived in Portland since attending Oregon State ... Real first name is Clarence, he goes by middle name ... Wife Janice is the daughter of Miami Heat GM Stu Inman, who used to be with the Blazers ... Has made many stops ... Was the No. 7 pick of Kansas City in 1981 ... Traded to Chicago and San Antonio before arriving in Pacific Northwest in exchange for Larry Krystowiak and Mychal Thompson in 1986 ... Is the all-time league leader for fouls in a season with 325 ... Can play the center spot in a pinch ... Just a solid pro ... Earns a solid $650,000.

Year	Team	G	FG	FG Pct.	FT	FT Pct.	Reb.	Ast.	TP	Avg.
1981-82	Kansas City.........	78	395	.613	212	.642	459	91	1002	12.8
1982-83	Kansas City.........	79	371	.624	186	.574	398	95	928	11.7
1983-84	K.C.-Chi..........	81	302	.559	165	.575	418	81	769	9.5
1984-85	Chicago............	74	281	.545	181	.718	437	64	743	10.0
1985-86	San Antonio........	71	362	.632	259	.694	462	95	983	13.8
1986-87	Portland...........	79	494	.556	342	.698	566	155	1330	16.8
1987-88	Portland...........	43	258	.529	146	.586	242	57	662	15.4
	Totals............	505	2463	.580	1491	.647	2982	638	6417	12.7

TERRY PORTER 25 6-3 195   Guard

Has one of those bodies that looks like it was chiseled from granite... Muscles everywhere ... Plays a pretty strong game in the back-court, too... Developed into a fine quarterback, an excellent defender and now is showing more and more offensive ability... Born April 8, 1963, in Milwaukee... Attracted his first national headlines at the 1984 Olympic Trials when he caught the eye of Bobby Knight ... Didn't make the gold-medal team, but became a second-round draft pick in 1985 and has paid immediate dividends... Attended tiny Wisconsin-Stevens Point, an NAIA school... Probably should have been a first-round pick (especially by guard-starved Houston), but teams were scared off by his small-college credentials... He'd steal your shadow if you turned your head... He's a steal for the Blazers at $251,000.

Year	Team	G	FG	FG Pct.	FT	FT Pct.	Reb.	Ast.	TP	Avg.
1985-86	Portland	79	212	.474	125	.806	117	198	562	7.1
1986-87	Portland	80	376	.488	280	.838	337	715	1045	13.1
1987-88	Portland	82	462	.519	274	.846	378	831	1222	14.9
	Totals	241	1050	.498	679	.835	832	1744	2829	11.7

RICHARD ANDERSON 27 6-10 240   Forward

Have jumper will travel... A Johnny-One-Note player who doesn't have any weapons in his arsenal except the long-range shot... Kind of a poor man's Kiki Vandeweghe... A very poor man... It's just amazing that people continue to carry him on their rosters... Portland was his fourth club in four NBA seasons... Born Nov. 19, 1960, in Anaheim, Cal.... Attended Cal-Santa Barbara and was the 32nd pick in the 1982 draft by the San Diego Clippers... Bounced to Denver, then played two years in Europe before returning to try to qualify for his NBA pension... Picked up for a year by Houston... Rockets waived him on Dec. 7, 1987, just before making the Ralph Sampson-for-Joe Barry Carroll-and-Sleepy Floyd deal.

Year	Team	G	FG	FG Pct.	FT	FT Pct.	Reb.	Ast.	TP	Avg.
1982-83	San Diego	78	174	.404	48	.696	272	120	403	5.2
1983-84	Denver	78	272	.426	116	.773	406	193	663	8.5
1986-87	Houston	51	59	.424	22	.759	79	33	144	2.8
1987-88	Hou.-Port.	74	171	.390	58	.753	303	112	448	6.1
	Totals	281	676	.410	244	.751	1060	458	1658	5.9

SAM BOWIE 27 7-2 237   Center

Give this guy a break...Oh no, he's had too many breaks already...Had to miss another entire season when he broke a leg during the exhibition season...Quickly becoming the re-incarnation of the oft-injured Bill Walton in Portland...You've got to start wondering if he'll ever pull it together and have a decent NBA career...It's a shame, because he's bright, articulate and wants very much to play ball...Injuries have dogged him since college days at Kentucky, where he missed two full seasons with foot ailments....Born March 17, 1961, in Lebanon, Pa....The No. 2 pick in the 1984 draft, just behind Akeem Olajuwon...The Blazers could have taken Michael Jordan and surely regret that choice every day...A fine shooter, solid rebounder and excellent passer who deserves at least one healthy year to show what he's got...In four NBA seasons, he's played in just 119 of a possible 328 games...Has a hefty salary of $1,055,000.

Year	Team	G	FG	FG Pct.	FT	FT Pct.	Reb.	Ast.	TP	Avg.
1984-85	Portland.	76	299	.537	160	.711	656	215	758	10.0
1985-86	Portland.	38	167	.484	114	.708	327	99	448	11.8
1986-87	Portland.	5	30	.455	20	.667	33	9	80	16.0
1987-88	Portland.					Injured				
	Totals.	119	496	.512	294	.707	1016	323	1286	10.8

CALDWELL JONES 38 6-11 225   Center

The Thin Man...One of the world's most prolific beer drinkers, he looks like he never touched the stuff...Second-oldest player in the league behind Kareem Abdul-Jabbar...He always comes back and gives you the solid defense, the all-out effort and virtually no points...The last time he averaged double figures in scoring was the 1975-76 season in the defunct ABA...Born July 4, 1950, in McGhee, Ark....Second-round pick of Philadelphia in 1973, he signed instead with the ABA and played with the San Diego Conquistadors, Kentucky Colonels and the Spirit of St. Louis before the league folded...Was a defensive specialist in Philly for six seasons...Traded to Houston for Moses Malone...Spent two years with Rockets, one with Bulls and the last three with the Blazers...He's always been there to step in the breach when Sam Bowie is injured . . . You keep thinking he's at the end of the line, but he always wins a job . . . Brothers Wil, Charles and Major all played pro ball.

Year	Team	G	FG	FG Pct.	FT	FT Pct.	Reb.	Ast.	TP	Avg.
1973-74	San Diego (ABA).....	79	507	.465	171	.743	1095	144	1187	15.0
1974-75	San Diego (ABA).....	76	606	.489	264	.788	1074	162	1479	19.5
1975-76	SD-Ky.-St.L. (ABA)...	76	423	.470	140	.753	853	147	986	13.0
1976-77	Philadelphia.........	82	215	.507	64	.552	666	92	494	6.0
1977-78	Philadelphia.........	80	169	.471	96	.627	570	92	434	5.4
1978-79	Philadelphia.........	78	302	.474	121	.747	747	151	725	9.3
1979-80	Philadelphia.........	80	232	.436	124	.697	950	164	588	7.4
1980-81	Philadelphia.........	81	218	.449	148	.767	813	122	584	7.2
1981-82	Philadelphia.........	81	231	.497	179	.817	708	100	641	7.9
1982-83	Houston.............	82	307	.453	162	.786	668	138	776	9.5
1983-84	Houston.............	81	318	.502	164	.837	582	156	801	9.9
1984-85	Chicago.............	42	53	.461	36	.766	211	34	142	3.4
1985-86	Portland............	80	126	.496	124	.827	355	74	376	4.7
1986-87	Portland............	78	111	.496	97	.782	455	64	319	4.1
1987-88	Portland............	79	128	.487	78	.736	408	81	334	4.2
	Totals.............	1155	3946	.475	1968	.757	10155	1721	9866	8.5

JERRY SICHTING 31 6-1 175   Guard

Made himself a little tough-guy reputation by goading Ralph Sampson into a fight in the 1986 NBA finals when he played for Boston . . . Had a kind of cult following, but it's now apparent that the Celts just made him look a lot better than he is . . . Did absolutely nothing to help the Blazers over the second half of the season . . . Sent to Portland in exchange for Jim Paxson . . . Born Nov. 29, 1956, in Martinsville, Ind. . . . Played at Purdue and Golden State made him a fourth-round pick in 1979 . . . Hooked on with Indiana and after five years died and went to heaven in Boston . . . Get a good look, he'll be gone very soon.

Year	Team	G	FG	FG Pct.	FT	FT Pct.	Reb.	Ast.	TP	Avg.
1980-81	Indiana.............	47	34	.358	25	.781	43	70	93	2.0
1981-82	Indiana.............	51	91	.469	29	.763	55	117	212	4.2
1982-83	Indiana.............	78	316	.478	92	.860	155	433	727	9.3
1983-84	Indiana.............	80	397	.532	117	.860	171	457	917	11.5
1984-85	Indiana.............	70	325	.521	112	.875	114	264	771	11.0
1985-86	Boston..............	82	235	.570	61	.924	104	188	537	6.5
1986-87	Boston..............	78	202	.508	37	.881	91	187	448	5.7
1987-88	Bos.-Port...........	52	93	.541	17	.739	36	93	213	4.1
	Totals.............	538	1693	.513	490	.858	769	1809	3918	7.3

CHARLES JONES 26 6-8 215   Forward

Journeyman... Spends most of his time on the bench and making the others work in practice ... Came out of Denny Crum's stable in Louisville, but he's not one of the thoroughbreds... Best attribute is willingness to bang on the boards, but gives up a lot in height to the big boys... Born Jan. 12, 1962, in Scooba, Miss.... Former all-state prep player... Injuries have held his pro career greatly in check... A second-round pick (36th overall) of Phoenix in 1984... Blazers signed him as a free agent in April 1987... But he appeared in just 37 games and made no impact on the team... Costs $200,000 to have him sit on the bench... No relation to Portland teammate Caldwell Jones.

Year	Team	G	FG	FG Pct.	FT	FT Pct.	Reb.	Ast.	TP	Avg.
1984-85	Phoenix............	78	236	.520	182	.648	394	128	654	8.4
1985-86	Phoenix............	43	75	.457	50	.510	193	52	200	4.7
1987-88	Portland...........	37	16	.400	19	.576	31	8	51	1.4
	Totals.............	158	327	.497	251	.609	618	188	905	5.7

TOP ROOKIE

MARK BRYANT 23 6-9 245   Forward

Brute strength... Strongman was able to flourish in the physical Big East Conference, so he should be able to add much-needed muscle to the Trail Blazers... Taken with the No. 21 overall pick in the draft... Born April 25, 1965... Excellent senior year caught the attention of pro scouts... Led the way for Seton Hall in taking Pirates to their first-ever NCAA tournament berth... Named top player in the New York City area last year... A very aggressive rebounder.

COACH MIKE SCHULER: Somebody tell him that the

playoffs are where it counts in the NBA... In two seasons on the job, he's taken the Blazers to a 102-62 regular-season mark, then been wiped out in the first round of the playoffs... Last season it was Utah that put an ugly early end to his season... Problem may be that Schuler has installed a nice wide-open offense that functions during the regular year, but gets chewed up when defenses pack it in tight in the playoffs...Still he had his contract picked up for two more years...The NBA Coach of the Year as a rookie...Fell off his chair at his introductory news conference...Born Sept. 22, 1940, in Portsmouth, Ohio...Attended Ohio University...Another of Bob Knight's students as assistant at Army...Took the head-coaching job at Rice, then got invaluable experience as Don Nelson's assistant with Milwaukee Bucks...Is very thorough in preparation... Could have a long and successful career as an NBA boss... Likes to think of himself as a real fashion plate, but he's never been confused with Pat Riley.

Quarterback Terry Porter has blossomed on all counts.

GREATEST THREE-POINT SHOOTER

Another one of those teams that has not had a specifically designated man from radar range. But through the years, the Blazers have never been afraid to use the three-point shot as a weapon. The most effective in terms of quantity was Jim Paxson, who was traded to Boston in the middle of last season. Paxson holds the club mark with 84 treys in one season.

Of those left on the Portland roster, Kiki Vandeweghe probably shoots from afar as naturally as anybody and led the league in percentage in 1986-87. But there are others who must be watched beyond the stripe. Clyde Drexler not only glides in for dunks, but has shown a penchant for the home-run ball.

And Jerry Sichting, acquired in the Paxson deal, is not a frequent practitioner, yet has a high percentage. For now, give the honor as best in club history to Paxson, though that title is not likely to last much longer.

ALL-TIME TRAIL BLAZER LEADERS

SEASON

Points: Clyde Drexler, 2,185, 1987-88
Assists: Terry Porter, 831, 1987-88
Rebounds: Lloyd Neal, 967, 1972-73

GAME

Points: Geoff Petrie, 51 vs. Houston, 2/16/73
          Geoff Petrie, 51 vs. Houston, 1/20/73
Assists: Terry Porter, 19 vs. Utah, 4/14/88
Rebounds: Sidney Wicks, 27 vs. Los Angeles, 2/26/75

CAREER

Points: Jim Paxson, 10,003, 1979-88
Assists: Geoff Petrie, 2,057, 1970-76
Rebounds: Mychal Thompson, 4,878, 1978-86

SACRAMENTO KINGS

TEAM DIRECTORY: General Partner: Gregg Lukenbill; Exec. VP-Mktg.: Joe Axelson; Exec. VP-Basketball Oper.: Bill Russell; Dir. Pub. Rel.: Julie Fie; Coach: Jerry Reynolds; Asst. Coach: Phil Johnson. Arena: Arco Arena (16,400). Colors: Red, white and blue.

SCOUTING REPORT

SHOOTING: As far as shooting is concerned, well, they can't. Now the situation would seem to be even bleaker since they traded away Reggie Theus, who was a big part of their offense. But they got Randy Wittman from Atlanta in return and he can shoot. Never mind that he's very, very slow. They plucked a 6-8 guard in San Jose State's Ricky Berry from the draft and he comes highly rated as a shooter.

And he'd better deliver, because of the returnees, only Otis Thorpe—who rarely shoots from more than eight feet out—and Ed Pinckney make half their shots. Their problem is that they don't have a big man to go to for the easy inside hoops, so they must rely far too much on the perimeter game.

PLAYMAKING: This is one area where the Kings should have a solid future. Despite a rookie season that didn't knock anybody's socks off, former North Carolina ace Kenny Smith should develop into a solid performer. He's got one strike against him with a lack of size in today's bigger game, but he has the speed and smarts to get the ball to the right people. If only he had the right people.

Smith is not going to fully blossom until the Kings get some better talent around him to convert his passes. As a backup performer, Michael Jackson is an okay ball-handler, but doesn't look nearly as good as he used to with Patrick Ewing at Georgetown.

DEFENSE: The defense was so bad last year that it drove Mr. Defense, Bill Russell, to lose his job midway through the season. Oh well, Russell had lost interest early on anyway and the Kings said they were promoting him upstairs. But what does any of that matter, since Sacramento probably couldn't keep a team of grandmothers from scoring less than 100 points in a game. It all goes back to the big guy in the middle. Joe Kleine and LaSalle Thompson can't stop penetration.

But if there is hope, it is in the person of All-Flake Team

... "When I'm open, I take my shot," he said. "Everybody has their view of what a passed-up shot is." ... Everybody has their view of open, too ... No range, no penetration. Has averaged less than two free throws per game in career ... Only starting NBA guard who didn't attempt a three-pointer ... Played in all 82 games ... Born Oct. 28, 1959, in Indianapolis ... Member of Indiana's NCAA championship team in 1981 ... First-round pick by Bullets in '83, then went to Hawks for Tom McMillen and second-rounder prior to that season ... Earns $350,000.

Year	Team	G	FG	FG Pct.	FT	FT Pct.	Reb.	Ast.	TP	Avg.
1983-84	Atlanta	78	160	.503	28	.609	71	71	350	4.5
1984-85	Atlanta	41	187	.531	30	.732	73	125	406	9.9
1985-86	Atlanta	81	467	.530	104	.770	170	306	1043	12.9
1986-87	Atlanta	71	398	.503	100	.787	124	211	900	12.7
1987-88	Atlanta	82	376	.478	71	.798	170	302	823	10.0
	Totals	353	1588	.507	333	.760	608	1015	3522	10.0

ED PINCKNEY 25 6-9 215   Forward

Overrated or just in over his head? ... Nickname in college was E-Z Ed ... But he's found nothing easy about the transition to the pro game ... Doesn't have the quickness to beat the little guys and lacks the strength to mix it up with the big guys ... May wind up having a strictly journeyman career ... That would be a disappointment after Phoenix made him the No. 10 pick in the 1985 draft ... Born March 27, 1963, in the Bronx, N.Y. ... Was the mainstay of Villanova's miracle championship team in 1985, outplaying Patrick Ewing in the title game ... Traded to the Kings in 1987 for Eddie Johnson ... Could be moving on again if he doesn't produce soon.

Year	Team	G	FG	FG Pct.	FT	FT Pct.	Reb.	Ast.	TP	Avg.
1985-86	Phoenix	80	255	.558	171	.673	308	90	681	8.5
1986-87	Phoenix	80	290	.584	257	.739	580	116	837	10.5
1987-88	Sacramento	79	179	.522	133	.747	230	66	491	6.2
	Totals	239	724	.558	561	.719	1118	272	2009	8.4

MIKE McGEE 29 6-5 190   Guard

One-trick pony ... He's a three-point shooting specialist whose percentage from the rest of the floor isn't very good ... Shows flashes of being a good defensive player, but does not exhibit consistency ... Born July 29, 1959, in Tyler, Tex. ... Big rep in college at Michigan ... Lakers made him the No. 19 pick in the 1981 draft and figured he'd contribute to the dynasty . . . Never could crack the lineup . . . Traded to Atlanta in 1986 for Billy Thompson and Ron Kellogg . . . Hawks gave up and sent him back west on Dec. 14 of last season for a pair of second-round draft choices in 1991 and 1995.

Year	Team	G	FG	FG Pct.	FT	FT Pct.	Reb.	Ast.	TP	Avg.
1981-82	Los Angeles.	39	80	.465	31	.585	49	16	191	4.9
1982-83	Los Angeles.	39	69	.423	17	.739	53	26	156	4.0
1983-84	Los Angeles.	77	347	.594	61	.540	193	81	757	9.8
1984-85	L.A. Lakers.	76	329	.538	94	.588	165	71	774	10.2
1985-86	L.A. Lakers.	71	252	.463	42	.656	140	83	587	8.3
1986-87	Atlanta.	76	311	.459	80	.584	159	149	788	10.4
1987-88	Atl.-Sac.	48	223	.421	76	.745	128	71	575	12.0
	Totals.	426	1611	.491	401	.615	887	497	3828	9.0

JOE KLEINE 26 6-11 255   Center

If he was a blind date, you'd say he has a nice personality . . . Nothing pretty about his game . . . He just works hard and it's unfortunate that he doesn't have a few more inches in height to use on the inside . . . Born Jan. 4, 1962, in Colorado Springs, Colo. . . . Started in college at Notre Dame and then transferred to Arkansas . . . Became an All-SWC performer for the Hogs . . . A nice touch on the perimeter shot . . . Pulled down $575,000 last season . . . Played on gold medal Olympic team in 1984 at LA . . . You've got to like his work ethic . . . To judge how far he's progressed in the pros, consider that in college he used to give Akeem Olajuwon fits. But no more.

Year	Team	G	FG	FG Pct.	FT	FT Pct.	Reb.	Ast.	TP	Avg.
1985-86	Sacramento.	80	160	.465	94	.723	373	46	414	5.2
1986-87	Sacramento.	79	256	.471	110	.786	483	71	622	7.9
1987-88	Sacramento.	82	324	.472	153	.814	579	93	801	9.8
	Totals.	241	740	.470	357	.779	1435	210	1837	7.6

JAWANN OLDHAM 31 7-1 230   Center

Beam him back up, Scotty . . . The classic space cadet . . . If you listen to him talk, you'd think he's a cross between Bill Russell, Wilt Chamberlain and Kareem Abdul-Jabbar . . . Actually he's just a big guy with leaping ability who can dunk the ball hard . . . Also very proficient at shot-blocking . . . Born July 4, 1957, in Seattle . . . He bounced from Denver to Houston to Chicago and New York before arriving in Sacramento ... Played at University of Seattle and was drafted 41st in 1980 by Denver ... Last season was the first of a five-year deal worth $1.7 million ... He's a real flake ... Could be a solid pro if he wasn't so impressed with himself.

Year	Team	G	FG	FG Pct.	FT	FT Pct.	Reb.	Ast.	TP	Avg.
1980-81	Denver	4	2	.333	0	.000	5	0	4	1.0
1981-82	Houston	22	13	.361	8	.571	24	3	34	1.5
1982-83	Chicago	16	31	.534	12	.545	47	5	74	4.6
1983-84	Chicago	64	110	.505	39	.591	233	33	259	4.0
1984-85	Chicago	63	89	.464	34	.680	236	31	212	3.4
1985-86	Chicago	52	167	.517	53	.582	306	37	387	7.4
1986-87	New York	44	71	.408	31	.544	179	19	173	3.9
1987-88	Sacramento	54	119	.476	59	.678	304	33	297	5.5
	Totals	319	602	.479	236	.610	1334	161	1440	4.5

HAROLD PRESSLEY 25 6-7 210   Guard-Forward

So he ain't a hound dog after all ... Came out of his rookie shell ... Showed ability to score, rebound and handle the ball ... Even was named NBA Player of the Week once ... Bounced back after a rookie season in which he didn't show much of anything ... Born July 14, 1963, in Uncasville, Conn. ... Versatile guy who played all five positions in college at Villanova ... Teamed with Kings' teammate Ed Pinckney on Villanova's miracle drive to the NCAA title in 1985 ... Is still learning to be a pro guard ... Says his biggest dream is to be James (007) Bond for one day.

Year	Team	G	FG	FG Pct.	FT	FT Pct.	Reb.	Ast.	TP	Avg.
1986-87	Sacramento	67	134	.423	35	.729	176	120	310	4.6
1987-88	Sacramento	80	318	.453	103	.792	369	185	775	9.7
	Totals	147	452	.444	138	.775	545	305	1085	7.4

TERRY TYLER 32 6-7 220   Forward

A bigger bust in Sacramento than Bill Russell as head coach ... Just hasn't delivered on the big free-agent contract he signed during the 1985-86 season ... Pulling down $475,000 to be a very marginal player off the bench ... Born Oct. 30, 1956, in Detroit ... Stayed home to attend the University of Detroit and was drafted by the Motown Pistons (No. 28 overall) in 1978 ... He has decent range on the 10- to 15-foot

shot, but must do more than that to earn the big money . . .
Excellent leaper . . . Should be getting more rebounds.

Year	Team	G	FG	FG Pct.	FT	FT Pct.	Reb.	Ast.	TP	Avg.
1978-79	Detroit..............	82	456	.482	144	.658	648	89	1056	12.9
1979-80	Detroit..............	82	430	.465	143	.765	627	129	1005	12.3
1980-81	Detroit..............	82	476	.532	148	.592	567	136	1100	13.4
1981-82	Detroit..............	82	336	.523	142	.740	493	126	815	9.9
1982-83	Detroit..............	82	421	.478	146	.745	540	157	990	12.1
1983-84	Detroit..............	82	313	.453	94	.712	285	76	722	8.8
1984-85	Detroit..............	82	422	.494	106	.716	423	63	950	11.6
1985-86	Sacramento.........	71	295	.455	84	.750	313	94	674	9.5
1986-87	Sacramento.........	82	329	.495	101	.721	328	73	760	9.3
1987-88	Sacramento.........	74	184	.452	41	.641	242	56	410	5.5
	Totals.............	801	3662	.483	1149	.701	4466	999	8482	10.6

MICHAEL JACKSON 24 6-2 180   Guard

No, not that one . . . He's the Jackson without
the white glove and the moonwalk . . . But he
can still be "bad" and was definitely a
"Thriller" in college . . . Working his way into
the league the hard way . . . Drafted as the last
pick on the second round (No. 47) in 1986 by
the Knicks, many thought to give Patrick
Ewing the company of a former Georgetown
teammate . . . Didn't make the team . . . Spent a year toiling in the
CBA and hooked on with the Kings as a free agent at the start of
the year . . . Had a make-good contract for $115,000 . . . A good
backup point guard who can deal the ball . . . But will have to
develop a much better shot to stick in the big time permanently.

Year	Team	G	FG	FG Pct.	FT	FT Pct.	Reb.	Ast.	TP	Avg.
1987-88	Sacramento.........	58	64	.374	23	.719	59	179	157	2.7

TOP ROOKIE

RICKY BERRY 24 6-8 207   Guard
Three-time honorable mention All-American . . . Was always on
the fringe of breaking into the big-time . . . Ranked 15th in the
nation in scoring as a senior at San Jose State . . . Has never shot
50 percent in his career, but is a good penetrator and runs the
floor well . . . Born Oct. 6, 1964, in Morgan Hill, Cal. . . . Started
out at Oregon State, then transferred after freshman season . . . At

Followed in Akeem Olajuwon's footsteps as the center at the University of Houston... Works out regularly against Olajuwon at Fonde Recreation Center and that has helped his game... Named to the All-Rookie team... Will be an even greater force at power forward when David Robinson arrives on the scene next season.

Year	Team	G	FG	FG Pct.	FT	FT Pct.	Reb.	Ast.	TP	Avg.
1987-88	San Antonio.........	82	379	.501	198	.604	513	79	957	11.7

ALBERT KING 29 6-6 215   Guard-Forward

After sad year as a Sixer, he was traded to the Spurs for Pete Myers... Had escaped New Jersey, where he had more contract disputes than contributions... Nice guy—too nice on court—who always was questionable streak shooter... No questions about his shooting last season. Hit just .391, his worst ever... Moved to Philly in November 1987 for a couple of draft picks, one of which was returned in Gminski-Hinson deal... New York City high-school legend in Brooklyn, went to Maryland and was Nets' first-round pick (10th overall) in 1981 ... Born Dec. 17, 1959, in Brooklyn, N.Y.

Year	Team	G	FG	FG Pct.	FT	FT Pct.	Reb.	Ast.	TP	Avg.
1981-82	New Jersey.........	76	391	.482	133	.778	312	142	918	12.1
1982-83	New Jersey.........	79	582	.475	176	.775	456	291	1346	17.0
1983-84	New Jersey.........	79	465	.492	232	.786	388	203	1165	14.7
1984-85	New Jersey.........	42	226	.491	85	.817	159	58	537	12.8
1985-86	New Jersey.........	73	438	.456	167	.823	366	181	1047	14.3
1986-87	New Jersey.........	61	244	.426	81	.810	214	103	582	9.5
1987-88	Philadelphia.........	72	211	.391	78	.757	216	109	517	7.2
	Totals.............	482	2557	.463	952	.791	2111	1087	6112	12.7

FRANK BRICKOWSKI 29 6-10 240   Center-Forward

Thick as a brick.... And tough.... But nowadays he doesn't have a shot like concrete... Surprised many with the strides he made last season... Developed a good shooting touch and showed an ability to penetrate... Now he's being looked at as an integral piece of the puzzle when David Robinson arrives in another year... Born Aug. 14, 1959, in Glen Cove, N.Y.... Has paid his dues... Third-round pick of the Knicks in 1981... After three years in Europe, hooked on with Seattle and then the Lakers... Came to San Antonio from LA with Petur Gudmundsson, a 1987 first-round pick, a 1990 second-round pick and cash for Mychal Thompson... May pay off big dividends with the Spurs in the next couple of years.

Year	Team	G	FG	FG Pct.	FT	FT Pct.	Reb.	Ast.	TP	Avg.
1984-85	Seattle	78	150	.492	85	.669	260	100	385	4.9
1985-86	Seattle	40	30	.517	18	.667	54	21	78	2.0
1986-87	LAL-S.A.	44	63	.508	50	.714	116	17	176	4.0
1987-88	San Antonio	70	425	.528	268	.768	483	266	1119	16.0
	Totals	232	668	.517	421	.735	913	404	1758	7.6

MIKE MITCHELL 32 6-7 215   Forward

A solid performer who has never been recognized as a superstar... It's only a matter of time until his beaten body wears down and he fades away into the woodwork... In prime was a great offensive threat from the baseline ... Always plays hurt and will give it all he's got... Admitted to having a cocaine problem two years ago, but entered the NBA rehab program and has had no problems since then... Born Jan. 1, 1956, in Atlanta... An unheralded college player at Auburn... A first-round pick by Cleveland in 1978... Arrived in San Antonio in 1982 and has become a fixture... Had a contract last year for $750,000 and that is way above what he's worth at this point in his career.

Year	Team	G	FG	FG Pct.	FT	FT Pct.	Reb.	Ast.	TP	Avg.
1978-79	Cleveland	80	362	.513	131	.736	329	60	855	10.7
1979-80	Cleveland	82	775	.523	270	.787	591	93	1820	22.2
1980-81	Cleveland	82	853	.476	302	.784	502	139	2012	24.5
1981-82	Clev.-S.A.	84	753	.510	220	.728	540	82	1726	20.5
1982-83	San Antonio	80	686	.511	219	.758	537	98	1591	19.9
1983-84	San Antonio	79	779	.488	275	.779	570	93	1839	23.3
1984-85	San Antonio	82	775	.497	269	.777	417	151	1824	22.2
1985-86	San Antonio	82	802	.473	317	.809	409	188	1921	23.4
1986-87	San Antonio	40	208	.435	92	.821	103	38	509	12.7
1987-88	San Antonio	68	378	.482	160	.825	198	68	919	13.5
	Totals	759	6371	.493	2255	.779	4246	1010	15016	19.8

DAVID GREENWOOD 31 6-9 220   Forward

Give this guy some healthy wheels... Looks and plays much older than his age due to succession of leg injuries that have kept him on the sidelines... Missed 37 games last season and you've got to wonder if he can get back to top form at this stage in his career... Born May 27, 1957, in Lynwood, Cal.... Developed solid reputation at UCLA and Chicago made him the No. 2 pick in the 1979 draft...Had six seasons of unfulfilled promise in the Windy City...Has been nothing but a burden on the franchise since coming to the Spurs ...They are not getting good return on a $700,000 salary...A great leaper and fine rebounder when he's 100 percent healthy ...But the sands of time are running out...Has not averaged 12 points a game in five seasons.

Year	Team	G	FG	FG Pct.	FT	FT Pct.	Reb.	Ast.	TP	Avg.
1979-80	Chicago	82	498	.474	337	.810	773	182	1334	16.3
1980-81	Chicago	82	481	.436	217	.748	724	218	1179	14.4
1981-82	Chicago	82	480	.473	240	.825	786	262	1200	14.6
1982-83	Chicago	79	312	.455	165	.708	765	151	789	10.0
1983-84	Chicago	78	369	.490	213	.737	786	139	951	12.2
1984-85	Chicago	61	152	.458	67	.713	388	78	371	6.1
1985-86	San Antonio	68	198	.510	142	.772	531	90	538	7.9
1986-87	San Antonio	79	336	.513	241	.785	783	237	916	11.6
1987-88	San Antonio	45	151	.460	83	.748	300	97	385	8.6
	Totals	656	2977	.481	1705	.749	5836	1454	7663	11.7

KURT NIMPHIUS 30 6-10 219   Center

Journeyman...It sums him up...As long as he can hustle up and down the floor, he'll keep drawing paychecks in this league for a few more years...Willing to bang and do the dirty work while coming off the bench... Back in Texas last year after a four-year stint with the Dallas Mavericks...Had bounced from Dallas to the LA Clippers and Detroit Pistons before landing in San Antonio...Looks like a lost flower child with his very long hair...Had a flaky reputation that he's trying to live down these days...Born March 13, 1958, in Milwaukee...Played college ball at Arizona State, where the entire starting five in his senior year—Byron Scott, Fat Lever, Alton Lister, Sam Williams—all made it to the NBA...Taken on the third round in 1980 by Denver...Signed a free-agent contract for $310,000 last season.

Year	Team	G	FG	FG Pct.	FT	FT Pct.	Reb.	Ast.	TP	Avg.
1981-82	Dallas	63	137	.461	63	.583	295	61	337	5.3
1982-83	Dallas	81	174	.490	77	.550	404	115	426	5.3
1983-84	Dallas	82	272	.520	101	.623	513	176	646	7.9
1984-85	Dallas	82	196	.452	108	.771	408	183	500	6.1
1985-86	Dal.-LAC	80	351	.506	194	.740	453	62	896	11.2
1986-87	LAC-Det	66	155	.470	81	.675	187	25	391	5.9
1987-88	San Antonio	72	128	.498	60	.723	153	53	316	4.4
	Totals	526	1413	.489	684	.674	2413	675	3512	6.7

PETUR GUDMUNDSSON 30 7-2 270   Center

How many guys can say they are the greatest players in the history of their country?... Call him the second Iceman to ever play for San Antonio... Born Oct. 30, 1958, in Reykjavik, Iceland, it's a long story of how he wound up eating tacos in the Alamo City... Just goes to show that when you have this big a body, they'll find room for you in the NBA... One of the seemingly countless players to be a backup for Kareem Abdul-Jabbar with the Lakers... Went to school at the University of Washington... Played three years of pro ball in Argentina, England and Iceland... A third-round pick of Portland in 1981 ... Spent time in the CBA with KC Sizzlers, then hooked on with the Lakers... Shipped with Frank Brickowski and draft choices in deal that gave Lakers Mychal Thompson.

Year	Team	G	FG	FG Pct.	FT	FT Pct.	Reb.	Ast.	TP	Avg.
1981-82	Portland............	68	83	.500	52	.684	186	59	219	3.2
1985-86	L.A. Lakers.........	8	20	.541	18	.667	38	3	58	7.3
1987-88	San Antonio.........	69	139	.496	117	.807	323	86	395	5.7
	Totals.............	145	242	.501	187	.754	547	148	672	4.6

ED NEALY 28 6-7 240   Forward

Testimony to hard work and hustle... Doesn't shoot or rebound or block shots or anything except give up his body and make his teammates try harder in practice... Journeyman has spent five seasons in the NBA and that's only about five longer than anybody figured ... Born Feb. 19, 1960, in Pittsburg, Kan.... Taken on the eighth round of the 1982 draft by KC Kings... A hometown choice... Just finished his second season in San Antonio, playing just above minimum wage at $100,000... You keep figuring there is no way he'll stick, but don't bet against him having another pro job for all of this season... Played college ball at Kansas State.

Year	Team	G	FG	FG Pct.	FT	FT Pct.	Reb.	Ast.	TP	Avg.
1982-83	Kansas City.........	82	147	.595	70	.614	485	62	364	4.4
1983-84	Kansas City.........	71	63	.500	48	.800	222	50	174	2.5
1984-85	Kansas City.........	22	26	.591	10	.526	44	18	62	2.8
1986-87	San Antonio.........	60	84	.438	51	.739	284	83	223	3.7
1987-88	San Antonio.........	68	50	.459	41	.651	222	49	142	2.1
	Totals.............	303	370	.515	220	.677	1257	262	965	3.2

TOP ROOKIE

WILLIE ANDERSON 21 6-7 190   **Guard**
A modern-day version of George Gervin?... He's got the same
kind of build and can play with the same versatility... Also is in
the same city as the Iceman, was taken No. 10 in the draft by the
Spurs... Great scoring ability, also can handle the ball and has
good floor vision... Born Jan. 8, 1967... Started out at Georgia
as a small forward, but switched in the backcourt and that's
where he caught the eye of the scouts... Could be a real sleeper.

COACH LARRY BROWN: The Travelin' Man... Back on the

road after spending what was an eternity for
him—five years—at Kansas University...
Says he missed the challenge of the pro game
... Probably just got bored and wanted a
change of scenery... It was also a good time
to bail out after winning an NCAA championship and seeing main man Danny Manning become the No. 1 pick in the draft by the LA
Clippers... He set a new standard for NBA coaches when he
signed a five-year, $3.5-million deal with the Spurs... Gets criti-
cized for changing jobs, but never shortchanges his teams or the
fans... Has never had a losing season at any level of coaching
... Born Sept. 14, 1940, in Long Beach, N.Y.... Captained one
of Dean Smith's early clubs at North Carolina and won an Olympic gold medal in 1964... After a five-year playing career in the
old ABA, he got into coaching at Carolina and Denver... Pro
coaching record is 446-225... Chalked up a 135-44 mark the last
five years at Kansas... Had also been 44-17 in two seasons at
UCLA, taking the Bruins to the 1980 NCAA title game... Now
he gets to build with a young team that will get a big boost from
David Robinson next year... It probably won't be his last job,
but you've got figure that based on his track record, he'll produce
a winner.

GREATEST THREE-POINT SHOOTER

Is there a team anywhere else in the NBA that conjures up
more visions of running and gunning and shooting from the hip

as the Spurs? This is a franchise that has never lacked for scorers, whether they were named George Gervin or James Silas or Louie Dampier or Mike Mitchell. Even point guard Johnny Moore got into the act of shooting the threes once he put himself through extra training sessions.

But while you'll find all of those names making up the top 10 lists of the Spurs' mad bombers, the man who ranks No. 1 all-time is Glen Combs. Who? That's right, the 1968 draft choice out of Virginia Tech could fire rainbows with the best of them. He played back in the ABA days when the franchise was still located in Dallas and was called the Chapparrals. You could look it up. The best of the franchise's three-point guys from 1968-71. Might even win you a bar bet.

ALL-TIME SPUR LEADERS

SEASON

Points: George Gervin, 2,585, 1979-80
Assists: Johnny Moore, 816, 1984-85
Rebounds: Swen Nater, 1,279, 1974-75

GAME

Points: George Gervin, 63 vs. New Orleans, 4/9/78
Assists: John Lucas, 24 vs. Denver, 4/15/84
Rebounds: Manny Leaks, 35 vs. Kentucky, 11/27/70

CAREER

Points: George Gervin, 23,602, 1974-85
Assists: Johnny Moore, 3,663, 1980-87
Rebounds: George Gervin, 4,841, 1974-85

SEATTLE SUPERSONICS

TEAM DIRECTORY: Chairman: Barry Ackerley; Pres.: Bob Whitsitt; Dir. Pub. Rel.: Jim Rupp; Coach: Bernie Bickerstaff; Asst. Coaches: Bob Klopperburg, Tom Newell. Arena: Seattle Center Coliseum (14,200). Colors: Green and yellow.

Dale Ellis (25.8 ppg) puts charge in Sonics.

SCOUTING REPORT

SHOOTING: One thing is for sure. There will certainly be a lot more shots to go around now that Tom Chambers has signed a free-agent contract with Phoenix. For a while, the Sonics liked to trumpet the fact they had the only trio in the league—Chambers, Dale Ellis and Xavier McDaniel—to average 20 points apiece; the truth is that those three also all took more than 1,300 shots last season.

Chambers' absence should help balance out coach Bernie Bickerstaff's offense, though the Sonics still should not be hurting for gunners, what with Derrick McKey and Michael Cage waiting in the wings. McKey may be—excuse the pun—the key here. If the second-year man can blossom fully, the Sonics might not even notice that Chambers is gone. Except, of course, that there will be less fussing over his selfish style of play. One thing the Sonics don't lack is people to put the ball in the hoop.

PLAYMAKING: So far, he's been an ironman. He's also a wonderful diamond in the rough. Nate McMillan, the 6-5 find down in the 30th spot in the 1986 draft, has the size and quickness to keep up with most of the guards in the league. He's not flashy, but still handed out about nine assists per game last season. He could use some work on his outside shot to make his game well-rounded. Danny Young has been a decent enough backup for the last couple of seasons, but now they've added 6-3 rookie Corey Gaines out of Loyola-Marymount and he'll challenge for a job.

DEFENSE: An area that will definitely have to be tightened up before anybody can truly take them seriously as contenders in the Western Conference. It's nice to score a lot of points, but when it gets down to crunch time, you've also got to be able to stop the other guys and the Sonics don't do that well enough at this point. Of course, Chambers was a prime culprit in the no-defense attack and he's gone now.

But at 6-7, McKey doesn't have the size to replace Chambers. Cage, having played the past four seasons with the Clippers, isn't playoff-tested. Center Alton Lister is currently the only shot-blocking threat on the roster and he just doesn't play enough minutes to be considered a consistent force. Seattle would be delighted if second-year man Olden Polynice could move up a level and become a regular contributor. McMillan is very capable in the backcourt, but Ellis is by no means a stopper. And the Sonics lost bulldog reserve Kevin Williams in the expansion draft.

SONIC ROSTER

No.	Veteran	Pos.	Ht.	Wt.	Age	Yrs. Pro	College
44	Michael Cage	F	6-9	230	26	4	San Diego State
3	Dale Ellis	G	6-7	213	28	5	Tennessee
53	Alton Lister	C	7-0	240	30	7	Arizona State
34	Xavier McDaniel	F	6-7	205	25	3	Wichita State
31	Derrick McKey	F	6-9	210	22	1	Alabama
10	Nate McMillan	G	6-5	190	24	2	North Carolina State
23	Olden Polynice	C	7-0	240	23	1	Virginia
40	Russ Schoene	F	6-10	215	28	3	Tenn.-Chattanooga
4	Sedale Threatt	G	6-2	181	27	5	West Virginia Tech
30	Danny Young	G	6-4	175	26	4	Wake Forest

Rd.	Top Rookies	Sel. No.	Pos.	Ht.	Wt.	College
3	Corey Gaines	65	G	6-3	195	Loyola Marymount

REBOUNDING: They were in the top fourth of the league in clearing the glass last season and shouldn't lose anything by losing Chambers, since Cage comes aboard with credentials as the NBA's top rebounder. Formerly the wimpish type for two years in LA, Cage has re-dedicated himself and now makes good use of his Adonis-like body. He'll have plenty of rebounding opportunities here, since his teammates love to put the ball up.

McDaniel is a jumping jack on the boards and the center combination of Lister and Polynice should enable these guys to keep up with any club in the rebounding department.

OUTLOOK: Just a year ago, they were being talked about as threats to the Lakers in the West. But as so often happens, they fell short this time around and were wiped out out in the first round of the playoffs. The subtraction of Chambers, elevation of McKey and addition of Cage should make them a more well-rounded club. They have got to develop more of an inside attack and stop relying on the bombs-away shooting of Ellis to go deeper in the playoffs. Right now, the second round would seem to be their limit.

SUPERSONIC PROFILES

DALE ELLIS 28 6-7 213   Guard

A top gun... After three years under wraps in Dallas, he's blossomed in the last two seasons in the Pacific Northwest... Ranked seventh in the league in scoring and ninth in three-point percentage last season... Has a gorgeous-looking jumper when he squares up to the basket... Originally projected as a small forward in the NBA, he's successfully made switch to the backcourt... Just deadly coming off screens... Combines with Tom Chambers and Xavier McDaniel to give Seattle three players averaging over 20 points a game the last two seasons... Born Aug. 6, 1960, in Marietta, Ga.... Taken in the No. 9 spot in the 1983 college draft... Could never get off Dick Motta's bench there... Came to Seattle in 1986 for Al Wood... A real steal.

Year	Team	G	FG	FG Pct.	FT	FT Pct.	Reb.	Ast.	TP	Avg.
1983-84	Dallas.............	67	225	.456	87	.719	250	56	549	8.2
1984-85	Dallas.............	72	274	.454	77	.740	238	56	667	9.3
1985-86	Dallas.............	72	193	.411	59	.720	168	37	508	7.1
1986-87	Seattle............	82	785	.516	385	.787	447	238	2041	24.9
1987-88	Seattle............	75	764	.503	303	.767	340	197	1938	25.8
	Totals.............	368	2241	.487	911	.765	1443	584	5703	15.5

MICHAEL CAGE 26 6-9 230   Forward

Did a 180 spin... No, not going for dunk, just in his attitude and approach to the game... OK, we'll take the credit, since he says the turnaround began when he read a description of himself as a wimp in this book two years ago... Decided to rededicate himself... It's paid off and he's now a wonderful success story... Uses that gift of a strong, powerful body to work inside for the tough hoops... Also led the league in rebounds, beating out Charles Oakley by .03 per game... Acquired from Clippers in draft-day trade for rights to Gary Grant and a 1989 first-round pick... Born Jan. 28, 1962, in West Memphis, Ark.... Teamed with Nets' Keith Lee in high school and starred for Smokey Gaines at San Diego State... Clips made him No. 14 overall pick in the 1985 draft and it looked like a bomb after his first two seasons... Now he's a steal and well worth his $810,000 salary . . . All we ask is a 10 percent commission for providing motivation.

Year	Team	G	FG	FG Pct.	FT	FT Pct.	Reb.	Ast.	TP	Avg.
1984-85	L.A. Clippers........	75	216	.543	101	.737	392	51	533	7.1
1985-86	L.A. Clippers........	78	204	.479	113	.649	417	81	521	6.7
1986-87	L.A. Clippers........	80	457	.521	341	.730	922	131	1255	15.7
1987-88	L.A. Clippers........	72	360	.470	326	.688	938	110	1046	14.5
	Totals............	305	1237	.501	881	.704	2669	373	3355	11.0

XAVIER McDANIEL 25 6-7 205   Forward

X . . . It's such a definitive nickname . . . Kind of sweet and powerful, just like his game . . . He's capable of devouring you on the inside or displaying a soft touch on the jumper . . . Teamed with Dale Ellis and Tom Chambers to give Seattle three 20-point-a-game scorers in the last two seasons . . . Shaves his head clean . . . But don't kid him about it . . . He's one of the league's big brawlers who'll fight at the slightest provocation . . . Born June 4, 1963, in Columbia, S.C. . . . Starred at Wichita State, where he became first player in history to lead the nation in scoring (27.2) and rebounding (14.8) in 1985 . . . Sonics made him No. 4 pick in the draft . . . Original nickname in high school was Mountain Man . . . Has been called X since childhood, because his grandmother couldn't pronounce Xavier . . . Has a measured vertical jump of 42 inches.

Year	Team	G	FG	FG Pct.	FT	FT Pct.	Reb.	Ast.	TP	Avg.
1985-86	Seattle............	82	576	.490	250	.687	655	193	1404	17.1
1986-87	Seattle............	82	806	.509	275	.696	705	207	1890	23.0
1987-88	Seattle............	78	687	.488	281	.715	518	263	1669	21.4
	Totals............	242	2069	.497	806	.700	1878	663	4963	20.5

NATE McMILLAN 24 6-5 190   Guard

Look what we found. . . . Sonics scooped him up on the second round of the draft in 1986 and he's become one of the best tall point guards in the league . . . Only member of the Sonics to start all 82 games last season . . . Outstanding passer who was sixth in the league in assists . . . Born Aug. 3, 1964, in Raleigh, N.C. . . . Attended junior college in home state, then spent two years under Jim Valvano at North Carolina State . . . No big rep coming out of college, but now a lot of NBA clubs would love to have him . . . Also can play solid defense . . . He'll never get mentioned in the same breath with Magic Johnson or Isiah Thomas, but he'll be around for a lot of years . . . An absolute steal at $129,000 last season.

Year	Team	G	FG	FG Pct.	FT	FT Pct.	Reb.	Ast.	TP	Avg.
1986-87	Seattle.............	71	143	.475	87	.617	331	583	373	5.3
1987-88	Seattle.............	82	235	.474	145	.707	338	702	624	7.6
	Totals.............	153	378	.474	232	.671	669	1285	997	6.5

DERRICK McKEY 22 6-9 210   Forward

Tried to change his mind . . . Declared himself eligible for the college draft after junior year at Alabama, then flip-flopped and wanted to stay in school . . . He had to turn pro when it was discovered that he accepted money from an agent . . . Eventually accepted $355,000 to play for the Sonics last season and there are indications that he might be worth it . . . A very uneven season . . . Has scoring ability, but at times appeared lost in the system . . . Born Oct. 10, 1966, in Meridian, Miss . . . The Southeastern Conference Player of the Year in 1987 . . . One of two first-round draft choices by Seattle in 1987 . . . Played on U.S. team that won gold medal in World Championships in 1986.

Year	Team	G	FG	FG Pct.	FT	FT Pct.	Reb.	Ast.	TP	Avg.
1987-88	Seattle.............	82	255	.491	173	.772	328	107	694	8.5

DANNY YOUNG 26 6-4 175   Guard

Cool Breeze . . . That's the nickname he's been given for his ability to perform under pressure . . . Can be a streaky shooter, though his overall percentage isn't very good . . . Decent enough to come off the bench for short stretches . . . Actually seems to have better range on three-pointers . . . Born July 26, 1962, in Raleigh, N.C. . . . Stayed home to play college ball at Wake Forest . . . A second-round pick (No. 39 overall) of Seattle in 1984 . . . Couldn't cut it and went to the CBA to play for the Wyoming Wildcatters . . . In return to Seattle he's worked to hang on to a spot. . . . He's always going to be fighting for a job.

Year	Team	G	FG	FG Pct.	FT	FT Pct.	Reb.	Ast.	TP	Avg.
1984-85	Seattle.............	3	2	.200	0	.000	3	2	4	1.3
1985-86	Seattle.............	82	227	.506	90	.849	120	303	568	6.9
1986-87	Seattle.............	73	132	.458	59	.831	113	353	352	4.8
1987-88	Seattle.............	77	89	.408	43	.811	75	218	243	3.2
	Totals.............	235	450	.466	192	.835	311	876	1167	5.0

ALTON LISTER 30 7-0 240   Center

Stats say he's a lot more effective than he looks... Got his most notoriety last season when wife Bobby Jo got into a fight outside Seattle locker room with the wife of teammate Dale Ellis... Not at all a big scorer for someone with $835,000 salary... He did lead the Sonics in rebounding again last season... Born Oct. 1, 1958, in Dallas... Owes his big contract and career to Don Nelson, who molded him into a player during five years together in Milwaukee... A first-round draft choice by the Bucks in 1981... Came to the Pacific Northwest in 1986 in the deal that shipped Jack Sikma to Milwaukee... Member of the 1980 U.S. Olympic team that boycotted the Moscow Games... Teammate at Arizona State with Fat Lever, Sam Williams, Kurt Nimphius and Byron Scott. All made it to the NBA.

Year	Team	G	FG	FG Pct.	FT	FT Pct.	Reb.	Ast.	TP	Avg.
1981-82	Milwaukee..........	80	149	.519	64	.520	387	84	362	4.5
1982-83	Milwaukee..........	80	272	.529	130	.537	568	111	674	8.4
1983-84	Milwaukee..........	82	256	.500	114	.626	603	110	626	7.6
1984-85	Milwaukee..........	81	322	.538	154	.588	647	127	798	9.9
1985-86	Milwaukee..........	81	318	.551	160	.602	592	101	796	9.8
1986-87	Seattle.............	75	346	.504	179	.675	705	110	871	11.6
1987-88	Seattle.............	82	173	.504	114	.606	627	58	461	5.6
	Totals.............	561	1836	.522	915	.599	4129	701	4588	8.2

RUSS SCHOENE 28 6-10 215   Forward

Big Red... Versatile enough to go inside for the rebounds or can consistently hit the jumper from the perimeter... Another guy who's stuck around the league through perseverance and hard work... Born April 16, 1960, in Trenton, Ill.... Came out of nowhere. Well, actually from Tennessee-Chattanooga... Drafted on the second round in 1982 by Philadelphia... Was traded to Indiana midway through his rookie year and missed a chance to get a championship ring that season with the Sixers... Waived out of the league... He went to Europe for three seasons and teamed with Joe Barry Carroll on Simac team that won the Italian League championship in 1986.

Year	Team	G	FG	FG Pct.	FT	FT Pct.	Reb.	Ast.	TP	Avg.
1982-83	Phil.-Ind............	77	207	.476	61	.735	255	59	476	6.2
1986-87	Seattle.............	63	71	.374	29	.630	117	27	173	2.7
1987-88	Seattle.............	81	208	.458	51	.810	198	53	484	6.0
	Totals.............	221	486	.450	141	.734	570	139	1155	5.1

OLDEN POLYNICE 23 7-0 245   Center

Raw...But tough and mean, too....Has been known to throw plenty of stray elbows, which made him fit right in on the rough-and-tumble Sonics...Followed Ralph Sampson as the starting center at Virginia...Had to leave school with eligibility remaining when implicated in incidents of cheating and stealing... Born Nov. 21, 1964, in New York...Played for one year in Europe with Rimini in the Italian League... Regarded as a project...Could make any team a real force inside if he learns the fundamentals of the game...Drafted on the first round in 1987 by Chicago and traded to Seattle on the same day in exchange for fellow rookie Scottie Pippen...Made $350,000 last season.

Year	Team	G	FG	FG Pct.	FT	FT Pct.	Reb.	Ast.	TP	Avg.
1987-88	Seattle	82	118	.465	101	.639	330	33	337	4.1

SEDALE THREATT 27 6-2 180   Guard

A designated shooter...For a couple of seasons in Philadelphia, it was thought he could blossom into a star...Now he's strictly a guy who can help you from time to time off the bench by hitting the open shot...Drafted by the Sixers on the sixth round in 1983 out of West Virginia Tech...Spent three years in Philly and has bounced around a bit...First went to Chicago for Steve Colter and then was shipped to Seattle late last season for Sam Vincent...Born Sept. 10, 1961, in Atlanta...Streaky kind of player...You never know whether he'll be trick or Threatt.

Year	Team	G	FG	FG Pct.	FT	FT Pct.	Reb.	Ast.	TP	Avg.
1983-84	Philadelphia	45	62	.419	23	.821	40	41	148	3.3
1984-85	Philadelphia	82	188	.452	66	.733	99	175	446	5.4
1985-86	Philadelphia	70	310	.453	75	.833	121	193	696	9.9
1986-87	Phil.-Chi.	68	239	.448	95	.798	108	259	580	8.5
1987-88	Chi.-Sea.	71	216	.508	57	.803	88	160	492	6.9
	Totals	336	1015	.460	316	.794	456	828	2362	7.0

TOP ROOKIE

COREY GAINES 23 6-3 195   Guard

Starting point guard for the fastest team in the West last season at

Loyola-Marymount... Finished up career at LMU after playing his first three college seasons at UCLA, then transferring... Born June 1, 1965, in Los Angeles... Averaged nearly nine assists a game as a senior... Possesses the speed and quickness to fit into an NBA running game... Taken with the No. 65 pick overall in the third round by the Sonics... Will be competing with Danny Young for a spot on the team.

Xavier McDaniel blends soft touch with aggressive game.

COACH BERNIE BICKERSTAFF: A star on the rise . . . Not

quite the overnight success story that many think . . . Certainly paid his dues with 12 years on the bench as an assistant coach under Dick Motta and Gene Shue . . . In three years in Seattle, he's turned the Sonics from losers into a Western Conference force . . . Two straight trips to the playoffs . . . He's a good communicator with his players, but is tough enough to get his message across when necessary . . . The only thing very flashy about him is his wardrobe . . . A GQ kind of guy . . . Born Nov. 3, 1943, in Benham, Ky. . . . Played at University of San Diego . . . Inherited the head job at alma mater from Hall of Famer Phil Woolpert . . . Turned down an opportunity to play with the Harlem Globetrotters in order to learn his lessons on the bench . . . Became the league's youngest assistant at age 29 when he hooked on with Motta in Washington . . . He's future Coach of the Year material . . . Has 114-132 coaching record.

GREATEST THREE-POINT SHOOTER

It would seem so obvious. How can you not say the best three-point shooter in history is a guy nicknamed "Downtown"? Well, it's true that Freddie Brown could toss in the bombs from a dinghy out in the middle of Puget Sound, but "Downtown" spent too much of his prime playing career in the days before the three-point shot.

If you're looking for the guy who has made the most of the rule—as well as the most buckets—from outside the arc, it's Dale Ellis, who has made his mark in Seattle in just two seasons. For the second straight season, Ellis tossed in more than 100 bombs, flicking the long shots with the ease of someone putting up a free throw.

Ellis once attempted as many as eight in one game, but ex-teammate Tom Chambers holds the club mark for successful three-pointers in one game with four. Give the nod to Ellis though, because he makes the most of the shot. And makes them most often.

ALL-TIME SUPERSONIC LEADERS

SEASON

Points: Spencer Haywood, 2,251, 1972-73
Assists: Lenny Wilkens, 766, 1971-72
Rebounds: Jack Sikma, 1,038, 1981-82

GAME

Points: Fred Brown, 58 vs. Golden State, 3/23/74
Assists: Nate McMillan, 25 vs. LA Clippers, 2/23/87
Rebounds: Jim Fox, 30 vs. Los Angeles, 12/26/73

CAREER

Points: Fred Brown, 14,018, 1971-84
Assists: Fred Brown, 3,160, 1971-84
Rebounds: Jack Sikma, 7,729, 1977-86

UTAH JAZZ

TEAM DIRECTORY: Owner: Larry H. Miller; Pres./GM: Dave Checketts; VP Basketball Oper./Coach: Frank Layden; Dir. Pub. Rel.: Bill Kreifeldt; Asst. Coaches: Jerry Sloan, Scott Layden. Arena: Salt Lake Palace (12,444). Colors; Purple, gold and green.

SCOUTING REPORT

SHOOTING: How about this for a turnaround? Two seasons ago, they needed help finding their way out of the locker room and now the Jazz are considered one of the dead-eye teams in the West. Of course, a lot of that has to do with the blossoming of John Stockton (.574 shooting percentage) in the backcourt. As a full-time starter and quarterback of the offense, Stockton makes the most of his scoring opportunities. He beats the defense down the floor for layups on the break, knifes through traffic to score and can hit the outside shot when he's open. And they keep hoping for a healthy return of Darrell Griffith and his three-point shot.

And what shot is too hard for Karl Malone to make? The Mailman, who connected at a .520 clip, now delivers from way out on the baseline as well as on the power moves to the hoop. They've got Thurl Bailey able to sling in those looping shots from the baseline and have now added rookie center Eric Leckner as a backup to Mark (No shot) Eaton. Leckner has a nice touch from medium range for a big man. The mistake often made when looking at this club is just giving them credit for their size. But the Jazz can now shoot it with the best of them.

PLAYMAKING: Consider this: During a halftime interview at the 1988 NBA Finals, Wilt Chamberlain was asked to name the one current pro player he would select to start a franchise. The answer was none other than Stockton. Of course, Wilt may have been slightly biased since he'd have loved to had had this little guy setting him up with perfect passes in scoring position night after night. Nevertheless, Stockton deserves consideration when ranking the game's best point guards. He broke Isiah Thomas' single-season assist record last year with 1,128.

Outside of Magic Johnson and Maurice Cheeks, he's as good a pure quarterback as there is today. Where the Jazz need help is backing up Stockton. The candidates for the job will be a pair of rookies, Jeff Moe out of Iowa and Ricky Grace from Oklahoma.

Assist champ John Stockton worked his own Magic.

DEFENSE: Eaton. It begins and ends there. You can talk all you want about Michael Jordan chasing guards around the perimeter. Still, no single player can change a game like Eaton, who stands taller than the Mormon Tabernacle and acts like King Kong, swatting down enemy shots.

Add in the 125 blocked shots last season by the sixth man Bailey and the fact that Malone can bang you around with that solid body and they've got defenders up front. Stockton ranked third in the league in steals (242) last season, though he can be victimized by taller guards. And then there is Bobby Hansen, who showed Magic in the Utah-LA playoff series that he is a tenacious defender in the backcourt.

Utah led the NBA by limiting opponents to just .449 shooting

JAZZ ROSTER

No.	Veteran	Pos.	Ht.	Wt.	Age	Yrs. Pro	College
41	Thurl Bailey	F	6-1	232	27	5	North Carolina State
40	Mike Brown	C	6-9	240	25	2	George Washington
53	Mark Eaton	C	7-4	290	41	6	UCLA
35	Darrell Griffith	G	6-4	190	30	7	Louisville
20	Bobby Hansen	G	6-6	200	27	5	Iowa
25	Eddie Hughes	G	5-10	164	28	1	Colorado State
43	Marc Iavoroni	F	6-10	225	32	6	Virginia
11	Bart Kofoed	G	6-5	205	24	1	Kearny State
32	Karl Malone	F	6-9	256	25	3	Louisiana Tech
33	Scott Roth	G	6-8	212	25	1	Wisconsin
12	John Stockton	G	6-1	175	26	4	Gonzaga
54	Mel Turpin	C	6-11	280	27	4	Kentucky

Rd.	Top Rookies	Sel. No.	Pos.	Ht.	Wt.	College
1	Eric Leckner	17	C	6-11	265	Wyoming
2	Jeff Moe	42	G	6-4	205	Iowa
3	Ricky Grace	67	G	6-1	175	Oklahoma

last season. So behind all that Jazz is definitely some solid defense.

REBOUNDING: This is an area where the Jazz can definitely improve. They have the size and the leaping ability (at least, everybody but Eaton has that). If they ever put their minds to it, this club should be able to almost shut out opponents on the backboards. The Jazz should be even stronger on the offensive glass and convert their own missed shots for easy hoops. When they do that, they'll become a very serious threat in the West.

OUTLOOK: Gone are the days when coach Frank Layden can sit back and poor-mouth his team all season long. They've now got two legitimate NBA stars in Malone and Stockton and possess enough surrounding talent to stand toe-to-toe with the rest of the league.

What Layden must do is develop more depth. His six-man rotation through last season's playoffs will just not cut it. If Leckner can fit in and Layden uses one of the rookie guards, they could go far in the playoffs. Because of the Jazz' size, nobody wants to face this team in the postseason. Go ahead, just ask the Lakers. A real darkhorse candidate.

JAZZ PROFILES

KARL MALONE 25 6-9 256   Forward

The Mailman...The U.S. Postal Service should deliver like this guy...Rough, tough, he'll lick your stamp, cancel your letter and give you an elbow to the face just for good measure...In three short seasons, he's gone from a question mark Dallas passed over in the draft to an All-NBA performer...Can hit the outside shot as well as make like a tank and clear a path to the hoop...Born July 24, 1963, in Summerfield, La....Attended Louisiana Tech...First thing he did with his signing bonus was pay off a student loan that he'd taken out during his freshman year...A real stand-up guy...Delights reporters with friendly personality and quick quotes...Guaranteed a Utah victory in Game 6 of Western Conference semifinal vs. the Lakers and delivered...Collects exotic animals as pets and has a mini zoo in his house...An all-star for years and years to come...Worth every cent of his $835,000 salary.

Year	Team	G	FG	FG Pct.	FT	FT Pct.	Reb.	Ast.	TP	Avg.
1885-86	Utah	81	504	.496	195	.481	718	236	1203	14.9
1986-87	Utah	82	728	.512	323	.598	855	158	1779	21.7
1987-88	Utah	82	858	.520	552	.700	986	199	2268	27.7
	Totals	245	2090	.511	1070	.617	2559	593	5250	21.4

JOHN STOCKTON 26 6-1 175   Guard

John Who?...That was the question on draft day of 1984 when the Jazz made him the No. 16 pick in the draft...Well, everybody knows the name now...Broke Isiah Thomas' single-season NBA assist record, then outplayed Magic Johnson in the head-to-head duel between Jazz and the Lakers in the playoffs...Probably the fastest player in the NBA...A real team leader, excellent quarterback in the running game or the set offense...Born March 26, 1962, in Spokane, Wash....Came out of nowhere—actually Gonzaga—to impress scouts at the 1984 Olympic Trials...Has never missed a game in four NBA seasons...A bargain at $278,000...John Who?

Year	Team	G	FG	FG Pct.	FT	FT Pct.	Reb.	Ast.	TP	Avg.
1984-85	Utah	82	157	.471	142	.736	105	415	458	5.6
1985-86	Utah	82	228	.489	172	.839	179	610	630	7.7
1986-87	Utah	82	231	.499	179	.782	151	670	648	7.9
1987-88	Utah	82	454	.574	272	.840	237	1128	1204	14.7
	Totals	328	1070	.521	765	.804	672	2823	2940	9.0

MARK EATON 31 7-4 290   Center

You've come a long way, baby . . . Had a college career of doing nothing but sitting on the bench at UCLA . . . But returned to LA last spring and gave fits to Kareem Abdul-Jabbar in the playoffs . . . Once again led the league in blocked shots with almost four a game . . . Almost single-handedly clogged the Laker attack in that classic seven-game series . . . Born Jan. 24, 1957, in Inglewood, Cal. . . . Had started on a career as an auto mechanic before Frank Layden convinced him to try pro ball . . . Can't jump over a sheet of paper, can't move faster than a brick wall and can't shoot anything more than a five-footer. But he can change a game like nobody else . . . Very foul-prone . . . Now makes $625,000.

Year	Team	G	FG	FG Pct.	FT	FT Pct.	Reb.	Ast.	TP	Avg.
1982-83	Utah	81	146	.414	59	.656	462	112	351	4.3
1983-84	Utah	82	194	.466	73	.593	595	113	461	5.6
1984-85	Utah	82	302	.449	190	.712	927	124	794	9.7
1985-86	Utah	80	277	.470	122	.604	675	101	676	8.5
1986-87	Utah	79	234	.400	140	.657	697	105	608	7.7
1987-88	Utah	82	226	.418	119	.623	717	55	571	7.0
	Totals	486	1379	.437	703	.647	4073	610	3461	7.1

BOB HANSEN 27 6-6 200   Guard

Favorite son? . . . . Not on your life . . . He's not a big-name point producer, but earns his starting job strictly on the basis of tough defense . . . Gave Magic Johnson all that he could handle in the playoff series with the Lakers . . . He can score when you need him . . . Born Jan. 18, 1961, in Des Moines, Iowa . . . A home-state star at Iowa in college . . . Jazz spotted him while watching scouting films of an opposing player . . . Utah got a steal on the third round (54th overall) of the 1983 draft . . . Got a raise last season to $200,000, but is still a bargain at that price . . . Might look like a fair-haired member of the Mormon Tabernacle Choir, but he'd stuff your organ pipes if it meant getting to a loose ball.

Year	Team	G	FG	FG Pct.	FT	FT Pct.	Reb.	Ast.	TP	Avg.
1983-84	Utah	55	65	.448	18	.643	48	44	148	2.7
1984-85	Utah	54	110	.489	40	.556	70	75	261	4.8
1985-86	Utah	82	299	.476	95	.720	244	193	710	8.7
1986-87	Utah	72	272	.453	136	.760	203	102	696	9.7
1987-88	Utah	81	316	.517	113	.743	187	175	777	9.6
	Totals	344	1062	.481	402	.714	752	589	2592	7.5

MARC IAVARONI 32 6-10 225   **Forward**

A gimmick starter... He got in for the opening minutes last year before Thurl Bailey came off the bench and played most of the game... Still serves a function as a hustler and a banger... Threw away inbounds pass for a crucial turnover to end Game 5 vs. the Lakers in the playoffs and may have cost the Jazz a chance to win the series... Born Sept. 15, 1956, in Bethpage, N.Y.... The center at Virginia before Ralph Sampson... Knicks made him the 55th pick in the 1978 draft and then cut him twice... Didn't make it to the NBA until 1982-83 season when hulking white guys out of the Kurt Rambis mold were in vogue... Played on Philadelphia title team as a rookie, then went to San Antonio for a year... Traded by Spurs to Jazz with Jeff Cook for Jeff Wilkins... No brain surgeon, he once wore his uniform pants backwards for the whole first half in a game against Portland. That's tough when they have a drawstring in the front.

Year	Team	G	FG	FG Pct.	FT	FT Pct.	Reb.	Ast.	TP	Avg.
1982-83	Philadelphia.........	80	163	.462	78	.690	329	83	404	5.1
1983-84	Philadelphia.........	78	149	.463	97	.740	310	95	395	5.1
1984-85	Phil.-S.A...........	69	162	.458	87	.680	304	119	411	6.0
1985-86	S.A.-Utah..........	68	110	.451	76	.661	209	82	296	4.4
1986-87	Utah..............	78	100	.465	78	.672	173	36	278	3.6
1987-88	Utah..............	81	143	.464	78	.788	268	67	364	4.5
	Totals.............	454	827	.460	494	.704	1593	482	2148	4.7

THURL BAILEY 27 6-11 232   **Forward**

The Utah PR department likes to call him the NBA's "true" sixth man... But truth in advertising would force the Jazz to admit that he's really a starter in sheep's clothing... Actually played more minutes last season than every team member but Karl Malone and John Stockton... A wonderful talent who has the height to go inside and the nice outside touch to stick the long jumper... Wears goggles like Kareem Abdul-Jabbar... Born April 7, 1961, in Washington, D.C.... Big college career at North Carolina State, where he gained notoriety beating up on Ralph Sampson... After capturing NCAA title in 1983, he was Jazz' top pick (No. 7 overall) in the draft... Says his ambition is to be a radio-TV announcer, but that will have to wait... Still has a long and productive career ahead... Salary is $549,000.

Year	Team	G	FG	FG Pct.	FT	FT Pct.	Reb.	Ast.	TP	Avg.
1983-84	Utah	81	302	.512	88	.752	464	129	692	8.5
1984-85	Utah	80	507	.490	197	.842	525	138	1212	15.2
1985-86	Utah	82	483	.448	230	.830	493	153	1196	14.6
1986-87	Utah	81	463	.447	190	.805	432	102	1116	13.8
1987-88	Utah	82	633	.492	337	.826	531	158	1604	19.6
	Totals	406	2388	.475	1042	.819	2445	680	5820	14.3

MEL TURPIN 27 6-11 280   Center

Have snacks will travel.... When traded to Utah in summer of 1987, he arrived in Salt Lake City weighing 15 pounds more than he supposedly weighed when he left. "I like airplane food," he explained... Just don't put your hands around his mouth or your fingers will be gone... Was so out of shape by the end of the year that Frank Layden didn't use him at all... Either that or he was too heavy to get up off the bench... Born Dec. 28, 1960, in Lexington, Ky.... A decent college career at Kentucky... The fat is what keeps him from being a player in the NBA... Washington made him No. 6 pick in the 1984 draft and was shipped to Cleveland for Cliff Robinson... Farmed out to Utah with Darryl Dawkins for Kent Benson and Dell Curry... He could probably eat the Mormon Tabernacle and use the Great Salt Lake to wash it down... Almost stealing money at $1 million a year.

Year	Team	G	FG	FG Pct.	FT	FT Pct.	Reb.	Ast.	TP	Avg.
1984-85	Cleveland	79	363	.511	109	.784	452	36	835	10.6
1985-86	Cleveland	80	456	.544	185	.811	556	55	1097	13.7
1986-87	Cleveland	64	169	.462	55	.714	190	33	393	6.1
1987-88	Utah	79	199	.512	71	.724	236	32	470	5.9
	Totals	302	1187	.515	420	.775	1434	156	2795	9.3

BART KOFOED 24 6-5 205   Guard

You've got to be kidding... That's what everybody was thinking in the playoffs every time he entered a game instead of Rickey Green... Frank Layden likes those unknown players... This guy certainly qualifies, coming out of NAIA's Kearny State (Neb.), where he was the team captain MVP of something called the Central States Conference... Born March 24, 1964, in Omaha, Neb.... Jazz dipped down deep to make him the 107th pick overall in the 1987 draft... Not much of a game, but he has managed to acquire an All-NBA tan... Salary: Are you kidding? He probably pays the Jazz to let him play.

Year	Team	G	FG	FG Pct.	FT	FT Pct.	Reb.	Ast.	TP	Avg.
1987-88	Utah.............	36	18	.375	8	.615	15	23	46	1.3

DARRELL GRIFFITH 30 6-4 190   Guard

Smitten by injuries... Sat out all of the 1985-86 season with a stress fracture in his foot and was kept down to very limited duty last season by a recurring knee problem... Played in only 52 games and started just 11 ... Sidelined for all of the playoffs... He was Dr. Dunkenstein in college, but became the Mad Bomber of the three-point shot in the NBA... Born June 1, 1958, in Louisville, Ky.... A homegrown product who led Louisville and coach Denny Crum to the NCAA title in 1980... Still a great leaper... He's faded from the headlines in recent seasons and that has made him a constant source of trade rumors for the last year... Salary of $685,000 is not justified by the minutes and the role he's played lately... The No. 2 pick in the 1980 draft. Jazz took him after Joe Barry Carroll (good) and ahead of Kevin McHale (bad).

Year	Team	G	FG	FG Pct.	FT	FT Pct.	Reb.	Ast.	TP	Avg.
1980-81	Utah.............	81	716	.464	229	.716	288	194	1671	20.6
1981-82	Utah.............	80	689	.482	189	.697	305	187	1582	19.8
1982-83	Utah.............	77	752	.484	167	.679	304	270	1709	22.2
1983-84	Utah.............	82	697	.490	151	.696	338	283	1636	20.0
1984-85	Utah.............	78	728	.457	216	.725	344	243	1764	22.6
1985-86	Utah.............					Injured				
1986-87	Utah.............	76	463	.446	149	.703	227	129	1142	15.0
1987-88	Utah.............	52	251	.429	59	.641	127	91	589	11.3
	Totals.............	526	4296	.469	1160	.700	1933	1397	10093	19.2

MIKE BROWN 25 6-9 240   Forward-Center

Well, he is big... Given Bulls' starting job in December, gave it back in February... Played four minutes in playoffs. Made a free throw, delighting folks back home in Newark, N.J., where he was born July 19, 1963... As pleasant and upbeat as they get... Has no offensive game to speak of... Became a cheerleader after starting job went back to Dave Corzine ... Had great junior year at George Washington, and had been projected as first-round pick until toe injury marred his senior year...Became Bulls' third-round pick in 1985...Played in Italy for two seasons...Hornets made him their fourth selection in expansion draft, then sent him to Jazz for Kelly Tripucka.

Year	Team	G	FG	FG Pct.	FT	FT Pct.	Reb.	Ast.	TP	Avg.
1986-87	Chicago	62	106	.527	46	.639	214	24	258	4.2
1987-88	Chicago	46	78	.448	41	.577	159	28	197	4.3
	Totals	108	184	.491	87	.608	373	52	455	4.2

TOP ROOKIE

ERIC LECKNER 22 6-11 265   **Center**
Big man with a nice shooting touch from the outside...Also has very good hands and a knack for making the right pass...Was overshadowed during his career at Wyoming by flamboyant teammate Fennis Dembo...Born May 27, 1966, in Manhattan Beach, Cal....Not much of a leaper, but he loves to bang on the inside...Finished up as third-leading scorer in Wyoming history...Utah made him the No. 17 pick overall in the first round...He'll stick around.

COACH FRANK LAYDEN: In India, they'd worship this body ...He once wore a blue and yellow suit and somebody thought he was a Fotomat store and tried to drop film in his pocket...One-liners, wisecracks, a laugh a minute...That's Fat Frank...But it's not all fun and games anymore...The Jazz have risen to the level of legitimate contender in the Western Conference instead of being an opening act at the Comedy Store...His club had its fifth-straight season of finishing at .500 or better, then took the defending champion Lakers to the seven-game limit before going down in the second round of the playoffs...Along the way, the coach lost a bit of his sense of humor...Was fined a total of $16,000 last season for criticizing refs and barring the media from the locker room following Game 5 in LA...Some of the fans are dissatisfied with him...Born Jan. 5, 1932, in Brooklyn, N.Y....He's a Big Apple classic... NBA Coach of the Year in 1983-84...Coached Calvin Murphy

ALTON LISTER 30 7-0 240   Center

Stats say he's a lot more effective than he looks... Got his most notoriety last season when wife Bobby Jo got into a fight outside Seattle locker room with the wife of teammate Dale Ellis... Not at all a big scorer for someone with $835,000 salary... He did lead the Sonics in rebounding again last season... Born Oct. 1, 1958, in Dallas... Owes his big contract and career to Don Nelson, who molded him into a player during five years together in Milwaukee... A first-round draft choice by the Bucks in 1981... Came to the Pacific Northwest in 1986 in the deal that shipped Jack Sikma to Milwaukee... Member of the 1980 U.S. Olympic team that boycotted the Moscow Games... Teammate at Arizona State with Fat Lever, Sam Williams, Kurt Nimphius and Byron Scott. All made it to the NBA.

Year	Team	G	FG	FG Pct.	FT	FT Pct.	Reb.	Ast.	TP	Avg.
1981-82	Milwaukee..........	80	149	.519	64	.520	387	84	362	4.5
1982-83	Milwaukee..........	80	272	.529	130	.537	568	111	674	8.4
1983-84	Milwaukee..........	82	256	.500	114	.626	603	110	626	7.6
1984-85	Milwaukee..........	81	322	.538	154	.588	647	127	798	9.9
1985-86	Milwaukee..........	81	318	.551	160	.602	592	101	796	9.8
1986-87	Seattle.............	75	346	.504	179	.675	705	110	871	11.6
1987-88	Seattle.............	82	173	.504	114	.606	627	58	461	5.6
	Totals.............	561	1836	.522	915	.599	4129	701	4588	8.2

RUSS SCHOENE 28 6-10 215   Forward

Big Red... Versatile enough to go inside for the rebounds or can consistently hit the jumper from the perimeter... Another guy who's stuck around the league through perseverance and hard work... Born April 16, 1960, in Trenton, Ill.... Came out of nowhere. Well, actually from Tennessee-Chattanooga... Drafted on the second round in 1982 by Philadelphia... Was traded to Indiana midway through his rookie year and missed a chance to get a championship ring that season with the Sixers... Waived out of the league... He went to Europe for three seasons and teamed with Joe Barry Carroll on Simac team that won the Italian League championship in 1986.

Year	Team	G	FG	FG Pct.	FT	FT Pct.	Reb.	Ast.	TP	Avg.
1982-83	Phil.-Ind............	77	207	.476	61	.735	255	59	476	6.2
1986-87	Seattle.............	63	71	.374	29	.630	117	27	173	2.7
1987-88	Seattle.............	81	208	.458	51	.810	198	53	484	6.0
	Totals.............	221	486	.450	141	.734	570	139	1155	5.1

OLDEN POLYNICE 23 7-0 245   Center

Raw... But tough and mean, too.... Has been known to throw plenty of stray elbows, which made him fit right in on the rough-and-tumble Sonics... Followed Ralph Sampson as the starting center at Virginia... Had to leave school with eligibility remaining when implicated in incidents of cheating and stealing... Born Nov. 21, 1964, in New York... Played for one year in Europe with Rimini in the Italian League... Regarded as a project... Could make any team a real force inside if he learns the fundamentals of the game... Drafted on the first round in 1987 by Chicago and traded to Seattle on the same day in exchange for fellow rookie Scottie Pippen... Made $350,000 last season.

Year	Team	G	FG	FG Pct.	FT	FT Pct.	Reb.	Ast.	TP	Avg.
1987-88	Seattle	82	118	.465	101	.639	330	33	337	4.1

SEDALE THREATT 27 6-2 180   Guard

A designated shooter... For a couple of seasons in Philadelphia, it was thought he could blossom into a star... Now he's strictly a guy who can help you from time to time off the bench by hitting the open shot... Drafted by the Sixers on the sixth round in 1983 out of West Virginia Tech... Spent three years in Philly and has bounced around a bit... First went to Chicago for Steve Colter and then was shipped to Seattle late last season for Sam Vincent... Born Sept. 10, 1961, in Atlanta... Streaky kind of player... You never know whether he'll be trick or Threatt.

Year	Team	G	FG	FG Pct.	FT	FT Pct.	Reb.	Ast.	TP	Avg.
1983-84	Philadelphia	45	62	.419	23	.821	40	41	148	3.3
1984-85	Philadelphia	82	188	.452	66	.733	99	175	446	5.4
1985-86	Philadelphia	70	310	.453	75	.833	121	193	696	9.9
1986-87	Phil.-Chi.	68	239	.448	95	.798	108	259	580	8.5
1987-88	Chi.-Sea.	71	216	.508	57	.803	88	160	492	6.9
	Totals	336	1015	.460	316	.794	456	828	2362	7.0

TOP ROOKIE

COREY GAINES 23 6-3 195   Guard

Starting point guard for the fastest team in the West last season at

at Niagara . . . Roommate at Niagara of Hubie Brown . . . Joined
the Jazz in 1979 and became the head coach in 1981 season . . .
Definitely one of a kind . . . Career record is 266-288.

GREATEST THREE-POINT SHOOTER

The name just doesn't go with the player. They used to call
him Dr. Dunkenstein, but Darrell Griffith has made his biggest
mark in the NBA not with the slam, but with the bomb. He holds
all of the club marks for attempts and three-pointers made and
just to watch Griffith release that beautifully arcing rainbow that
seems to touch the sky is a thing of beauty.

The Jazz had to make do without Griffith's touch much of last
season due to injury and had a number of other candidates try
to fill the void. Griffith's closest competition for best long-
range gunner came from Kelly Tripucka, who makes up in
accuracy what he lacks in quantity. Tripucka ranked in the top 10
(percentage-wise) in the NBA, but the Jazz' best bomber
remains Dr. Dunkenstein, even if the nickname doesn't fit.

ALL-TIME JAZZ LEADERS

SEASON

Points: Adrian Dantley, 2,457, 1981-82
Assists: John Stockton, 1,128, 1987-88
Rebounds: Len Robinson, 1,288, 1977-78

GAME

Points: Pete Maravich, 68 vs. New York, 2/25/77
Assists: John Stockton, 26 vs. Portland, 4/14/88
Rebounds: Len Robinson, 27 vs. Los Angeles, 11/11/77

CAREER

Points: Adrian Dantley, 13,545, 1979-86
Assists: Rickey Green, 4,159, 1980-88
Rebounds: Mark Eaton, 4,073, 1982-88

ATLANTA HAWKS

TEAM DIRECTORY: Pres./GM: Stan Kasten; Dir. Pub. Rel: Bill Needle; Coach: Mike Fratello; Asst. Coaches: Brendan Suhr, Brian Hill, Cazzie Russell. Arena: The Omni (16,451). Colors: Red and white.

SCOUTING REPORT

SHOOTING: It'll get better. The Hawks' .485 placed them 10th in field-goal percentage. And they managed that with Dominique Wilkins hoisting up 28 percent of their shots and settling in at .464. 'Nique fired away 1,957 times, more than twice as many as the Hawks' No. 2 man, Doc Rivers. There was sniping all season from both sides. Dominique said he didn't get enough offensive help; the other Hawks felt he was too much of the offense.

The addition of 14-year vet Moses Malone and Reggie Theus, a certified shooter, should have a big impact. Malone averaged 20.3 ppg last year with the Bullets. Theus cost a No. 1 pick and Randy Wittman, who was the only starting guard in the league not to even attempt a three-pointer. Unlike Wittman, Theus has superb range and can create his own shots.

PLAYMAKING: Steady Rivers (747 assists) continues to blossom and proved he can handle playoff pressure. But after him, the Hawks' passing game is hurting. Wilkins dishes off well, but he doesn't do it enough. And after him, assists along the Hawk frontline usually come by accident. Kevin Willis is just a bad passer. The Hawks ranked closer to the bottom than the top with 2,062 assists, but should improve as the offensive burden is lifted from 'Nique.

DEFENSE: An area where the Hawks don't get enough credit. They're a hard-working bunch who conjure up images of skilled offensive players rather than tenacious defenders. Still, they forced foes into .471 shooting, fifth best in the league, and their yield of 104.3 was fourth best. The Hawks employ all sorts of switches and traps—and with an athletic, physical front line, they make you pay the price.

REBOUNDING: With stallions like Willis, Wilkins and Cliff Levingston complementing horses like Antoine Carr and Jon Koncak, the Hawks have been one of the better offensive rebounding teams in the league. And now they have one of the

All-Star Doc Rivers keeps Hawk offense flowing.

all-time bangers in Malone, who was second in the NBA in offensive rebounds last season.

OUTLOOK: If not for Larry Bird's spectacular fourth quarter in Game 7 of their second-round playoff series, Mike Fratello's Hawks would have been in the Eastern Conference finals. Even in defeat, they answered a lot of questions about their heart. They are still young, still athletic and still one of the league's most dangerous forces. Pencil in another 50-victory season and further advancement in the playoffs.

HAWK PROFILES

DOMINIQUE WILKINS 28 6-8 200   **Forward**

U'Nique's best season . . . Averaged career-high 30.7 points per game and continued all-around improvement . . . Took 28 percent of team's shots . . . Still the Human Highlight Film . . . Electrifying leaper, owns spin moves he hasn't used . . . Had Game 7 shootout with Larry Bird in Eastern Conference semis that is destined for legend status. Scored 16 fourth-quarter points to finish with 47; Bird got 20 for 34 . . . Wants to work on lefty shot . . . Still gets carried away offensively . . . Superb on finishing the break . . . Doesn't get enough credit for defense . . . Is he too much of Hawk offense? "Dominique is

HAWK ROSTER

No.	Veteran	Pos.	Ht.	Wt.	Age	Yrs. Pro	College
12	John Battle	G	6-2	175	25	3	Rutgers
33	Antoine Carr	F	6-9	235	27	4	Wichita State
55	Jon Koncak	C	7-0	250	25	3	SMU
53	Cliff Levingston	F	6-8	210	27	6	Wichita State
—	Moses Malone	C	6-10	255	33	14	None
25	Glenn (Doc) Rivers	G	6-4	185	27	5	Marquette
24	Reggie Theus	G	6-7	205	31	10	Nevada-Las Vegas
50	Chris Washburn	C	6-11	235	23	2	North Carolina State
4	Spud Webb	G	5-6	133	25	3	North Carolina State
21	Dominique Wilkins	F	6-8	200	28	6	Georgia
42	Kevin Willis	F	7-0	235	26	4	Michigan State

Rd.	Top Rookies	Sel. No.	Pos.	Ht.	Wt.	College
2	Anthony Taylor	44	G	6-4	175	Oregon
3	Jorge Gonzalez	54	C	7-6	370	Argentina
3	Darryl Middleton	68	F	6-9	230	Baylor

Dominique," coach Mike Fratello said. "When you try to do too much to change a player, you're only hurting his game. Dominique has grown as a player every year."... Earns $1.46 million a year... Born Jan. 12, 1960, in Sorbonne, France. Air Force brat... Real name Jacques... Starred at Georgia, and Jazz made him third player selected in 1982 draft... Dealt to Hawks prior to '82 season for John Drew, Freeman Williams and cash.

Year	Team	G	FG	FG Pct.	FT	FT Pct.	Reb.	Ast.	TP	Avg.
1982-83	Atlanta	82	601	.493	230	.682	478	129	1434	17.5
1983-84	Atlanta	81	684	.479	382	.770	582	126	1750	21.6
1984-85	Atlanta	81	853	.451	486	.806	557	200	2217	27.4
1985-86	Atlanta	78	888	.468	577	.818	618	206	2366	30.3
1986-87	Atlanta	79	828	.463	607	.818	494	261	2294	29.0
1987-88	Atlanta	78	909	.464	541	.826	502	224	2397	30.7
	Totals	479	4763	.468	2823	.798	3231	1146	12458	26.0

KEVIN WILLIS 26 7-0 235   Forward

Get the Windex. Another streaky season, typified in playoffs vs. Celts... In Games 3-5, scored 23, 19 and 27. Then managed only 8 and 10 after that... Struggled after December knee injury... Late bloomer, still developing. Didn't play organized ball until junior year in high school... Small hands partially responsible for meager 7.3-rebound average... Still, an asset... Eleventh draft pick in '84 out of Michigan State... Game suffered last season when he was forced to play a lot of backup center because of Jon Koncak injury... Passing must improve...Has averaged one assist every 52 minutes...Sees the court with blinders...Good on break...Nice jump hook ...When he's on, he's fierce. When he's off, he breaks pollution laws...Earned $395,000...Born Sept. 6, 1962, in Los Angeles.

Year	Team	G	FG	FG Pct.	FT	FT Pct.	Reb.	Ast.	TP	Avg.
1984-85	Atlanta............	82	322	.467	119	.657	522	36	765	9.3
1985-86	Atlanta............	82	419	.517	172	.654	704	45	1010	12.3
1986-87	Atlanta............	81	538	.536	227	.709	849	62	1304	16.1
1987-88	Atlanta............	75	356	.518	159	.649	547	28	871	11.6
	Totals............	320	1635	.512	677	.671	2622	171	3950	12.3

GLENN (DOC) RIVERS 27 6-4 185   Guard

Walking quote machine...Good point guard getting better...Rebounded from 1987 playoff spanking by Isiah Thomas and heavy criticism to post best season as pro (14.2 points, 9.3 assists)...Set team record with 22 assists in playoff game against Celtics last season, including NBA playoff-tying 15 in first half...Blocked 41 shots—same total as 7-foot teammate Kevin Willis...Downright likable, sincere guy ...Honest to a fault...Goes to his right too often...Jumper sometimes erratic, but is one of finest penetrating guards in game...Selected to first All-Star Game...Averaged 18.5 points after break...Was 31st pick in 1983 draft out of Marquette as undergraduate eligible...Born Oct. 13, 1961, in Chicago... Earned $450,000.

Year	Team	G	FG	FG Pct.	FT	FT Pct.	Reb.	Ast.	TP	Avg.
1983-84	Atlanta............	81	250	.462	255	.785	220	314	757	9.3
1984-85	Atlanta............	69	334	.476	291	.770	214	410	974	14.1
1985-86	Atlanta............	53	220	.474	172	.608	162	443	612	11.5
1986-87	Atlanta............	82	342	.451	365	.828	299	823	1053	12.8
1987-88	Atlanta............	80	403	.453	319	.758	366	747	1134	14.2
	Totals............	365	1549	.462	1402	.759	1261	2737	4530	12.4

MOSES MALONE 33 6-10 255   Center

Sought long-term Bullets' contract after his $2.1-million deal ran out, but he didn't figure in Wes Unseld's long-range plans. ... So he ended up with a Hawks' pact for three years that could bring him, with bonuses, an estimated $1.5 million a year...Average of 20.3 points per game was lowest since second NBA season in 1977-78...But the man is still a rebounding clinic...Only Charles Barkley (385) had more offensive rebounds than Moses' 372. Ranks 10th on all-time NBA rebounding list, second in active players to Kareem Abdul-Jabbar... Didn't foul out for 10th straight season... Three-time league MVP wants to exit with a winner... Had been 1-of-34 in three-pointers, until he heated up last season with 2-of-7... But his average of 18.6 points in playoffs was lowest in 10 years... One of three players to jump to pros from high school (Darryl Dawkins and Bill Willoughby are the others)... Began career with two-year ABA stint... Came to Bullets in June 1986 deal with Philadelphia with Terry Catledge and first-round pick for Cliff Robinson, Jeff Ruland and 1988 first-round pick... Born March 23, 1955, in Petersburg, Va.

Year	Team	G	FG	FG Pct.	FT	FT Pct.	Reb.	Ast.	TP	Avg.
1974-75	Utah (ABA)	83	591	.571	375	.635	1209	82	1557	18.8
1975-76	St. Louis (ABA)	43	251	.512	112	.612	413	58	614	14.3
1976-77	Buf.-Hou.	82	389	.480	305	.693	1072	89	1083	13.2
1977-78	Houston	59	413	.499	318	718	886	31	1144	19.4
1978-79	Houston	82	716	.540	599	.739	1444	147	2031	24.8
1979-80	Houston	82	778	.502	563	.719	1190	147	2119	25.8
1980-81	Houston	80	806	.522	609	.757	1180	141	2222	27.8
1981-82	Houston	81	945	.519	630	.762	1188	142	2520	31.1
1982-83	Philadelphia	78	654	.501	600	.761	1194	101	1908	24.5
1983-84	Philadelphia	71	532	.483	545	.750	950	96	1609	22.7
1984-85	Philadelphia	79	602	.469	737	.815	1031	130	1941	24.6
1985-86	Philadelphia	74	571	.458	617	.787	872	90	1759	23.8
1986-87	Washington	73	595	.454	570	.824	824	120	1760	24.1
1987-88	Washington	79	531	.487	543	.788	884	112	1607	20.3
	Totals	1046	8374	.500	7123	.752	14337	1486	23874	22.8

REGGIE THEUS 31 6-7 205   Guard

Escape from purgatory... Delighted to join one of NBA's elite teams when Atlanta acquired him for Randy Wittman and first-round pick hours prior to June draft... Went from Chicago to KC and then Sacramento, but despite being out of the bright lights he's managed to shine... Was the Kings' best scorer and assist man the past two seasons... Born Oct. 13, 1957, in Inglewood, Cal.... He'd have fit right at home with the Lakers... Has always felt unappreciated and he's got a point... Both size and speed make him a good defender when he wants to be... Probably should concentrate less on the outside bombing and more on going to the hoop... Always on the cutting edge of fashion, he's had numerous modeling assignments... Traded to the Kings in 1984 for Steve Johnson... Not the bad guy he was made out to be in Chicago... Bulls drafted him on first round as a Nevada-Las Vegas undergrad in 1978.

Year	Team	G	FG	FG Pct.	FT	FT Pct.	Reb.	Ast.	TP	Avg.
1978-79	Chicago	82	537	.480	264	.761	228	429	1338	16.3
1979-80	Chicago	82	566	.483	500	.838	329	515	1660	20.2
1980-81	Chicago	82	543	.495	445	.809	287	426	1549	18.9
1981-82	Chicago	82	560	.469	363	.808	312	476	1508	18.4
1982-83	Chicago	82	749	.478	434	.801	300	484	1953	23.8
1983-84	Chi.-K.C.	61	262	.419	214	.762	129	352	745	12.2
1984-85	Kansas City	82	501	.487	334	.863	270	656	1341	16.4
1985-86	Sacramento	82	546	.480	405	.827	304	788	1503	18.3
1986-87	Sacramento	79	577	.472	429	.867	266	692	1600	20.3
1987-88	Sacramento	73	619	.470	320	.831	232	463	1574	21.6
	Totals	787	5460	.476	3708	.820	2657	5281	14771	18.8

JOHN BATTLE 25 6-2 175   Guard

Soars to new heights on jump shot . . . Human elevator . . . Showed true grit last season. Stricken by hepatitis, he returned to club a month later . . . Another example of how scouts mess up . . . Was the 84th player selected in 1985 draft, out of Rutgers . . . His emergence enabled Hawks to ship out Mike McGee . . . Hit career-high 27 points three times . . . His 10.6 average was fourth highest on team . . . Basketball body . . . Perseverance pays. Has fought and hustled to make it since rookie season. Now he's made it . . . Terrific streak shooter . . . Born Nov. 9, 1962, in Washington, D.C. . . . Has degree in criminal justice. His $100,000 salary is something of a crime.

Year	Team	G	FG	FG Pct.	FT	FT Pct.	Reb.	Ast.	TP	Avg.
1985-86	Atlanta	64	101	.455	75	.728	62	74	277	4.3
1986-87	Atlanta	64	144	.457	93	.738	60	124	381	6.0
1987-88	Atlanta	67	278	.454	141	.750	113	158	713	10.6
	Totals	195	523	.455	309	.741	235	356	1371	7.0

ANTOINE CARR 27 6-9 235   Forward

Keep him away from the Twinkies . . . Almost ate himself into oblivion. Reached 260 at one point . . . When he slimmed down, his superb low-post game came back . . . Still, his overall season was mediocre . . . Had a career-high 8.8 point per game average, but Hawks expected more . . . In Game 5 of Eastern Conference semis in Boston, he hit three straight spinning moves, reminding Celtics why they gave him offer sheet . . . Will earn $454,250. Salary escalates 15 percent thanks to that offer sheet . . . Ejected from game for shattering backboard in pregame warmup. Busted eight while playing in Italy in 1983-84 . . . Good soft touch and strong on offensive boards . . . Out of Wichita State, he was eighth pick overall by Pistons in 1983. Obtained with Cliff Levingston for aging Dan Roundfield in June 1984. An absolute steal . . . Born July 23, 1961, in Oklahoma City.

Year	Team	G	FG	FG Pct.	FT	FT Pct.	Reb.	Ast.	TP	Avg.
1984-85	Atlanta.	62	198	.528	101	.789	232	80	499	8.0
1985-86	Atlanta.	17	49	.527	18	.667	52	14	116	6.8
1986-87	Atlanta.	65	134	.506	73	.709	156	34	342	5.3
1987-88	Atlanta.	80	281	.544	142	.780	289	103	705	8.8
	Totals.	224	662	.530	334	.759	729	231	1662	7.4

SPUD WEBB 25 5-6 133   Guard

May be faster than a speeding bullet . . . No one stays with him coast to coast . . . An injection of adrenaline laced with caffeine off the bench . . . Can hit the 15-foot jumper consistently . . . Career threatened by damaged knee in 1986-87 . . . That season was more an exercise in physical rehab. . . . Obvious fan favorite. Gets tons of letters from appreciative small people . . . Makes $225,000 . . . Born July 13, 1963, in Dallas . . . Was fourth-round pick by Pistons in 1985 . . . Thrilled ACC fans with exploits at North Carolina State . . . Signed as free agent prior to '85 season.

Year	Team	G	FG	FG Pct.	FT	FT Pct.	Reb.	Ast.	TP	Avg.
1985-86	Atlanta.	79	199	.483	216	.785	123	337	616	7.8
1986-87	Atlanta.	33	71	.438	80	.762	60	167	223	6.8
1987-88	Atlanta.	82	191	.475	107	.817	146	337	490	6.0
	Totals.	194	461	.472	403	.789	329	841	1329	6.9

CLIFF LEVINGSTON 27 6-8 210   Forward

Getting better and better. First forward off bench, probably would start for a lot of teams . . . Perfect reserve in Hawks' scheme . . . Good leaper and active player. Solid off the offensive glass. Plays bigger and stronger than size . . . Good defense, too . . . But one shot may forever haunt him. In Game 6 against Celtics, he had chance to force overtime, but his driving, off-balance attempt fell way short . . . Another in the "good, young athlete" mold that seem to typify the Hawks . . .

Averaged 10 points and 6.1 rebounds per 26 minutes... Tied career high for rebounds (17) vs. Knicks in December 1987... Played with Antoine Carr at Wichita State and both arrived in Pistons' deal for Dan Roundfield after 1983-84 season... Born Jan. 4, 1961, in San Diego... Has $350,000 salary.

Year	Team	G	FG	FG Pct.	FT	FT Pct.	Reb.	Ast.	TP	Avg.
1982-83	Detroit	62	131	.485	84	.571	232	52	346	5.6
1983-84	Detroit	80	229	.525	125	.672	545	109	583	7.3
1984-85	Atlanta	74	291	.527	145	.653	566	104	727	9.8
1985-86	Atlanta	81	294	.534	164	.678	534	72	752	9.3
1986-87	Atlanta	82	251	.506	155	.731	533	40	657	8.0
1987-88	Atlanta	82	314	.557	190	.772	504	71	819	10.0
	Totals	461	1510	.526	863	.688	2914	448	3884	8.4

CHRIS WASHBURN 23 6-11 255   Center

Can this guy pan out? Does he care?... Disastrous rookie season in Golden State included stint in drug rehab and bizarre escapades that would have been comical had situation not been so sad (he was late for one game because of "a slow elevator")... Was given new lease in Atlanta... Probably blew it... Sent into one game and was quickly yanked when he didn't have sneakers tied... "I didn't think I'd get in," he said... Did nothing on court last season worth mentioning... Warriors wasted No. 2 pick of 1987 draft by selecting former North Carolina State product... Warriors sent him to Hawks for rights to Kenny Barlow in December 1987... Contract reworked to fit $770,000 salary slot... Size guarantees someone will always gamble.

Year	Team	G	FG	FG Pct.	FT	FT Pct.	Reb.	Ast.	TP	Avg.
1986-87	Golden State	35	57	.393	18	.353	101	16	132	3.8
1987-88	G.S.-Atl.	37	36	.444	18	.581	75	6	90	2.4
	Totals	72	93	.412	36	.439	176	22	222	3.1

JON KONCAK 25 7-0 250   Center

Torn right knee ligaments limited him to 49 games after two seasons of 82 each... His absence in playoffs against Celtics severely hurt Hawks... Was beginning to show promise that made him first-round pick (No. 5 overall) from SMU in 1985 draft... Only averaged 5.7 points per game, but had 6.0 average in 23.2 minutes... Highly coveted by Knicks. But

Hawks refused to part with him, nixing trade involving Bill Cartwright . . . Won starting job from Tree Rollins with early-season surge, then went back to sub status because of slump and injury . . . Watching playoffs made him angry and hungry . . . Born May 17, 1963, in Cedar Rapids, Iowa . . . Member of U.S. 1984 Olympic team that won gold medal.

Year	Team	G	FG	FG Pct.	FT	FT Pct.	Reb.	Ast.	TP	Avg.
1985-86	Atlanta............	82	263	.507	156	.607	467	55	682	8.3
1986-87	Atlanta............	82	169	.480	125	.654	493	31	463	5.6
1987-88	Atlanta............	49	98	.483	83	.610	333	19	279	5.7
	Totals............	213	530	.493	364	.623	1293	105	1424	6.7

TOP ROOKIE

ANTHONY TAYLOR 22 6-4 175   Guard

Second all-time leading scorer at Oregon . . . A two-time All-Pac 10 selection, he'll be tried by Hawks as point guard . . . Was 44th overall selection as Hawks had traded away first pick . . . Shot .502 as a freshman, but never approached that again . . . But he's a solid athlete with good all-around skills and fits into Hawks' mold . . . Member of U.S. squad in World University Games in '86 . . . "He'll have a longer and more prosperous career if he can play point guard," said Pacers' director of player personnel George Irvine . . . Born Nov. 30, 1965, in Beaverton, Ore.

COACH MIKE FRATELLO: He'll diagram Judgment Day lineups . . . Master coach . . . In fourth year at helm, directed third straight 50-victory season . . . Franchise never had back-to-back 50 wins before Fratello . . . Coached Eastern Conference to All-Star Game victory. Actually set up some plays, too . . . Intense every second of every game . . . Usually worn out at game's end, hoarse voice, completely drained . . . Four-year record of 231-179 . . . Former assistant to Hubie Brown, he's a tireless worker who has developed his own flair and identity . . . Parents Vincent and Marie remain his biggest fans . . . Dad was a Golden Gloves champion and pro middleweight . . . At 5-7 he's smallest coach in NBA . . . Played football, basketball and baseball at Montclair State (N.J.) . . . His sideline yelling sometimes wears thin on his players . . . But respect is definitely there . . . Born Feb. 24, 1947, in Hackensack, N.J. . . . A snappy dresser.

GREATEST THREE-POINT SHOOTER

The Hawks have traditionally been nearly non-existent from long distance. Last season, for example, only three teams attempted fewer three-point shots than the 282 hoisted by the Hawks. Since the NBA first measured off 23 feet, 9 inches in 1979, the Hawks have managed only one season in which they've ranked closer to the top of the league, rather than the bottom. That was in 1986-87, when they hit a team-record 135, thanks to Mike McGee.

With 86 three-pointers that season, McGee broke the Hawks' team record. Not just the team individual record, but the entire *team* mark. Before McGee, the Hawks' highest output in a season was 73 in 1984-85. McGee, whose 229 attempts in 1986-87 were by far an individual team high, added five more three-pointers in 19 attempts last season before his trade to Sacramento in December 1987.

ALL-TIME HAWK LEADERS

SEASON

Points: Bob Pettit, 2,429, 1961-62
Assists: Glenn Rivers, 823, 1986-87
Rebounds: Bob Pettit, 1,540, 1960-61

GAME

Points: Dominique Wilkins, 57 vs. Chicago, 11/10/86
Dominique Wilkins, 57 vs. New Jersey, 4/10/86
Lou Hudson, 57 vs. Chicago, 11/10/69
Bob Pettit, 57 vs. Detroit, 2/18/61
Assists: Glenn Rivers, 21 vs. Philadelphia, 3/4/86
Rebounds: Bob Pettit, 35 vs. Cincinnati, 3/2/58
Bob Pettit, 35 vs. New York, 1/6/56

CAREER

Points: Bob Pettit, 20,880, 1954-65
Assists: Lenny Wilkins, 3,048, 1960-68
Rebounds: Bob Pettit, 12,851, 1954-65

BOSTON CELTICS

TEAM DIRECTORY: Chairman: Don F. Gaston; Pres.: Arnold (Red) Auerbach; VP/GM Jan Volk; VP-Basketball Operations: K.C. Jones; Dir. Pub. Rel.: Jeff Twiss; Coach: Jimmy Rodgers; Asst. Coaches: Chris Ford, Lanny Van Eman. Arena: Boston Garden (14,890) and Hartford Civic Center (15,134). Colors: Green and white.

SCOUTING REPORT

SHOOTING: How often did two guys from the same team rank 1-2 in shooting? Never, until last year when Kevin McHale (.604) and Robert Parish (.589) did just that as the Celts were runaway leaders in field-goal percentage, their fifth straight year over 50 percent (.521). Yet their shooting deserted them in the playoffs thanks in part to the hounding by the Pistons. Larry Bird, a 53 percent marksman in regular season, was a very un-Bird-like 35 percent.

The Celtics' touch-passing ways drive opponents crazy and result in quality shot attempts. But their half-court offense often stagnated; Danny Ainge's three-point bombs was their only real versatility. With Jimmy Rodgers taking over as head coach, the Celtics figure to get back to more running and better opportunities.

PLAYMAKING: Good shots come from good passes. Simple. When the Celtics are moving the ball around, they do it better than anyone. Bird is Bird, a passing forward without peer. The Celtics are hoping No. 1 pick Brian Shaw will be a legit playmaker in time. Until he assumes the mantle from Dennis Johnson, the Celts will continue their share-the-wealth approach with everybody touching the ball. D.J. topped in assists with 598, followed by Ainge (503) and Bird (467).

DEFENSE: Opponents shot .482 against the Celtics. That's somewhat alarming considering the low percentages over the last two years. McHale again was voted to the All-Defensive team, Johnson showed he's still tough on "D" and—again—Bird is Bird. The Celtics can disguise a zone better than most. But age and the endless minutes played by regulars—which the Celts deny are factors—were very real factors in the defensive cracks.

REBOUNDING: No Celtic appeared among the league leaders and Bird's 703 boards were a team high. Like their passing, re-

Despite Bird feeds, the Celts were consumed by Pistons.

bounding is usually a democratic procedure. After Bird, Parish checked in with 628 and McHale added 536. Three years ago, they led the league in rebounds but last season they finished 16th. They need help here and figure it should come from second-year men Brad Lohaus and Mark Acres plus 7-2 Yugoslavian Stojko Vrankovic if he sticks after the Olympics.

OUTLOOK: A positively critical year for Boston. They are a step beyond aging. The insistence of sticking with the starters and

CELTIC ROSTER

No.	Veteran	Pos.	Ht.	Wt.	Age	Yrs. Pro	College
42	Mark Acres	F	6-11	225	25	1	Oral Roberts
44	Danny Ainge	G	6-5	185	29	7	Brigham Young
33	Larry Bird	F	6-9	220	31	9	Indiana State
53	Artis Gilmore	C	7-2	265	39	17	Jacksonville
3	Dennis Johnson	G	6-4	202	34	12	Pepperdine
35	Reggie Lewis	G	6-7	195	23	1	Northeastern
54	Brad Lohaus	F	7-0	230	24	1	Iowa
32	Kevin McHale	F	6-10	235	30	8	Minnesota
11	Dirk Minniefield	G	6-3	180	27	3	Kentucky
00	Robert Parish	C	7-0	230	35	12	Centenary
4	Jim Paxson	G	6-6	210	31	9	Dayton
5	Bill Walton	C	6-11	235	35	13	UCLA

Rd.	Top Rookies	Sel. No.	Pos.	Ht.	Wt.	College
1	Brian Shaw	24	G	6-6	190	Cal-Santa Barbara
3	Gerald Paddio	74	F-G	6-7	197	Nevada-Las Vegas

not working in the youth was devastating in the playoffs. Rodgers will make some changes—lessening starters' minutes and giving more minutes to the likes of Reggie Lewis. Too bad Rodgers doesn't have mineral rights to the Fountain of Youth. Still, the Celtics remain a superb team and they will win their 50. But after failing to make the NBA Finals for the first time since 1983, they lost some respect from the league. They want that back.

CELTIC PROFILES

LARRY BIRD 31 6-9 220   Forward

Bow head in reverence...One of greatest ever—many say THE greatest ever—who had perhaps his best season end with "my worst series ever."...Shot awful 36 percent as Celtics were bounced by Pistons in Eastern Conference final...Carried team in semifinals with incredible fourth-quarter, Game 7 shootout with Hawks' Dominique Wilkins.

Scored 20 points in final quarter, making shots heretofore deemed impossible...Cut long hair, lost 10 pounds, lifted weights before season. Wanted to be better. Scary part, he was ...Shot .527 from floor, .916 from line. Averaged 29.9 points, 9.3 rebounds, 6.1 assists...Second all-time Celtic scorer behind John Havlicek...Scored 2,000-plus points for fourth straight season...Set team records with 53 straight free throws and seven three-pointers in one game...Simply an outstanding passer...Accepted responsibility for team failing to make finals fifth straight year. "My shots don't go in and it carries over to everybody else. If I score and I'm on, everybody plays well. They're more confident. They know they can go to me if they're off."...Remarkable press relations turnaround since joining league. Went from introvert, often arrogant, to candid and utterly patient interview...Opened hotel in home state of Indiana...Born Dec. 7, 1956, in West Baden, Ind....Put Indiana State on map in 1979, leading Sycamores to NCAA championship game ...Drafted by Celts as junior eligible (sixth pick) in 1978... Earned $1.8 million and is underpaid.

Year	Team	G	FG	FG Pct.	FT	FT Pct.	Reb.	Ast.	TP	Avg.
1979-80	Boston............	82	693	.474	301	.836	852	370	1745	21.3
1980-81	Boston............	82	719	.478	283	.863	895	451	1741	21.2
1981-82	Boston............	77	711	.503	328	.863	837	447	1761	22.9
1982-83	Boston............	79	747	.504	351	.840	870	458	1867	23.6
1983-84	Boston............	79	758	.492	374	.888	796	520	1908	24.2
1984-85	Boston............	80	918	.522	403	.882	842	531	2295	28.7
1985-86	Boston............	82	796	.496	441	.896	805	557	2115	25.8
1986-87	Boston............	74	786	.525	414	.910	682	566	2076	28.1
1987-88	Boston............	76	881	.527	415	.916	703	467	2275	29.9
	Totals............	711	7009	.503	3310	.879	7282	4367	17783	25.0

KEVIN McHALE 30 6-10 225   Forward

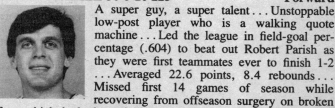

A super guy, a super talent...Unstoppable low-post player who is a walking quote machine...Led the league in field-goal percentage (.604) to beat out Robert Parish as they were first teammates ever to finish 1-2 ...Averaged 22.6 points, 8.4 rebounds... Missed first 14 games of season while recovering from offseason surgery on broken foot which had plagued him in 1987 playoffs...Has a good word for everybody, except Pistons' Rick Mahorn, "the only player in the league I can say I don't like."...Knows every down-low move in book, plus those that haven't yet been written ... Hockey freak ... Dry, rapid-fire wit ... Was named to NBA's All-Defensive team ... Broad shoulders and octopus-like arms make him quality shot-blocker ... When Celtic offense went south vs. Pistons, he was lone constant, averaging 26.8 ppg. Led Celtics throughout playoffs with 25.4 average ... Born Dec. 19, 1957, in Hibbing, Minn. ... Was third pick by Celts in '80 draft, out of Minnesota ... Earned $1.3 million ... May resemble Herman Munster, but he's a monster of a power forward.

Year	Team	G	FG	FG Pct.	FT	FT Pct.	Reb.	Ast.	TP	Avg.
1980-81	Boston	82	355	.533	108	.679	359	55	818	10.0
1981-82	Boston	82	465	.531	187	.754	556	91	1117	13.6
1982-83	Boston	82	483	.541	193	.717	553	104	1159	14.1
1983-84	Boston	82	587	.556	336	.765	610	104	1511	18.4
1984-85	Boston	79	605	.570	355	.760	712	141	1565	19.8
1985-86	Boston	68	561	.574	326	.776	551	181	1448	21.3
1986-87	Boston	77	790	.604	428	.836	763	198	2008	26.1
1987-88	Boston	64	550	.604	346	.797	536	171	1446	22.6
	Totals	616	4396	.567	2279	.773	4640	1045	11072	18.0

DENNIS JOHNSON 34 6-4 202   Guard

One of the top money players of all time ... One of few times he failed to find way to win was Game 6 in Eastern Conference final vs. Pistons ... Maybe it was because he was wearing pain-alleviating device for sore lower back ... Averaged 15.9 points in playoffs ... In regular season, had career-high 598 assists while averaging 12.6 points ... Shot just .438, low even by his standards ... "There are some people you just never worry about," said teammate Kevin McHale. "D.J. is one of those." ... When foes double-team, he invariably is left open. And he invariably buries the jumper ... Chronic right shoulder slowed him by end of regular season ... Always shone in postseason: MVP of 1978-79 playoffs; he made driving basket after Larry Bird's memorable steal in 1987 conference finals vs. Pistons ... Became Celt in June 1983 when Suns traded him and two draft picks for Rick Robey and two second-rounders ... Drafted out of Pepperdine on second round as hardship case in 1976 by Seattle. Went to Suns for Paul Westphal in June 1980 ... Born Sept. 18, 1954, in San Pedro, Cal. ... Earns $832,000.

Year	Team	G	FG	FG Pct.	FT	FT Pct.	Reb.	Ast.	TP	Avg.
1976-77	Seattle.............	81	285	.504	179	.624	302	123	749	9.2
1977-78	Seattle.............	81	367	.417	297	.732	294	230	1031	12.7
1978-79	Seattle.............	80	482	.432	306	.781	374	280	1270	15.9
1979-80	Seattle.............	81	574	.422	380	.780	414	332	1540	19.0
1980-81	Phoenix............	79	532	.436	411	.820	363	291	1486	18.8
1981-82	Phoenix............	80	577	.470	399	.806	410	369	1561	19.5
1982-83	Phoenix............	77	398	.462	292	.791	335	388	1093	14.2
1983-84	Boston.............	80	384	.437	281	.852	280	338	1053	13.2
1984-85	Boston.............	80	493	.462	261	.853	317	543	1254	15.7
1985-86	Boston.............	78	482	.455	243	.818	268	456	1213	15.6
1986-87	Boston.............	79	423	.444	209	.833	261	594	1062	13.4
1987-88	Boston.............	77	352	.438	255	.856	240	598	971	12.6
	Totals.............	953	5349	.446	3513	.795	3858	4542	14283	15.0

ROBERT PARISH 35 7-0 230   Center

Aging Chief...When he suffered bruised knee in Game 6 of Eastern Conference finals, Celtics were doomed...Finished regular season with highest field-goal percentage (.589) of career...Age and injuries have slowed him, so he picks his spots to run. When he does—or when "time-honored" (they don't like being called "old") Celts run, Parish is often first guy on break...Good first baseline step, quality turnaround jumper...Great passer, a Celtic must...With Bird and McHale, makes double-teams almost impossible...As chatty as a wall. "He said 13 words to me," said Pistons' John Salley, "and said that was it forever."...Intelligent pro who knows all the tricks...Laid savage attack on Bill Laimbeer two years ago in playoffs...Earns $2 million with incentives...Born Aug. 30, 1953, in Shreveport, La....Was going nowhere with Warriors, who sent him to Celts with first-round pick (which became Kevin McHale) for two first-round picks in 1980.

Year	Team	G	FG	FG Pct.	FT	FT Pct.	Reb.	Ast.	TP	Avg.
1976-77	Golden State........	77	288	.503	121	.708	543	74	697	9.1
1977-78	Golden State........	82	430	.472	165	.625	680	95	1025	12.5
1978-79	Golden State........	76	554	.499	196	.698	916	115	1304	17.2
1979-80	Golden State........	72	510	.507	203	.715	783	122	1223	17.0
1980-81	Boston.............	82	635	.545	282	.710	777	144	1552	18.9
1981-82	Boston.............	80	669	.542	252	.710	866	140	1590	19.9
1982-83	Boston.............	78	619	.550	271	.698	827	141	1509	19.3
1983-84	Boston.............	80	623	.546	274	.745	857	139	1520	19.0
1984-85	Boston.............	79	551	.542	292	.743	840	125	1394	17.6
1985-86	Boston.............	81	530	.549	245	.731	770	145	1305	16.1
1986-87	Boston.............	80	588	.566	227	.735	851	173	1403	17.5
1987-88	Boston.............	74	442	.589	177	.734	628	115	1061	14.3
	Totals.............	941	6439	.534	2705	.714	9338	1528	15583	16.6

DANNY AINGE 29 6-5 185   **Guard**

A real pest... "If I were on the other team, I wouldn't like me, either," said Danny Boy, who has a face mothers love and opponents want to bash... Good ball-hawker, still has cry-baby image... Really a great guy with terrific wit... Had miserable playoffs vs. Pistons. Shot 1-for-17 in last two games and was embarrassed by Isiah Thomas. "I was pitiful," he said... Few knew he played with strained back, though... Established NBA regular-season record for three-pointers with 147... Had streaks of 43 and 25 straight games with at least one three-pointer... Was three-sport All American in high school... Started pro career in baseball with Blue Jays, but had offensive numbers similiar to Piston series so he found new work... Born March 17 (fitting for guy named Danny), 1959 in Eugene, Ore ... Attended Brigham Young and was Celtics' second-round pick in 1981. Earns about $625,000.

Year	Team	G	FG	FG Pct.	FT	FT Pct.	Reb.	Ast.	TP	Avg.
1981-82	Boston	53	79	.357	56	.862	56	87	219	4.1
1982-83	Boston	80	357	.496	72	.742	214	251	791	9.9
1983-84	Boston	71	166	.460	46	.821	116	162	384	5.4
1984-85	Boston	75	419	.529	118	.868	268	399	971	12.9
1985-86	Boston	80	353	.504	123	.904	235	405	855	10.7
1986-87	Boston	71	410	.486	148	.897	242	400	1053	14.8
1987-88	Boston	81	482	.491	158	.878	249	503	1270	15.7
	Totals	511	2266	.490	721	.863	1380	2207	5543	10.8

JIM PAXSON 31 6-6 210   **Guard**

Don't ask how Celtics fit him in under salary cap. All the league's GMs are wondering the same thing... Portland contract called for about $875,000 last season, $1 million in the next two... And suddenly, he's a Celt because of February 1988 trade for Jerry Sichting... Father was former NBAer, younger brother John plays for Chicago... Used to be a Larry Bird in miniature and one of finest guards in league... Became resident of Portland bench before parole... Brought movement to often stagnant Celt offense... Played 27 games for Boston, averaged 8.7 points... Started playoffs strong, hurt back, became semi-useless... Had incredible streak in Game 4 vs. Pistons. Managed to get his first four shots blocked... Born July 9, 1957, in Kettering, Ohio... Played at Dayton before Blazers made him No. 12 pick in 1979 draft.

Year	Team	G	FG	FG Pct.	FT	FT Pct.	Reb.	Ast.	TP	Avg.
1979-80	Portland...........	72	189	.411	64	.711	109	144	443	6.2
1980-81	Portland...........	79	585	.536	182	.734	211	299	1354	17.1
1981-82	Portland...........	82	662	.526	220	.767	221	276	1552	18.9
1982-83	Portland...........	81	682	.515	388	.812	174	231	1756	21.7
1983-84	Portland...........	81	680	.514	345	.841	173	251	1722	21.3
1984-85	Portland...........	68	508	.514	196	.790	222	264	1218	17.9
1985-86	Portland...........	75	372	.470	217	.889	148	278	981	13.1
1986-87	Portland...........	72	337	.460	174	.806	139	237	874	12.1
1987-88	Port.-Bos...........	45	137	.460	68	.861	45	76	347	7.7
	Totals............	655	4152	.502	1854	.806	1442	2056	10247	15.6

REGGIE LEWIS 23 6-7 195   Guard

Another who K.C. Jones felt wasn't ready for prime time ... Smooth shooter who can find lots of ways to score ... Played just 405 minutes in regular season ... When he saw time during playoffs, some goods things happened.... Be patient, he's a player ... Three speeds: fast, faster and out of control ... Celtics' first-round pick in 1987 (22d overall) from nearby Northeastern ... Out of famed Dunbar High in Baltimore, where he was sixth man on team that included Reggie Williams and Muggsy Bogues. Should be better than both ... Scored 2,709 collegiate points, ninth-best total ever ... Top all-time scorer at Northeastern, which was 102-26 in his four years there ... Born Nov. 21, 1965, in Baltimore.

Year	Team	G	FG	FG Pct.	FT	FT Pct.	Reb.	Ast.	TP	Avg.
1987-88	Boston............	49	90	.466	40	.702	63	26	220	4.5

BRAD LOHAUS 24 7-0 230   Forward

Part of Celtics' future ... One of those not used enough during regular season as Celtic starters died in playoff ... Had Game 6 fight with Pistons' Dennis Rodman and was fined $1,500 ... Was thrust into game when Robert Parish hurt knee. Scored six points in 10 minutes. "He showed he's as good as I thought he was," said Larry Bird ... Nice kid ... Was good find on second round (45th pick) out of Iowa ... Wasn't a star there, either ... Registered team high with five blocks (in just 18 minutes against San Antonio) ... If he gets himself into the weight room, he has a chance ... Born Sept. 29, 1964, in New Ulm, Minn ... Paid $75,000.

Year	Team	G	FG	FG Pct.	FT	FT Pct.	Reb.	Ast.	TP	Avg.
1987-88	Boston............	70	122	.496	50	.806	138	49	297	4.2

MARK ACRES 25 6-11 225   Forward

Showed he can play . . . But he was top front-court sub, which also showed Celtics were in trouble . . . Signed by Celts last season as a free agent after European tour with Belgium . . . Prime expansion-team material . . . Good inside type who can bang bodies . . . Shot high percentage (.532), but was foul-prone . . . Averaged 3.6 points, 2.9 rebounds . . . Played for Dick Acres, his dad, at Oral Roberts, where brother Jeff was a teammate . . . Was a second-round draft pick of Dallas in 1985 . . . Born Nov. 15, 1962, in Inglewood, Cal. . . . Got minimum wage of $75,000 as a Celt.

Year	Team	G	FG	FG Pct.	FT	FT Pct.	Reb.	Ast.	TP	Avg.
1987-88	Boston	79	108	.532	71	.640	270	42	287	3.6

BILL WALTON 35 6-11 235   Center

How good could he have been if he stayed healthy? . . . Has missed more games due to injury than he has played since leaving UCLA after legendary career. Many proclaim him greatest collegian ever . . . Missed entire season for fourth time as pro because of never-ending foot injuries. Also had seasons of 14 and 10 games . . . Last year of contract paid him $450,000. Next move seems like retirement . . . Acquired by Celtics from Clippers in September 1985 for Cedric Maxwell and first-round pick . . . Born Nov. 5, 1952, in La Mesa, Cal. . . . First pick of 1974 draft by Trail Blazers . . . Led Portland to 1977 NBA title and was playoff MVP . . . One of greatest passing big men ever.

Year	Team	G	FG	FG Pct.	FT	FT Pct.	Reb.	Ast.	TP	Avg.
1974-75	Portland	35	177	.513	94	.686	441	167	448	12.8
1975-76	Portland	51	345	.471	133	.583	681	220	823	16.1
1976-77	Portland	65	491	.528	228	.697	934	245	1210	18.6
1977-78	Portland	58	460	.522	177	.720	766	291	1097	18.9
1978-79	Portland					Injured				
1979-80	San Diego	14	81	.503	32	.593	126	34	194	13.9
1980-81	San Diego					Injured				
1981-82	San Diego					Injured				
1982-83	San Diego	33	200	.528	65	.536	323	120	465	14.1
1983-84	San Diego	55	288	.556	92	.597	477	183	668	12.1
1984-85	L.A. Clippers	67	269	.521	138	.680	600	156	676	10.1
1985-86	Boston	80	231	.562	144	.713	544	165	606	7.6
1986-87	Boston	10	10	.385	8	.533	31	9	28	2.8
1987-88	Boston					Injured				
	Totals	468	2552	.521	1111	.660	4923	1590	6215	13.3

ARTIS GILMORE 39 7-2 265   Center

Should hang it up before someone gets killed ... Celtics were looking for a couple minutes per from pivot with Bill Walton again out for season. Signed on with Celts two weeks after Christmas Eve release by Bulls ... Wouldn't admit best decades were behind him ... Can be tough inside by pure strength, but has no moves, quickness, stamina left ... Got no respect last season from refs who called him for rookie fouls ... Played 47 games for Celts, averaged 3.6 points, first time in 17-year career he was not in double figures ... After helping Jacksonville to NCAA finals, started career with Kentucky of ABA. Selected by Chicago in ABA dispersal draft. Went to Spurs, back to Chicago, then Celts ... All-time NBA field-goal leader (.599) who won't face reality.

Year	Team	G	FG	FG Pct.	FT	FT Pct.	Reb.	Ast.	TP	Avg.
1971-72	Kentucky (ABA)......	84	806	.598	391	.646	1491	230	2003	23.8
1972-73	Kentucky (ABA)......	84	687	.559	368	.643	1476	295	1743	20.9
1973-74	Kentucky (ABA)......	84	621	.494	326	.667	1538	329	1568	18.7
1974-75	Kentucky (ABA)......	84	784	.580	412	.696	1361	208	1081	23.1
1975-76	Kentucky (ABA)......	84	773	.552	521	.682	1303	211	2067	24.6
1976-77	Chicago............	82	570	.522	387	.660	1070	199	1527	18.6
1977-78	Chicago............	82	704	.559	471	.704	1071	263	1879	22.9
1978-79	Chicago............	82	753	.575	434	.739	1043	274	1940	23.7
1979-80	Chicago............	48	305	.595	245	.712	432	133	855	17.8
1980-81	Chicago............	82	547	.670	375	.705	828	172	1469	17.9
1981-82	Chicago............	82	546	.652	424	.768	835	136	1517	18.5
1982-83	San Antonio........	82	556	.626	367	.740	984	126	1479	18.0
1983-84	San Antonio........	64	351	.631	280	.718	662	70	982	15.3
1984-85	San Antonio........	81	532	.623	484	.749	846	131	1548	19.1
1985-86	San Antonio........	71	423	.618	338	.701	600	102	1184	16.7
1986-87	San Antonio........	82	346	.597	242	.680	579	150	934	11.4
1987-88	Chi.-Bos...........	71	99	.547	67	.523	211	21	265	3.7
	Totals............	1329	9403	.582	6132	.698	16330	3050	24941	18.8

DIRK MINNIEFIELD 27 6-3 180   Guard

Ultimate journeyman ... Was picked up last season after being waived by Warriors, so that shows you how much Celtics were slipping ... Played in 61 games for Boston, averaging 3.6 points and 14 minutes ... In playoffs vs. Atlanta, had one of the most rotten five minutes in memory. Even numbers don't do justice just how bad it was. For the record, he shot 1-of-3, had two turnovers and two fouls as Hawks attacked him like sharks sniffing blood ... Lots and lots of weaknesses. Can penetrate, though. ... Second-round draft choice by Dallas in 1983 out of Kentucky. Has been traded or waived by almost everybody: Mavs, Nets, Bulls, Cavs, Rockets, Warriors... Born Jan. 17, 1961, in Lexington, Ky.... Earns $75,000... Cousin Frank Minnifield a standout cornerback with Cleveland Browns.

Year	Team	G	FG	FG Pct.	FT	FT Pct.	Reb.	Ast.	TP	Avg.
1985-86	Cleveland	76	167	.481	73	.785	131	269	417	5.5
1986-87	Clev.-Hou.	74	218	.452	62	.689	140	348	509	6.9
1987-88	G.S.-Bos.	72	108	.489	41	.745	96	228	261	3.6
	Totals	222	493	.470	176	.739	367	845	1187	5.3

TOP ROOKIE

BRIAN SHAW 22 6-6 190   Guard
Celtics delighted he was still available at No. 24... First point guard in history of Pacific Coast Athletic Conference to lead conference in rebounding (9.1 per game)... Quick, decent shooter, good defensively... "He reminds me of Michael Cooper," said Bucks' director of player personnel Bob Zuffelato... Averaged 13.3 points, 8.8 boards and 6.1 assists as senior... With Dennis Johnson getting another year closer to the end, this kid is expected to become Celts' point guard of the future... He'll watch and learn from the great ones this season... Born March 22, 1966, in Richmond, Cal.

COACH JIMMY RODGERS: There is justice in this life after all... For years, he's been the loyal soldier. For years, he got offers for head-coaching jobs. For years, he got shafted by Celts, who wouldn't let him go... Knicks wanted him after 1986 season, but Red Auerbach requested not one, but two pounds of flesh... Finally, after eight years as assistant with Celts (including four as director of player personnel), he gets his shot as K.C. Jones moves upstairs... Felt Jones should have used younger players more and may have been right... Superb basketball mind. Calling him just an assistant coach is like labeling Everest a big hill... Oozes class and draws respect... Tremendous judge of talent... Followed Bill Fitch as an assistant from North Dakota University to Cleveland to Boston. Then became a perennial coach-in-waiting... Born March 12, 1943, in Oak Park, Ill., and played guard at Iowa for four years... Of his years with Fitch, he said "each day was a learning experience."

GREATEST THREE-POINT SHOOTER

When you have Danny Ainge, who last season set an NBA record for three-point shots made (148), only someone special would stop him from ranking as the team's all-time three-point king. "Special" pretty well sums up Larry Bird.

Ainge has a better lifetime percentage (.389), but Bird (.377) is the unquestioned master. He has made more NBA career three-pointers (455-of-1206) than anybody. The All-Star Long Distance Shootout has become nothing more than a way for him to pocket a fast $12,500. They've held it three times. Bird has won it three times.

"There's too much money to be made," Bird said in predicting his Shootout victory last season. When asked about players who felt they should have been invited but weren't, Bird said they "wouldn't have a chance anyway." No one did. Not even Ainge. "I kinda felt sorry for Danny because he's been practicing for two months," Bird said.

One other player deserves mention: Chris Ford, currently a Celtic assistant coach. From 1979-82, Ford had 126, including the first ever in the NBA.

ALL-TIME CELTIC LEADERS

SEASON

Points: John Havlicek, 2,388, 1970-71
Assists: Bob Cousy, 715, 1959-60
Rebounds: Bill Russell, 1,930, 1963-64

GAME

Points: Larry Bird, 60 vs. Atlanta, 3/12/85
Assists: Bob Cousy, 28 vs. Minneapolis, 2/27/59
Rebounds: Bill Russell, 51 vs. Syracuse, 2/5/60

CAREER

Points: John Havlicek, 26,395, 1962-78
Assists: Bob Cousy, 6,945, 1950-63
Rebounds: Bill Russell, 21,620, 1956-69

CHARLOTTE HORNETS

TEAM DIRECTORY: Owner: George Shinn; VP-GM: Carl Scheer; Dir. Player Personnel: Gene Littles; Dir. Basketball Adm.: Ed Badger; Dir. Pub. Rel.: Andy Warfield; Coach: Dick Harter; Asst. Coaches: Ed Badger, Gene Littles. Arena: Charlotte Coliseum (23,500).

SCOUTING REPORT

SHOOTING: This may be the only thing Dick Harter's Hornets do. Kelly Tripucka, penciled in for small forward, was never shy about hoisting 'em up before he went to rot on the Utah bench the past two seasons. Dell Curry's reputation has always been that of a streak shooter. And Rex Chapman—in time—will supposedly shoot the lights out, if his arm doesn't fall off first.

As expected, the first-year roster will be dotted with certified bricklayers: Tyrone Bogues and Michael Holton, etc. Unless some serious help is found for Dave Hoppen, the only drafted player over 6-7, this gang could set some kind of unofficial record for attempted perimeter shots.

PLAYMAKING: They better do something with all the guards they've got. Since they pre-sold all those tickets, why in the world they took Bogues is anybody's guess. Sedric Toney, the last player selected in the expansion draft, is a gutsy little guy who can pass. Along with shooting, this is an area where the expansionists may be abysmal.

DEFENSE: They should see a lot of defense. They just won't play it that much, however. Tripucka will have to get a lot of minutes because he's the one guy who can score. But defense has never been emblazoned on his calling card. Robert Reid, at 33, is too old to play all-out defense for 40 minutes anymore. They could always walk the ball up and keep scores respectable.

Next category, please.

REBOUNDING: They think they can, they think they can, they think . . .

The Hornets will get some by accident, a few others off the long rebounds from the outside shots they miss. Earl Cureton and Kurt Rambis are both over 30 and both rusty from lack of playing time the last couple of seasons with the Clippers and Lakers, respectively. Michael Brooks was last healthy five years ago.

All that Jazz behind him, Kelly Tripucka eyes a fresh start.

Unfortunately, height is a nice thing to have for rebounding and the Hornets have very little. They have indicated they'll trade some of their guards for big men. And farmers in the Midwest would like to trade some dust and dirt for rain.

OUTLOOK: Start scouring those scouting reports now for next season's lottery. The most interesting competition could be between the Hornets and Heat to see who loses fewer games. Rebuilt knees are the standard battle scar with Brooks and Hoppen. Since it's their first year, victories may be as rare as scoring totals over 100.

HORNET ROSTER

No.	Veteran	Pos.	Ht.	Wt.	Age	Yrs. Pro	College
30	Dell Curry	G	6-5	195	24	2	Virginia Tech
1	Tyrone Bogues	G	5-4	140	23	2	Wake Forest
35	Michael Brooks	F	6-7	220	30	6	LaSalle
25	Earl Cureton	F-C	6-9	215	31	8	Detroit
14	Rickey Green	G	6-0	175	34	10	Michigan
6	Michael Holton	G	6-4	185	27	4	UCLA
52	Dave Hoppen	C	6-11	235	24	1	Nebraska
35	Ralph Lewis	F-G	6-6	205	25	1	LaSalle
31	Kurt Rambis	F	6-8	218	30	7	Santa Clara
33	Robert Reid	G-F	6-8	215	33	10	St. Mary's
11	Sedric Toney	G	6-2	178	26	2	Dayton
7	Kelly Tripucka	G-F	6-6	220	29	7	Notre Dame
5	Clinton Wheeler	G	6-1	185	29	1	William Paterson

Rd.	Top Rookies	Sel. No.	Pos.	Ht.	Wt.	College
1	Rex Chapman	8	G	6-4	185	Kentucky
2	Tom Tolbert	34	F	6-8	235	Arizona
3	Jeff Moore	58	F	6-7	240	Auburn

HORNET PROFILES

KELLY TRIPUCKA 29 6-6 220　　　　Guard-Forward

It just never worked out for him in Utah... This New Jersey boy had been completely out of place in Salt Lake City since arriving there two years ago... New chance in Charlotte (Hornets gave Jazz expansion pick Mike Brown, ex-Bull, in exchange) may be just what the doctor ordered... Traded in August 1986 to Jazz along with Kent Benson for Adrian Dantley and second-round draft choices in 1987 and 1990... His hairstyle—going from a long perm to a skinhead—isn't the only thing that's changed radically... Former 20-point scorer played in just 49 games last season and failed to average double figures for the first time in his career... Made no secret of his dislike for coach Frank Layden... Had been an anchor around the Jazz payroll at $971,000... Born Feb. 16, 1959, in Bloomfield, N.J... Played at Notre Dame with Orlando Woolridge... Father Frank was former Notre Dame quarterback... This will be his eighth NBA season and we're still waiting to see him play defense just one time down the floor.

Year	Team	G	FG	FG Pct.	FT	FT Pct.	Reb.	Ast.	TP	Avg.
1981-82	Detroit............	82	636	.496	495	.797	443	270	1772	21.6
1982-83	Detroit............	58	565	.489	392	.845	264	237	1536	26.5
1983-84	Detroit............	76	595	.459	426	.815	306	228	1618	21.3
1984-85	Detroit............	55	396	.477	255	.885	218	135	1049	19.1
1985-86	Detroit............	81	615	.498	380	.856	348	265	1622	20.0
1986-87	Utah............	79	291	.469	197	.872	242	243	798	10.1
1987-88	Utah............	49	139	.459	59	.868	117	105	368	7.5
	Totals............	480	3237	.481	2204	.837	1938	1483	8763	18.3

DELL CURRY 24 6-5 195   Guard

Change of scenery helped... Had disappointing rookie year with Utah, but became solid contributor off Cavalier bench in regular season... Playoffs were another story as he played just 17 minutes... Acquired in three-team deal from Jazz in October 1987, he matched rookie scoring high on opening night with 20 points at New Jersey... Career high of 27 came last December at Golden State... Earned rep as Otis Birdsong-type shooter out of Virginia Tech... Was 15th player selected in 1986 draft... But he just idled away in Salt Lake... Not a bad rebounder for a guard... Third on Cavs with 94 steals ... Good three-point shooter, making 28 of 81... Born June 25, 1964, in Grottoes, Va.... Hornets' first pick in expansion draft.

Year	Team	G	FG	FG Pct.	FT	FT Pct.	Reb.	Ast.	TP	Avg.
1986-87	Utah............	67	139	.426	30	.789	78	58	325	4.9
1987-88	Cleveland..........	79	340	.458	79	.782	166	149	787	10.0
	Totals............	146	479	.449	109	.784	244	207	1112	7.6

DAVE HOPPEN 24 6-11 235   Center

Hornets' only expansion list choice over 6-7 ... Originally drafted by Atlanta in third round of 1986 draft after he received All-American honors at Nebraska... Senior season cut short by devastating knee injury... First Cornhusker ever to have jersey retired... After his release from Hawks, he signed a 10-day contract with Bucks last January, was released, then picked up by Golden State... Hornets made him their first pick from expansion heap... A golf freak whose favorite movie is *Caddyshack*... Played for a high-school team nicknamed the "Bunnies"... Strictly minimum wage last season.

Year	Team	G	FG	FG Pct.	FT	FT Pct.	Reb.	Ast.	TP	Avg.
1987-88	Mil.-G.S............	39	84	.459	54	.871	174	32	222	5.7

TYRONE BOGUES 23 5-4 140   Guard

Muggsy didn't justify his No. 12 pick by the Bullets in the 1987 draft and he wound up as No. 6 in the expansion draft... His listed height vaulted an inch once he turned pro... Quickly proved he's not Spud Webb II... Sure, he's quick... But he's simply a poor shooter (.390)... Led Bullets in assists with 404 (5.1 per game), but every team (except Clippers) had assist-maker with more assists... Playing time decreased as season wore on. Saw total of two minutes in playoffs, setting up his place on unprotected list... Born Jan. 9, 1965, in Baltimore... Entertained ACC crowds during career at Wake Forest... Played at Dunbar High in Baltimore, where he was teammate of Reggie Lewis and Reggie Williams.

Year	Team	G	FG	FG Pct.	FT	FT Pct.	Reb.	Ast.	TP	Avg.
1987-88	Washington	79	166	.390	58	.784	136	404	393	5.0

EARL CURETON 31 6-9 215   Forward-Center

Earl the Twirl... An unlikely nickname for a guy who is simply a blue-collar worker... Had a flamboyant reputation in college at the University of Detroit, but now he's just a role player... A member of the Philadelphia 76ers' championship team in 1983... Has since played for Detroit, Chicago, LA Clippers and now Charlotte, where he signed as a free agent in July... Born Sept. 3, 1957, in Detroit... Drafted on the third round in 1979 by the Sixers... Clippers got him from the Bulls for a 1989 draft pick... He can be moody and has had problems with a couple of coaches... But mostly it's his lack of overall talent that sends him packing every couple of years... Coming to the end of the line.

Year	Team	G	FG	FG Pct.	FT	FT Pct.	Reb.	Ast.	TP	Avg.
1980-81	Philadelphia	52	93	.454	33	.516	155	25	219	4.2
1981-82	Philadelphia	66	149	.487	51	.543	270	32	349	5.3
1982-83	Philadelphia	73	108	.419	33	.493	269	43	249	3.4
1983-84	Detroit	73	81	.458	31	.525	287	36	193	2.6
1984-85	Detroit	81	207	.484	82	.569	419	83	496	6.1
1985-86	Detroit	80	285	.505	117	.555	504	137	687	8.6
1986-87	Chi.-LAC	78	243	.476	82	.539	452	122	568	7.3
1987-88	L.A. Clippers	69	133	.429	33	.524	271	63	299	4.3
	Totals	572	1299	.471	462	.541	2627	541	3060	5.3

ROBERT REID 33 6-8 215   Guard-Forward

You decide... He's either a cool veteran contributor or a slick-talking con man... He has been to the NBA Finals twice with the Rockets, but you always get the feeling that he should be doing a little bit more... Seems to get benefit of doubt with the media because of his outgoing personality... Can go on torrid shooting streaks... Born Sept. 30, 1955, in Atlanta... Lived all over the world when father was in the military... Stops in Crete and Hawaii before settling in tiny Shertz, Tex.... Rockets made a smart move by making him No. 40 pick in 1977 out of St. Mary's in San Antonio... Left NBA for one season to follow beliefs of Pentecostal religion... Has definitely lost a step... But still can dig in and play some defense... And now he's a Hornet, traded for Bernard Thompson.

Year	Team	G	FG	FG Pct.	FT	FT Pct.	Reb.	Ast.	TP	Avg.
1977-78	Houston	80	261	.455	63	.656	359	121	585	7.3
1978-79	Houston	82	382	.492	131	.704	483	230	895	10.9
1979-80	Houston	76	419	.487	153	.736	441	244	991	13.0
1980-81	Houston	82	536	.482	229	.756	583	344	1301	15.9
1981-82	Houston	77	437	.456	160	.748	511	314	1035	13.4
1983-84	Houston	64	406	.474	81	.659	341	217	895	14.0
1984-85	Houston	82	312	.481	88	.698	273	171	713	8.7
1985-86	Houston	82	409	.464	162	.757	301	222	986	12.0
1986-87	Houston	75	420	.417	136	.768	289	323	1029	13.7
1987-88	Houston	62	165	.463	50	.794	125	67	393	6.3
	Totals	762	3747	.467	1253	.733	3706	2253	8823	11.6

KURT RAMBIS 30 6-8 218   Forward

Is it possible to be a 30-year-old dinosaur?... It seems like millions of years ago when this guy was a crucial element of the Lakers' championship mixture... Last season he was part of the starting lineup for only the last quarter of the season and then went back to being a deep sub through all of the playoffs... Had lost his starting job to the younger and more mobile A.C. Green... Signed free-agent contract in July with Hornets, which is light years away from the fabulous Forum... Born Feb. 25, 1958, in Cupertino, Cal.... Played college ball at Santa Clara... Drafted and cut by the New York Knicks... Played a couple of years in Greece and then returned stateside when the Lakers needed a muscular body to bang their way to the title... Carved out a niche and started a trend of hulking white forwards for a couple of seasons... Had his own fan club—Rambis Youth—that used to emulate him and wear black-rimmed Clark Kent-style glasses... Now that fad is as out of date as the Nehru jacket... Made $525,000 last year, but hardly earned it.

Year	Team	G	FG	FG Pct.	FT	FT Pct.	Reb.	Ast.	TP	Avg.
1981-82	Los Angeles.........	64	118	.518	59	.504	348	56	295	4.6
1982-83	Los Angeles.........	78	235	.569	114	.687	531	90	584	7.5
1983-84	Los Angeles.........	47	63	.558	42	.636	266	34	168	3.6
1984-85	L.A. Lakers.........	82	181	.554	68	.660	528	69	430	5.2
1985-86	L.A. Lakers.........	74	160	.595	88	.721	517	69	408	5.5
1986-87	L.A. Lakers.........	78	163	.521	120	.764	453	63	446	5.7
1987-88	L.A. Lakers.........	70	102	.548	73	.785	268	54	277	4.0
	Totals.............	493	1022	.553	564	.684	2911	435	2608	5.3

RICKEY GREEN 34 6-0 175   Guard

What happened?... Went from being one of Utah's mainstays to a bench-warmer... Rarely got out of his seat late in the season and did not play at all in the playoffs against the Lakers... Word was that there were personality problems with coach Frank Layden... So he was expendable and he became 10th player chosen in expansion draft... Still can outrun most players in league. Born Aug. 18, 1954, in Chicago... Made big name for himself in college at Michigan... Drafted on the first round by Golden State... Cut by the Warriors and took the long way back through Detroit, then Billings (Mont.) and Hawaii of CBA... Hooked on with Utah in 1981... Went from starting 80 games two years ago to just three last season... Might still have one or two decent years left... Makes $312,000.

Year	Team	G	FG	FG Pct.	FT	FT Pct.	Reb.	Ast.	TP	Avg.
1977-78	Golden State........	76	143	.381	54	.600	116	149	340	4.5
1978-79	Detroit..............	27	67	.379	45	.672	40	63	179	6.6
1980-81	Utah...............	47	176	.481	70	.722	116	235	422	9.0
1981-82	Utah...............	81	500	.493	202	.765	243	630	1202	14.8
1982-83	Utah...............	78	464	.493	185	.797	223	697	1115	14.3
1983-84	Utah...............	81	439	.486	192	.821	230	748	1072	13.2
1984-85	Utah...............	77	381	.477	232	.869	189	597	1000	13.0
1985-86	Utah...............	80	357	.471	213	.852	135	411	932	11.7
1986-87	Utah...............	81	301	.467	172	.827	163	541	781	9.6
1987-88	Utah...............	81	157	.424	75	.904	80	300	393	4.9
	Totals.............	709	2985	.470	1440	.804	1535	4371	7436	10.5

MICHAEL HOLTON 27 6-4 185   Guard

One of those guys you're always surprised to find is still in the league . . . A very low-profile player, despite getting into all 82 regular-season and all four playoff games for the Blazers last season . . . A former *Parade Magazine* All-American . . . Made a big name at UCLA . . . Never unpacks his suitcase, because he's always on the move . . . Now it's on to Charlotte . . . Drafted on the third round by Golden State in 1984 . . . He's played with Phoenix and Chicago and also spent time in the CBA with Puerto Rico Coquis, Tampa Bay Thrillers and Florida Stingers . . . Born Aug. 4, 1961, in Seattle, but was raised in Pasadena, Cal. . . . Plays cheap at $120,000, so he might be around a few more seasons.

Year	Team	G	FG	FG Pct.	FT	FT Pct.	Reb.	Ast.	TP	Avg.
1984-85	Phoenix............	74	257	.446	96	.814	132	198	624	8.4
1985-86	Phoe.-Chi..........	28	77	.440	28	.636	33	55	183	6.5
1986-87	Portland..........	58	70	.409	44	.800	38	73	191	3.3
1987-88	Portland..........	82	163	.462	107	.829	149	211	436	5.3
	Totals.............	242	567	.445	275	.795	352	537	1434	5.9

SEDRIC TONEY 26 6-2 178   Guard

No, he's not related to Andrew. Yes, first name begins with an "S" . . . That answers most-asked questions about 1985 third-round Atlanta pick . . . Served as Mark Jackson's caddy with Knicks last season . . . Paid by the hour, played by the minute . . . Was playing in amateur league in Ohio when Knicks reached out 61 games into season. GM Al Bianchi remembered him from brief stint with Suns . . . Gutsy type . . . Chose AAU over CBA so he could complete communications degree at Dayton . . . Averaged 2.7 points in 21 games. Played 15 minutes in playoffs, but sank trio of three-pointers . . . Was Hornets' last pick in expansion draft . . . Born April 13, 1962, in Columbus, Miss.

Year	Team	G	FG	FG Pct.	FT	FT Pct.	Reb.	Ast.	TP	Avg.
1985-86	Atl.-Phoe..........	13	28	.424	21	.677	25	26	80	6.2
1987-88	New York..........	21	21	.438	10	.909	8	24	57	2.7
	Totals.............	34	49	.430	31	.738	33	50	137	4.0

RALPH LEWIS 25 6-6 205   Forward-Guard

Maybe Hornets thought this was Reggie...Free agent out of LaSalle, he was originally drafted by Celtics in 1985...Did two-year CBA tour before latching on to Pistons in preseason... Good leaper who is not bad defensively, not so good offensively ...When used, he played either big guard or small forward...Averaged slightly over six minutes in 50 games...Saw 17 minutes of cameo playoff appearances...Born March 28, 1963, in Philadelphia...No. 18 in expansion draft.

Year	Team	G	FG	FG Pct.	FT	FT Pct.	Reb.	Ast.	TP	Avg.
1987-88	Detroit	50	27	.310	29	.604	51	14	83	1.7

MICHAEL BROOKS 30 6-7 220   Forward

Can he stage a comeback?...Was rising star with Clippers in early 1980s until shattered knee curtailed career...Hasn't been the same...Sat out two straight seasons (1984-85 and 1985-86) ...Hit the CBA trail with Tampa Bay and Charlestown in 1986-87 and again last season until he got a late-season call from Denver...Hornets made him their sixth pick...Was 1980 U.S. Olympian...An excellent college talent who was named second-team All-American at LaSalle in his senior season ...Drafted by Clippers on first round (No. 9 overall)...Born Aug. 17, 1958, in Philadelphia.

Year	Team	G	FG	FG Pct.	FT	FT Pct.	Reb.	Ast.	TP	Avg.
1980-81	San Diego	82	488	.479	226	.706	442	208	1202	14.7
1981-82	San Diego	82	537	.504	202	.757	624	236	1276	15.6
1982-83	San Diego	82	402	.484	193	.697	521	262	1002	12.2
1983-84	San Diego	47	213	.479	104	.689	342	88	530	11.3
1986-87	Indiana	10	13	.351	7	.700	28	11	33	3.3
1987-88	Denver	16	20	.408	3	.750	44	13	43	2.7
	Totals	319	1673	.486	735	.714	2001	818	4086	12.8

CLINTON WHEELER 29 6-1 185   Guard

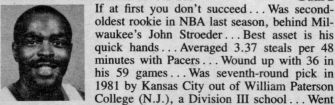

If at first you don't succeed...Was second-oldest rookie in NBA last season, behind Milwaukee's John Stroeder...Best asset is his quick hands...Averaged 3.37 steals per 48 minutes with Pacers...Wound up with 36 in his 59 games...Was seventh-round pick in 1981 by Kansas City out of William Paterson College (N.J.), a Division III school...Went on world tour after release and played in the Philippines from 1981-84...Hit the CBA for three seasons and the USBL for

Young Rex Chapman, No. 9 in draft, must grow up in a hurry.

two . . . Was MVP of CBA championships for Rapid City in 1986-87 . . . Scored personal-high 18 points at Houston last January . . . Was 18th pick in expansion draft . . . Born Oct. 27, 1959, in Neptune, N.J.

Year	Team	G	FG	FG Pct.	FT	FT Pct.	Reb.	Ast.	TP	Avg.
1987-88	Indiana.............	59	62	.470	25	.735	40	103	149	2.5

TOP ROOKIE

REX CHAPMAN 21 6-4 185   Guard

Left Kentucky after sophomore season at family's urging . . .
Considered a few years away, but also considered a can't-miss
talent . . . Vertical leap of about 36 stories . . . Terrific perimeter
shooter . . . Ninth player selected in last summer's draft . . . Was
only third player in Kentucky history to surpass 1,000 points in
first two years . . . Led Wildcats to regular-season SEC title and
into NCAA's Sweet 16 . . . SEC tourney MVP . . . Averaged 19.0
ppg as senior . . . Member of U.S. squad in 1983 Pan Am Games
which won silver medal . . . Will probably play right away, which
may or may not deter development . . . "Enormous physical talent," said Philadelphia GM John Nash . . . Born Oct. 5, 1967, in
Owensboro, Ky.

COACH DICK HARTER: Be gentle with him. This won't be

easy . . . In expansion draft, he was stocked
with more guards than any team could ever
possibly need . . . Then Hornets went out and
made a guard their first pick in draft . . . First
NBA head-coaching job . . . Born Oct. 14,
1930, in Pottstown, Pa. . . . An ex-Marine . . .
Fortunately, he has patience and temperament
necessary for expansion team . . . Came over
from Indiana, where he was assistant to Jack Ramsay for two
seasons . . . Prior to that he was assistant at Detroit for three years
under Chuck Daly . . . Successful college coaching career . . .
Began as head coach at Rider (N.J.) College in 1966 . . . As head
coach at Pennsylvania from 1967-71, he compiled 88-44 record,
including staggering 55-3 mark in his last two seasons . . . Then
went on to Oregon from 1972-78 and coached the team that broke
John Wooden's UCLA team's 98-game home win streak at Pau-
ley Pavilion . . . Went back east to Penn State for five seasons
. . . Owns 315-194 record in 18-year college coaching career . . .
Graduate of Penn ('53), he was a three-sport letterman and
helped Quakers to pair of Ivy basketball titles . . . Sound basketball mind, stresses defensive strategy.

CHICAGO BULLS

TEAM DIRECTORY: Chairman: Jerry Reinsdorf; VP-Operations: Jerry Krause; Dir. Media Services: Tim Hallam; Coach: Doug Collins; Asst. Coaches: John Bach, Tex Winter, Phil Jackson. Arena: Chicago Stadium (17,500). Colors: Red, white and black.

SCOUTING REPORT

SHOOTING: Drastic improvement. After two straight seasons of ranking third from the bottom in field-goal accuracy, the Bulls

The Bulls took wing on Air Jordan's league-leading 35.0 ppg.

improved to .490, a three-way tie for sixth. Of course, 'shooting and 'Chicago' mean MVP Michael Jordan, who attempted a league-high 1,998 shots, connecting on 1,069 for a career-high .535. Two others, rookie Horace Grant and midseason acquisition Sedale Threatt, also bettered 50 percent.

The Bulls acquired another high-percentage man in low-post threat Bill Cartwright (.544 with the Knicks). And Cartwright, the center the Bulls have long sought, may well shoulder much of the offensive burden which has been planted on Jordan, particularly late in games.

PLAYMAKING: Whatever Michael wants, Michael does is the general rule in Chicago. Jordan was the team's top assist man (485) as the Bulls again had an assembly-line format at point guard. The Bulls haven't been satisfied with any of the half-dozen candidates who have applied and ultimately received pink slips for the starting job. The passing game will miss Charles Oakley up front. Power forward of the future Grant isn't the passer Oakley is. Scottie Pippen as a rookie showed he can move it around, but his availability is much in doubt following offseason back surgery. And the Bulls must also settle on a point guard.

DEFENSE: The best in the league last season. Opponents managed a league-low 101.6 points a game while shooting just .470.

Again, the focal point is Mr. Jordan, last year's Defensive Player of the Year when he became the first player ever to lead the league in scoring and steals (259). Jordan plays passing lanes better than anyone. And he proved it picking off pass after pass, game after game. He also led the team in blocks with 131.

REBOUNDING: To acquire Cartwright, Doug Collins was forced to part with Oakley, who grabbed more rebounds in the past two seasons than anyone in the NBA. And he was a big reason why the Bulls ranked behind only Dallas in the board department.

The Bulls feel Grant is ready to burst into monster status: he averaged 5.5 boards off the bench, one every 4.1 minutes, which roughly translates to 12 a game. Chicago believes No. 1 pick Will Perdue, who averaged 10.1 boards as a senior at Vanderbilt, is the real thing.

OUTLOOK: In the playoffs, the Bulls saw exactly what happens when Air Jordan is hauled down from Olympus and placed among the mortals. When Detroit blanketed Jordan, the Bulls averaged an embarrassing 87.6 points in their second-round

BULL ROSTER

No.	Veteran	Pos.	Ht.	Wt.	Age	Yrs. Pro	College
40	Dave Corzine	C	6-11	265	32	10	DePaul
25	Bill Cartwright	C	7-1	230	31	8	San Francisco
54	Horace Grant	F	6-10	220	23	1	Clemson
23	Michael Jordan	G	6-6	198	25	4	North Carolina
5	John Paxson	G	6-2	185	28	5	Notre Dame
33	Scottie Pippin	F	6-7	210	23	1	Central Arkansas
6	Brad Sellers	F	7-0	227	25	2	Ohio State
2	Rory Sparrow	G	6-2	175	30	8	Villanova
21	Elston Turner	G	6-5	220	29	7	Mississippi
11	Sam Vincent	G	6-2	185	25	7	Michigan State
31	Granville Waiters	C	6-11	225	27	5	Ohio State

Rd.	Top Rookies	Sel. No.	Pos.	Ht.	Wt.	College
1	Will Perdue	11	C	7-0	240	Vanderbilt
3	Derrick Lewis	62	F	6-7	195	Maryland

playoff series. The price was high, but they had to get Cartwright for offensive help. The Bulls are a rising team whose horizon appears brighter than ever, and they have two more first-round picks next season.

BULL PROFILES

MICHAEL JORDAN 25 6-6 198   Guard

Words don't do him justice . . . Most dynamic offensive weapon in game today . . . Defensive Player of the Year . . . Only player to top NBA in scoring and steals in same year . . . But of all his numbers, including NBA highs of 35.0 ppg average and 3.16 steals, the most comforting to Bulls is his age: 25 . . . "I'd rather score 10 points a game and be known as a great all-around player," he said . . . Teammates miffed early in season about him taking high number of shots. He got message and his superlative team play got even better . . . No one on this team should ever grumble a syllable about him . . . Led Bulls in every offensive category except three pointers . . . Established five-game playoff record vs. Cavs with 226 points, including 55-point night...NBA scoring champ two straight years...Hit 14 field goals in one half vs. Celtics last January for team record... Scored 50 points four times, including season-high 59 at Detroit ...Earned $845,000, but Bulls working on pact to make him highest-paid athlete in team sports at $3 million per...And he makes more from endorsements...Won Slam Dunk title (with hometown officiating help) and was All-Star Game MVP... Born Feb. 17, 1963, in Brooklyn, N.Y....Was 1984-85 Rookie of Year, after Bulls made him No. 3 pick of draft out of North Carolina.

Year	Team	G	FG	FG Pct.	FT	FT Pct.	Reb.	Ast.	TP	Avg.
1984-85	Chicago	82	837	.515	630	.845	534	481	2313	28.2
1985-86	Chicago	18	150	.457	105	.840	64	53	408	22.7
1986-87	Chicago	82	1098	.482	833	.857	430	377	3041	37.1
1987-88	Chicago	82	1069	.535	723	.841	449	485	2868	35.0
	Totals	264	3154	.506	2291	.848	1477	1396	8630	32.7

HORACE GRANT 23 6-10 220   Forward

Stud in the making...Was consensus ACC Player of Year for Clemson before Bulls made him first-round (10th overall) pick in 1987... Decent rookie season, but Bulls are looking for bigger things...Out of Charles Oakley mold, board crasher who works until he drops ...Missed just one game, the season finale, with ankle sprain...Averaged 5.5 rebounds, 7.7 points in 22.6 minutes...Turnover and foul-prone...Played some small forward and some center, but is best suited at power forward...Hit season-high 20 points at Philadelphia last February...Makes $500,000 with incentives...Born July 4, 1965, in Augusta, Ga.

Year	Team	G	FG	FG Pct.	FT	FT Pct.	Reb.	Ast.	TP	Avg.
1987-88	Chicago	81	254	.501	114	.626	447	89	622	7.7

BILL CARTWRIGHT 31 7-1 230   Center

No more Medical Bill...Played all 82 games for Knicks, finally shedding injury hex of previous years...Was rumored in trades to 12 different teams before deadline, but he finished season in New York. Then he was sent to Chicago for Charles Oakley the day before the June draft...Failed as part of Twin Towers experiment in previous season, but worked wonders in selected spots with Patrick Ewing . . . Now Bulls expect him to take scoring burden off Michael Jordan . . . Very potent low-post threat who draws loads of fouls . . . Has quickness of a lamp post, though . . . Hardly an intimidator on defense . . . Averaged 11.1 points a game, but 28 per 48 minutes . . . Class act despite rough media criticism . . . Born July 30, 1957, in Lodi, Cal. . . . Third player selected in 1979 draft, out of San Francisco . . . Will soon receive master's degree in sociology.

Year	Team	G	FG	FG Pct.	FT	FT Pct.	Reb.	Ast.	TP	Avg.
1979-80	New York.	82	665	.547	451	.797	726	165	1781	21.7
1980-81	New York.	82	619	.554	408	.788	613	111	1646	20.1
1981-82	New York.	72	390	.562	257	.763	421	87	1037	14.4
1982-83	New York.	82	455	.566	380	.744	590	136	1290	15.7
1983-84	New York.	77	453	.561	404	.805	649	107	1310	17.0
1984-85	New York.					Injured				
1985-86	New York.	2	3	.429	6	.600	10	5	12	6.0
1986-87	New York.	58	335	.531	346	.790	445	96	1016	17.5
1987-88	New York.	82	287	.544	340	.798	384	85	914	11.1
	Totals.	537	3207	.552	2592	.784	3838	792	9006	16.8

SAM VINCENT 25 6-2 185   Guard

If Bulls don't watch it, they may have a starting point guard here . . . Bulls were 19-8 after handing starting job to Vincent following trade with Seattle for Sedale Threatt last February . . . In the 27 games he started, Bulls scored under 103 points only once . . . That changed in the playoffs when Pistons threw wet blanket over Bulls' offense . . . Had career-high 17 assists vs. Knicks and career-high 23 points vs. Bullets in April . . . Didn't miss a free throw in first 10 games as Bull (19-for-19) . . . Was Boston's first-round pick (No. 20) out of Michigan State in 1985 . . . Wound up in Seattle before trade to Bulls. "If God had sent me all around the league for 10 years and still had me end up in Chicago, I wouldn't mind. I can play my game here, uninhibited." . . . Earned $392,500 . . . Born May 18, 1963, in East Lansing, Mich.

Year	Team	G	FG	FG Pct.	FT	FT Pct.	Reb.	Ast.	TP	Avg.
1985-86	Boston.	57	59	.364	65	.929	48	69	184	3.2
1986-87	Boston.	46	60	.441	51	.927	27	59	171	3.7
1987-88	Sea.-Chi.	72	210	.456	145	.868	152	381	573	8.0
	Totals.	175	329	.433	261	.894	227	509	928	5.3

SCOTTIE PIPPEN 23 6-7 210   Forward

Another baby Bull with a bright future... Terrific athleticism... Runs, leaps, defends ... Central Arkansas product who became the darling of 1987 draft. Went from "Scottie Who?" to a household name in postseason all-star games... Seattle made him No. 5 pick overall, dealt him to Bulls for draft rights to Olden Polynice, a second-rounder and option to swap future first-rounder... Had tough time early as his ability to play with pain—any pain—was questioned... Got down on himself, compounding problem... Picked up game immensely down the stretch and replaced Brad Sellers as starter in last six playoff games... But rehabilitation from offseason back surgery will cause him to miss at least the first month of the season... Contract with incentives worth $725,000... Born Sept. 25, 1965, in Hamburg, Ark.

Year	Team	G	FG	FG Pct.	FT	FT Pct.	Reb.	Ast.	TP	Avg.
1987-88	Chicago............	79	261	.463	99	.576	298	169	625	7.9

BRAD SELLERS 25 7-0 227   Forward

Gives soft a bad name... Makes butter seem like steel... Nice jump shot, though... Just don't expect him to follow a miss. They throw elbows under there, ya know... Averaged 3.0 rebounds, most by accident... Started 76 games, finally yanked in playoffs when Bulls went against physical Pistons... Bulls were trying to deal him, but few were interested... Can run floor and is effective on wing on break... Ought to talk to Mel Turpin about how to put on some weight... Did not have one double-figure rebound game, despite averaging 27 minutes and despite 7-foot size... Averaged 4.5 points in playoffs... Earned $382,000... Born Dec. 17, 1962, in Cleveland... Starred at Ohio State before Bulls picked him No. 9 in 1986 draft—ahead of Johnny Dawkins, John Salley and John Williams.

Year	Team	G	FG	FG Pct.	FT	FT Pct.	Reb.	Ast.	TP	Avg.
1986-87	Chicago............	80	276	.455	126	.728	373	102	680	8.5
1987-88	Chicago............	82	326	.457	124	.790	250	141	777	9.5
	Totals.............	162	602	.456	250	.758	623	243	1457	9.0

DAVE CORZINE 32 6-11 265 Center

Flashy as rust ... Good passer, nice outside touch, physical underneath, but lacks strong post-up game ... Seems to have always been in the league ... Didn't play well in playoffs ... Down-to-earth guy with a nice beard ... Gives honest, blue-collar effort and bangs with the best ... An ironman who rarely misses a game. In six of his 11 years since leaving De-Paul, he's made it through all 82 ... Was personal whipping boy of Chicago fans for years, but hung tough ... Heard cheers this year and his game didn't change one iota ... Troubled by the Akeems and Ewings and other quick centers ... Earned $700,000 ... Born April 25, 1956, in Arlington Heights, Ill. ... Was first-round (No. 18 overall) pick of Washington in 1978 ... Went to Spurs for draft choices, came to Bulls in 1982 with Mark Olberding for Artis Gilmore.

Year	Team	G	FG	FG Pct.	FT	FT Pct.	Reb.	Ast.	TP	Avg.
1978-79	Washington	59	63	.534	49	.778	147	49	175	3.0
1979-80	Washington	78	90	.417	45	.662	270	63	225	2.9
1980-81	San Antonio	82	366	.490	125	.714	636	117	857	10.5
1981-82	San Antonio	82	336	.519	159	.746	629	130	832	10.1
1982-83	Chicago	82	457	.497	232	.720	717	154	1146	14.0
1983-84	Chicago	82	385	.467	231	.840	575	202	1004	12.2
1984-85	Chicago	82	276	.486	149	.745	422	140	701	8.5
1985-86	Chicago	67	255	.491	127	.743	433	150	640	9.6
1986-87	Chicago	82	294	.475	95	.736	540	209	683	8.3
1987-88	Chicago	80	344	.481	115	.752	527	154	804	10.1
	Totals	776	2866	.486	1327	.750	4896	1368	7067	9.1

JOHN PAXSON 28 6-2 185 Guard

Name everybody on the Titanic, then name all the guys who have held and lost Bulls' starting point guard job in past two seasons. Second question ain't so easy, either ... Became just another seldom-used player after starting first 27 games ... Wracked by injuries: tendinitis in knee, ankle sprains, dislocated thumb ... Became permanent bench material by late February ... Can stick the outside jumper, but he's a step slow ... Brother Jim plays with Celtics, dad Jim Sr. played for Cincinnati and Minneapolis in late 1950s ... Enters second season of three-year deal with $300,000 guaranteed in each of first two seasons, plus option year of $350,000 ... Born Sept. 9, 1960, in

Kettering, Ohio . . . San Antonio made him 12th player selected in 1983 draft . . . Joined Bulls as free agent in October 1985.

Year	Team	G	FG	FG Pct.	FT	FT Pct.	Reb.	Ast.	TP	Avg.
1983-84	San Antonio	49	61	.445	16	.615	33	149	142	2.9
1984-85	San Antonio	78	196	.509	84	.840	68	215	486	6.2
1985-86	Chicago	75	153	.466	74	.804	94	274	395	5.3
1986-87	Chicago	82	386	.487	106	.809	139	467	930	11.3
1987-88	Chicago	81	287	.493	33	.733	104	303	640	7.9
	Totals	365	1083	.487	313	.794	438	1408	2593	7.1

ELSTON TURNER 29 6-5 220   Guard

Defense can keep you employed . . . Veteran was brought back as free agent last March, two days after Bulls were burned by Gerald Henderson's last-second drive in one-point Sixer win . . . "He plays strong defense, we could have used somebody with his size," Michael Jordan said . . . But when playoffs came around, "E.T." needed to phone home and find out why he was essentially ignored by coach Doug Collins . . . After release from Bulls following 1986-87 season, he bounced around CBA . . . Dallas made him 43d selection in 1981 out of Mississippi . . . Degree in TV and radio communications . . . Born June 10, 1959, in Knoxville, Tenn.

Year	Team	G	FG	FG Pct.	FT	FT Pct.	Reb.	Ast.	TP	Avg.
1981-82	Dallas	80	282	.441	97	.703	301	189	661	8.3
1982-83	Dallas	59	96	.403	20	.667	152	88	214	3.6
1983-84	Dallas	47	54	.360	28	.824	93	59	137	2.9
1984-85	Denver	81	181	.466	51	.785	216	158	414	5.1
1985-86	Denver	73	165	.435	39	.736	201	165	369	5.1
1986-87	Chicago	70	112	.444	23	.742	115	102	248	3.5
1987-88	Chicago	17	8	.267	1	.500	10	9	17	1.0
	Totals	427	898	.433	259	.734	1088	770	2060	4.8

RORY SPARROW 30 6-2 175   Guard

Solid citizen . . . One of *Sports Illustrated's* Sportspersons of the Year . . . Tireless charity worker, his Foundation has helped hundreds of inner-city kids . . . Came to Bulls from Knicks (where he was pushed out by Mark Jackson) and eventually was pushed out in Chicago by Sam Vincent . . . Collected splinters at end of season and in playoffs . . . Averaged only 7.2

minutes in March and did not play in three playoff games... Good court presence, but limited by athletic deficiencies... Born June 12, 1958, in Suffolk, Va.... Fourth-round pick out of Villanova by Nets in 1980... Managed $325,000 pact from Knicks before trade.

Year	Team	G	FG	FG Pct.	FT	FT Pct.	Reb.	Ast.	TP	Avg.
1980-81	New Jersey	15	22	.349	12	.750	18	32	56	3.7
1981-82	Atlanta	82	366	.501	124	.838	224	424	857	10.5
1982-83	Atl.-N.Y.	81	392	.484	147	.739	230	397	936	11.6
1983-84	New York	79	350	.474	108	.824	189	539	818	10.4
1984-85	New York	79	326	.492	122	.865	169	557	781	9.9
1985-86	New York	74	345	.477	101	.795	170	472	796	10.8
1986-87	New York	80	263	.446	71	.798	115	432	608	7.6
1987-88	N.Y.-Chi.	58	117	.399	24	.727	72	167	260	4.5
	Totals	548	2181	.473	709	.802	1187	3020	5112	9.3

GRANVILLE WAITERS 27 6-11 225   Center

This guy never got off the bench in the playoffs. Bulls were eliminated. A connection?... Be serious... He's slow, can't jump and is not aggressive... So what's he doing in the NBA?... You figure... Was a free agent and the Bulls came to him last summer. "They said they needed me," he said... They never said for what... Seems destined for CBA or Europe... Sad thing is, he's a hard worker, non-complainer... He's just not too talented... Out of Ohio State, Portland picked him 39th in 1983 draft... Originally came to Bulls from Rockets in October 1986 for a fourth-round draft choice... Born Jan. 8, 1961, in Columbus, Ohio... Earned $100,000.

Year	Team	G	FG	FG Pct.	FT	FT Pct.	Reb.	Ast.	TP	Avg.
1983-84	Indiana	78	123	.517	31	.608	227	60	277	3.6
1984-85	Indiana	62	85	.447	29	.580	170	30	199	3.2
1985-86	Houston	43	13	.333	1	.167	28	8	27	0.6
1986-87	Chicago	44	40	.430	5	.556	87	22	85	1.9
1987-88	Chicago	22	9	.310	0	.000	28	1	18	0.8
	Totals	249	270	.458	66	.559	540	121	606	2.4

TOP ROOKIE

WILL PERDUE 23 7-0 240   Center

Southeastern Conference Player of the Year at Vanderbilt...

Averaged 18.3 ppg on sizzling .634 shooting . . . Also broke own school record with 74 blocks . . . Not a bad passer, he may be used in a Twin Tower set-up with Bill Cartwright . . . Bulls plucked him at No. 11 on first round with pick acquired in Charles Oakley trade for Cartwright . . . Vandy coach C.M. Newton says Big Will "has developed a completeness" in his game. "He runs the court well, plays strong post-up defense and has improved his passing and ball-handling skills dramatically." . . . Born Aug. 29, 1965, at Merritt Island, Fla.

COACH DOUG COLLINS: Many touted him for Coach of Year after 50-victory season, Bulls' first since 1973-74 . . . Has two-year mark of 90-74 . . . No-nonsense, no-grudge guy . . . TV analyst before becoming ninth Chicago head coach . . . Was a superlative 6-6 guard whose career was wracked with knee surgeries . ... Still averaged 17.9 points and shot .501 in eight-year stint with 76ers . . . Four-time all-star . . . Averaged 21.5 points a game in playoffs on .526 shooting . . . Got coaching experience as an assistant at Penn and Arizona State . . . Was the No. 1 pick in 1973 draft out of Illinois State, where his 2,240 career points and 29.1 scoring average still stand as school marks . . . Member of 1972 U.S. Olympic team whose gold was stolen by international refs.

GREATEST THREE-POINT SHOOTER

What? An offensive category in Chicago where Michael Jordan isn't king? Blasphemy!

But it's true. For three-pointers, John Paxson is the reigning Bull. That's John, not Jim. Half the people in America can't get it right. John ended last season on the Bulls' bench, but not before hitting 33-of-95 missiles to hike his three-year total to 100-of-286 (.350). And he passed Reggie Theus (92) for all-time Chicago three-pointers. Hey, Jordan can't lead everything.

ALL-TIME BULL LEADERS

SEASON

Points: Michael Jordan, 3,041, 1986-87
Assists: Guy Rodgers, 908, 1966-67
Rebounds: Tom Boerwinkle, 1,133, 1970-71

GAME

Points: Michael Jordan, 61 vs. Detroit, 3/4/87
　　　　　 Michael Jordan, 61 vs. Atlanta, 4/16/87
Assists: Ennis Whatley, 22 vs. New York, 1/14/84
　　　　　 Ennis Whatley, 22 vs. Atlanta, 3/3/84
Rebounds: Tom Boerwinkle, 37 vs. Phoenix, 1/8/70

CAREER

Points: Bob Love, 12,623, 1968-76
Assists: Norm Van Lier, 3,676, 1971-78
Rebounds: Tom Boerwinkle, 5,745, 1968-78

CLEVELAND CAVALIERS

TEAM DIRECTORY: Chairmen: George Gund III, Gordon Gund; GM: Wayne Embry; Dr. Pub. Rel.: Bob Price; Coach: Lenny Wilkens; Asst. Coaches: Brian Winters, Dick Helm. Arena: The Coliseum (20,900). Colors: Blue, white and orange.

SCOUTING REPORT

SHOOTING: The Cavs finished with a respectable .490 field-goal percentage, using a good balance of inside and outside

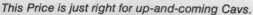

This Price is just right for up-and-coming Cavs.

shooting. Mark Price finished second in the league with .484 accuracy on three-point shots—the second highest trey mark ever. Ironically, the loss of Ron Harper probably helped the percentage. As a rookie, Harper was slightly out of control, but his numbers improved to .464 in 57 games last season—still nothing to write home about.

Still, the Cavs possess scoring threats at every position, and had six guys average in double figures. And they brought in another shooter, small forward Randolph Keys of Southern Mississippi, with their first-round pick.

PLAYMAKING: Price is the floor general and he's a good one. He does a solid job of penetrating, finding the open man and finding his own spots to unleash long-range missiles. Brad Daugherty is the top passing center in the league: he finished with 333 assists and no other center was even close. Overall, the Cavs were 12th in the league in assists. The Cavs cut their turnovers down to 17.5, but there's room for more improvement.

DEFENSE: Good, getting better. Only the Bulls surrendered less than the Cavs' nightly yield of 103.7 points. And opponents shot .476, middle-of-the-pack numbers. The addition of 7-1 Tree Rollins, the Hawks' all-time leading shot-blocker, is a plus. The Cavs have a good pair of shot-blocking forwards in John Williams and Larry Nance, but could use some more rejections from Daugherty, who blocked just 56 shots in 79 games, the third-lowest total by a starting center in the league.

REBOUNDING: The Cavs still seek a rebound monster. Individually, their front-line players are all good, but none spectacular off the glass. Nance averaged 9.0 overall, Daugherty had 8.4 and Williams got 6.6. Still, Cleveland ranked 17th in the league in rebounds and got little boardwork from the bench.

OUTLOOK: The Cavs' future is so bright it hurts the eyes. They need some bench holes plugged here and there and lost Dell Curry to expansion, but that starting five—Price, Harper, Daugherty, Nance and Williams—is frightening with its youth and talent. Harper needed almost all season to get over an ankle sprain. So if he's healthy, the Cavs—who were two games over .500—will be even more of a force. It took a while for both sides to get acclimated to Nance, but now everybody's comfortable. Price is a terrific point guard, Daugherty continues to emerge into a first-rate all-around center and Williams is a comer. Lenny Wilkens' Cavs may well be the team of the future.

CAVALIER ROSTER

No.	Veteran	Pos.	Ht.	Wt.	Age	Yrs. Pro	College
43	Brad Daugherty	C	7-1	255	23	2	North Carolina
22	Chris Dudley	C	6-11	235	23	1	Yale
3	Craig Ehlo	G	6-7	195	27	5	Washington State
4	Ron Harper	G	6-6	205	24	2	Miami (Ohio)
12	Kevin Henderson	G	6-4	195	24	2	Cal-Fullerton
35	Phil Hubbard	F	6-8	215	31	9	Michigan
6	Larry Nance	F	6-10	217	29	7	Clemson
25	Mark Price	G	6-1	175	24	2	Georgia Tech
32	Johnny Rogers	F	6-1	231	24	2	Cal-Irvine
30	Tree Rollins	C	7-1	245	33	11	Clemson
11	Mike Sanders	F	6-6	215	28	6	UCLA
1	Darnell Valentine	G	6-2	185	29	7	Kansas
18	John Williams	F	6-11	230	26	2	Tulane

Rd.	Top Rookies	Sel. No.	Pos.	Ht.	Wt.	College
1	Randolph Keys	22	F	6-9	195	So. Mississippi
3	Winston Bennett	64	F	6-7	210	Kentucky

CAVALIER PROFILES

MARK PRICE 24 6-1 175   Guard

Price was very right . . . A star in second season. More than doubled rookie scoring average from 6.9 to 16 points per game . . . Took over quarterbacking duties with departure of John Bagley and Cavs picked it up a couple beats . . . One of quickest guards in league . . . Second in NBA on three-pointers (72-of-148, .486), second-best mark ever . . . Only second time a Cav ranked as high as second in anything (Lenny Wilkens was No. 2 in assists in 1972-73) . . . Drives defenses nuts. Superb penetrator who dishes off well . . . Terrific in open court . . . Had best field-goal percentage (.506) ever by a Cleveland guard . . . Scored career-high 32 points vs. Pacers last April . . . Excellent foul shooter, his .877 percentage is also a Cavalier record. Made 31 straight at one point . . . Raised game in playoffs, averaging 21 points . . . Dallas took him on second round (25th overall) in 1986 out of Georgia Tech, where he's school's second-leading all-time scorer. Never played for Mavericks, who gave him away for second-rounder and cash...Honest-to-gosh choir boy...Born Feb. 15, 1964, in Enid, Okla....Underpaid at $175,000.

Year	Team	G	FG	FG Pct.	FT	FT Pct.	Reb.	Ast.	TP	Avg.
1986-87	Cleveland............	67	173	.408	95	.833	117	202	464	6.9
1987-88	Cleveland............	80	493	.506	221	.877	180	480	1279	16.0
	Totals.............	147	666	.476	316	.863	297	682	1743	11.9

RON HARPER 24 6-6 205   Guard

Injury tarnished much of the luster from his game...Severely sprained left ankle in second game of season knocked him out of 24 games...Upon return, didn't have spring needed for Jordanesque dunks and struggled terribly...Scoring average dropped seven points from remarkable rookie season...Not to worry. He'll be back...Another ankle sprain kept him out of Game 1 in first round of Eastern Conference playoffs vs. Bulls. Came back to average 17.6 points in playoffs, including 30-point game...Cavaliers tried him at small forward early last season, didn't work. Went back to off guard and led team in steals (122 in 57 games) for second straight season. Had 209 as rookie, only second ever to get 200 in first year...Has enormous hands...Was eighth player selected in 1986 draft...Born Jan. 20, 1964, in Dayton, Ohio...Attended Miami (Ohio) and became Mid-America Conference's all-time scorer (2,377 points)...Earns $555,000.

Year	Team	G	FG	FG Pct.	FT	FT Pct.	Reb.	Ast.	TP	Avg.
1986-87	Cleveland............	82	734	.455	386	.684	392	394	1874	22.9
1987-88	Cleveland............	57	340	.464	196	.705	223	281	879	15.4
	Totals.............	139	1074	.458	582	.691	615	675	2753	19.8

BRAD DAUGHERTY 23 7-1 255   Center

The complete center. Scores, rebounds and passes...His 333 assists led NBA centers for second straight year...Basketball baby getting better by the minute...Was youngest member of All-Star team...First Cavalier selected to annual event since 1981...Registered career-high 44 points vs. Celtics last April, including 17-point fourth quarter ...In last eight games of regular season, he outscored opposing starting center, 170-71...Averaged 15.8 in playoffs vs. Bulls, but had miserable Game 1, missing several gimmes down the stretch...Quickly shedding the soft label...Grandpa was a full-blooded Cherokee. But fantasy is to be old western-style cowboy...Hunts rattlesnakes to relax...Was No. 1 pick in 1986 draft after Cavaliers sent Roy Hinson and $750,000 to Philadelphia for the choice...Was 16-year-old freshman starter at North Carolina...Born Oct. 19, 1965, in Ashville, N.C....Has $857,500 salary.

Year	Team	G	FG	FG Pct.	FT	FT Pct.	Reb.	Ast.	TP	Avg.
1986-87	Cleveland...........	80	487	.538	279	.696	647	304	1253	15.7
1987-88	Cleveland...........	79	551	.510	378	.716	665	333	1480	18.7
	Totals.............	159	1038	.523	657	.707	1312	637	2733	17.2

JOHN WILLIAMS 26 6-11 230   Forward

Rocky past behind him, great future ahead... Settled in as sixth man over last 23 games and averaged 11 points...Can be a fearsome rebounder...Led team in boards 21 times. Great at getting them in traffic...Had season-high 15 rebounds last March vs. San Antonio, but his best night may have been eight rebounds in 10 minutes vs. New York last January...Led team in blocks (1.88 per game) for second straight season...Set Cavalier record with nine rejections in game at Washington...Did two years in USBL, sweating out Tulane point-shave scandal. Acquitted on all counts...Former GM Harry Weltman gets credit for showing faith in his innocence and drafting him on second round in 1985...In last season of three-year $750,000 contract...Born Aug. 9, 1962, in Sorrento, La...."Hot Rod"...Got nickname as toddler for scooting across floor.

Year	Team	G	FG	FG Pct.	FT	FT Pct.	Reb.	Ast.	TP	Avg.
1986-87	Cleveland...........	80	435	.485	298	.745	629	154	1168	14.6
1987-88	Cleveland...........	77	316	.477	211	.756	506	103	843	10.9
	Totals.............	157	751	.481	509	.750	1135	257	2011	12.8

LARRY NANCE 29 6-10 217   Forward

Pogo sticks in his socks...His acquisition gave Cavaliers very impressive first five... Came from Phoenix last February with Mike Sanders for Mark West, Kevin Johnson, Ty Corbin, two second-round picks and a swap of 1988 first-rounders...Cavs went into immediate dive, losing 11 of 14. But they won 11 of last 13...Started 26 of 27 games with Cavs, and gave them needed inside strength . . . NBA Player of Month for December with Suns (averaged 26.3 points for month) . . . Scored career-high 45 points at Sacramento last December, had career-high 10 blocked shots at Philadelphia in January and career-high 18 rebounds at New York the next night . . . Magnificent leaper with murderous inside game . . . Generally underrated. Made All-Star Game just once . . . Was 1984 Slam Dunk champ . . . Divisional dunking duels with Michael Jordan should spice up regular season . . . Suns made him 20th selection in 1981 draft out of Clemson . . . Born Feb. 12, 1959, in Anderson, S.C. . . . Car collector . . . Earned $625,000.

Year	Team	G	FG	FG Pct.	FT	FT Pct.	Reb.	Ast.	TP	Avg.
1981-82	Phoenix	80	227	.521	75	.641	256	82	529	6.6
1982-83	Phoenix	82	588	.550	193	.672	710	197	1370	16.7
1983-84	Phoenix	82	601	.576	249	.707	678	214	1451	17.7
1984-85	Phoenix	61	515	.587	180	.709	536	159	1211	19.9
1985-86	Phoenix	73	582	.581	310	.698	618	240	1474	20.2
1986-87	Phoenix	69	585	.551	381	.773	599	233	1552	22.5
1987-88	Phoe.-Clev.	67	487	.529	304	.779	607	207	1280	19.1
	Totals	514	3585	.559	1692	.724	4004	1332	8867	17.3

CRAIG EHLO 27 6-7 195 Guard

Has earned some respect . . . An opposing coach once said NBA needs this guy so coaches can tell players after a mistake, "You stink worse than Craig Ehlo." . . . Hung on to job by fingertips in Houston and got a life-preserver from Cavaliers, who signed him as free agent in January 1987 . . . Scored more points last season (563) than in previous four combined . . . Versatile, plays three positions adequately . . . Sometimes starter . . . Twice scored 20 points . . . Nice rebounder from backcourt, had career-high 14 boards vs. Dallas last December . . . Good outside shooter, a favorite target for Mark Price off the penetration . . . Soap-opera looks . . . Born Aug. 11, 1961, in Lubbock, Tex. . . . Worth the $175,000 base pay investment.

Year	Team	G	FG	FG Pct.	FT	FT Pct.	Reb.	Ast.	TP	Avg.
1983-84	Houston	7	11	.407	1	1.000	9	6	23	3.3
1984-85	Houston	45	34	.493	19	.633	25	26	87	1.9
1985-86	Houston	36	36	.429	23	.793	46	29	98	2.7
1986-87	Cleveland	44	99	.414	70	.707	161	92	273	6.2
1987-88	Cleveland	79	226	.466	89	.674	274	206	563	7.1
	Totals	211	406	.449	202	.694	515	359	1044	4.9

PHIL HUBBARD 31 6-8 215   Forward

Takes no prisoners... He only takes off your ear underneath the basket... Not dirty, just physical. Opposing forwards hate to play him ... Stayed healthy last season in an injury-plagued career... However, against Knicks last March he had his first "did not play, coach's decision" since becoming a Cavalier in 1982... The only holdover from Cavs' 1984-85 playoff team... Acquired in deal from Pistons that also brought Paul Mokeski and first-and second-round picks in 1982 for Kenny Carr and Bill Laimbeer... Scored 7,000th career point at Milwaukee last February... Over last four years, Cavs are 98-105 (.483) when he starts, 40-85 (.320) when he doesn't... Overlooked, underrated... Feeling pinch of youth. Averaged 20.9 minutes, down from 30.6... Hit season-high 25 points vs. Bulls last February... Played at Michigan, but knee woes stripped a lot of his mobility... Still became first-rounder (No. 15) as junior eligible by Pistons in 1979... Does lots of work for charity... Wife Jackie a dentist... Earned $450,000... Born Dec. 13, 1956, in Canton, Ohio.

Year	Team	G	FG	FG Pct.	FT	FT Pct.	Reb.	Ast.	TP	Avg.
1979-80	Detroit	64	210	.466	165	.750	320	70	585	9.1
1980-81	Detroit	80	433	.492	294	.690	586	150	1161	14.5
1981-82	Det.-Clev.	83	326	.490	191	.682	473	91	843	10.2
1982-83	Cleveland	82	288	.482	204	.689	471	89	780	9.5
1983-84	Cleveland	80	321	.511	221	.739	380	86	863	10.8
1984-85	Cleveland	76	415	.505	371	.751	479	114	1201	15.8
1985-86	Cleveland	23	93	.470	76	.679	120	29	262	11.4
1986-87	Cleveland	68	321	.531	162	.596	388	136	804	11.8
1987-88	Cleveland	78	237	.489	182	.749	281	81	656	8.4
	Totals	634	2644	.496	1866	.706	3498	846	7155	11.3

DARNELL VALENTINE 29 6-2 185   Guard

Who would want this guy to be their valentine?... At one time regarded as a top-flight point guard, he's slid rapidly to mediocrity or worse... Selected by Miami in expansion draft and then traded to Cavs for second-round pick in 1990 or 1992... Turned on the juices one night when he burned the Houston Rockets for a season-high 30 points late in the year... Evidence of how bad the Clippers were last season is the fact that he started 31 games for them... Born Feb. 3, 1959, in Chicago... A star at Kansas... Member of the 1980 U.S. Olympic team that was a victim of the Moscow boycott...

Portland made him the No. 16 pick in the 1981 draft . . . Clips were buffaloed into giving up a first-round draft pick for him in 1986 . . . Legs like tree trunks, but so what?

Year	Team	G	FG	FG Pct.	FT	FT Pct.	Reb.	Ast.	TP	Avg.
1981-82	Portland.	82	187	413	152	.760	149	270	526	6.4
1982-83	Portland.	47	209	.454	169	.793	117	293	587	12.5
1983-84	Portland.	68	251	.447	194	.789	127	395	696	10.2
1984-85	Portland.	75	321	.473	230	.793	219	522	872	11.6
1985-86	Port.-LAC.	62	161	.415	130	.743	125	246	456	7.4
1986-87	L. A. Clippers	65	275	.410	163	.815	150	447	726	11.2
1987-88	L.A. Clippers	79	223	.418	101	.743	156	382	562	7.1
	Totals.	478	1627	.434	1139	.780	1043	2555	4425	9.3

JOHNNY ROGERS 24 6-11 231   Forward

Reportedly a shooter . . . Reportedly still in the NBA . . . Started 15 games in 1986-87 for Kings, who released him . . . Signed by Cavs as free agent last November when Ron Harper was hurt . . . Played 168 minutes, averaged 2.6 points, shot .426 . . . Never left bench in playoffs . . . Injury list with ankle sprain for 12 games . . . Deeply religious . . . Pac-10 Freshman of Year at Stanford in 1981-82, transferred after soph season to Cal-Irvine . . . Had .538 shooting percentage in college, while averaging 21.2 points a game at Cal-Irvine . . . Second-round pick of Kings in 1986 . . . Born Dec. 30, 1963, in Fullerton, Cal. . . . Makes minimum wage.

Year	Team	G	FG	FG Pct.	FT	FT Pct.	Reb.	Ast.	TP	Avg.
1986-87	Sacramento.	45	90	.486	9	.600	77	26	189	4.2
1987-88	Cleveland.	24	26	.426	10	.769	27	3	62	2.6
	Totals.	69	116	.472	19	.679	104	29	.251	3.6

MIKE SANDERS 28 6-6 215   Forward

It's the little things that count . . . Versatile guy who sticks his nose in, gets dirty, gets no acclaim . . . Every team needs one, not every team has one . . . Good quickness, tough in pressing defense . . . Came to Cleveland from Phoenix in Larry Nance trade last February . . . Scored career-high 29 points with Suns against Nets in November 1987 . . . Started 11 games with Cavaliers at small forward, and Cavs went 8-3 . . . Injured hand put him back on bench until playoffs when he averaged 12.8 points, 5.0 rebounds . . . Two-year team captain at

UCLA. With Kiki Vandeweghe and Rod Foster, he helped Bruins to 1980 NCAA championship game... Fourth-round pick of Kings in 1982... Released... CBA All-Star... Signed by Spurs. Broke hand, released. Signed by Suns in December 1983 ... Born May 7, 1962, in Vidalia, La.... Is paid $240,000.

Year	Team	G	FG	FG Pct.	FT	FT Pct.	Reb.	Ast.	TP	Avg.
1982-83	San Antonio	26	76	.484	31	.721	94	19	183	7.0
1983-84	Phoenix	50	97	.478	29	.690	103	44	223	4.5
1984-85	Phoenix	21	85	.486	45	.763	89	29	215	10.2
1985-86	Phoenix	82	347	.513	208	.809	273	150	905	11.0
1986-87	Phoenix	82	357	.494	143	.781	271	126	859	10.5
1987-88	Phoe.-Clev.	59	153	.505	59	.776	109	56	365	6.2
	Totals	320	1115	.499	515	.769	939	424	2750	8.6

KEVIN HENDERSON 24 6-4 195   Guard

Roster fodder... Played 20 minutes in regular season for Cavs, who signed him as free agent last March after he was waived by Warriors ... Was 50th player chosen in 1986 draft by Cavaliers. Was released before season... Then got to know how to read CBA road maps... Hung on Warrior roster via a couple 10-day pacts... Minimum wage earner...

Was Fullerton State backcourt mate of Leon Wood, one of great travelin' men in recent NBA seasons... Born March 22, 1964, in Baltimore... There's always expansion and more minimum wage.

Year	Team	G	FG	FG Pct.	FT	FT Pct.	Reb.	Ast.	TP	Avg.
1986-87	Golden State	5	3	.375	2	1.000	3	11	8	1.6
1987-88	G.S.-Clev.	17	21	.396	15	.577	21	23	57	3.4
	Totals	22	24	.393	17	.607	24	34	65	3.0

TREE ROLLINS 33 7-1 245   Center

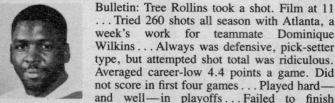

Bulletin: Tree Rollins took a shot. Film at 11 ... Tried 260 shots all season with Atlanta, a week's work for teammate Dominique Wilkins... Always was defensive, pick-setter type, but attempted shot total was ridiculous. Averaged career-low 4.4 points a game. Did not score in first four games... Played hard— and well—in playoffs... Failed to finish among top 10 shot-blockers for only second time in 11-year career...Paid $1.17 million in final year of contract...Played in more games in Hawk uniform (820) than anyone in club history, passing Bob Pettit...Born June 15, 1955, in Winter Haven, Fla....First-round pick (No. 14 overall) from Clemson in 1977...Free agent signed two-year contract with Cavs in July for estimated $1.6 million.

Year	Team	G	FG	FG Pct.	FT	FT Pct.	Reb.	Ast.	TP	Avg.
1977-78	Atlanta	80	253	.487	104	.703	552	79	610	7.6
1978-79	Atlanta	81	297	.535	89	.631	588	49	683	8.4
1979-80	Atlanta	82	287	.558	157	.714	774	76	731	8.9
1980-81	Atlanta	40	116	.552	46	.807	286	35	278	7.0
1981-82	Atlanta	79	202	.584	79	.612	611	59	483	6.1
1982-83	Atlanta	80	261	.510	98	.726	743	75	620	7.8
1983-84	Atlanta	77	274	.518	118	.621	593	62	666	8.6
1984-85	Atlanta	70	186	.549	67	.720	442	52	439	6.3
1985-86	Atlanta	74	173	.499	69	.767	458	41	415	5.6
1866-87	Atlanta	78	171	.546	63	.724	488	22	405	5.4
1987-88	Atlanta	76	133	.512	70	.875	459	20	336	4.4
	Totals	817	2353	.529	960	.701	5994	570	5666	6.9

CHRIS DUDLEY 23 6-11 235   Center

The Dudley family legend continues...Background more interesting than his game, although he can get some rebounds...Learned to get down and dirty in the basketball jungle at Yale...Only third Yalie—Tony Lavelli and Butch Graves the others—ever to play in NBA...Boola Boola...Mater, pater, grandpater and uncle Eli alums...Grandfather Guilford Dudley was ambassador to Denmark...Four cameos in playoffs...Pulled down 10 rebounds twice in regular season, including his only start last February at Phoenix...Was second in nation in rebounding (13.3) as senior to Pitt's Jerome Lane...Fourth-round pick in 1987...Born Feb. 22, 1965, in Stamford, Conn....Makes minimum at $75,000.

Year	Team	G	FG	FG Pct.	FT	FT Pct.	Reb.	Ast.	TP	Avg.
1987-88	Cleveland	55	65	.474	40	.563	144	23	170	3.1

TOP ROOKIE

RANDOLPH KEYS 22 6-9 195   Forward

Good-shooting small forward out of Southern Mississippi...Cavaliers made him No. 22 selection in first round...Can leap,

but he'll have to bulk up in pros to be factor off the boards . . .
Averaged 17.7 points a game and 7.9 rebounds as senior . . . Was
named NIT MVP as junior . . . Cavs took him "largely because of
his perimeter shooting," said GM Wayne Embry . . . His stock
dropped slightly when he didn't quite meet expectations as
senior . . . One area he did improve in was free-throw shooting,
upping percentage to .765.

COACH LENNY WILKENS: Took his lumps in 1986-87 with
51 defeats. But patience paid off . . . Brought
Cavs into playoffs and now figures to have a
young terror at his disposal . . . Reclaimed the
necessary understanding, patient attitude that
had slipped away following 11-year-plus stint
in Seattle . . . Solid work ethic, good sidelines
thinker . . . First goal was to establish Coliseum as a pit and Cavs responded with best-
ever 31-10 home mark. In his two seasons there, Cavs 56-26 at
home . . . Fifteen years as NBA coach has brought 626 wins,
eighth all-time mark, 582 defeats . . . Head coach at Seattle for
three years, starting in 1969. Moved to Portland for two, then
back to Seattle for eight . . . Won championship with Sonics in
1978-79 after advancing to finals in previous year . . . Was
GM-VP for Sonics for four months before changing zip code to
Richfield . . . Had 15-year playing career (St. Louis, Seattle,
Cleveland) after two All-American college seasons at Providence
. . . No. 2 all-time in assists (7,211) . . . Born Oct. 28, 1937, in
Brooklyn, N.Y.

GREATEST THREE-POINT SHOOTER

Back in those rollicking days from 1982-86 when the Cavs
were a sure-shot to miss the playoffs, the team needed something
to keep the fans' minds off the 212 defeats suffered in those four
seasons. World B. Free was part of that something.

Mark Price (95-of-218 in two seasons) one day figures to rank
as the Cavs' all-time three-point champ, but he still must stand in
the three-point line behind Free, who fired in 179 three-pointers
in his four-year stay with the Cavs. Free would shoot from anywhere—he'd be a five-point king if there were such an animal.

Free, whose soft, high-arcing jumper was a thing of beauty, made 71 three-pointers in each of his last two campaigns in Cleveland. In 1984-85, he made 71-of-193 three-point attempts (.368), hoisting more bombs than anyone that year other than Utah's Darrell Griffith.

ALL-TIME CAVALIER LEADERS

SEASON

Points: Mike Mitchell, 2,012, 1980-81
Assists: John Bagley, 735, 1985-86
Rebounds: Jim Brewer, 891, 1975-76

GAME

Points: Walt Wesley, 50 vs. Cincinnati, 2/19/71
Assists: Geoff Huston, 27 vs. Golden State, 1/27/82
Rebounds: Rick Roberson, 25 vs. Houston, 3/4/72

CAREER

Points: Austin Carr, 10,265, 1971-80
Assists: John Bagley, 2,311, 1982-87
Rebounds: Jim Chones, 3,790, 1974-79

DETROIT PISTONS

TEAM DIRECTORY: Pres.: Bill Davidson; GM: Jack McCloskey; Dir. Pub. Rel.: Matt Dobek; Coach: Chuck Daly; Asst. Coaches: Brendan Malone, Dick Versace. Arena: The Palace, Auburn Hills (21,519). Colors: Red, white and blue.

SCOUTING REPORT

SHOOTING: Only the Lakers and Celtics checked in with better shooting numbers than the Pistons' club-record .493. Detroit's effective inside game racked up gaudy numbers for forwards Dennis Rodman (.561), Rick Mahorn (.574) and John Salley (.566). And small forward Adrian Dantley shot over 50 percent (.514) for the 12th straight year. Bill Laimbeer is the deadliest perimeter threat among league centers. And guards Isiah Thomas, Joe Dumars and Vinnie Johnson are all capable of carrying a team all by themselves.

PLAYMAKING: Isiah usually decides when and where the ball goes. When he's enveloped in the team concept, he's as good a playmaker as there is. When he's enveloped in the individual concept, well, things can get out of hand. Dumars, who is rocksolid at off-guard, also has point-guard capabilities.

DEFENSE: The Pistons were third in the league—behind Central Division foes Chicago and Cleveland—in points allowed with 104.1. And they were third in best point differential at +5.2. Individually and collectively, this is a solid defensive team. Isiah can turn it up several notches and become a thief of wild abandon. Rodman is a defensive gem. He showed those skills in the finals against Magic Johnson, performing as well as humanly possible against the Laker superstar.

Salley, Laimbeer, Dantley and Mahorn are all sound. But the best is probably Dumars. Much of the Piston defense comes from physical and psychological intimidation.

Yes, they play hard. Yes, they play aggressive. And yes, they'll play dirty if need be. But all the banging keeps foes thinking twice about entering the lane. Popular or not, it works.

REBOUNDING: The Pistons just keep getting better. Laimbeer is always up there. Rodman is, perhaps, the finest offensive rebounding small forward in the game. And Salley isn't too far behind. The Pistons keep the ball alive around the offensive glass

Adrian Dantley & Co. look for new way to dethrone Lakers.

and wear down opponents with their never-ending supply of bodies. Detroit tied for fourth in league rebounding last season.

OUTLOOK: The only way for Chuck Daly's gang to improve is to win everything. Of course they came mighty close last season. A healthy Isiah in Game 7 and who knows? The Pistons are now firmly established among the league's elite. Last season, their primary goal was to bounce the Celtics and make the finals. Done. This year, it's that final step. Hope abounds that Wyoming's Fennis Dembo will emerge as a terror at big guard since Johnson, still a lethal threat, had his second straight season with longer-than-usual cold shooting spells.

PISTON ROSTER

No.	Veteran	Pos.	Ht.	Wt.	Age	Yrs. Pro	College
25	William Bedford	C	7-1	235	24	2	Memphis State
45	Adrian Dantley	F	6-5	210	32	12	Notre Dame
4	Joe Dumars	G	6-3	190	25	3	McNeese State
53	James Edwards	C	7-1	252	33	11	Washington
15	Vinnie Johnson	G	6-2	200	32	9	Baylor
40	Bill Laimbeer	C	6-11	260	31	8	Notre Dame
44	Rick Mahorn	F	6-10	255	30	8	Hampton Institute
10	Dennis Rodman	F	6-8	210	27	2	SE Oklahoma State
23	Walker Russell	G	6-5	195	28	6	Western Michigan
22	John Salley	F	6-11	231	24	2	Georgia Tech
11	Isiah Thomas	G	6-1	185	27	7	Indiana

Rd.	Top Rookies	Sel. No.	Pos.	Ht.	Wt.	College
2	Fennis Dembo	30	F-G	6-6	215	Wyoming
2	Michael Williams	48	G	6-2	175	Baylor
3	Lee Johnson	72	F	6-9	210	Norfolk State

PISTON PROFILES

ISIAH THOMAS 27 6-1 185   Guard

Only thing, thank goodness, he didn't suffer in NBA Finals vs. Lakers was amputation... So he managed to play in Game 7 after spending day and a half on crutches for severely sprained ankle... Also suffered severely bruised back in Game 3... Inspiration and leadership aside, probably hurt team more than helped in Game 7. Ankle stiffened at halftime and Lakers ran past him for 11-1 run to start third quarter. Pistons never caught up... Greatest munchkin ever to play the game... Example of his dominant traits exhibited in Game 6. Scored 43 points, record 25 in third. "He was unconscious," raved pal Magic Johnson... NBA Finals almost became love match: Isiah vs. Magic. Pushed and shoved each other in Game 3, then literally kissed and made up... Wife Lynn gave birth to couple's first child, Joshua, during Finals... Shows why middle name is "Lord" when he runs the team... But "Pocket Magic" sometimes gets carried away as his penetrating becomes aimless kamikazi charges. He'll burn you at any time, or go silly with 1-on-5 drives... Seems to be loved or hated by public and media, no middle ground... Will have to live with awful Game 5 pass in 1987 semis vs. Celts till ashes are planted... Scoring slipped below 20 ppg for first time since 1981-82 rookie season... Was No. 2 player selected in 1981 draft out of Indiana... Born April 30, 1961, in Chicago... Earned $750,000, but renegotiation expected to bring him over a million.

Year	Team	G	FG	FG Pct.	FT	FT Pct.	Reb.	Ast.	TP	Avg.
1981-82	Detroit	72	453	.424	302	.704	209	565	1225	17.0
1982-83	Detroit	81	725	.472	368	.710	328	634	1854	22.9
1983-84	Detroit	82	669	.462	388	.733	327	914	1748	21.3
1984-85	Detroit	81	646	.458	399	.809	361	1123	1720	21.2
1985-86	Detroit	77	609	.488	365	.790	277	830	1609	20.9
1986-87	Detroit	81	626	.463	400	.768	319	813	1671	20.6
1987-88	Detroit	81	621	.463	305	.774	278	678	1577	19.5
	Totals	555	4349	.462	2527	.755	2099	5557	11404	20.5

JOE DUMARS 25 6-3 190   Guard

The Piston nobody hates... Career bests in scoring and steals... The "other guy" in backcourt with Isiah... A blend of an off and point guard... All-around player and a very good one. Can dominate with offense, but was superb in second playoff round defensively vs. Michael Jordan... Instrumental in Eastern Conference victory over Celtics, including a playoff-high 29-point game... Comes away with bad memory of Finals, though. Missed running five-footer in lane with :08 left in Game 6. "I should have taken it all the way," he admitted later ... A steal in 1985 draft when Pistons made him 18th player chosen... Played at little-known McNeese State, where he was sixth in nation in scoring in 1984... Born May 5, 1963, in Natchitoches, La.... Earns $400,000.

Year	Team	G	FG	FG Pct.	FT	FT Pct.	Reb.	Ast.	TP	Avg.
1985-86	Detroit	82	287	.481	190	.798	119	390	769	9.4
1986-87	Detroit	79	369	.493	184	.748	167	352	931	11.8
1987-88	Detroit	82	453	.472	251	.815	200	387	1161	14.2
	Totals	243	1109	.481	625	.789	486	1129	2861	11.8

BILL LAIMBEER 31 6-11 260   Center

Who's hated more, Laimbeer or teammate Rick Mahorn?... Knows every sly trick in book... He probably wrote the book... He loves to act and is rather good at it, too. When detected for an elbow or a shove, he pleads so convincingly with that crybaby mug, you think he's the one being picked on... Contends he just plays hard and aggressive. Which he does ... "Anybody who plays golf and drinks beer can't be all bad," said Celtics' Kevin McHale... Besides the naughty-boy rep, he's a heckuva player... Despite vertical leap of three-quarters of an inch, he's one of best rebounders in NBA, finishing 10th in league last year after five seasons of placing no lower than fifth. Led league in 1985-86... Legitimate perimeter shooter, but his low-post game is nearly non-existent... Has played in 646 straight regular-season games, starting last 522. Both current NBA highs... Became a Piston regular in 1982-83 after trade from Cleveland with Kenny Carr for Phil Hubbard, Paul Mokeski plus first- and second-round picks... Was third-round pick by Cavs in 1979 (65th overall), out of Notre Dame... Born May 19, 1957, in Boston, where shrine of him will never be built, and grew up in Palos Verdes, Cal.... Earns $650,000.

Year	Team	G	FG	FG Pct.	FT	FT Pct.	Reb.	Ast.	TP	Avg.
1980-81	Cleveland	81	337	.503	117	.765	693	216	791	9.8
1981-82	Clev.-Det.	80	265	.494	184	.793	617	100	718	9.0
1982-83	Detroit	82	436	.497	245	.790	993	263	1119	13.6
1983-84	Detroit	82	553	.530	316	.866	1003	149	1422	17.3
1984-85	Detroit	82	595	.506	244	.797	1013	154	1438	17.5
1985-86	Detroit	82	545	.492	266	.834	1075	146	1360	16.6
1986-87	Detroit	82	506	.501	245	.894	955	151	1263	15.4
1987-88	Detroit	82	455	.493	187	.874	832	199	1110	13.5
	Totals	653	3692	.503	1804	.830	7181	1378	9221	14.1

ADRIAN DANTLEY 32 6-5 210   Forward

You watching, Frank Layden?... Was exiled from Utah with pair of draft choices for Kelly Tripucka and Kent Benson prior to 1986-87 season after old-fashioned hate relationship with Jazz coach... Tripucka and Benson are now footnotes to one of NBA's most lopsided trades as A.D. remains an unstoppable low-post player... Eleventh-best scorer in NBA history. Two-time league scoring champ... Listed at 6-5, he's more like 6-3... Can foul anybody out and almost lives on the foul line . . . Was on way to 1988 NBA Playoffs MVP when funny thing happened: Lakers won . . . Chuck Daly provided second-guess heaven when he kept him on bench for final 10:22 of Game 7 . . . Embarrassed A.C. Green in front of national audience with 34-point night in Game 1 . . . Has now averaged 20 points a game for nine straight years . . . Left Notre Dame as hardship case after junior year in 1976 and was sixth player chosen overall by Buffalo. Went to Indiana and Lakers before landing in Utah in '79 . . . Product of DeMatha High in Washington D.C., where he teamed with ex-NBAer Kenny Carr . . . Born Feb. 28, 1956, in Hyattsville, Md. . . . Will get about $1 million this year.

Year	Team	G	FG	FG Pct.	FT	FT Pct.	Reb.	Ast.	TP	Avg.
1976-77	Buffalo	77	544	.520	476	.818	587	144	1564	20.3
1977-78	Ind.-L.A.	79	578	.512	541	.796	620	253	1697	21.5
1978-79	Los Angeles	60	374	.510	292	.854	342	138	1040	17.3
1979-80	Utah	68	730	.576	443	.842	516	191	1903	28.0
1980-81	Utah	80	909	.559	632	.806	509	322	2452	30.7
1981-82	Utah	81	904	.570	648	.792	514	324	2457	30.3
1982-83	Utah	22	233	.580	210	.847	140	105	676	30.7
1983-84	Utah	79	802	.558	813	.859	448	310	2418	30.6
1984-85	Utah	55	512	.531	438	.804	323	186	1462	26.6
1985-86	Utah	76	818	.563	630	.791	395	264	2267	29.8
1986-87	Detroit	81	601	.534	539	.812	332	162	1742	21.5
1987-88	Detroit	69	444	.514	492	.860	227	171	1380	20.0
	Totals	827	7449	.546	6154	.820	4953	2570	21058	25.5

RICK MAHORN 30 6-10 255   Forward

No more calls. We have a winner. This guy is the most hated player in NBA . . . Mr. Maim . . . He's Jason of "Friday the 13th" on a basketball court . . . Actually, he's a nice guy off the court . . . But his future's clouded by off-season disc surgery . . . Bum back kept him sprawled on floor in front of Piston bench for last two months and he was almost a complete non-factor in playoffs . . . Was off to best season ever when injury struck, and still finished with highest scoring (10.7) and rebounding (8.4) averages in his three years as Piston . . . Shot career-best .574 from the floor . . . A major force when he's healthy and at reasonable weight. Almost ate way out of league two years ago . . . Became another Bullet blunder, when Pistons acquired him with Mike Gibson for over-the-hill Dan Roundfield in June 1985 . . . Was highly recruited for football skills out of high school . . . Born Sept. 21, 1958, in Hartford, Conn. . . . Second-round pick (35th overall) by Washington in

1980 draft...Three-time NAIA All-American at Hampton Institute...Earns $575,000.

Year	Team	G	FG	FG Pct.	FT	FT Pct.	Reb.	Ast.	TP	Avg.
1980-81	Washington	52	111	.507	27	.675	215	25	249	4.8
1981-82	Washington	80	414	.507	148	.632	704	150	976	12.2
1982-83	Washington	82	376	.490	146	.575	779	115	898	11.0
1983-84	Washington	82	307	.507	125	.651	738	131	739	9.0
1984-85	Washington	77	206	.499	71	.683	608	121	483	6.3
1985-86	Detroit	80	157	.455	81	.681	412	64	395	4.9
1986-87	Detroit	63	144	.447	96	.821	375	38	384	6.1
1987-88	Detroit	67	276	.574	164	.756	565	60	717	10.7
	Totals	583	1991	.502	858	.672	4396	704	4841	8.3

JOHN SALLEY 24 6-11 231 Forward

Long, tall Salley...Tentacles for arms... Outstanding shot-blocker (362 in two seasons coming off the bench), and outstanding offensive rebounder...Part of Pistons' second-unit running team...Superb passer from high post and his overall game is improving by the second...Was a real raw talent out of Georgia Tech when Pistons made him No. 11 pick in 1986 draft...All he could really do back then was pass... Credit Chuck Daly for tons of patience and confidence-building ...Was considered as one of nation's top prospects after junior year in college but "my stock fell because I didn't average 35 points," he said...Became a national media darling in NBA Finals with most quotable quotes this side of Mychal Thompson ...Downright funny guy...And a true force off the bench... Final contract year will bring $335,000...Will be playing for bigger bucks very soon...Born May 16, 1964, in Brooklyn, N.Y.

Year	Team	G	FG	FG Pct.	FT	FT Pct.	Reb.	Ast.	TP	Avg.
1986-87	Detroit	82	163	.562	105	.614	296	54	431	5.3
1987-88	Detroit	82	258	.566	185	.709	402	113	701	8.5
	Totals	164	421	.564	290	.671	698	167	1132	6.9

VINNIE JOHNSON 32 6-2 200 Guard

The Microwave was only lukewarm...Had worst shooting season (.443) since rookie year...And his 12.2 ppg was lowest in 6½ seasons as Piston...Was left open for expansion and not claimed, which was rather surprising even if he is 32...Still the most lethal streak shooter in game who can pour in line-drive jumpers by the bushel...When he's on, nothing known to man can stop him...Among the strongest of guards, he's a powerful rebounder, especially on offensive glass ...Born in Brooklyn, N.Y., one of eight children, on Sept. 1, 1956...Celtics' Danny Ainge coined his nickname...Best suited for reserve role due to his streakiness. And when he hits his first two shots, opponents can light novena candles...Seattle made Baylor product No. 7 pick of '79 draft...Acquired from Sonics for Greg Kelser in November 1981...Earns $633,000.

Year	Team	G	FG	FG Pct.	FT	FT Pct.	Reb.	Ast.	TP	Avg.
1979-80	Seattle.	38	45	.391	31	.795	55	54	121	3.2
1980-81	Seattle.	81	419	.534	214	.793	366	341	1053	13.0
1981-82	Sea.-Det.	74	217	.489	107	.754	159	171	544	7.4
1982-83	Detroit.	82	520	.513	245	.778	353	301	1296	15.8
1983-84	Detroit.	82	426	.473	207	.753	237	271	1063	13.0
1984-85	Detroit.	82	428	.454	190	.769	252	325	1051	12.8
1985-86	Detroit.	79	465	.467	165	.771	226	269	1097	13.9
1986-87	Detroit.	78	533	.462	158	.786	257	300	1228	15.7
1987-88	Detroit.	82	425	.443	147	.677	231	267	1002	12.2
	Totals.	678	3478	.476	1464	.763	2136	2299	8455	12.5

DENNIS RODMAN 27 6-8 210   Forward

The Worm...Made scouts look foolish after being second-round (27th overall) pick out of Southeastern Oklahoma State in 1986... Swings to big guard for defense...Suffocating defensive player who denies penetration...Another jumping-jack off offensive glass, 45 percent of his 715 rebounds were on offensive end...An endless supply of energy, wind him up and watch him go...One of most memorable sights of NBA Finals was his near-vault over Lakers' Kurt Rambis as he caught his foot on Rambis' nose...Scintillating dunker, but he has no outside shot to speak of...He's also one of the worst free-throw shooters who ever walked on a basketball court...Will always be remembered for his inane remarks about Larry Bird after 1987 semifinals when he said Larry Legend was overrated because he was white...It was a surprising comment from someone with his background. During college days, he virtually lived with blue-collar white family and helped troubled pre-teen kids...Underpaid at $160,000...Born May 13, 1961, in Dallas.

Year	Team	G	FG	FG Pct.	FT	FT Pct.	Reb.	Ast.	TP	Avg.
1986-87	Detroit.	77	213	.545	74	.587	332	56	500	6.5
1987-88	Detroit.	82	398	.561	152	.535	715	110	953	11.6
	Totals.	159	611	.555	226	.551	1047	166	1453	9.1

JAMES EDWARDS 33 7-1 252   Center

Another part of Suns' broom job... Was sent to Pistons for a project named Ron Moore and a second-round pick last February... Sparsely used by Detroit in regular season, he became a low-post scoring force in playoffs... Was key contributor off Piston bench which humiliated Celtic reserves in Eastern Conference finals ... Charmin-soft during his tenure in Phoenix as a starter, he fit in nicely in reserve role with Pistons... Named in grand-jury probe in Phoenix, but was cleared of all drug charges... Still, it tainted his reputation and Suns sent him away as part of housecleaning... An NBA vagabond. Was drafted out of Washington on third round (46th overall) by Lakers in 1977, then sent to Indiana, then to Cleveland, where he played for then-coach Chuck Daly. Then on to Phoenix... Born Nov. 22, 1955, in Seattle... Earned $600,000.

Year	Team	G	FG	FG Pct.	FT	FT Pct.	Reb.	Ast.	TP	Avg.
1977-78	L.A.-Ind............	83	495	.453	272	.646	615	85	1252	15.2
1978-79	Indiana............	82	534	.501	298	.676	693	92	1366	16.7
1979-80	Indiana............	82	528	.512	231	.681	578	127	1287	15.7
1980-81	Indiana............	81	511	.509	244	.703	571	212	1266	15.6
1981-82	Cleveland..........	77	528	.511	232	.684	581	123	1288	16.7
1982-83	Clev.-Phoe.........	31	128	.487	69	.639	155	40	325	10.5
1983-84	Phoenix............	72	438	.536	183	.720	348	184	1059	14.7
1984-85	Phoenix............	70	384	.501	276	.746	387	153	1044	14.9
1985-86	Phoenix............	52	318	.542	212	.702	301	74	848	16.3
1986-87	Phoenix............	14	57	.518	54	.771	60	19	168	12.0
1987-88	Phoe.Det..........	69	302	.470	210	.654	412	78	814	11.8
	Totals.............	713	4223	.502	2281	.689	4701	1187	10727	15.0

WILLIAM BEDFORD 24 7-1 235   Center

There were the rumors in college. There was the messy drug situation in Phoenix. Then he finally admitted to cocaine problem, reportedly with strong-arm "suggestion" from teammates following players-only meeting in March... Before being placed on suspended list, he had 38 undistinguished appearances ... One of the greatest disappointments in recent years... When Phoenix made him sixth player chosen in 1986 draft as an undergraduate from Memphis State, he was supposed to be aggressive, a shot-blocker and the best "pure center" in the nation... The Suns thought they could build the franchise around him . . . But after he dogged his way through rookie year, they shipped him to Motown for a 1989 first-round pick . . . Earns $637,500 . . . Born Dec. 14, 1963, in Memphis, Tenn. . . . Despite his track record, there will always be a team willing to take a shot with him because he's 7-1.

Year	Team	G	FG	FG Pct.	FT	FT Pct.	Reb.	Ast.	TP	Avg.
1986-87	Phoenix.	50	142	.397	50	.581	246	57	334	6.7
1987-88	Detroit.	38	44	.436	13	.565	65	4	101	2.7
	Totals.	88	186	.405	63	.578	311	61	435	4.9

WALKER D. RUSSELL 28 6-5 195   Guard

D stands for Downright Lucky . . . Was in CBA when Pistons signed him for final game of regular season and playoffs to fill William Bedford's roster spot and give Pistons 12 guys for playoffs . . . Had an assist in regular season, played 10 playoff minutes and earned nice postseason check . . . Journeyman right from the beginning . . . Played at three colleges, finishing at Western Michigan. Drafted on fourth round by Pistons (78th overall) in 1982. Free-agent signings with Atlanta, Detroit (again) and Indiana followed . . . Born Oct. 26, 1960, in Pontiac, Mich. Plays about five minutes from doorstep . . . Shouldn't unpack luggage . . . Brother of former NBA forward Campy and guard Frank.

Year	Team	G	FG	FG Pct.	FT	FT Pct.	Reb.	Ast.	TP	Avg.
1982-83	Detroit.	68	67	.364	47	.810	73	131	183	2.7
1983-84	Detroit.	16	14	.333	12	.923	19	22	41	2.6
1984-85	Atlanta.	21	34	.540	14	.824	40	66	83	4.0
1985-86	Detroit.	1	0	.000	0	.000	0	1	0	0.0
1986-87	Indiana.	48	64	.388	27	.730	55	129	157	3.3
1987-88	Detroit.	1	0	.000	0	.000	0	1	0	0.0
	Totals.	155	179	.393	100	.800	187	350	464	3.0

TOP ROOKIE

FENNIS DEMBO 22 6-6 215   Forward-Guard

Is this a name or is this a name? Consensus preseason All-American and *Sports Illustrated* coverboy had disappointing senior season after huge hype and successful junior campaign at

Wyoming . . . Cost him first-round selection status and big, big bucks . . . Averaged 20.4 ppg as senior . . . Pistons took him on second round, 30th overall . . . Good passer, but his shooting slipped from .540 as sophomore to .512 as junior to .477 as senior . . . "The thing people don't emphasize about him is his unselfishness," said Wyoming coach Benny Dees . . . Led Wyoming to NIT finals in 1987.

COACH CHUCK DALY: Gentleman's Quarterly threads. Voted best-dressed coach in league . . . Obviously, there's a lot more than sartorial splendor . . . Didn't get the credit he truly deserved for magnificent coaching job with team filled with sensitive and reclamation types . . . Nice, pleasant guy . . . Never met a golf course he didn't like . . . After the groundhog, he's the most famous product of Punxsutawney, Pa.  "They have a groundhog, a golf course and a special hamburger that they put on a hot dog roll. After that, well, that's about it," he said . . . Born July 20, 1930, in St. Mary's, Pa. . . . Winningest coach in Pistons' history. Compiled franchise's first back-to-back 50-win seasons . . . Before he arrived, Pistons never had back-to-back winning seasons, let alone a 50-win year . . . In five years in Motown, he has 247-163 record, five winning seasons, five playoff appearances . . . Coached in playoffs without a contract. Finally, Piston hierarchy saw light and rewarded him with three-year, $1.2-million deal . . . Spent four seasons as assistant to Billy Cunningham in Philly before going to Detroit . . . Took head coaching job with Cavs, lasted 41 disastrous games in utterly futile situation . . . Began coaching at Punxsutawney High following graduation from Bloomsburg (Pa.) State in '55 . . . After assisting at Duke, coached Boston College for two years and Pennsylvania for six years, winning four Ivy League titles.

GREATEST THREE-POINT SHOOTER

In seven years with the Pistons, a lot of good Isiah Thomas has done has been tarnished due to sub-par playoff performances. But let's face it. The guy can dazzle with his passing and shooting. And he can also connect from three-point land.

His percentage of .279 won't frighten anybody out of their commercially endorsed footwear, but Thomas has converted more three-pointers (179) than any Piston ever. The fact that he has attempted more (641) than any Piston sort of helped him achieve that status. For accuracy, Thomas' best season was 1983-84 (22-of-65, .338). For quantity, his top season was 1982-83 (36-of-125). Last season, however, Isiah played less one-on-one and that was reflected in his 30-of-97 (.309) total.

ALL-TIME PISTON LEADERS

SEASON

Points: Dave Bing, 2,213, 1970-71
Assists: Isiah Thomas, 1,123, 1984-85
Rebounds: Bob Lanier, 1,205, 1972-73

GAME

Points: Kelly Tripucka, 56 vs. Chicago, 1/29/83
Assists: Kevin Porter, 25 vs. Phoenix, 4/1/79
         Kevin Porter, 25 vs. Boston, 3/9/79
         Isiah Thomas, 25 vs. Dallas, 2/13/85
Rebounds: Bob Lanier, 33 vs. Seattle, 12/22/72

CAREER

Points: Bob Lanier, 15,488, 1970-80
Assists: Isiah Thomas, 5,557, 1981-88
Rebounds: Bob Lanier, 8,033, 1970-80

INDIANA PACERS

TEAM DIRECTORY: Owners: Herb Simon, Melvin Simon: GM: Donnie Walsh; Dir. Player Personnel: George Irvine; Media Rel. Dir.: Dale Ratermann; Coach: Jack Ramsay; Asst. Coaches: Dave Twardzik, Mel Daniels. Arena: Market Square Arena (16,912). Colors: Blue and yellow.

Chuck Person: Small forward, big mouth, huge talent.

SCOUTING REPORT

SHOOTING: The Pacers went from bad (.472, fifth worst) to so-so (.480, 11th best) last season, despite a second-year dip from Chuck Person and an invisible campaign from Herb Williams. But Wayman Tisdale checked in at .512 and constantly-improving guard Vern Fleming shot a team-high .523. Steve Stipanovich, who virtually stopped trying to score down the stretch, shot .496 while again roaming the high post.

Rookie Reggie Miller shot .488, despite all those three-point attempts. On two-point shots, Miller was an impressive .538 (245-of-455). The addition of No. 1 pick Rik Smits should bring some low-post scoring from center as Stipanovich slides over to big forward.

PLAYMAKING: The Pacers, in a patient, work-ethic offense, were sixth worst in the league with 1,997 assists. Individually, they have good passers—Fleming (team-high 568 assists), Person (309) and Stipanovich—but collectively they need a little work. They were tied with the Lakers for sixth best in turnovers committed (16.1), but were fifth worst in turnovers forced (15.5).

DEFENSE: A Jack Ramsay team will always play defense. The Pacers yielded 105.4 points a game, the seventh-best mark in the league. Trouble was, they scored only 104.6 per, fourth worst in the NBA. And only the Warriors blocked fewer shots than the Pacers' 345. That should change with the addition of Smits.

REBOUNDING: Forward failure. That explains why the Pacers were hurting on the boards (ranking 17th) last season. Person dipped from a team-high 8.2 rebounds in 1987 to 6.8 last season. And Williams, usually a force on the boards, didn't supply much power with just 6.2 per. Help was provided by Fleming, who rebounds well from his point-guard post. The 7-4 Smits should be a big help.

OUTLOOK: The Pacers' chances of a repeat postseason trip weren't dashed until the very last second of the season. It was especially disappointing considering their fine 41-41 campaign of 1986-87. They folded in the last two months, going from playoff lock to the lottery with alarming ineptness. Many questions loom. Can Person and Jack Ramsay co-exist without homicide investigators being called in before season's end? How long will it take Smits to develop? Will the Pacers get anything out of

PACER ROSTER

No.	Veteran	Pos.	Ht.	Wt.	Age	Yrs. Pro	College
15	Ron Anderson	F	6-7	215	30	4	Fresno State
54	Greg Dreiling	C	7-1	250	24	2	Kansas
10	Vern Fleming	G	6-5	195	26	4	Georgia
55	Stuart Gray	C	7-0	245	25	4	UCLA
25	John Long	G	6-5	195	32	10	Detroit
31	Reggie Miller	G-F	6-7	190	23	1	UCLA
45	Chuck Person	F	6-8	225	24	2	Auburn
3	Scott Skiles	G	6-1	190	24	2	Michigan State
40	Steve Stipanovich	C	7-0	250	27	5	Missouri
23	Wayman Tisdale	F	6-7	240	24	3	Oklahoma
32	Herb Williams	F	6-11	240	30	7	Ohio State

Rd.	Top Rookies	Sel. No.	Pos.	Ht.	Wt.	College
1	Rik Smits	2	C	7-4	250	Marist
3	Herbert Crook	61	F	6-7	195	Louisville
3	Michael Anderson	73	G	5-11	184	Drexel

Williams this year? And how much improvement will come from Miller in his second season? The Pacers are aligned in the murderous Central Division, which certainly won't help, but with a curious mixture of talent they are one of those teams whose chances of going either way are equally strong.

PACER PROFILES

CHUCK PERSON 24 6-8 225   Forward

Missing Person in stretch drive . . . Led team in scoring 30 times—but only once in last nine games; twice in last 14; three times in last 20 . . . Finished as Pacers' leading scorer and one of their leading headaches . . . Wanted to be a leader, but few wanted to follow. He didn't see eye-to-eye with coach Jack Ramsay. Or many of players in league . . . Not in Bill Laimbeer's or Rick Mahorn's class for being despised, but more than a few players around league would dearly like to put a hurting on him ...First team All-Talkin' Trash...Says he doesn't mean to upset, nothing personal, just his style...Enormous natural talent...Second on team in rebounds, second in assists, fourth in steals. But first in turnovers...Nicknamed "The Rifleman." Full name is Chuck Connors Person...Mom was a big fan of the old TV show starring the guy who was once a Celtic and briefly a major leaguer in baseball...Tremendous range...Can stick the three-pointer; has 104 in two seasons...Was overwhelming choice as Rookie of the Year in 1986-87 after Pacers grabbed him fourth overall in draft...Left Auburn as the school's all-time leading scorer with 2,311 points in four seasons...Born June 27, 1964, in Brantley, Ala....GM Donnie Walsh said no one on team was "untradeable" but said Person would have to bring "an Olajuwon or Jordan."...Earned $565,500.

Year	Team	G	FG	FG Pct.	FT	FT Pct.	Reb.	Ast.	TP	Avg.
1986-87	Indiana	82	635	.468	222	.747	677	295	1541	18.8
1987-88	Indiana	79	575	.459	132	.670	536	309	1341	17.0
	Totals	161	1210	.464	354	.717	1213	604	2882	17.9

VERN FLEMING 26 6-5 195   Guard

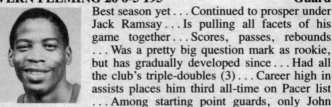

Best season yet...Continued to prosper under Jack Ramsay...Is pulling all facets of his game together...Scores, passes, rebounds ...Was a pretty big question mark as rookie, but has gradually developed since...Had all the club's triple-doubles (3)...Career high in assists places him third all-time on Pacer list ...Among starting point guards, only John Stockton shot better than his .523...Scored career-high 30 points at Denver last November...Was rewarded with contract extension prior to training camp. Earned $257,500...Bigger bucks ahead...Good rebounder from point guard spot...Born Feb. 4, 1961, in Long Island City, N.Y....Drafted by Pacers on first round (No. 18 overall) in 1984...All-American at Georgia, where he finished as all-time scorer, ahead of Dominique Wilkins.

Year	Team	G	FG	FG Pct.	FT	FT Pct.	Reb.	Ast.	TP	Avg.
1984-85	Indiana	80	433	.470	260	.767	323	247	1126	14.1
1985-86	Indiana	80	436	.506	263	.745	386	505	1136	14.2
1986-87	Indiana	82	370	.509	238	.788	334	473	980	12.0
1987-88	Indiana	80	442	.523	227	.802	364	568	1111	13.9
	Totals	322	1681	.501	988	.774	1407	1793	4353	13.5

REGGIE MILLER 23 6-7 190 Guard-Forward

Reggie, Reggie, Reggie. Threes dominated his rookie season... Outstanding outside shooter broke Larry Bird's rookie record with 61 three-point shots... Earned his $254,000 pay by being only Pacer to play all 82 games... When Pacers were self-destructing in stretch, he came up with big 31-point (4-of-7 on three-pointers) effort in victory over Philly last April that looked like it might turn Pacers back into playoff team... It didn't... Started season impressively. Scored in double figures in first 11 games. Cooled off, but finished strong... Was Pacers' first-round pick in 1987... Second only to Kareem-Abdul Jabbar (then Lew Alcindor) in scoring at UCLA... Outstanding sports family: sister Cheryl was mega-star in basketball at USC and Olympics; brother Darrell catches for the Angels; sister Tammy is volleyball standout at Cal-State Fullerton. Born Aug. 24, 1965, in Riverside, Cal.

Year	Team	G	FG	FG Pct.	FT	FT Pct.	Reb.	Ast.	TP	Avg.
1987-88	Indiana............	82	306	.488	149	.801	190	132	822	10.0

WAYMAN TISDALE 24 6-7 240 Forward

Another consolation prize... Was selected right behind Patrick Ewing in 1985 lottery... Awful rookie season... Stock has skyrocketed as he has become first front-line player off bench... Used at each forward post... Was *the* man who kept Pacers in playoff hunt until very last second... Averaged team-high 18.4 points in second half of season... A lefty... Great low-post game and his range is ever creeping outwards... Good, only getting better... Good rebounder, too... Was college center at Oklahoma and became Big Eight's all-time scorer in just three seasons. Was first conference player ever to earn All-American honors as frosh, soph and junior... Son of a preacher... Donates lots of time and money to anti-substance abuse programs... Affable and pleasant, an easy guy to root for ... Earned $983,300 last year. His contract will surpass $1 million this season... Born June 9, 1964, in Tulsa, Okla.

Year	Team	G	FG	FG Pct.	FT	FT Pct.	Reb.	Ast.	TP	Avg.
1985-86	Indiana............	81	516	.515	160	.684	584	79	1192	14.7
1986-87	Indiana............	81	458	.513	258	.709	475	117	1174	14.5
1987-88	Indiana............	79	511	.512	246	.783	491	103	1268	16.1
	Totals............	241	1485	.513	664	.728	1550	299	3634	15.1

HERB WILLIAMS 30 6-11 240   Forward

What happened?...A model of consistency for six seasons, he was terribly inconsistent in his seventh...Worst of his career. Trade rumors swirled...Didn't score 20 points in a game until 79th game. Then had another in Game 80...Until last season, his previous scoring low was 11.5 in rookie season...Also had career lows in rebounds, minutes and shooting (.425). Disappointment came after hefty raise upped salary to $1-million atmosphere ($983,000)...Stayed solid in one area: blocks, with 146, to again finish in NBA's top 10 (eighth with 1.95). Is all-time Pacer leader in blocks...Great power-forward physique includes tentacle-like arms...Was 14th player selected in 1981 draft, out of Ohio State...Born Feb. 16, 1958, in Columbus, Ohio.

Year	Team	G	FG	FG Pct.	FT	FT Pct.	Reb.	Ast.	TP	Avg.
1981-82	Indiana............	82	407	.477	126	.670	605	139	942	11.5
1982-83	Indiana............	78	580	.499	155	.705	583	262	1315	16.9
1983-84	Indiana............	69	411	.478	207	.702	554	215	1029	14.9
1984-85	Indiana............	75	575	.475	224	.657	634	252	1375	18.3
1985-86	Indiana............	78	627	.492	294	.730	710	174	1549	19.9
1986-87	Indiana............	74	451	.480	199	.740	543	174	1101	14.9
1987-88	Indiana............	75	311	.425	126	.737	469	98	748	10.0
	Totals............	531	3362	.478	1331	.705	4098	1314	8059	15.2

RON ANDERSON 30 6-7 215   Forward

Another strong, solid season—in reserve... Had two great back-to-back games last April when he had 14-point fourth quarter against Nets, and then season-high 25 points against Knicks...In previous season, he ripped Jersey for a 23-point fourth quarter...Had his best shooting season ever...An instant offense, high-energy type who's caught in numbers squeeze behind Chuck Person. With Wayman Tisdale also getting some small-forward time, he saw just 14.8 minutes a game...Another "Can You Top This?" story...Didn't play in high school and originally bypassed college to pursue the exciting field of supermarket stock managing...A friend talked him into entering a community college and he wound up at Fresno State. Drafted by Cleveland on second round in 1984...Was given away to Pacers for fourth-rounder in December 1985...Born

Oct. 15, 1957, in Chicago... Earned $200,000 last season, a tad more than your neighborhood stock manager.

Year	Team	G	FG	FG Pct.	FT	FT Pct.	Reb.	Ast.	TP	Avg.
1984-85	Cleveland...........	36	84	.431	41	.820	88	34	210	5.8
1985-86	Clev.-Ind...........	77	310	.494	85	.669	274	144	707	9.2
1986-87	Indiana............	63	139	.473	85	.787	151	54	363	5.8
1987-88	Indiana............	74	217	.498	108	.766	216	78	542	7.3
	Totals............	250	750	.483	319	.749	729	310	1822	7.3

STEVE STIPANOVICH 29 7-0 250   Center

Stipo... He missed the last shot of the Pacers' season and team missed playoffs. Knicks' Kenny Walker got a tiny piece of his driving scoop at the buzzer and the Pacers were in the lottery... He knows about lotteries, being the consolation prize in the Ralph Sampson lottery of 1983... Ultra-consistent, has averaged between 13.2 and 13.7 points per game last four years... Plays higher post than most... Excellent passer. Moves a lot, too. Gives opposing defenses trouble... Another who faded in stretch, particularly in scoring. Led team with 21 double-doubles (rebounds and points), but had just three in last 17 games as Pacers played themselves out of playoffs... Sound, steady player, but not a championship-caliber center, unless supporting cast improves rather dramatically... Earned $710,000 ... Born Nov. 17, 1960, in St. Louis... Left Missouri as the leading scorer, rebounder and shot-blocker in school's history.

Year	Team	G	FG	FG Pct.	FT	FT Pct.	Reb.	Ast.	TP	Avg.
1983-84	Indiana............	81	392	.480	183	.753	562	170	970	12.0
1984-85	Indiana............	82	414	.475	297	.798	614	199	1126	13.7
1985-86	Indiana............	79	416	.470	242	.768	623	206	1076	13.6
1986-87	Indiana............	81	382	.503	307	.837	670	180	1072	13.2
1987-88	Indiana............	80	411	.496	254	.809	662	183	1079	13.5
	Totals............	403	2015	.484	1283	.796	3131	938	5323	13.2

JOHN LONG 32 6-5 195   Guard

Appropriate name... Can bury 'em from anywhere... Established Pacer record for three-point accuracy (.442). Had 34 three-pointers, one less than he managed in nine previous seasons combined... Excellent free-throw shooter. Set club standard .907 from line... Ended season with run of 30 straight free throws. Was one of four NBA players to finish at 90 percent... Don't say apple to him, though. Rap has been that he doesn't handle pressure too well ... In win-or-go home-season finale, was yanked with 7:42 left after shooting 4-for-12 ... Family man ... Does youth counseling in offseason ... Born Aug. 28, 1956, in Romulus, Mich., suburb of Detroit ... Went to high school and college, plus started pro career in Motown ... Second-round pick of Pistons in 1978 ... Was dealt to Seattle in October 1986 and then shipped to Pacers the next day for Russ Schoene and Terence Stansbury ... Earned $375,000.

Year	Team	G	FG	FG Pct.	FT	FT Pct.	Reb.	Ast.	TP	Avg.
1978-79	Detroit	82	581	.469	157	.826	266	121	1319	16.1
1979-80	Detroit	69	588	.505	160	.825	337	206	1337	19.4
1980-81	Detroit	59	441	.461	160	.870	197	106	1044	17.7
1981-82	Detroit	69	637	.492	238	.865	257	148	1514	21.9
1982-83	Detroit	70	312	.451	111	.760	180	105	737	10.5
1983-84	Detroit	82	545	.472	243	.884	289	205	1334	16.3
1984-85	Detroit	66	431	.487	106	.862	190	130	973	14.7
1985-86	Detroit	62	264	.482	89	.856	98	82	620	10.0
1986-87	Indiana	80	490	.419	219	.890	217	258	1218	15.2
1987-88	Indiana	81	417	.474	166	.907	229	173	1034	12.8
	Totals	720	4706	.471	1649	.859	2260	1534	11130	15.5

SCOTT SKILES 24 6-1 190   Guard

Grown-up Spanky McFarland in looks and attitude ... Won't back down from anyone ... Absolutely, positively hates losing ... Tremendous heart and desire—with a temper to match ... Career was threatened by disc problems ... First two pro seasons have been spent heavily on injured list (twice last season) ... "My back's a mess, my knee's a wreck and my hair's falling out," he once said ... Tremendous passer with exciting look-that-way, pass-that-way vision ... Pushes the ball extremely well and is fine penetrator ... A real throwback ... Had career-high 13 assists vs. Cavs last April and was third on team in assists despite averaging only 14.9 minutes ... Was 22th selection in 1986 draft by Milwaukee, out of Michigan State ... Teams shied away because of his rocky past with booze and drugs that landed him in jail for 15 days ... Born March 5, 1964, in LaPorte, Ind. ... Acquired by Pacers in June 1987 for second-round pick ... If health holds up, he'll be solid contributor.

Year	Team	G	FG	FG Pct.	FT	FT Pct.	Reb.	Ast.	TP	Avg.
1986-87	Milwaukee	13	18	.290	10	.833	26	45	49	3.8
1987-88	Indiana	51	86	.411	45	.833	66	180	223	4.4
	Totals	64	104	.384	55	.833	92	225	272	4.3

STUART GRAY 25 7-0 245   Center

See Greg Dreiling and wasted height... Does have toughness, though... Lost a tooth this year to prove it... Left UCLA as a junior following a blistering 9.9-point and 7.9-rebound season in 1983-84... Shouldn't that be cause to re-enroll, rather than go hardship?... But the Pacers welcomed him with open checkbook and gave guaranteed money after making him a second-round pick (29th overall)... Earned $200,000 last year... Scored 10 points with career-high 12 boards against Lakers last February... Career high in minutes and blocked shots... Another big white guy who'll find employment somewhere... Born May 27, 1963, in the Panama Canal Zone ... Maybe that's why U.S. gave it away.

Year	Team	G	FG	FG Pct.	FT	FT Pct.	Reb.	Ast.	TP	Avg.
1984-85	Indiana	52	35	.380	32	.681	123	15	102	2.0
1985-86	Indiana	67	54	.500	47	.635	118	15	155	2.3
1986-87	Indiana	55	41	.406	28	.718	129	26	110	2.0
1987-88	Indiana	74	90	.466	44	.603	250	44	224	3.0
	Totals	248	220	.445	151	.648	620	100	591	2.4

GREG DREILING 24 7-1 250   Center

Stiffer than Julius Caesar... Should be a law passed prohibiting people from wasting seven feet of height... Mostly a garbage-time contributor... Has played in only 44 games in two seasons since becoming Pacers' second-round pick in 1986... Tallest player in Pacer history... College teammate of Danny Manning for a couple of seasons at Kansas... Typical collegiate star who won't pan out in NBA but will always find a job because of his height... Was considered only true senior center in nation his last year... Which means there was serious shortage of true senior centers... All-time prep scorer in Kansas schoolboy history... Best assets are his hands... Born Nov. 7, 1964, in Wichita, Kan.... Gets $180,000.

Year	Team	G	FG	FG Pct.	FT	FT Pct.	Reb.	Ast.	TP	Avg.
1986-87	Indiana	24	16	.432	10	.833	43	7	42	1.8
1987-88	Indiana	20	8	.471	18	.692	17	5	34	1.7
	Totals	44	24	.444	28	.737	60	12	76	1.7

TOP ROOKIE

RIK SMITS 22 7-4 250   **Center**

The chance to draft a top-notch center comes along once every decade and a half... Pacers weren't about to wait any longer, so they made the Dunkin' Dutchman out of Marist College the No. 2 selection after Danny Manning... He's regarded as a project, but that's only because he's been playing just six years... "I have nowhere to go but up," he said. "Give me time and a place to play and I'll be a great player."... Averaged 24.7 points as senior, which helps dispel notion he'll be "next Mark Eaton" defense-only type. "He'll be a real force in three or four years," said NBA superscout Marty Blake... Born Aug. 23, 1966, in Eindhoven, Holland.

COACH JACK RAMSAY: Enters 21st year as NBA head coach... But his second one in Indiana was pretty disappointing... He won 41 games and made playoffs with team that had no business doing so in 1986-87, a 15-game turnaround ... Last season's 38-victory, non-playoff campaign didn't set well with this incredibly intense guy... After Pacers were ousted by Knicks on last day, New York assistant Jim O'Brien was afraid to talk to him. And O'Brien's his son-in-law ... In 20-year career as bench boss, Ramsay's teams have made playoffs 16 times... His 864 NBA coaching victories (776 losses) are second only to Red Auerbach's 938... Physical fitness fanatic who jumps rope, jogs, rides a bicycle, lifts weights and swims... Coached 10 years in Portland, winning NBA in his first season in 1977... Began pro coaching career with Philadelphia in 1968 after 17 years coaching high school and college (11 years at St. Joe's, where teams were 234-72)... Authored two books on coaching... Used to be known for his outrageously loud sports coats and pants and storming down the sidelines... Clothes have toned down, but not his coaching demeanor... Born Feb. 21, 1925, in Philadelphia, but grew up in Milford, Conn., shooting hoops at basket nailed to a barn... Fascinating guy.

GREATEST THREE-POINT SHOOTER

Back in the ABA, when defensive struggles were about as commonplace as beach days in Iceland, the three-point shot was a coveted weapon. Indiana, which once scored 177 points in a game, used the three-pointer better than most. And Bill Keller used it best as a Pacer.

Keller, a 5-10 fireplug drafted from Purdue in 1969, shot more three-pointers (1,498) and made more (506) than any Pacer in history. His seven Pacer seasons, all in the ABA, produced a career three-point percentage of .338, fourth best in the Indiana record book. In his final ABA campaign in 1975-76, Keller hit a personal-high 123 (in 349 attempts). Aided by Keller's long bombs, the Pacers won three ABA titles.

ALL-TIME PACER LEADERS

SEASON

Points: George McGinnis, 2,353, 1974-75
Assists: Don Buse, 689, 1975-76
Rebounds: Mel Daniels, 1,475, 1970-71

GAME

Points: George McGinnis, 58 vs. Dallas, 11/28/72
Assists: Don Buse, 20 vs. Denver, 3/26/76
Rebounds: George McGinnis, 37 vs. Carolina, 1/12/74

CAREER

Points: Billy Knight, 10,780, 1974-83
Assists: Don Buse, 2,747, 1972-77, 1980-82
Rebounds: Mel Daniels, 7,622, 1968-74

MILWAUKEE BUCKS

TEAM DIRECTORY: Pres.: Herb Kohl; VP-Bus. Oper.: John Steinmiller; Dir. Player Personnel: Bob Zuffelato; Dir. Pub. Rel.: Bill King II; Coach: Del Harris. Arena: Bradley Center. Colors: Forest green, red and white.

The Bucks are well-armed with floor leader Paul Pressey.

SCOUTING REPORT

SHOOTING: The defense-oriented Bucks finished at .475 for the second straight season, after a .493 campaign in 1985-86. A staggering slew of injuries swelled the number of players used to 20, tying the Nets for the most in the Eastern Conference. Of all those players, only Ricky Pierce (.510) was over 50 percent. Jay Humphries, who finished at .528, was a disappointing .370 in Milwaukee after his arrival from Phoenix.

Jack Sikma and Terry Cummings look to rebound after sub-par seasons. Randy Breuer cooled off after a nice start. No. 1 pick Jeff Grayer, who fits into the Moncrief-Pressey shooter-passer mold, should help this plodding, methodical offense.

PLAYMAKING: As long as there's Paul Pressey (523 assists), there's a playmaking threat in Milwaukee. John Lucas, who became a backcourt savior two years ago, didn't do quite as much this time around. But in the Bucks' system, everything's a share-the-wealth proposition. The club's 2,194 assists (seventh best in NBA) were amply spread around.

DEFENSE: The franchise's trademark for years. The numbers were still decent last season as the Bucks yielded just 105.5 points per, eighth best in the league. But as in every other area, the Bucks slipped a bit. Since 1981-82 Milwaukee has *always* been in the top five, twice finishing as league leaders. The cracks have come through age and injuries. The Bucks are still a good defensive team, but the dip started in earnest last season and could continue.

REBOUNDING: Big disappointment. The Bucks were 15th in the league, despite good numbers from Sikma (8.6 per) and Cummings (7.3). Breuer averaged 6.8 boards, which isn't bad if he was six inches shorter. The Bucks went through horrifying rebounding slumps and were one of two Eastern playoff teams (Cleveland was the other) to be outrebounded by opponents during the regular season. The Bucks drafted a real physical specimen in 7-1 Tito Horford on the second round, but he's in no way ready. In time he could help. Problem is, the Bucks don't have a heckuva lot of time. As insurance they acquired Fred Roberts, the veteran Celtic forward who'd gone to Miami in the expansion draft.

OUTLOOK: Del Harris' Bucks had to struggle to finish two games over .500. Injuries marred any semblance of consistency;

BUCK ROSTER

No.	Veteran	Pos.	Ht.	Wt.	Age	Yrs. Pro	College
45	Randy Breuer	C	7-3	258	28	5	Minnesota
34	Terry Cummings	F	6-9	235	27	6	DePaul
24	Jay Humphries	G	6-3	199	26	4	Colorado
42	Larry Krystkowiak	F	6-10	240	24	2	Montana
10	John Lucas	G	6-3	185	35	12	Maryland
44	Paul Mokeski	C	7-0	255	31	9	Kansas
4	Sidney Moncrief	G	6-3	183	31	9	Arkansas
22	Ricky Pierce	G-F	6-4	205	29	6	Rice
25	Paul Pressey	G-F	6-5	201	29	6	Tulsa
35	Jerry Reynolds	F-G	6-8	198	25	3	Louisiana State
31	Fred Roberts	F	6-10	220	28	5	Brigham Young
43	Jack Sikma	C-F	7-0	250	32	11	Illinois-Wesleyan

Rd.	Top Rookies	Sel. No.	Pos.	Ht.	Wt.	College
1	Jeff Grayer	13	G	6-5	200	Iowa State
2	Tito Horford	39	C	7-1	245	Miami
3	Mike Jones	63	F	6-7	238	Auburn

there were some good streaks; there were some awful streaks. The decline in Milwaukee has been subtle, but last year subtlety came to a halt. This year it could be worse. A lot worse.

BUCK PROFILES

TERRY CUMMINGS 27 6-9 235   **Forward**

Mr. Inside and Mr. Outside . . . Potent at both power and small forward spots . . . Absolutely lethal from 15 feet and in . . . Led Bucks in scoring for third time in last four seasons . . . Doesn't particularly care to bang inside, but drives well and is solid on boards . . . Again upped average in playoffs, scoring 25.8 ppg while shooting .562 in first-round loss to Hawks . . . Scored 10,000th NBA point last March . . . Fewest turnovers (170, 2.24 per) of career . . . Clippers drafted him No. 2 overall in 1982, out of DePaul . . . Named NBA Rookie of the Year in 1982-83 . . . But career really blossomed since coming to Bucks with Craig Hodges and Ricky Pierce for Junior Bridgeman, Marques Johnson, Harvey Catchings and cash prior to 1984-85 . . . Born March 15, 1961, in Chicago . . . Ordained Pentecostal minister. Bible college speaker, anti-substance abuse preacher, basketball camp teacher . . . Earns $1.33 million.

Year	Team	G	FG	FG Pct.	FT	FT Pct.	Reb.	Ast.	TP	Avg.
1982-83	San Diego	70	684	.523	292	.709	744	177	1660	23.7
1983-84	San Diego	81	737	.494	380	.720	777	139	1854	22.9
1984-85	Milwaukee	79	759	.495	343	.741	716	228	1861	23.6
1985-86	Milwaukee	82	681	.474	265	.656	694	193	1627	19.8
1986-87	Milwaukee	82	729	.511	249	.662	700	229	1707	20.8
1987-88	Milwaukee	76	675	.485	270	.665	553	181	1621	21.3
	Totals	470	4265	.497	1799	.695	4184	1147	10330	22.0

PAUL PRESSEY 29 6-5 201　　　　　　Guard-Forward

Indispensable Buck . . . Mr. Do-it-all . . . Has missed 28 games in two seasons and Bucks were 10-18 (.357) without him. With him, they were 82-54 (.603) . . . Registered team's only two triple doubles and they came 20 days apart last December . . . Outstanding defensive player . . . Recorded 112 steals, fourth straight year of 100-plus thefts . . . All-time club leader in assists (2,589) . . . Was 20th overall pick in 1982 draft, out of Tulsa . . . Cut from high-school team as soph and didn't play as senior because he was too old . . . Born Dec. 24, 1958, in Richmond, Va. . . . Earned $750,000 last year.

Year	Team	G	FG	FG Pct.	FT	FT Pct.	Reb.	Ast.	TP	Avg.
1982-83	Milwaukee	79	213	.457	105	.597	281	207	532	6.7
1983-84	Milwaukee	81	276	.523	120	.600	282	252	674	8.3
1984-85	Milwaukee	80	480	.517	317	.758	429	543	1284	16.1
1985-86	Milwaukee	80	411	.488	316	.806	399	623	1146	14.3
1986-87	Milwaukee	61	294	.477	242	.738	296	441	846	13.9
1987-88	Milwaukee	75	345	.491	285	.798	375	523	983	13.1
	Totals	456	2019	.494	1385	.740	2062	2589	5465	12.0

RANDY BREUER 28 7-3 258　　　　　　　　　　Center

Was headed to Most Improved honors . . . Then he got hurt and turned back into the stiff he's always been . . . Works hard, he just doesn't know what to do with his big body . . . Was averaging 15.8 points through December, but suffered rib injury and slip-slided rest of way . . . Back to sub status for last six games of season and playoffs, where he was non-factor: 47 minutes, 4.8 ppg . . . Set career high in scoring (12.0), first time he made double figures in unfulfilling five-year career . . . Bucks drafted him 18th overall out of Minnesota in 1983 . . . Ranks fifth in blocked shots (404) in Milwaukee team history . . . Earned spot in trivia annals last December when he guarded Kareem Abdul-Jabbar the night his streak of 787 straight double-figure scoring games ended . . . Born Oct. 11, 1960, in Lake City, Minn. . . . Earned $312,500 last season.

Year	Team	G	FG	FG Pct.	FT	FT Pct.	Reb.	Ast.	TP	Avg.
1983-84	Milwaukee..........	57	68	.384	32	.696	109	17	168	2.9
1984-85	Milwaukee..........	78	162	.511	89	.701	256	40	413	5.3
1985-86	Milwaukee..........	82	272	.477	141	.712	458	114	685	8.4
1986-87	Milwaukee..........	76	241	.485	118	.584	350	47	600	7.9
1987-88	Milwaukee..........	81	390	.495	188	.657	551	103	968	12.0
	Totals.............	374	1133	.482	568	.661	1724	321	2834	7.6

JACK SIKMA 32 7-0 250   Center-Forward

Still grand . . . Bucks got him to plug the middle, but he has spent more time at big forward . . . Second in team in scoring (16.5), first in rebounds (8.6), fourth in assists (3.4), second in blocks (80) . . . Scored 14,000th NBA point last February at Boston . . . Great touch. Has frustrated foes for years with virtually unblockable fallaway shot . . . Averaged 19.0 ppg, 12.4 rebounds in playoffs . . . Won NBA free-throw title (.922) which was also a club record, bettering Flynn Robinson's .898 of 1969-70 . . . Durable . . . Played full 82 games for eighth time . . . Has missed just 23 games in 11 years . . . Was steal of 1977 draft, when Seattle drafted him eighth overall out of Ilinois Wesleyan . . . Went to Bucks as part of trade for Alton Lister prior to 1986-87 season . . . He and Mike Gminski are the only centers to finish in top 10 free-throw percentage since 1964-65. He has done it four times . . . Helped lead Sonics to 1979 NBA championship . . . Accounting degree, avid golfer, is active at Seattle Children's Orthopedic Hospital . . . Two-time All-Defense . . . Seven-time all-star . . . Born Nov. 14, 1955, in Kankakee, Ill. . . . Earned $1.6 million.

Year	Team	G	FG	FG Pct.	FT	FT Pct.	Reb.	Ast.	TP	Avg.
1977-78	Seattle.............	82	342	.455	192	.777	678	134	876	10.7
1978-79	Seattle.............	82	476	.460	329	.814	1013	261	1281	15.6
1979-80	Seattle.............	82	470	.475	235	.805	908	279	1175	14.3
1980-81	Seattle.............	82	595	.454	340	.823	852	248	1530	18.7
1981-82	Seattle.............	82	581	.479	447	.855	1038	277	1611	19.6
1982-83	Seattle.............	75	484	.464	400	.837	858	233	1368	18.2
1983-84	Seattle.............	82	576	.499	411	.856	911	327	1563	19.1
1984-85	Seattle.............	68	461	.489	335	.852	723	285	1259	18.5
1985-86	Seattle.............	80	508	.462	355	.864	748	301	1371	17.1
1986-87	Milwaukee..........	82	390	.463	265	.847	822	203	1045	12.7
1987-88	Milwaukee..........	82	514	.486	321	.922	709	279	1352	16.5
	Totals.............	879	5397	.472	3630	.844	9260	2827	14431	16.4

SIDNEY MONCRIEF 31 6-3 183   Guard

Sad... The knees are shot... Missed 26 games in second straight injury-riddled season ... Had knee surgery to remove bone fragment, then developed tendinitis... A shell of former excellence... About to call it quits... Averaged 10.8 ppg., lowest since rookie season, but as usual he sucked it up in playoffs and scored 15.0... Superb leader... Boulevard-length arms helped him notch two Defensive Player of the Year honors... Magnificent post-up guard... Five-time all-star... Earned $784,000 base pay, but began collecting $1.4 million in deferred payments... Fifth player selected in 1979 draft, out of Arkansas... One of classiest individuals in game... Born Sept. 21, 1957, in Little Rock, Ark.... Civic-minded, he works with underprivileged kids and numerous charity groups.

Year	Team	G	FG	FG Pct.	FT	FT Pct.	Reb.	Ast.	TP	Avg.
1979-80	Milwaukee	77	211	.468	232	.795	338	133	654	8.5
1980-81	Milwaukee	80	400	.541	320	.804	406	264	1122	14.0
1981-82	Milwaukee	80	556	.523	468	.817	534	382	1581	19.8
1982-83	Milwaukee	76	606	.524	499	.826	437	300	1712	22.5
1983-84	Milwaukee	79	560	.498	529	.848	528	358	1654	20.9
1984-85	Milwaukee	73	561	.483	454	.828	391	382	1585	21.7
1985-86	Milwaukee	73	470	.489	498	.859	334	357	1471	20.2
1986-87	Milwaukee	39	158	.488	136	.840	127	121	460	11.8
1987-88	Milwaukee	56	217	.489	164	.837	180	204	603	10.8
	Totals	633	3739	.504	3300	.830	3275	2501	10842	17.1

JOHN LUCAS 35 6-3 185   Guard

He's come clean... Now living a healthy life off drugs and that's his greatest accomplishment... Has established a nationwide network of support systems for athletes recovering from drug and alcohol addiction which includes a model facility in Houston... On the court, he gave Bucks a little bit of everything ... Mostly he gave them stability and experience... Shooting was very erratic, though... Tenth on NBA's all-time assist list with 5,956... Singed one-year, $600,000 contract last November... Became No. 1 pick of 1976 draft by Rockets after standout career at Maryland... Made road back after two stints in rehab and CBA followed before last-chance free-agent signing... Born Oct. 31, 1953, in Durham, N.C.... Founder of STAND: Students Taking Action Not Drugs.

Year	Team	G	FG	FG Pct.	FT	FT Pct.	Reb.	Ast.	TP	Avg.
1976-77	Houston............	82	388	.477	135	.789	219	463	911	11.1
1977-78	Houston............	82	412	.435	193	.772	255	768	1017	12.4
1978-79	Golden State.......	82	530	.462	264	.822	247	762	1324	16.1
1979-80	Golden State.......	80	388	.467	222	.768	220	.602	1010	12.6
1980-81	Golden State.......	66	222	.439	107	.738	154	464	555	8.4
1981-82	Washington........	79	263	.426	138	.784	166	551	666	8.4
1982-83	Washington........	35	62	.473	21	.500	29	102	145	4.1
1983-84	San Antonio........	63	275	.462	120	.764	180	673	689	10.9
1984-85	Houston............	47	206	.462	103	.798	85	318	536	11.4
1985-86	Houston............	65	365	.446	231	.775	143	571	1006	15.5
1986-87	Milwaukee..........	43	285	.457	137	.787	125	290	753	17.5
1987-88	Milwaukee..........	81	281	.445	130	.802	159	392	743	9.2
	Totals.............	805	3677	.454	1801	.778	1982	5956	9355	11.6

JAY HUMPHRIES 26 6-3 199   Guard

Is he legit or just so-so?... Overall game has stagnated in last two years... But Bucks think he's gonna be just fine, which is why they gave up their best three-point shooter for him ... Acquired from Suns for Craig Hodges and a second-round pick obtained from Warriors as compensation for Don Nelson... Can play either guard spot... Suns were disappointed in his leadership, and became part of housecleaning process... Didn't get into groove in Milwaukee; didn't learn new system quickly, then missed 11 games with groin and hamstring injuries ...Had 18 scoreless playoff minutes... Can direct offense, has good quickness... Phoenix' first-round pick (No. 13 overall) in 1984, out of Colorado... Born Oct. 17, 1962, in Inglewood, Cal.... Salary at $290,000.

Year	Team	G	FG	FG Pct.	FT	FT Pct.	Reb.	Ast.	TP	Avg.
1984-85	Phoenix............	80	279	.446	141	.829	164	350	703	8.8
1985-86	Phoenix............	82	352	.479	197	.767	260	526	905	11.0
1986-87	Phoenix............	82	359	.477	200	.769	260	632	923	11.3
1987-88	Phoe.-Mil..........	68	284	.528	112	.732	174	395	683	10.0
	Totals.............	312	1274	.480	650	.774	858	1903	3214	10.3

RICKY PIERCE 29 6-4 205   Guard-Forward

Potent sixth man... Got in ugly contract hassle and Bucks tried to unload him... Missed first 42 games of season... But he finished year in Suds City after finally signing two-year deal that brought him $225,000 last year and will bring $250,000 this season... Deadly from 18-20 feet... Was coming off his best season ever in 1986-87, hence the holdout... Get it while you can... Came to Bucks from Clippers with Terry Cummings and Craig Hodges in super 1984 deal for Milwaukee... Born Aug. 19, 1959, in Dallas... Was a first-round pick (No. 18 overall) by Detroit in 1982, out of Rice... Wife Joyce was former lead singer for the Fifth Dimension.

Year	Team	G	FG	FG Pct.	FT	FT Pct.	Reb.	Ast.	TP	Avg.
1982-83	Detroit	39	33	.375	18	.563	35	14	85	2.2
1983-84	San Diego	69	268	.470	149	.861	135	60	685	9.9
1984-85	Milwaukee	44	165	.537	102	.823	117	94	433	9.8
1985-86	Milwaukee	81	429	.538	266	.858	231	177	1127	13.9
1986-87	Milwaukee	79	575	.534	387	.880	266	144	1540	19.5
1987-88	Milwaukee	37	248	.510	107	.877	83	73	606	16.4
	Totals	349	1718	.517	1029	.857	867	562	4476	12.8

LARRY KRYSTKOWIAK 24 6-10 240   Forward

Proceed with caution... This well-traveled guy can bump, grind and make you ache all over... After scoring season-high 23 vs. Knicks last April, coach Del Harris said he'll be "part of the Bucks for years to come."... We'll see... Was drafted by Bulls on second round (28th pick) in 1986. Traded within hours to Trail Blazers, who traded him three days later to Spurs. Stayed in San Antonio for a season until last November when he was dealt to Milwaukee for Charles Davis and cash... Blue-collar work ethic... Bumped Randy Breuer from starting lineup in playoffs... Born Sept. 23, 1964, in Missoula, Mont., where he still makes his home... Was Big Sky MVP three times at Montana... Makes $125,000.

Year	Team	G	FG	FG Pct.	FT	FT Pct.	Reb.	Ast.	TP	Avg.
1986-87	San Antonio	68	170	.456	110	.743	239	85	451	6.6
1987-88	Milwaukee	50	128	.481	103	.811	231	50	359	7.2
	Totals	118	298	.466	213	.775	470	135	810	6.9

FRED ROBERTS 28 6-10 220   Forward

Well, at least he has staying power... Was only non-starter still with Celts from previous season... Now he's in Milwaukee, where he should get more playing time... Not afraid to mix it up inside, but has hands of stone... In Game 5 of Eastern Conference finals vs. Pistons, his little post-up shot with 1:09 forced overtime. The bad news was he managed to foul out in 12 minutes as Celtics lost anyway... Began season starting as Kevin McHale recovered from foot woes and averaged

11.4 points in first 12 games . . . Obtained by Celtics from Jazz in September 1986 for third-round pick . . . Was Bucks' second-round pick in 1982 out of Brigham Young . . . Draft rights traded to Nets, who eventually gave draft right to Spurs as compensation for signing coach Stan Albeck . . . Born Aug. 14, 1960, in Provo, Utah . . . Earns $200,000 with incentives.

Year	Team	G	FG	FG Pct.	FT	FT Pct.	Reb.	Ast.	TP	Avg.
1983-84	San Antonio	79	214	.536	144	.837	304	98	573	7.3
1984-85	S.A.-Utah	74	208	.498	150	.824	186	87	567	7.7
1985-86	Utah	58	74	.443	67	.770	80	27	216	3.7
1986-87	Boston	73	139	.515	124	.810	190	62	402	5.5
1987-88	Boston	74	161	.488	128	.776	162	81	450	6.1
	Totals	358	796	.503	613	.808	922	355	2208	6.2

JERRY REYNOLDS 25 6-8 198   Forward-Guard

Opportunity finally knocked. And this guy tripped and hurt himself answering the door . . . After getting cold shoulder from Don Nelson, "Ice" finally got his chance when Nellie departed . . . Began season as starter in backcourt and averaged 11.4 points through 12 games . . . Then came a rash of ailments . . . Missed 18 of next 28 with sprained ankle, bum back, flu . . . Born Dec. 23, 1962, in Brooklyn, N.Y. . . . A 1,000-point scorer in three years at LSU . . . Was Bucks' first-round pick (22d overall) in 1985 . . . Contract of $181,333.

Year	Team	G	FG	FG Pct.	FT	FT Pct.	Reb.	Ast.	TP	Avg.
1985-86	Milwaukee	55	72	.444	58	.558	80	86	203	3.7
1986-87	Milwaukee	58	140	.393	118	.641	173	106	404	7.0
1987-88	Milwaukee	62	188	.449	119	.773	160	104	498	8.0
	Totals	175	400	.427	295	.667	413	296	1105	6.3

PAUL MOKESKI 31 7-0 255   Center

Used to be mobile . . . But injuries have rendered him nearly useless . . . Missed 19 games through hamstring and knee woes . . . Has missed 79 in last three years . . . One of three white seven-footers on same team, has got to be some kind of record . . . A banger . . . Has thrown body willingly around for nine seasons . . . Lots of fouls . . . Vanilla ice-cream type. Absolutely nothing flashy or special, but he does what's asked . . . When Milwaukee Symphony asked him to be guest conductor a few years ago, he did that, too . . . Houston made him 42nd selection in 1979 draft, out of Kansas . . . Milwaukee got on waivers from Cleveland in 1982... Born Jan. 3, 1957, in Spokane, Wash.... Journalism degree... A $350,000 paycheck.

Year	Team	G	FG	FG Pct.	FT	FT Pct.	Reb.	Ast.	TP	Avg.
1979-80	Houston	12	11	.333	7	.778	29	2	29	2.4
1980-81	Detroit	80	224	.489	120	.600	418	135	568	7.1
1981-82	Det.-Clev.	67	84	.435	48	.762	208	35	216	3.2
1982-83	Clev.-Mil.	73	119	.458	50	.735	260	49	288	3.9
1983-84	Milwaukee	68	102	.479	50	.694	166	44	255	3.8
1984-85	Milwaukee	79	205	.478	81	.698	410	99	491	6.2
1985-86	Milwaukee	45	59	.424	25	.735	139	30	143	3.2
1986-87	Milwaukee	62	52	.403	46	.719	138	22	150	2.4
1987-88	Milwaukee	60	100	.476	51	.708	221	22	251	4.2
	Totals	546	956	.463	478	.685	1989	438	2391	4.4

TOP ROOKIE

JEFF GRAYER 23 6-5 200   Guard
Played small forward at Iowa State, but he's a top guard prospect in pros... Iowa State's all-time leading scorer with 2,502 points, he averaged 25.3 as a senior... "He's great, a lot of people don't realize what kind of player he is, except in the Big Eight. He's one of my favorites," said Spurs' coach Larry Brown, who was tormented by Grayer while coaching Kansas... Bucks loved him, too, and picked him No. 13... Solid, all-around player who'll play decent minutes as Sidney Moncrief's classic act runs its course in Suds City... Born Dec. 17, 1965, in Flint, Mich.

COACH DEL HARRIS: Faced unenviable task of following the legend of Nellie in Milwaukee... Despite injury-riddled campaign, Bucks finished with 42-40 record and customary playoff berth... There were rumors about his security, however... Only third Bucks' head coach since franchise inception in 1968... Coached four years in Houston from 1979-83 and brought Rockets to NBA Finals in 1981... Bounced after rotten 14-68 mark in 1982-83, his only sub-.500 record as head coach... Joined Bucks as head scout for three seasons and assistant coach for three seasons before assuming the position... Nice fellow, calm approach but bristled over Bucks' laissez-faire attitude toward end of regular season... Looks just like the Man from Glad... Honors graduate of Milligan College (Tenn.) with degree in religion in 1959. Later earned master's in history from Indiana... Was coach at Earlham College in Richmond, Ind. . . . Coached Bayama Cowboys to three national titles in Puerto Rico . . . In second year of three-year contract . . . Born June 18, 1937, in Orlean, Ind.

GREATEST THREE-POINT SHOOTER

The Bucks' history is spiced with outstanding three-point shooters: Brian Winters, Mike Dunleavy, Kevin Grevey. But all pale in comparison to one of the greatest ever in that category: Craig Hodges.

The 6-2 guard from Long Beach State came to the Bucks from the Clippers as part of the blockbuster Terry Cummings deal in 1984. In 3½ seasons with the Bucks, Hodges was 260-of-643 (.404). He led the league in three-point percentage in 1985-86, when he beat New York's Trent Tucker on the last day of the season (.4506 to .4505) by making four-of-six three-pointers. Hodges made 85-of-228 attempts that season; both are Buck records.

He was traded to Phoenix in midseason last year, but the change of scenery didn't hurt Hodges' accuracy. His .491 percentage (86-of-175) was an all-time NBA high. Lifetime, Hodges is 321-of-836 for .384 accuracy.

ALL-TIME BUCK LEADERS

SEASON

Points: Kareem Abdul-Jabbar, 2,822, 1971-72
Assists: Oscar Robertson, 668, 1970-71
Rebounds: Kareem Abdul-Jabbar, 1,346, 1971-72

GAME

Points: Kareem Abdul-Jabbar, 55 vs. Boston, 12/10/71
Assists: Guy Rodgers, 22 vs. Detroit, 10/31/68
Rebounds: Swen Nater, 33 vs. Atlanta, 12/19/76

CAREER

Points: Kareem Abdul-Jabbar, 14,211, 1969-75
Assists: Paul Pressey, 2,589, 1982-87
Rebounds: Kareem Abdul-Jabbar, 7,161, 1969-75

NEW JERSEY NETS

TEAM DIRECTORY: Chairman: Alan Aufzien; Pres.: Bernie Mann; Exec. VP-Chief Operating Officer: Bob Casciola; GM: Harry Weltman; Dir. Player Personnel: Al Menendez; Asst. GM: Bob MacKinnon; Dir. Pub. Rel.: John Mertz; Coach: Willis Reed; Asst. Coaches: Lee Rose, Butch Beard. Arena: Brendan Byrne Meadowlands Arena (20,039). Colors: Red, white and blue.

SCOUTING REPORT

SHOOTING: The third-worst shooting team in the league. The Netsies were a gagging .468, averaging a paltry 100.4 points per game. Dennis Hopson, the third player selected in the 1987 draft, immediately disproved his reputation of being a guy who could shoot the lights out. Buck Williams (the most tortured soul in sports?) had one of his finest shooting seasons (.560). Roy Hinson arrived near midseason and hit .502 as a Net while fellow traveler Tim McCormick shot .543 as a Net. Nice numbers. But the dreadful showing of the guards negated the front line's efforts. Playmaker John Bagley lacks range, Hopson shot an awful .404 and former deadeye Otis Birdsong (.458) has been waived. But the coming of Walter Berry, .563 with the Spurs last year, should give the Nets a big boost.

PLAYMAKING: After Bagley (479 assists) and Birdsong (222), there was nothing. The Nets were dead last in assists last season. The best way to sum up the Nets' offensive flow came in the form of a question from a female fan late in the season. After watching the confusion that led the Nets to pile up 1,503 turnovers (third highest in the league), she asked, "The Nets don't look very professional, do they?"

DEFENSE: Ugh. That's probably the nicest thing you can say. Opponents shot .497 (fifth worst) and scored 108.5 (14th best). It got better after Hinson, a proven shot-blocker, arrived as did part-timer Dudley Bradley. The problem was Bradley also had to play some offense. Defense is one area Willis Reed specialized in as a player—and he'll now have to get it across as a coach.

REBOUNDING: Finally, a bright spot. Actually two, Williams and Hinson. Buck is Buck, one of the best year in and year out,

Eight-year vet Buck Williams remains Net stalwart.

although injuries caused him to miss 1,000 boards for the second time in three seasons. Still, he pulled down 11.9 boards (fifth best), while Hinson grabbed 7.3 per after arriving from Philly.

OUTLOOK: "Welcome to the Meadowlands, ladies and gentlemen. Please don't make any noise while the game is in progress —you wouldn't want to stand out. And use the exit ramps when you leave, like always, after the third quarter."

The Nets have tried and tried and tried. And failed and failed and failed. Name a disaster and it has befallen Franchise Chaos. Drug problems (Micheal Ray Richardson, Orlando Woolridge) have struck twice in three years. They drafted a Pearl and wound up with costume jewelry. They firmly believe Keith Lee has value. For three straight years, the Nets have set team records for manpower games lost to injury. And they play before what is perhaps the deadest crowd in all of sports.

The Nets must make the playoffs or hari-kari may become

NET ROSTER

No.	Veteran	Pos.	Ht.	Wt.	Age	Yrs. Pro	College
5	John Bagley	G	6-0	192	28	6	Boston College
6	Walter Berry	F	6-8	215	24	2	St. John's
22	Dudley Bradley	F	6-6	195	31	8	North Carolina
35	Tony Brown	G	6-6	185	28	4	Arkansas
50	Chris Engler	C	7-0	248	29	6	Wyoming
21	Roy Hinson	F	6-9	215	27	5	Rutgers
23	Dennis Hopson	G	6-5	205	23	1	Ohio State
24	Keith Lee	F	6-10	220	25	3	Memphis State
12	Kevin McKenna	G	6-6	195	29	6	Creighton
40	Tim McCormick	C	7-0	240	26	4	Michigan
3	Mike O'Koren	F	6-7	225	30	8	North Carolina
14	Duane Washington	G	6-4	195	24	1	Middle Tenn. State
52	Buck Williams	F	6-8	225	28	7	Maryland

Rd.	Top Rookies	Sel. No.	Pos.	Ht.	Wt.	College
1	Chris Morris	4	F	6-8	210	Auburn
2	Charles Shackleford	32	F	6-10	225	North Carolina State
3	Derek Hamilton	52	G	6-6	197	So. Mississippi

fashionable. They won't have a first-round pick in '89. They gave it up to Chicago for Woolridge, who after a rehab stint announced he wanted no further part of the Nets and he went on to sign with the Lakers in August.

The Nets grabbed a talent on the first round in Chris Morris, a reported head case. On the second round, they plucked Lynn Shackleford, described by one scout as "a dog, but a talented dog." They should fit right in. Williams, the classy vet, has become downright frustrated amid the insanity, but won't publicly admit it. Who blamed Custer's horse for running away?

NET PROFILES

BUCK WILLIAMS 28 6-8 225   Forward

Living proof life ain't fair . . . Should be recognized as a superstar. Instead, he suffers year in, year out with loser . . . A pro's pro . . . One of NBA's best rebounders since leaving Maryland after junior year as Nets' No. 3 pick in 1981 . . . Put him on the Lakers or Celtics (both have hungered for his services for years) and watch endorsements, recognition soar . . .

Help him, before it's too late . . . For first time in seven-year career, sat because of injury. Missed eight games with ankle sprain, four more with hamstring pull . . . Prior to that, had missed one game in career—suspended because of fight . . . Another standout season; career-high 18.3 ppg; fifth in NBA in rebounding (11.9) . . . One of only eight players to get 1,000 boards in first four seasons . . . All-Defense second team . . . Complete class . . . Strong advocate of anti-drug programs . . . Born March 8, 1960, in Rocky Mount, N.C. . . . Deserves his $1.5 million.

Year	Team	G	FG	FG Pct.	FT	FT Pct.	Reb.	Ast.	TP	Avg.
1981-82	New Jersey	82	513	.582	242	.624	1005	107	1268	15.5
1982-83	New Jersey	82	536	.588	324	.620	1027	125	1396	17.0
1983-84	New Jersey	81	495	.535	284	.570	1000	130	1274	15.7
1984-85	New Jersey	82	577	.530	336	.625	1005	167	1491	18.2
1985-86	New Jersey	82	500	.523	301	.676	986	131	1301	15.9
1986-87	New Jersey	82	521	.557	430	.731	1023	129	1472	18.0
1987-88	New Jersey	70	466	.560	346	.668	834	109	1279	18.3
	Totals	561	3608	.552	2263	.647	6880	898	9481	16.9

TIM McCORMICK 26 7-0 240   Center

You could do worse . . . Give Willis Reed some time with him. He won't be Akeem, but won't be Randy Breuer, either . . . Former Sixer was part of January trade which sent Mike Gminski and Ben Coleman to Philly . . . Shot .543 in 47 Net games . . . Shows lots of hustle and intelligence . . . In first three games after Reed's arrival, opposing centers averaged more than six turnovers a game . . . Nets could let him roam outside a little more with Buck Williams and Roy Hinson crashing boards, but he's a willing banger, too . . . A $675,000 paycheck . . . Has gone coast to coast in trades . . . As undergraduate from Michigan, was Cavaliers' first-round pick (12th overall) in 1984 draft . . . Was dealt to Washington with Cliff Robinson, cash and draft rights to Mel Turpin. Then was immediately sent with Rickey Sobers to Seattle for Gus Williams. On to Philly with Danny Vranes for Clemon Johnson and 1989 first-rounder . . . Born March 10, 1962, in Detroit.

Year	Team	G	FG	FG Pct.	FT	FT Pct.	Reb.	Ast.	TP	Avg.
1984-85	Seattle	78	269	.557	188	.715	398	78	726	9.3
1985-86	Seattle	77	253	.570	174	.713	403	83	681	8.8
1986-87	Philadelphia	81	391	.545	251	.719	611	114	1033	12.8
1987-88	Phil-N.J.	70	348	.537	145	.647	467	118	841	12.0
	Totals	306	1261	.550	758	.708	1879	393	3281	10.7

JOHN BAGLEY 28 6-0 192   Guard

Pillsbury Doughboy of the backcourt . . . Lack of height hurts . . . But he's silenced a lot of critics since leaving Boston College a year early in 1982 when Cavaliers chose him 12th overall . . . Came from Cleveland with Keith Lee in three-way October 1987 trade that sent Darryl Dawkins and James Bailey out of New Jersey . . . Only Net to suffer through all 82 games . . . Still lacks consistency . . . Averaged career-high 12.0 points and led club with 479 assists, but he's capable of more . . . Was fourth in NBA in assists (735) in 1986-87 . . . Does well against pressure defenses . . . Born April 23, 1960, in Bridgeport, Conn. . . . Earns $475,000.

Year	Team	G	FG	FG Pct.	FT	FT Pct.	Reb.	Ast.	TP	Avg.
1982-83	Cleveland	68	161	.432	64	.762	96	167	386	5.7
1983-84	Cleveland	76	257	.423	157	.793	156	333	673	8.9
1984-85	Cleveland	81	338	488	125	.749	291	697	804	9.9
1985-86	Cleveland	78	366	.423	170	.791	275	735	911	11.7
1986-87	Cleveland	72	312	.426	113	.831	252	379	768	10.7
1987-88	New Jersey	82	393	.439	148	.822	257	479	981	12.0
	Totals	457	1827	.439	777	.793	1327	2790	4523	9.9

ROY HINSON 27 6-9 215   Forward

Okay, he's not Brad Daugherty . . . Didn't meet expectations in Philadelphia, where he was traded for No. 1 pick in 1986 draft, which was Daugherty . . . But he's a good, sound player and superb shot-blocker . . . Huge hands, tough rebounder . . . Came to New Jersey from Philly last January with Tim McCormick for Mike Gminski and Ben Coleman . . . That gave Nets two dependable power forwards (Buck Williams the other), so Hinton was played out of position at center and small forward . . . Still was 10th in league in blocked shots at 1.82 per . . . Solid citizen . . . Played at Rutgers and was 20th overall pick by Cavs in 1983 . . . Born May 2, 1961, in Trenton, N.J. . . . Earns $420,000.

Year	Team	G	FG	FG Pct.	FT	FT Pct.	Reb.	Ast.	TP	Avg.
1983-84	Cleveland	80	184	.496	69	.590	499	69	437	5.5
1984-85	Cleveland	76	465	.503	271	.721	596	68	1201	15.8
1985-86	Cleveland	82	621	.532	364	.719	639	102	1606	19.6
1986-87	Philadelphia	76	393	.478	273	.758	488	60	1059	13.9
1987-88	Phil.-N.J.	77	453	.487	272	.775	517	99	1178	15.3
	Totals	391	2116	.502	1249	.730	2739	398	5481	14.0

Ex-76er Roy Hinson added shot-blocking and inside moves.

DENNIS HOPSON 23 6-5 205   Guard

Don't give up on him yet . . . Seemed too good to be true when Nets made him No. 3 pick in 1987 draft, but only showed what he's capable of on rare occasions . . . Needn't fear sophomore jinx because rookie season was a washout . . . Lost his confidence . . . A scoring machine at Ohio State . . . But he lost his shooting touch early in season and never found it . . . Shot .404, averaged 9.6 points . . . Jerked around most of season and missed 20 games to injury . . . Began season as starter, yanked from front five after 10 games . . . Struggled and sat under interim coach Bob MacKinnon, who elected to play Otis Birdsong . . . Willis Reed took over and played him a little more . . . Got in just 1,365 minutes . . . Just too talented to be a flop . . . All-American-boy-next-door type. Carpentry skills, electronics whiz, helps old ladies across street... Born April 22, 1965, in Toledo, Ohio... Signed two-year deal, potentially worth $800,000.

Year	Team	G	FG	FG Pct.	FT	FT Pct.	Reb.	Ast.	TP	Avg.
1987-88	New Jersey.........	61	222	.404	131	.740	143	118	587	9.6

WALTER BERRY 24 6-8 215   Forward

Earth to Walter, Earth to Walter... Nobody's sure whether this guy will turn out to be a real NBA player or an honest-to-goodness space cadet before it's all over... Certainly has the physical tools to be an effective low-post scorer... But his concentration and desire are very much in question... Born May 14, 1964, in the Bronx, N.Y.... The 1986 College Player of the Year at St. John's... Taken as the 14th pick on the first round in 1986 by Portland and barely had time to unpack before getting shipped to the Alamo City... People thought it might be a steal for the Spurs, since they only gave up fat boy Kevin Duckworth... But now the Duck is a player and this fella is an enigma... Ranked fifth in the league in field-goal percentage... It's amazing to think what he might accomplish if he tried harder... Traded by the Spurs for Dallas Comegys in August.

Year	Team	G	FG	FG Pct.	FT	FT Pct.	Reb.	Ast.	TP	Avg.
1986-87	Port.-S.A...........	63	407	.531	187	.649	309	105	1001	15.9
1987-88	San Antonio.........	73	540	.563	192	.600	395	110	1272	17.4
	Totals.............	136	947	.549	379	.623	704	215	2273	16.7

KEITH LEE 25 6-10 220   Forward

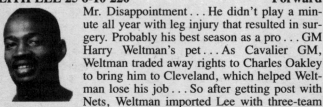

Mr. Disappointment... He didn't play a minute all year with leg injury that resulted in surgery. Probably his best season as a pro... GM Harry Weltman's pet... As Cavalier GM, Weltman traded away rights to Charles Oakley to bring him to Cleveland, which helped Weltman lose his job... So after getting post with Nets, Weltman imported Lee with three-team trade last October... Lee and John Bagley came to Meadowlands, Darryl Dawkins and James Bailey departed... Deal was made after NBA ruled Lee's knee injury a liability and voided Cavs' deal with Portland for Jim Paxson... Vastly overrated at Memphis State, he was 11th pick in 1985 draft... Can't run floor, hands of stone, rotten work ethic, foul prone. Otherwise, he's solid... Paid $301,666... Born Dec. 28, 1962, in W. Memphis, Ark.

Year	Team	G	FG	FG Pct.	FT	FT Pct.	Reb.	Ast.	TP	Avg.
1985-86	Cleveland...........	58	177	.466	75	.781	351	67	431	7.4
1986-87	Cleveland...........	67	170	.455	72	.713	251	69	412	6.1
	Totals.............	125	347	.460	147	.746	602	136	843	6.7

DUDLEY BRADLEY 31 6-6 195   Forward

Has been picked off more scrap heaps than sheet metal... Solid defensive player, poor shooter... He always finds a home, if not for long... Has spent time in Indiana, Phoenix, Chicago, Washington, Milwaukee and New Jersey with obligatory CBA stop thrown in to complete journeyman resume... Started 15 games at three different positions for Nets, which is a) tribute to his versatility or b) indictment of Nets' talent. (It's b)... Signed as free agent last December and led Nets in steals (114 for a 1.34 average) in 65 games... Defensive whiz at North Carolina, he was Indiana's first-round pick (No. 13 overall) in 1979... His 211 steals is still a rookie mark... Minimum wage... Born March 19, 1957, in Baltimore.

Year	Team	G	FG	FG Pct.	FT	FT Pct.	Reb.	Ast.	TP	Avg.
1979-80	Indiana.............	82	275	.452	136	.782	223	252	688	8.4
1980-81	Indiana.............	82	265	.474	125	.702	193	188	657	8.0
1981-82	Phoenix............	64	125	.445	74	.740	87	80	325	5.1
1982-83	Chicago............	58	82	.516	36	.800	105	106	201	3.5
1984-85	Washington.........	73	142	.475	54	.684	134	173	358	4.9
1985-86	Washington.........	70	73	.349	32	.571	95	107	195	2.8
1986-87	Milwaukee..........	68	76	.357	47	.810	102	66	212	3.1
1987-88	Mil.-N.J............	65	156	.427	74	.763	127	151	423	6.5
	Totals.............	562	1194	.445	578	.734	1066	1123	3059	5.4

TONY BROWN 28 6-6 185   Guard

Another member of the hospital ward... Played three minutes in training-camp opener, tore up Achilles tendon, underwent surgery, had courtside seat for rest of season. Didn't play a lick... Had shown he's a decent role player and good defender... Worked hard to improve on shooting after leaving Arkansas in 1982... Originally a fourth-round pick of Nets, then became a regular on waiver wire... Released by Nets,

Pistons, Pacers and Bulls...Gained notoriety when he went through Pacers' "Walter Mitty Camp" and earned a roster spot ...Utah coach Frank Layden once said, "That Tony What's His Name is a pretty good player...Born July 29, 1960, in Chicago ...Earns $125,000.

Year	Team	G	FG	FG Pct.	FT	FT Pct.	Reb.	Ast.	TP	Avg.
1984-85	Indiana	82	214	.460	116	.678	288	159	544	6.6
1985-86	Chicago	10	18	.439	9	.692	16	14	45	4.5
1986-87	New Jersey	77	358	.442	152	.738	219	259	873	11.3
	Totals	169	590	.448	277	.710	523	432	1462	8.7

KEVIN McKENNA 29 6-6 195   Guard

All players should have his heart...Plays tougher than his body—or brain—says he should...Limited to just 31 games with torn Achilles tendon...Decent long-range shooter ...First time in career he was with same team in back-to-back seasons...Originally fourth-round pick (88th overall) of Lakers in 1981 ...Has spent time with Lakers, Pacers, Bullets, Nets (twice), as well as CBA stops in Las Vegas-Albur-querque and Kansas City...Had three-point frenzy in 1986-87 when he hit 52, including 5-of-6 in one game...Born Jan. 8, 1959, in St. Paul, Minn....Earns $150,000 with incentives.

Year	Team	G	FG	FG Pct.	FT	FT Pct.	Reb.	Ast.	TP	Avg.
1981-82	Los Angeles	36	28	.322	11	.647	29	14	67	1.9
1983-84	Indiana	61	152	.410	80	.816	95	114	387	6.3
1984-85	New Jersey	29	61	.455	38	.884	49	58	165	5.7
1985-86	Washington	30	61	.367	25	.833	36	23	174	5.8
1986-87	New Jersey	56	153	.454	43	.754	77	93	401	7.2
1987-88	New Jersey	31	43	.394	24	.960	31	40	126.	4.1
	Totals	243	498	.414	221	.819	317	342	1320	5.4

MIKE O'KOREN 30 6-7 225   Forward

Was Nets' first-round pick (No. 6 overall) out of North Carolina in 1980, largely for his New Jersey appeal...Born Feb. 7, 1958, in Jersey City, he still has a following in the area... Played six seasons with Nets before being traded to Washington for Leon Wood in swap that didn't help anybody...Released, picked up in preseason by Celtics, released, picked up by Nets. Refused to report at first on agent's advice...Dumped agent, reported last December. Got hurt four games later... Doesn't have best perimeter shot to support living outside the fast lane... Is a pro wrestling fanatic... Earns $100,000.

Year	Team	G	FG	FG Pct.	FT	FT Pct.	Reb.	Ast.	TP	Avg.
1980-81	New Jersey	79	365	.486	135	.637	478	252	870	11.0
1981-82	New Jersey	80	383	.492	135	.714	305	192	909	11.4
1982-83	New Jersey	46	136	.525	34	.708	114	82	308	6.7
1983-84	New Jersey	73	186	.483	53	.609	175	95	430	5.9
1984-85	New Jersey	43	194	.494	42	.627	166	102	438	10.2
1985-86	New Jersey	67	160	.476	23	.590	135	118	350	5.2
1986-87	Washington	15	16	.381	0	.000	14	13	32	2.1
1987-88	New Jersey	4	9	.563	0	.000	4	2	18	4.5
	Totals	407	1449	.490	422	.651	1391	856	3355	8.2

CHRIS ENGLER 29 7-0 248   Center

King of the 10-day contracts... Remember, you can't teach size... Commits a foul every five minutes... But he's one of nicest guys you'll ever meet... A realist... He's trying to make as much money as he can before gravy train runs dry. Hopes to enter medical school and become one of the tallest internists anywhere... Helped recruit Randy Breuer to Minnesota, then realized he gave his job away so he transferred to Wyoming... Was third round pick (60th overall) by Golden State in 1982... From 1984-87, went from Warriors to CBA to Nets to Bulls to Bucks to Blazers, back to Bucks, back to Nets... Born March 1, 1959, in Stillwater, Minn.

Year	Team	G	FG	FG Pct.	FT	FT Pct.	Reb.	Ast.	TP	Avg.
1982-83	Golden State	54	38	.404	5	.313	104	11	81	1.5
1983-84	Golden State	46	33	.398	14	.609	97	11	80	1.7
1984-85	N.J.-Chi.-Mil.	11	8	.400	5	.556	30	0	21	1.9
1986-87	Mil.-Port.-N.J.	30	23	.451	12	.750	57	8	58	1.9
1987-88	New Jersey	54	36	.409	31	.886	98	15	103	1.9
	Totals	195	138	.411	67	.677	386	45	343	1.8

TOP ROOKIE

CHRIS MORRIS 22 6-8 210   Forward

Fourth player selected in draft... No question about this guy's talent—he scores inside and he scores outside. The questions concern his head and his heart; he's been known to disappear during games... Some say he's more talented than fellow Auburn products Charles Barkley and Chuck Person... Was first-team All-Southeastern Conference, averaging 20.7 points and 9.8 rebounds per game... This is an immense talent who has to keep his head screwed on. "I was kind of a wacko in college, I guess I'll have to be less of a wacko in the pros," he said on draft day... Born Jan. 20, 1966, in Atlanta.

COACH WILLIS REED: Starts first full season with Nets...

Named head coach on Feb. 29, 1988, replacing interim Bob MacKinnon, who replaced the fired Dave Wohl... Nets went 7-21 under Reed... Actually, that was good considering the material he had... Made people aware Nets even existed when he won his first three games... One of the all-time great players... Was Knicks' second-round pick (No. 10 overall) in 1964 draft out of Grambling... Became a legend in New York, where he averaged 18.7 points and 12.9 rebounds in 10-year career that included two NBA titles (1969-70 and 1972-73) ... That New York popularity certainly didn't escape Nets... Elected to Hall of Fame in 1981... His appearance at start of Game 7 of 1970 NBA final against Lakers with heavily braced knee following Game 5 injury was one of great moments in Knick history. Hit first two shots of game and LA was history ... Coached Knicks to second-place finish in 1977-78, was unceremoniously dumped 14 games into next season... Did four-year stint at Creighton before joining Mike Fratello as assistant for two years in Atlanta when Hawks won 50 each season ... Started last season as assistant to Bill Russell in Sacramento... Has 56-68 record as NBA coach... Classy guy who commands respect... Born June 25, 1942, in Hico, La.

GREATEST THREE-POINT SHOOTER

New Jersey has never been the stomping grounds for three-point specialists. In fact, to find the Nets' greatest three-point shooter, you have to go back to when the team played in the ABA in that odd basketball outpost, Commack, Long Island. The setting may have been strange, but the name was familiar: Rick Barry.

In two seasons (1970-71 and 1971-72), Barry sank 92 three-pointers in 323 attempts. That's 29 percent, hardly a rousing number. But then "rousing" and "Nets" have rarely been synonymous.

ALL-TIME NET LEADERS

SEASON

Points: Rick Barry, 2,518, 1971-72
Assists: Kevin Porter, 801, 1977-78
Rebounds: Billy Paultz, 1,035, 1971-72

GAME

Points: Julius Erving, 63 vs. San Diego (4 OT), 2/14/75
Assists: Kevin Porter, 29 vs. Houston, 2/24/78
Rebounds: Billy Paultz, 33 vs. Pittsburgh, 2/17/71

CAREER

Points: Buck Williams, 9,481, 1981-88
Assists: Billy Melchionni, 2,251, 1969-75
Rebounds: Buck Williams, 6,880, 1981-88

NEW YORK KNICKS

TEAM DIRECTORY: Pres.: Richard Evans; VP-GM: Al Bianchi; VP-Administration: Jack Diller; Dir. Administration: Hal Childs; Dir. Scouting Services: Dick McGuire; Dir. Communications: John Cirillo; Dir. Inf.: Dennis D'Agostino; Coach: Rick Pitino; Asst. Coach: Stu Jackson. Arena: Madison Square Garden (19,591). Colors: Orange, white and blue.

SCOUTING REPORT

SHOOTING: Ouch. If it weren't for the Clippers, the Knicks, at .465, would have ranked dead last in field-goal percentage. And the Clippers (.443) were so bad, it's almost unfair to count them.

Knick shooting did pick up late in the season as Patrick Ewing showed some smarts, quit forcing shots and began kicking the ball outside. Still, the Knicks' perimeter game doesn't scare anyone. Ewing (.555) and Bill Cartwright (.544) were the only ones above 50 percent. And now Cartwright's gone.

A shooting forward became the priority the moment they were eliminated in the first round of the playoffs. But the Knicks traded for a rebounding forward and drafted a point guard to back up Mark Jackson. Both moves solidify weak areas, but didn't address the No. 1 need. After the centers, Kenny Walker (.473) was the leading marksman—and that's scary. Gerald Wilkins (.446) was erratic at best and if a discouraging word could be said about Mark Jackson (.432), it's his outside touch.

PLAYMAKING: Basketball like it oughta be.

With the single addition of Jackson, the Knicks became a good passing team. And that's quite an improvement since they were the worst passing team on the planet the previous season. Jackson, a dream set-up man for Rick Pitino's motion offense, will get badly needed rest with the addition of top draft pick Rod Strickland.

DEFENSE: This is why nobody was particularly anxious to face the Knicks in the playoffs. When the Knicks went into their frantic, pressing, trapping alignments, they gave teams fits. They surrendered 106.0 points a game—only seven teams did better. Ewing has developed into a certified monster underneath, blocking 245 shots, altering countless others. The Knicks forced more turnovers (1,631) than any team—but negated that by committing more turnovers than everybody except the Clippers. Still, defense is a strong point and it will only get better.

REBOUNDING: Improving. Last year's addition of Sidney Green (7.9 per) helped, but the one-dimensional forward wasn't a force down the stretch. Ewing shredded all the rebounding raps and helped the Knicks finish tied for eighth in the league—a huge jump from dead last for two seasons running.

Now the fun begins. The acquisition of Charles Oakley, who grabbed more rebounds than any NBA player the past two years, could make the Knicks ferocious off the boards.

Revitalized Patrick Ewing shot career-best .555.

KNICK ROSTER

No.	Veteran	Pos.	Ht.	Wt.	Age	Yrs. Pro	College
3	Rick Carlisle	G	6-5	207	29	4	Virginia
33	Patrick Ewing	C	7-0	240	26	3	Georgetown
44	Sidney Green	F	6-9	220	27	5	Nevada-Las Vegas
13	Mark Jackson	G	6-3	205	23	1	St. John's
4	Johnny Newman	G	6-7	190	24	2	Richmond
—	Charles Oakley	F	6-9	245	24	3	Virginia Union
6	Trent Tucker	G	6-5	200	28	6	Minnesota
34	Kenny Walker	F	6-8	217	24	2	Kentucky
21	Gerald Wilkins	G	6-6	200	25	3	Tenn.-Chattanooga

Rd.	Top Rookies	Sel. No.	Pos.	Ht.	Wt.	College
1	Rod Strickland	19	G	6-3	175	DePaul
2	Greg Butler	37	F-C	6-11	240	Stanford
3	Phil Stinnie	69	F	6-8	222	Va. Commonwealth

OUTLOOK: The Knicks looked destined for lottery status last season, but they surprised people by clinching the final Eastern Conference playoff spot. The good times should continue.

Consider that the Knicks went from junk to "good" in just half a season. After Feb. 1, they had the third-best record (24-16) in the East. At home, they ran up a 13-game win streak and won 20 of their last 24. They finished with a 14-game overall improvement. Add another five this season, and they're over .500.

KNICK PROFILES

MARK JACKSON 23 6-3 205   **Guard**

Landing him as 18th selection in 1987 draft was greatest theft since Brink's Job... Phenomenal coming-out season... Had Rookie of Year Award in pocket by December ... Shattered rookie assist marks: 868 for 10.6 average, bettering Oscar Robertson's all-time marks of 690 and 9.7... Third rookie ever with over 200 steals (205). Only Dudley Bradley and Ron Harper had more... Poised and confident, he won three games at buzzer... "What I see in him is myself," praised

Magic Johnson . . . Became starter in third game. Played all 82, averaged 39.6 minutes, 13.6 points . . . Superb court intelligence, uses body well on drives. Jumper needs work . . . Signed two-year, $450,000 pact . . . Born in New York City on April Fool's Day, 1965. Joke was on most teams who ignored him . . . Skipped all-star games to get St. John's degree, hurting draft position.

Year	Team	G	FG	FG Pct.	FT	FT Pct.	Reb.	Ast.	TP	Avg.
1987-88	New York	82	438	.432	206	.774	396	868	1114	13.6

PATRICK EWING 26 7-0 240   Center

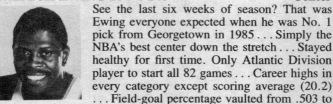

See the last six weeks of season? That was Ewing everyone expected when he was No. 1 pick from Georgetown in 1985 . . . Simply the NBA's best center down the stretch . . . Stayed healthy for first time. Only Atlantic Division player to start all 82 games . . . Career highs in every category except scoring average (20.2) . . . Field-goal percentage vaulted from .503 to .555 . . . Averaged 19 points, 12.8 rebounds in playoffs . . . Simple case of experience. Learned to read defenses and improved passing out of post . . . Defensive monster, altered scores of shots . . . Small hands hurt rebound numbers, but he had 20-board playoff game vs. Celts . . . Great on break . . . Quickness in motion offense negates attempts to body him . . . Nice guy whose "Hoya Paranoia" rep dissolved as he smelled playoffs . . . Actually became quotable . . . Born Aug. 5, 1962, in Kingston, Jamaica . . . Fourth season of 10-year, $30-million contract.

Year	Team	G	FG	FG Pct.	FT	FT Pct.	Reb.	Ast.	TP	Avg.
1985-86	New York	50	386	.474	226	.739	451	102	998	20.0
1986-87	New York	63	530	.503	296	.713	555	104	1356	21.5
1987-88	New York	82	656	.555	341	.716	676	125	1653	20.2
	Totals	195	1572	.515	863	.721	1682	331	4007	20.5

CHARLES OAKLEY 24 6-9 245   Forward

Manster on the boards: half man, half monster . . . Tremendous strength, hands as big as Nebraska . . . Came to Knicks in blockbuster trade last June which sent Bill Cartwright to Bulls . . . Had more boards than anybody (1,066 in 82 games) but lost rebounding title to Clippers' Michael Cage on last day (13.03 to 13.00) . . . Had led from opening night when he bruised 76ers for 21 . . . But he's turnover-prone with 241, 11th in league . . . A relentless, sacrificing worker . . . Had 248 assists, only Charles Barkley and Otis Thorpe had more among power forwards...Led NCAA Division II in rebounding while at Virginia Union...Was ninth player selected overall in 1985 draft by Cavaliers, who dealt him on draft day for Ennis Whatley and the rights to Keith Lee. An outright swindle...Paid $465,000...Born Dec. 18, 1963, in Cleveland.

Year	Team	G	FG	FG Pct.	FT	FT Pct.	Reb.	Ast.	TP	Avg.
1985-86	Chicago	77	281	.519	178	.662	664	133	740	9.6
1986-87	Chicago	82	468	.445	245	.686	1074	296	1192	14.5
1987-88	Chicago	82	375	.483	261	.727	1066	248	1014	12.4
	Totals	241	1124	.474	684	.694	2804	677	2946	12.2

GERALD WILKINS 25 6-6 200   Guard

Major improvement...Though scoring average dipped from 19.1 to 17.4 points a game, he became an all-around player...Averaged 20 in playoffs...Can dominate with exciting scoring bursts...Needs elephant tranquilizer if he gets out of control...Would be even better if he didn't have burden of being Dominique's little brother...Sensitive guy, was hurt by rumors of trade for Chris Mullin...Began hitting perimeter shot to open driving lanes...In trouble when outside game fails...Erratic passer...Defense could be better, but vastly improved from start of season...Best quote on team...Coach Rick Pitino said Wilkins went "from being a one-dimensional player to a basketball player."...Due for contract extension/raise from $246,000 pay...A super find in 1985 draft (47th pick) out of Tennessee-Chattanooga...Born Sept. 11, 1963, in Baltimore.

Year	Team	G	FG	FG Pct.	FT	FT Pct.	Reb.	Ast.	TP	Avg.
1985-86	New York	81	437	.468	132	.557	208	161	1013	12.5
1986-87	New York	80	633	.486	235	.701	294	354	1527	19.1
1987-88	New York	81	591	.446	191	.786	270	326	1412	17.4
	Totals	242	1661	.467	558	.685	772	841	3952	16.3

KENNY WALKER 24 6-8 217   Forward

Terrific personality...Great leaper, rotten shooter...Too mechanical...Tense guy who seems bothered by boos...Decent defensively, but foul-prone...Back-to-basket type at Kentucky, given face-up role by former Knick brass who are now unemployed...Didn't make fans forget Bernard King—or even Ken Bannister...Only starting small forward in Eastern Conference to score less was Bulls' Brad

Sellers... Averaged 10.1... Fifth pick in '86 lottery, right behind Chuck Person... Saw less playing time, but accepted role player status... Made *the* defensive play of season for Knicks. Got piece of Steve Stipanovich's last-second shot to preserve playoff-clincher in last game vs. Pacers... Disappeared in playoffs... Has $575,000 contract... Pro wrestling freak... Born Aug. 18, 1964, in Roberta, Ga.

Year	Team	G	FG	FG Pct.	FT	FT Pct.	Reb.	Ast.	TP	Avg.
1986-87	New York	68	285	.491	140	.757	338	75	710	10.4
1987-88	New York	82	344	.473	138	.775	389	86	826	10.1
	Totals	150	629	.481	278	.766	727	161	1536	10.2

JOHNNY NEWMAN 24 6-7 190   Forward

If only his size matched his heart... Tremendous waiver pickup five games into season after release by Cavaliers... Knicks picked up his two-year, $275,000 per contract and got a quality part-time starter/sixth man ... Fatigued late in season and his shooting and strength suffered... Hit 11-of-11 from field in Boston... Put into starting lineup for offense in last two playoff games vs. Celts and scored 59 points, including career-high 34... Limited moves but he fears no one. Would try to dunk on King Kong... Good outside touch... Can be posted up by bigger-shooting forwards in half-court offense, but is quick, deny-pass pest in up-tempo game... Was recruited out of high school by Rick Pitino for Boston University, but elected for Richmond to stay near Danville, Va., where he was born Nov. 28, 1963.

Year	Team	G	FG	FG Pct.	FT	FT Pct.	Reb.	Ast.	TP	Avg.
1986-87	Cleveland	59	113	.411	66	.868	70	27	293	5.0
1987-88	New York	77	270	.435	207	.841	159	62	773	10.0
	Totals	136	383	.428	273	.848	229	89	1066	7.8

TRENT TUCKER 28 6-5 200   Guard

Only midseason surge salvaged his season... Offseason routine of tennis and less basketball put him in early doghouse... Again solid on three-pointers, shooting .413... Ignites offense off bench with perimeter game. Began driving more, which has been career rap... Sixth overall pick from Minnesota in 1982... Tough defensively, a very underrated part of his game... Became a subtle clubhouse leader for young team during drive for playoffs... Used in three-guard plus Twin

Towers setup...Contract hassle (signed two years, $650,000) and early-season knee slowed him...All-time Knicks' three-point shot leader...Born Dec. 20, 1959, in Tarboro, N.C.

Year	Team	G	FG	FG Pct.	FT	FT Pct.	Reb.	Ast.	TP	Avg.
1982-83	New York	78	299	.462	43	.672	216	195	655	8.4
1983-84	New York	63	225	.500	25	.758	130	138	481	7.6
1984-85	New York	77	293	.483	38	.792	188	199	653	8.5
1985-86	New York	77	349	.472	79	.790	169	192	818	10.6
1986-87	New York	70	325	.470	77	.762	135	166	795	11.4
1987-888	New York	71	193	.424	51	.718	119	117	506	7.1
	Totals	436	1684	.469	313	.751	957	1007	3908	9.0

SIDNEY GREEN 27 6-9 220   Forward

First in a long line to admit he was a disappointment...Piston non grata in Detroit, he received three-year, $2.25-million offer sheet in preseason from Knicks, who handed him Bernard King's salary slot. When Pistons matched, Knicks acquired him for Ron Moore and second-round pick...Knicks got him to rebound and he had same number of points as rebounds (642)...One of league's most inconsistent players... Can be a fearsome rebounder; had 31 against Knicks while with Bulls in 1986 game...Also can be cause of coaching ulcers as he insists on putting ball on floor...Weak driving moves... Averaged one board every 3.1 minutes...Starred at Nevada-Las Vegas, then Bulls made him fifth player chosen in 1983 draft... Born Jan. 4, 1961, in Brooklyn, N.Y., where he was schoolyard legend.

Year	Team	G	FG	FG Pct.	FT	FT Pct.	Reb.	Ast.	TP	Avg.
1983-84	Chicago	49	100	.439	55	.714	174	25	255	5.2
1984-85	Chicago	48	108	.432	79	.806	246	29	295	6.1
1985-86	Chicago	80	407	.465	262	.782	658	139	1076	13.5
1986-87	Detroit	80	256	.472	119	.672	653	62	631	7.9
1987-88	New York	82	258	.441	126	.663	642	93	642	7.8
	Totals	339	1129	.455	641	.731	2373	348	2899	8.6

RICK CARLISLE 29 6-5 207   Guard

Every team needs a 12th man...Minuteman ...Ready at a minute's notice and that's about how much he gets to play...Rescued from CBA after release from Celts. Racked up career highs in points (21) and minutes (34) in Knick debut in December 1987 after overnight cram course in system...Then playing time plummeted...Ball-handling   and   speed suspect . . . Super guy, never whined. Chief cheerleader . . . Very heady, good shooter . . . Self-taught pianist who finds hotel piano immediately after check-in . . . Earned $100,000 in one-year contract . . . Born Oct. 27, 1959 in Ogdensburg, N.Y. Split collegiate career between Maine and Virginia . . . Prime expansion material.

Year	Team	G	FG	FG Pct.	FT	FT Pct.	Reb.	Ast.	TP	Avg.
1984-85	Boston............	38	26	.388	15	.882	21	25	67	1.8
1985-86	Boston............	77	92	.487	15	.652	77	104	199	2.6
1986-87	Boston............	42	30	.326	15	.750	30	35	80	1.9
1987-88	New York..........	26	29	.433	10	.909	13	32	74	2.8
	Totals............	183	177	.427	55	.775	141	196	420	2.3

Knicks got DePaul's Rod Strickland, 19th selection.

TOP ROOKIE

ROD STRICKLAND 22 6-3 175   **Guard**

Knicks raised lots of eyebrows when they took DePaul product No. 19... They had made another point guard, Mark Jackson, their first pick the year before and last season's Rookie of the Year is expected to hold down the job for the next 10 years... But they did have a gaping hole at backup point and "he was the best player available," said GM Al Bianchi, who rated Strickland the best point guard in the draft... Didn't see eye to eye with DePaul coach Joey Meyer and some have questioned this guy from shoulders up... Never met a classroom he didn't like to cut and left school after three years... A definite talent who averaged 20.0 points as junior... Born July 11, 1966, in the Bronx, N.Y.

COACH RICK PITINO: After one season, enters 1988-89 as dean of Atlantic Division coaches... His rah-rah, college system worked, silencing legions of skeptics... Brought Knicks to 14-game turnaround and first playoff bid in four seasons... Year was incredibly successful professionally, incredibly tragic personally. After leading Providence to Final Four, landed Knick job. Suffered through deaths of infant son and father... At 36, is one of bright young minds in the game... Former Hubie Brown assistant... Lives and dies with each possession... Coaching trail brought him to Hawaii, Boston U., Syracuse, Providence and back to hometown New York, where he was born Sept. 18, 1952, just four blocks from the old Madison Square Garden... Was a guard at St. Dominic High School in Oyster Bay, N.Y., before going to the University of Massachusetts, where he was a teammate of Julius Erving... Workaholic in Lombardi mold. Motto is Vince's "The harder you work, the tougher it is to surrender."

GREATEST THREE-POINT SHOOTER

Larry Bird and Craig Hodges—maybe Byron Scott—are the names that flash through people's minds when guessing the all-

Gerald Wilkins added new dimensions to his game.

time percentage leader for three-point shots.

But flash, they're wrong. The leader is Trent Tucker of the Knicks. Tucker's numbers are 227-of-537, a .423 percentage, the best among those who've made a minimum of 100 three-pointers. Last season, Tucker was 69-of-167 (.413), eighth best in the league.

"It's just a normal shot for me," said Tucker, the Minnesota product who was the sixth player selected in the 1982 draft. "Some take pride in rebounding, others in steals, but I've got three-pointers. It's the same feeling other players get with the slam dunk."

ALL-TIME KNICK LEADERS

SEASON

Points: Richie Guerin, 2,303, 1961-62
Assists: Mark Jackson, 868, 1987-88
Rebounds: Willis Reed, 1,191, 1968-69

GAME

Points: Bernard King, 60 vs. New Jersey, 12/25/84
Assists: Richie Guerin, 21 vs. St. Louis, 12/12/58
Rebounds: Harry Gallatin, 33 vs. Ft. Wayne, 3/15/53
Willis Reed, 33 vs. Cincinnati, 2/2/71

CAREER

Points: Walt Frazier, 14,617, 1967-77
Assists: Walt Frazier, 4,791, 1967-77
Rebounds: Willis Reed, 8,414, 1964-74

PHILADELPHIA 76ERS

TEAM DIRECTORY: Owner: Harold Katz; GM: John Nash; Dir. Player Personnel: Bob Weinhauer; Dir. Press Rel.: Dave Coskey; Coach: Jim Lynam; Asst. Coach: Fred Carter. Arena: The Spectrum (17,967). Colors: Red, white and blue.

SCOUTING REPORT

SHOOTING: The Sixers shot just .474—and helped shoot themselves right out of the playoff money. Much of the time, the problem wasn't so much shooting, as simply getting shots. Entry passes were generally a disaster and led to 17.5 turnovers a game.

The shooting guard, Andrew Toney, was again little more than an ornament as injuries wrecked another season. Albert King,

Is there a more underrated point guard than Mo Cheeks?

acquired from New Jersey, was moved to guard from small forward, shot an awful .391 and was traded in August to San Antonio for Pete Myers. The hope is that No. 1 pick Hersey Hawkins, the nation's leading scorer, will fit right into the baseline screen plays run for Toney. And always, there is Charles Barkley, the league's third-best shooter at .587.

PLAYMAKING: Maurice Cheeks for years has been vastly underrated. He had another quality year with 8.0 assists per game. But after him, the Sixers' passing is pretty poor. Either they can't (the Sixers committed nearly two full turnovers a game more than opponents) or they just don't (only three teams had less assists than Philly).

DEFENSE: This wasn't exactly what you'd call swell. Opponents shot .496 while scoring 107.1 points. Sure, they got some steals from Cheeks and Barkley and some blocks from Mike Gminski and Barkley. But overall team defense is a sorely lacking area.

OUTLOOK: The aftershocks of Julius Erving's retirement left Philadelphia without playoff basketball for the first time since 1975. There were critical injuries plus a getting-to-know-each-other period as bodies came and went.

The Sixers appeared to have helped themselves in the draft with Hawkins, Everette Stephens (a projected first-rounder whom they grabbed on the second) and Hernan Montenegro, who could emerge as a sleeper, in the third. Jim Lynam is expecting big things from 1987 top pick, center Chris Welp, who missed all but the first 10 games last season. With the decline of the Milwaukees and the Washingtons, the Sixers should fight back into the playoff picture.

76ER PROFILES

CHARLES BARKLEY 25 6-6 263   **Forward**

Sir Charles . . . Runs like a caterpillar—not the bug, the thing that moves mountains . . . "He's frightening," says Knick coach Rick Pitino . . . Fourth season was his most productive: Schick Pivotal Player Award third straight year; fourth in NBA in scoring (28.3), sixth in boards (11.9), third in shooting percentage (.587) . . . Scored over 40 points seven times

SIXER ROSTER

No.	Veteran	Pos.	Ht.	Wt.	Age	Yrs. Pro	College
34	Charles Barkley	F	6-6	263	25	4	Auburn
10	Maurice Cheeks	G	6-1	181	32	10	West Texas State
54	Ben Coleman	F	6-9	235	26	2	Maryland
42	Mike Gminski	C	6-11	260	29	8	Duke
3	David Henderson	G	6-6	200	24	1	Duke
12	Gerald Henderson	G	6-2	180	32	9	Va. Commonwealth
31	Mark McNamara	C	6-11	235	29	4	California
—	Pete Myers	F	6-7	190	25	2	Ark-Little Rock
4	Cliff Robinson	F	6-9	240	28	9	USC
45	Bob Thornton	F	6-10	225	26	3	Cal-Irvine
22	Andrew Toney	G	6-3	190	30	8	SW Louisiana
20	Danny Vranes	F	6-9	220	30	7	Utah
44	Chris Welp	C	7-0	245	24	1	Washington
25	David Wingate	G-F	6-5	185	25	2	Georgetown

Rd.	Top Rookies	Sel. No.	Pos.	Ht.	Wt.	College
1	Hersey Hawkins	6	G	6-3	190	Bradley
2	Everette Stephens	31	G	6-3	175	Purdue
3	Hernan Montenegro	57	F	6-10	246	Louisiana State

. . . Had staggering two-game output with career-high 47 points at Atlanta and 46 vs. Milwaukee next game . . . One of the few who are worth the price of admission . . . Players voted him All-NBA . . . Don't get him mad. Only if it can get him ejected . . . As usual, mouth caused problems. Said Sixers were "a bad team" after December blowout by Lakers and got fined by owner Harold Katz . . . But Barkley repeated contention all season . . . Vowed last season's All-Star appearance would be his last: "I got better things to do with my Sundays." . . . Master of taking the ball coast to coast. Only foolish or brain-dead get in his way . . . Entering third year of eight-year, $13-million pact . . . Fifth pick in 1984 draft after bypassing senior year at Auburn . . . Would you believe Bobby Knight took Jeff Turner over him for 1984 Olympics? . . . Born Feb. 20, 1963, in Leeds, Ala.

Year	Team	G	FG	FG Pct.	FT	FT Pct.	Reb.	Ast.	TP	Avg.
1984-85	Philadelphia	82	427	.545	293	.733	703	155	1148	14.0
1985-86	Philadelphia	80	595	.572	396	.685	1026	312	1603	20.0
1986-87	Philadelphia	68	557	.594	429	.761	994	331	1564	23.0
1987-88	Philadelphia	80	753	.587	714	.751	951	254	2264	28.3
	Totals	310	2332	.577	1832	.735	3674	1052	6579	21.2

MAURICE CHEEKS 32 6-1 181   Guard

People finally getting around to recognize this class act... An all-star for second straight year (fourth in 10 seasons)... Had Sixers' only triple-double (17 points, 10 rebounds, 12 assists vs. Utah)... Eighth in NBA in assists (8.0); seventh in steals (2.11)... Shot under 50 percent (.495) for first time in career... Only missed three games... Struggled after suffering concussion in March. "Post-concussion syndrome" caused dizziness, nausea plus decline in numbers... Barely shot 40 percent in spell... Still played second-most minutes (2,871) of career... Unselfish to a fault... Was second-round pick (36th overall) out of West Texas State in 1978... Born Sept. 8, 1956, in Chicago.

Year	Team	G	FG	FG Pct.	FT	FT Pct.	Reb.	Ast.	TP	Avg.
1978-79	Philadelphia.........	82	292	.510	101	.721	254	431	685	8.4
1979-80	Philadelphia.........	79	357	.540	180	.779	274	556	898	11.4
1980-81	Philadelphia.........	81	310	.534	140	.787	245	560	763	9.4
1981-82	Philadelphia.........	79	352	.521	171	.777	248	667	881	11.2
1982-83	Philadelphia.........	79	404	.542	181	.754	209	543	990	12.5
1983-84	Philadelphia.........	75	386	.550	170	.733	205	478	950	12.7
1984-85	Philadelphia.........	78	422	.570	175	.879	217	497	1025	13.1
1985-86	Philadelphia.........	82	490	.537	282	.842	235	753	1266	15.4
1986-87	Philadelphia.........	68	415	.527	227	.777	215	538	1061	15.6
1987-88	Philadelphia.........	79	428	.495	227	.825	253	635	1086	13.7
	Totals............	782	3856	.532	1854	.792	2355	5658	9605	12.3

MIKE GMINSKI 29 6-11 260   Center

Finally lost "best backup center in league" label... But he shouldn't be used as a 40-minute player. At his best when teamed with a pivot bruiser... Came to Sixers in January 1988 swap with Nets that sent Roy Hinson to East Rutherford... Thirsted for playoff success and stability, then Sixers fizzled. "I brought the curse with me down the [New Jersey] Turnpike," he said... Heckuva nice guy with lots of smarts ... Had most productive numbers ever: Averaged 16.9 points in both Jersey and Philly. First double-digit rebound season... Good perimeter game, outstanding free-throw shooter. Shot

best-ever .906 from line . . . Great quote . . . Earned $700,000 . . .
Helped Duke to NCAA title game in 1978 . . . Was 7th overall
pick by Nets in 1980 . . . Wife Stacey was one of first women to
get swimming scholarship to Duke . . . Dream was always to be
baseball star . . . Born Aug. 3, 1959, in Monroe, Conn. . . .
Crossword puzzle freak.

Year	Team	G	FG	FG Pct.	FT	FT Pct.	Reb.	Ast.	TP	Avg.
1980-81	New Jersey	56	291	.423	155	.767	419	72	737	13.2
1981-82	New Jersey	64	119	.441	97	.822	186	41	335	5.2
1982-83	New Jersey	80	213	.500	175	.778	382	61	601	7.5
1983-84	New Jersey	82	237	.513	147	.799	433	92	621	7.6
1984-85	New Jersey	81	380	.465	276	.841	633	158	1036	12.8
1985-86	New Jersey	81	491	.517	351	.893	668	133	1333	16.5
1986-87	New Jersey	72	433	.457	313	.846	630	99	1179	16.4
1987-88	N.J.-Phil.	81	505	.448	355	.906	814	139	1365	16.9
	Totals	597	2669	.469	1869	.844	4165	795	7207	12.1

ANDREW TONEY 30 6-3 190   Guard

The sun rose in the East, consumer prices did
not go down, Andrew Toney was hurt. So
what's new? . . . Chronic foot problems have
limited him to 87 games in last three seasons
. . . Philly patience worn out, but what to do
with a guy making $700,000? . . . Don't invite
him and owner Harold Katz to the same party
. . . Back in healthy days he was fearsome per-
former with lethal shot . . . Picked No. 8 by Philly in 1980 draft
out of Southwest Louisiana . . . Nets' scouts begged brass to take
him over Mike O'Koren . . . Could find work with expansion, but
not at this high salary . . . Born Nov. 23, 1957, in Birmingham,
Ala.

Year	Team	G	FG	FG Pct.	FT	FT Pct.	Reb.	Ast.	TP	Avg.
1980-81	Philadelphia	75	399	.495	161	.712	143	273	968	12.9
1981-82	Philadelphia	77	511	.522	227	.742	134	283	1274	16.5
1982-83	Philadelphia	81	626	.501	324	.788	225	365	1598	19.7
1983-84	Philadelphia	78	593	.527	390	.839	193	373	1588	20.4
1984-85	Philadelphia	70	450	.492	306	.862	177	363	1245	17.8
1985-86	Philadelphia	6	11	.306	3	.375	5	12	25	4.2
1986-87	Philadelphia	52	197	.451	133	.796	85	188	549	10.6
1987-88	Philadelphia	29	72	.421	58	.806	47	108	211	7.3
	Totals	468	2859	.500	1602	.797	1009	1965	7458	15.9

CLIFF ROBINSON 28 6-9 240   Forward

Has played two years with Sixers . . . If history holds, he'll be traded soon . . . Has been with six teams, never more than 2½ seasons . . . Loves to shoot. *Really* loves to shoot . . . Missed 20 games, 15 with back injury . . . Disciplined his offense a tad, but not enough . . . New Jersey drafted him as 19-year-old undergraduate draft pick from USC in 1979. Also has played for Kings, Cavs and Bullets . . . Came to Philly from Washington in blockbuster trade with since-retired Jeff Ruland for Moses Malone, Terry Catledge and two first-round draft picks . . . Fine open-court scorer who does the dirty work on boards, too . . . While with Nets in March 1980, he scored 23 points in fourth quarter against Bullets . . . Born March 13, 1960, in Oakland, Cal. . . . Earned $680,000.

Year	Team	G	FG	FG Pct.	FT	FT Pct.	Reb.	Ast.	TP	Avg.
1979-80	New Jersey	70	391	.469	168	.694	506	98	951	13.6
1980-81	New Jersey	63	525	.491	178	.718	481	105	1229	19.5
1981-82	K.C.-Clev.	68	518	.453	222	.709	609	120	1258	18.5
1982-83	Cleveland	77	587	.477	213	.708	856	145	1387	18.0
1983-84	Cleveland	73	533	.450	234	.701	753	185	1301	17.8
1984-85	Washington	60	422	.471	158	.742	546	149	1003	16.7
1985-86	Washington	78	595	.474	269	.762	680	186	1460	18.7
1986-87	Philadelphia	55	338	.464	139	.755	307	169	815	14.8
1987-88	Philadelphia	62	483	.464	210	.717	405	131	1178	19.0
	Totals	606	4392	.468	1791	.722	5143	1208	10582	17.5

CHRIS WELP 24 7-0 245   Center

Career may be endangered before ever beginning . . . Played in 10 games, went down in December with knee injury that required surgery . . . Suffered partial tear of the lateral meniscus cartilage and complete tear of the anterior cruciate ligament . . . In layman's terms, this isn't good . . . Still, he's expected to play this season . . . Paid $257,000 after Philly made him No. 16 pick in 1987 draft . . . Scored 18 points against Seattle before injury . . . Just scratching surface of skills . . . All-time leading scorer at Washington, three-time All-Pac 10 performer . . . Born Jan. 2, 1964, at Delmenhorst, West Germany . . . College teammate of fellow Deutschlander Detlef Schrempf.

Year	Team	G	FG	FG Pct.	FT	FT Pct.	Reb.	Ast.	TP	Avg.
1987-88	Philadelphia.........	10	18	.581	12	.667	24	5	48	4.8

DANNY VRANES 30 6-9 220   Forward

Yes, Virginia, there is a Santa Claus. Santa dresses as an NBA businessman and hands out $520,000 contracts to guys like this who average 2.1 points a game . . . Never lived up to rep that made him fifth overall pick by Seattle in 1981 draft . . . Plays good defense, but even that may be overrated . . . Soap commerical star. Has that Ivory look, ya know? . . . Played 772 minutes, career low . . . Should be just fine when he decides on a line of work . . . Born Oct. 28, 1958, in Salt Lake City . . . Stayed at home and became a star at University of Utah.

Year	Team	G	FG	FG Pct.	FT	FT Pct.	Reb.	Ast.	TP	Avg.
1981-82	Seattle.............	77	143	.546	89	.601	198	56	375	4.9
1982-83	Seattle.............	82	226	.527	115	.550	425	120	567	6.9
1983-84	Seattle.............	80	258	.521	153	.648	395	132	669	8.4
1984-85	Seattle.............	76	186	.463	67	.528	436	152	440	5.8
1985-86	Seattle.............	80	131	.461	39	.520	281	68	301	3.8
1986-87	Philadelphia.........	58	59	.428	21	.467	146	30	140	2.4
1987-88	Philadelphia.........	57	53	.438	15	.429	117	36	121	2.1
	Totals.............	510	1056	.496	499	.570	1998	594	2613	5.1

DAVID WINGATE 24 6-5 185   Guard-Forward

Showed signs of becoming a terror . . . Started season in great form (tied career high with 28 points vs. Spurs in December) . . . Suffered groin pull and missed 14 games . . . Didn't get back up to his earlier level . . . Great individual defensive player . . . Held St. John's Chris Mullin to eight points during NCAA semifinal game while a junior at Georgetown . . . An asset off anybody's bench...He's a player, pure and simple. Utilizes skills to maximum...Super find as 44th selection in 1986 draft...All-American at Dunbar High School in Washington, D.C....Still learning...Born Dec. 15, 1963, in Baltimore ...Incentives bring pact to $250,000.

Year	Team	G	FG	FG Pct.	FT	FT Pct.	Reb.	Ast.	TP	Avg.
1986-87	Philadelphia.........	77	259	.430	149	.741	156	155	680	8.8
1987-88	Philadelphia.........	61	218	.400	99	.750	101	119	545	8.9
	Totals.............	138	477	.416	248	.745	257	274	1225	8.9

DAVID HENDERSON 24 6-6 200　　　　Guard

As long as there are injuries in the NBA, guys like this find jobs...Brought in from CBA for 10-day look as free agent when Andrew Toney got hurt in March. Then was signed for rest of season...Defensive sort, averaged 5.7 points in 22 games... Contributed down the stretch and coach Jim Lynam liked his effort...Third-round pick out of Duke by Washington in 1986. Released and went CBA route...Re-signed by Bullets and released and back to CBA...Made All-ACC tourney team as senior...Was 1985 NIT MVP with 31 points in 30 minutes in title-game win vs. Kansas...Scored career-high 15 points vs. Bucks on March 30, 1988...Born July 21, 1964, in Henderson, N.C.

Year	Team	G	FG	FG Pct.	FT	FT Pct.	Reb.	Ast.	TP	Avg.
1987-88	Philadelphia.........	22	47	.405	32	.681	35	34	126	5.7

GERALD HENDERSON 32 6-2 180　　　　Guard

Somehow this guy was traded twice for No. 1 picks. Seattle and New York brass never heard end of it, either...Still can quarterback a team...Didn't feel happy about playing behind Mark Jackson with Knicks and was released outright before serious sulk set in...Signed one-year, $330,000 pact with Sixers last December...Rewarded faith, if not money, with 8.4 points, 3.2 assists in 44 games...Became ardent three-point freak, hitting 69-of-163 (67 with Sixers) for .423 percentage, fourth best in league. Had made 74 in eight previous seasons...Starred at Virginia Commonwealth and was third-round pick by San Antonio in 1978...Rescued from now-defunct Western Basketball Association by Celtics and was member of 1981 and 1984 championship teams... Never was really appreciated in Seattle and New York... Born Jan. 16, 1956, in Richmond, Va.

Year	Team	G	FG	FG Pct.	FT	FT Pct.	Reb.	Ast.	TP	Avg.
1979-80	Boston	76	191	.500	89	.690	83	147	473	6.2
1980-81	Boston	82	261	.451	113	.720	132	213	636	7.8
1981-82	Boston	82	353	.501	125	.727	152	252	833	10.2
1982-83	Boston	82	286	.463	96	.722	124	195	671	8.2
1983-84	Boston	78	376	.524	136	.768	147	300	908	11.6
1984-85	Seattle	79	427	.479	199	.780	190	559	1062	13.4
1985-86	Seattle	82	434	.482	185	.830	187	487	1071	13.1
1986-87	Sea.-N.Y.	74	298	442	190	.826	175	471	805	10.9
1987-88	N.Y.-Phil.	75	194	.428	138	.812	107	231	595	7.9
	Totals	710	2820	.476	1271	.772	1297	2855	7054	9.9

BEN COLEMAN 26 6-9 235   Forward

If only he were one-half as good as he thinks he is... Does have a decent low-post game ... Property of four teams since being drafted on second round, 37th overall, by Chicago in 1984... Benny refined his game in Italy after playing two years under Lefty Driesell at Maryland... Came to Sixers in January 1988 from Nets with Mike Gminski for Roy Hinson and Tim McCormick... Real strong, real wide... Averaged 6.9 points, 4.1 boards in 43 games with Sixers... Gets lots of garbage-point followups... Born Nov. 14, 1961, in Minneapolis.

Year	Team	G	FG	FG Pct.	FT	FT Pct.	Reb.	Ast.	TP	Avg.
1986-87	New Jersey	68	182	.581	88	.727	288	37	452	6.6
1987-88	N.J.-Phil.	70	226	.499	141	.762	350	62	593	8.5
	Totals	138	408	.533	229	.748	638	99	1045	7.6

MARK McNAMARA 29 6-11 235   Forward

Was born to be placed in an expansion pool ... Size is greatest, perhaps only, asset... Second stint with Sixers. Was their first-round pick (22d overall) in 1982. Traded to Spurs, who traded him to Kings, who traded him to Bucks, who waived him... Sixers said what the heck and signed him as free agent in March 1987, rescuing him from Europe... Started when Tim McCormick was hurt and averaged 6.8 points,

7.3 rebounds. Scored career-high 22 at Clippers last December ... Insured another contract that night ... Earns $100,000 with incentives ... Led nation in field-goal percentage (.702) at California in 1981-82 ... Born June 8, 1959, in San Jose, Cal.

Year	Team	G	FG	FG Pct.	FT	FT Pct.	Reb.	Ast.	TP	Avg.
1982-83	Philadelphia.........	36	29	.453	20	.444	76	7	78	2.2
1983-84	San Antonio.........	70	157	.621	74	.471	317	31	388	5.5
1984-85	S.A.-K.C...........	45	40	.526	32	.516	74	6	112	2.5
1986-87	Philadelphia.........	11	14	.467	7	.368	36	2	35	3.2
1987-88	Philadelphia.........	42	52	.391	48	.727	157	18	152	3.6
	Totals.............	204	292	.525	181	.519	660	64	765	3.8

BOB THORNTON 26 6-10 225   Forward

"Now starting for your Minnesota Timberwolves" ... Goes about a week and a half between ankle sprains ... Nice guy but personality only gets you so far ... Looks like Superman, plays like Clark Kent ... Released by Knicks after two ankle injuries last season and picked up by Sixers last December in apparent move to gain monopoly on white forwards ... He'll bang on the boards if nothing else ... Buck Williams once said, "There's a place in the league for Bob Thornton." Some folks still looking ... Earned $100,000 ... Not a half-bad offensive rebounder ... Born July 10, 1962, in Mission Viejo, Cal. ... Fourth-round pick by Knicks out of Cal-Irvine in 1984.

Year	Team	G	FG	FG Pct.	FT	FT Pct.	Reb.	Ast.	TP	Avg.
1985-86	New York...........	71	125	.456	86	.531	290	43	336	4.7
1986-87	New York...........	33	29	.433	13	.650	56	8	71	2.2
1987-88	N.Y.-Phil...........	48	65	.500	34	.618	112	15	164	3.4
	Totals.............	152	219	.465	133	.561	458	66	571	3.8

TOP ROOKIE

HERSEY HAWKINS 23 6-3 190   Guard

Nation's leading scorer (36.3 ppg) and consensus first-team All-American from Bradley ... Obviously a shooter, but some question if he creates his own shot in pros ... "Whoever drafts Hersey will get a perimeter player," said his college coach Stan Albeck ... Hawkins was grabbed sixth by Clippers, but was object of

Sixers' affections at No. 3 all along . . . Went to Philly on draft day, three-team trade . . . Averaged 24.1 during his four years in Peoria . . . Good passer and defender . . . Scored single-game school record 63 points vs. Detroit . . . Born Sept. 25, 1965, in Chicago.

COACH JIM LYNAM: Took over for fired Matt Goukas on

Feb. 8 . . . Guided a team riddled with injuries to 16-23 mark, but still was in contention for playoffs until final weekend . . . Rehired with three-year deal worth $600,000 . . . Set interior and perimeter defense as priority and quelled rumors of possible Charles Barkley trade . . . Well-respected in NBA circles . . . Good communicator. "After he speaks, you feel inspired," Maurice Cheeks said . . . Lynam was in heavy demand by expansion teams. Nets wanted to interview him in February, right before Guokas firing. Sixer brass didn't want to lose him . . . Head coach of San Diego/L.A. Clippers from 1983-85 . . . Spent 10 years in college ranks at Fairfield, American and St. Joseph's . . . Played for Jack Ramsay at St. Joseph's, where he was a gutsy guard, and later became Ramsay's assistant at Portland . . . Born Sept. 15, 1941, in Philadelphia . . . Has career NBA record of 68-114.

GREATEST THREE-POINT SHOOTER

When he wasn't hurt, when he wasn't feuding with owner Harold Katz, guard Andrew Toney was, among other things, establishing himself as the Sixers' all-time three-point shooter. He was just 9-of-27 last season, another injury-riddled campaign in which he missed 38 games. But Toney, a 6-3 guard from Southwestern Louisiana, who began his NBA career with Philly in 1980-81, now has 138 three-pointers for his career (403 attempts, a .342 percentage, both representing highs by a Sixer).

Gerald Henderson, thrown a career saver after his release by the Knicks, posted the best individual season ever by a Sixer when he canned 67-of-159 for a .421 percentage last season.

ALL-TIME 76ER LEADERS

SEASON

Points: Wilt Chamberlain, 2,649, 1965-66
Assists: Maurice Cheeks, 753, 1985-86
Rebounds: Wilt Chamberlain, 1,957, 1966-67

GAME

Points: Wilt Chamberlain, 68 vs. Chicago, 12/16/67
Assists: Wilt Chamberlain, 21 vs. Detroit, 2/2/68
　　　　　Maurice Cheeks, 21 vs. New Jersey, 10/30/82
Rebounds: Wilt Chamberlain, 43 vs. Boston, 3/6/65

CAREER

Points: Hal Greer, 21,586, 1958-73
Assists: Maurice Cheeks, 5,023, 1978-87
Rebounds: Dolph Schayes, 11,256, 1948-64

WASHINGTON BULLETS

TEAM DIRECTORY: Pres.: Abe Pollin; Vice Chairman: Jerry Sachs; Exec. VP: Garnett Flatton; GM: Bob Ferry; Dir. Pub. Rel.: Mark Pray; Coach: Wes Unseld; Asst. Coaches: Bill Blair, Jeff Bzdelik. Arena: Capital Centre (18,643). Colors: Red, white and blue.

SCOUTING REPORT

SHOOTING: Abominable, pure and simple. Terry Catledge's limited-range attempts brought a .506 mark and Bernard King's valiant comeback produced .501 accuracy, but after that no one smelled .500. Streaky Jeff Malone (.476) can hit jumpers with his eyes closed on certain nights, but some nights he looks like he shoots with, well, his eyes closed. Aside from King and Jeff Malone, the Bullets were bereft of a perimeter game. They took

Jeff Malone is one of NBA's sweetest shooters.

6-9 small forward Harvey Grant with their first pick, but his range is strictly from 15 feet and in.

PLAYMAKING: The Bullets went up-tempo after Wes Unseld replaced Kevin Loughery as coach. But he spent much of the year trying to find a point guard, settling for journeyman Steve Colter, hardly the answer. When the playoff berth was on the line, Darrell Walker, a combo-type guard, became the playmaker. This area is of major concern: the Bullets had fewer assists than any team except New Jersey.

DEFENSE: Not bad. Opponents shot .478 and scored 106.3 points. Both respectable, both better than anything the Bullets' offense managed. Shot-blocking reserve Manute Bol is gone and the Bullets made it eminently clear Moses Malone was not welcome back. Washington has some good pressure types in Walker and John Williams (a superstar waiting to blossom), but they have little in the middle.

REBOUNDING: Mediocre. The Bullets were 13th in the league. Malone was their chief party animal underneath with 11.2 per (eighth best in the league) but there wasn't a heckuva lot after that. Williams will get better, but the Bullets didn't have many other board-crashers and didn't find any in the draft.

OUTLOOK: The Bullets may pay this season for some grievous sins, like the absurd drafting of Tyrone Bogues with the 12th pick two years ago and the disastrous Jay Vincent and Michael Adams for Mark Alarie and Walker swap. Moses Malone's departure creates a huge question mark in the middle. The Bullets could very possibly—no, very probably—sink to lottery status this year.

BULLET PROFILES

JEFF MALONE 27 6-4 205   Guard

Streaky, streaky, streaky... When he's on, he's magnificent. When he's off, he's capable of stinking out any landfill... After two straight abysmal playoffs, he shot a sterling .520 in first-round series vs. Pistons... Led Bullets in scoring with 20.5 points per game, 17th best in league... All-time scorer at Mississippi State with 2,030 points, surpassing

BULLET ROSTER

No.	Veteran	Pos.	Ht.	Wt.	Age	Yrs. Pro	College
31	Mark Alarie	F	6-8	247	24	2	Duke
33	Terry Catledge	F	6-8	230	25	3	South Alabama
20	Steve Colter	G	6-3	175	26	4	New Mexico State
—	Dave Feitl	C	7-0	240	26	2	Texas-El Paso
15	Frank Johnson	G	6-3	185	29	7	Wake Forest
23	Charles Jones	F	6-9	215	31	5	Albany State (Ga.)
30	Bernard King	F	6-7	205	31	11	Tennessee
24	Jeff Malone	G	6-4	205	27	5	Mississippi State
42	Jay Murphy	F	6-9	220	26	3	Boston College
5	Darrell Walker	G	6-4	180	27	5	Arkansas
34	John Williams	F	6-9	237	22	2	Louisiana State

Rd.	Top Rookies	Sel. No.	Pos.	Ht.	Wt.	College
1	Harvey Grant	12	F	6-9	205	Oklahoma
2	Ledell Eackles	36	G	6-5	220	New Orleans
3	Ed Davender	60	G	6-3	165	Kentucky

Bailey Howell ... Was first-round pick (10th overall) by Bullets in 1983 ... Renegotiated contract to three years at $600,000 per ... Born June 28, 1961 in Mobile, Ala. ... Scorched Phoenix with season-high 47 points last February, including 28-point third quarter, most ever by Bullet, or by Suns' foe ... Education major in college ... Fun player to watch, especially when he's hot, hot, hot.

Year	Team	G	FG	FG Pct.	FT	FT Pct.	Reb.	Ast.	TP	Avg.
1983-84	Washington.........	81	408	.444	142	.826	155	151	982	12.1
1984-85	Washington.........	76	605	.499	211	.844	206	184	1436	18.9
1985-86	Washington.........	80	735	.483	322	.868	288	191	1795	22.4
1986-87	Washington.........	80	689	.457	376	.885	218	298	1758	22.0
1987-88	Washington.........	80	648	.476	335	.882	206	237	1641	20.5
	Totals.............	397	3085	.473	1386	.867	1073	1061	7612	19.2

JOHN WILLIAMS 22 6-9 237 Forward

Superstar in the making? ... Still a baby, was youngest player in NBA for second straight year ... Left LSU after sophomore year and Bullets grabbed him No. 12 on first round in 1986 ... Awesome raw talent ... Has played four positions: both forward and guard spots, but he's settling in at power forward ... Experiment to make him Magic East at point guard was wisely canned... Gave Pistons problems in the playoffs... Second on team in steals (1.43 per)... Jumper needs work... Has to drop some more baby fat... But remember, this should be his rookie year... Only Bullet to play all 82 games ... Born Oct. 26, 1966, in Los Angeles, where he attended Crenshaw High (same as Darryl Strawberry)... Earned $308,000 last season.

Year	Team	G	FG	FG Pct.	FT	FT Pct.	Reb.	Ast.	TP	Avg.
1986-87	Washington.........	78	283	.454	144	.646	366	191	718	9.2
1987-88	Washington.........	82	427	.469	188	.734	444	232	1047	12.8
	Totals.............	160	710	.463	332	.693	810	423	1765	11.0

DARRELL WALKER 27 6-4 180　　　　Guard

Ankle injury slowed him, coach's decisions stopped him most of season... Played just 940 minutes, lowest by far of his five-year career... Came alive in stretch drive, and helped land Bullets in the playoffs... Hit last-second jumper to beat Hawks and last-minute steal and layup to beat Celtics in waning days of April... Good defensively and a strong rebounder... Obtained from Denver last November with Mark Alarie for Jay Vincent and Michael Adams in what became the most lopsided deal of season. Adams and Vincent each scored 1,100 points, Walker and Alarie combined for 637... Former member of Hubie Brown's doghouse after Knicks made him No. 12 pick out of Arkansas in 1983... Base pay of $400,000.

Year	Team	G	FG	FG Pct.	FT	FT Pct.	Reb.	Ast.	TP	Avg.
1983-84	New York...........	82	216	.417	208	.791	167	284	644	7.9
1984-85	New York...........	82	430	.435	243	.700	278	408	1103	13.5
1985-86	New York...........	81	324	.430	190	.686	220	337	838	10.3
1986-87	Denver.............	81	358	.482	272	.745	327	282	988	12.2
1987-88	Washington.........	52	114	.392	82	.781	127	100	310	6.0
	Totals.............	378	1442	.438	995	.733	1119	1411	3883	10.3

BERNARD KING 31 6-7 205　　　　Forward

Comeback, Inc... Award was changed to Most Improved Player because guys bounding back from substance-abuse problems kept winning it... But his was a Comeback of the Year story all the way... After waiting for him to rehabilitate his knee for two years, Knicks let their team captain go without compensation... He signed $2.2-million offer sheet and became Bullet on Oct. 31, 1987... Knee was sound but back caused problems at end of season and he missed 13 games... Greatest game face in league, perhaps in all sports... Averaged 17.2 points, lowest full-season total of career... Bullets moved him to second unit for a spell to get bench productivity... Explosiveness from wing, which was compelling sight, is gone... But his ego never left... Asked why he took Washington over Boston, where as sixth man he could have been title piece, he said, "Who said I wouldn't start?"—ignoring a guy named Bird... Still has ultra-quick release, but it's a mega-second off what it was... Was 1984-85 scoring champ... Born Dec. 4, 1956, in Brooklyn, N.Y.... Nets made him seventh overall pick in 1977 out of Tennessee... Knicks got him from Warriors prior to 1982-83 season for Micheal Ray Richardson.

Year	Team	G	FG	FG Pct.	FT	FT Pct.	Reb.	Ast.	TP	Avg.
1977-78	New Jersey	79	798	.479	313	.677	751	193	1909	24.2
1978-79	New Jersey	82	710	.522	349	.564	669	295	1769	21.6
1979-80	Utah	19	71	.518	34	.540	88	52	176	9.3
1980-81	Golden State	81	731	.588	307	.703	551	287	1771	21.9
1981-82	Golden State	79	740	.566	352	.705	469	282	1833	23.2
1982-83	New York	68	603	.528	280	.722	326	195	1486	21.9
1983-84	New York	77	795	.572	437	.779	394	164	2027	26.3
1984-85	New York	55	691	.530	426	.772	317	204	1809	32.9
1985-86	New York					Injured				
1986-87	New York	6	52	.495	32	.744	32	19	136	22.7
1987-88	Washington	69	470	.501	247	.762	280	192	1188	17.2
	Totals	615	5661	.535	2777	.703	3877	1883	14104	22.9

DAVE FEITL 26 7-0 240   Center

Big body... That's his claim to fame and that alone will surely be enough to keep him in the NBA for a nice career as a reserve... Decent touch on the outside shot... Also shows a willingness to go inside and bang... Came to Washington in June in exchange for Manute Bol.... Born June 8, 1962, in Butler, Pa.... First team All-WAC as a senior at Texas-El Paso.... Drafted by Houston on the second round in 1986... Spent a year with the Rockets, then traded to Golden State prior to last season along with a first-round draft choice for Purvis Short... Comes from a large family of four sisters and five brothers... Started 18 games when Ralph Sampson went on the injured list... Not flashy, but functional.

Year	Team	G	FG	FG Pct.	FT	FT Pct.	Reb.	Ast.	TP	Avg.
1986-87	Houston	62	88	.436	53	.746	117	22	229	3.7
1987-88	Golden State	70	182	.450	94	.701	335	53	458	6.5
	Totals	132	270	.446	147	.717	452	75	687	5.2

CHARLES JONES 31 6-9 215   Forward

Makes Tree Rollins look like a scoring machine...Has played for about as many teams as he has career points...Well, almost ...Has 968 points in 261 games. Should crack 1,000 any week after the All-Star Game ...Defense and rebounding his specialty... Started 49 games...Pick a state or country, he's probably played there: Maine, Rhode Island, Florida in CBA; France and Italy in European leagues... Drafted 165th overall by Phoenix in 1979 out of Albany State (Ga.), he didn't play first NBA game until 1983-84...Led CBA in blocks three times...Had stints with Portland, New York, San Antonio, Philadelphia, Chicago and finally Washington... Earned $250,000...Brother of Caldwell, Major and Wil, all NBA players at one time or another.

Year	Team	G	FG	FG Pct.	FT	FT Pct.	Reb.	Ast.	TP	Avg.
1983-84	Philadelphia	1	0	.000	1	.250	0	0	1	1.0
1984-85	Chi.-Wash.	31	67	.528	40	.690	184	26	174	5.6
1985-86	Washington	81	129	.508	54	.628	321	76	312	3.9
1986-87	Washington	79	118	.474	48	.632	356	80	284	3.6
1987-88	Washington	69	72	.407	53	.707	325	59	197	2.9
	Totals	261	386	.478	196	.656	1186	241	968	3.7

MARK ALARIE 24 6-8 217   Forward

Washout in Washington...Played fewest minutes (769) of any Bullet who spent more than 10 days out of hospital...Can shoot and get some boards, but was forgotten man... Highlight was season-high 18 points vs. Celts last January...Everything else was a lowlight...Came over from Nuggets with Darrel Walker last November in disastrous deal in which Denver got Michael Adams and Jay Vincent... Starred at Duke, where he used solid court sense to find holes in zones...Too bad NBA has no zone defenses (the legal ones)... Denver made him 18th selection in 1986 draft...Base pay of $232,500...Born Dec. 11, 1963, in Phoenix.

Year	Team	G	FG	FG Pct.	FT	FT Pct.	Reb.	Ast.	TP	Avg.
1986-87	Denver	64	217	.490	67	.663	214	74	503	7.9
1987-88	Washington	63	144	.480	35	.714	160	39	327	5.2
	Totals	127	361	.486	102	.680	374	113	830	6.5

STEVE COLTER 26 6-3 175   Guard

How chaotic was Bullets' point guard situation?... This journeyman became regular-season starter after release by Sixers... Signed a couple of 10-day pacts, and then Bullets signed him for rest of year last January... A toothpick with legs... Needs work on his shot... Started all five games in playoffs vs. Pistons, but played just 86 minutes as lion's share of work went to Darrell Walker... Earned $150,000... Portland made him second-round pick in 1984 out of New Mexico State... Had brief stops in Chicago and Philly... Born July 24, 1962, in Phoenix.

Year	Team	G	FG	FG Pct.	FT	FT Pct.	Reb.	Ast.	TP	Avg.
1984-85	Portland..........	78	216	.453	98	.754	150	243	556	7.1
1985-86	Portland..........	81	272	.456	135	.823	177	257	706	8.7
1986-87	Chi.-Phil.	70	169	.426	82	.766	108	210	424	6.1
1987-88	Phil.-Wash.........	68	203	.460	75	.789	173	261	484	7.1
	Totals.............	297	860	.450	390	.786	608	971	2170	7.3

FRANK JOHNSON 29 6-3 185   Guard

Did not break his foot last season... Which in his case is man-bites-dog news... After suffering four recent breaks in his foot, he managed to get in 78 games—just three less than in three previous seasons combined... Health didn't help numbers, though... Averaged only 17 minutes and 7.4 points a game... In his prime, he was super quick with uncanny leaping ability... No longer... Foot problems date back to career at Wake Forest, where he was second-team team All-American in 1981... Became Bullets' first-round choice (No. 11) that June ... Good genes: brother of Eddie Johnson, cousin of Tree Rollins... Born Nov. 23, 1958, in Weirsdale, Fla.... Earned $325,000 in final year of contract.

Year	Team	G	FG	FG Pct.	FT	FT Pct.	Reb.	Ast.	TP	Avg.
1981-82	Washington.........	79	336	.414	153	.750	147	380	842	10.7
1982-83	Washington.........	68	321	.408	196	.751	178	549	852	12.5
1983-84	Washington.........	82	392	.467	187	.742	184	567	982	12.0
1984-85	Washington.........	46	175	.489	72	.750	63	143	428	9.3
1985-86	Washington.........	14	69	.448	38	.704	28	76	176	12.6
1986-87	Washington.........	18	59	.461	35	.714	30	58	153	8.5
1987-88	Washington.........	75	216	.434	121	.812	121	188	554	7.4
	Totals.............	382	1568	.438	802	.753	751	1961	3987	10.4

TERRY CATLEDGE 25 6-8 230 Forward

Started slow and never got going. Felt effects of fractured neck in offseason auto accident ...Strong inside player with awfully weak range...Scoring average plummeted from 13.1 to 10.7 points per game...Shot team-high .506 from floor, but had more turnovers (101) than assists (63) and steals (33) combined...Played just 45 minutes in five-game series vs. Pistons...Received hefty contract extension in preseason: $410,000 with incentives, up from $150,000...Says he's nicknamed "Cadillac" because he's "long, black and lovely."...Came to Bullets with Moses Malone in June 1986 heist of Philadelphia...At 6-8, had just four blocks—one more than Tyrone Bogues...Born Aug. 22, 1963, in Houston, Miss. ...Sixers chose him No. 21 overall, out of South Alabama, in 1985 draft.

Year	Team	G	FG	FG Pct.	FT	FT Pct.	Reb.	Ast.	TP	Avg.
1985-86	Philadelphia	64	202	.469	90	.647	272	21	494	7.7
1986-87	Washington	78	413	.495	199	.594	560	56	1025	13.1
1987-88	Washington	70	296	.506	154	.655	397	63	746	10.7
	Totals	212	911	.492	443	.625	1229	140	2265	10.7

JAY MURPHY 26 6-9 220 Forward

Helps keep medical insurance rates soaring ...Played in nine games before suffering a herniated disc...Placed on injured list last January and didn't return...For a 6-9 guy who can shoot outside, he's always worth a gamble...Showed immense improvement during collegiate career at Boston College... Was 31st pick in 1984 draft by Warriors, who traded rights to Clippers for Jerome Whitehead...Had arthroscopic surgery as rookie...Waived by Clippers (who have a nerve waiving anybody) after 14 games in 1985-86. Signed by Bullets as free agent in September 1986...Is usually on injury list when not playing sparingly...Born June 26, 1962, in Meriden, Conn....Makes $150,000 with incentives.

Year	Team	G	FG	FG Pct.	FT	FT Pct.	Reb.	Ast.	TP	Avg.
1984-85	L.A. Clippers	23	8	.160	12	.571	41	4	28	1.2
1985-86	L.A. Clippers	14	16	.356	9	.643	15	3	41	2.9
1986-87	Washington	21	31	.431	9	.563	39	5	71	3.4
1987-88	Washington	9	8	.348	4	.800	16	1	20	2.2
	Totals	67	63	.331	34	.607	111	13	160	2.4

TOP ROOKIE

HARVEY GRANT 23 6-9 205   **Forward**

Twin brother of Chicago's Horace . . . Bullets made this small forward, who some think could be a Bob McAdoo-type, the 12th selection on first round . . . Helped Oklahoma to NCAA finals averaging 20.9 points and 9.4 rebounds a game . . . "Harvey did everything we asked," said Sooners' coach Billy Tubbs. "I could tell him to go out and do nothing but rebound and not take a shot and he would do that." . . . First team All-Big Eight selection . . . He'll have to improve his movement without the ball, but he's a nice inside and outside scoring threat . . . Bullets' crying need was point guard but couldn't pass on him.

COACH WES UNSELD: Like he did as a player, had immediate impact as a coach . . . Took over for the fired Kevin Loughery last January when Bullets were hopeless, helpless and hapless at 8-19 . . . Led them to 30-25 record rest of the way and into playoffs . . . One of the NBA's all-time players . . . Only the second player ever to win MVP and Rookie of the Year in same season (Wilt Chamberlain was the other) . . . Inducted into Hall of Fame last May . . . At 6-7, he was one of smallest centers vertically but a behemoth horizontally at 245 pounds . . . Had strength of an ox . . . Perfect coaching temperment . . . Never dwells on past mistakes . . . But don't cross him . . . Bullets made him the No. 2 pick overall in 1968 draft out of Louisville . . . That's the city where he was born March 14, 1946 . . . In 13-year career with Bullets, he averaged 14 rebounds and 10.8 points . . . Set terrifying picks and became legendary for his outlet passes . . . MVP of 1978 NBA Finals when Bullets beat Sonics for championship.

GREATEST THREE-POINT SHOOTER

You think three-pointers, you don't think Washington. Last season, the Bullets pumped in a grand total of 29, roughly a week and a half's work for Danny Ainge, and far and away the lowest

Bernard King is still deadly as a Bullet.

total in the league. In fact, nine teams *made* more than the Bullets even *attempted* (138).

But it wasn't always that way. Not when streak-shooting Kevin Grevey played for Washington. Grevey converted 122-of-348 three-pointers (.351) with the Bullets (1979–83) before moving on to Milwaukee. The Bullets made Grevey, a Kentucky product, the 18th player drafted in 1975 and he contributed to Washington's NBA title team of 1977-78. And he's still the Bullets' all-time three-point master.

ALL-TIME BULLET LEADERS

SEASON

Points: Walt Bellamy, 2,495, 1961-62
Assists: Kevin Porter, 734, 1980-81
Rebounds: Walt Bellamy, 1,500, 1961-62

GAME

Points: Earl Monroe, 56 vs. Los Angeles, 2/3/68
Assists: Kevin Porter, 24 vs. Detroit, 3/23/80
Rebounds: Walt Bellamy, 37 vs. St.Louis, 12/4/64

CAREER

Points: Elvin Hayes, 15,551, 1972-81
Assists: Wes Unseld, 3,822, 1968-81
Rebounds: Wes Unseld, 13,769, 1968-81

1988 NBA COLLEGE DRAFT

Sel. No.	Team	Name	College	Ht.
	FIRST ROUND			
1.	LA Clippers	Danny Manning	Kansas	6-10
2.	Indiana	Rik Smits	Marist	7-4
3.	*Philadelphia	Charles Smith	Pittsburgh	6-10
4.	New Jersey	Chris Morris	Auburn	6-8
5.	Golden State	Mitch Richmond	Kansas State	6-5
6.	#LA Clippers (from Sacramento)	Hersey Hawkins	Bradley	6-3
7.	Phoenix	Tim Perry	Temple	6-9
8.	Charlotte	Rex Chapman	Kentucky	6-4
9.	Miami	Rony Seikaly	Syracuse	6-11
10.	San Antonio	Willie Anderson	Georgia	6-7
11.	Chicago (from New York)	Will Perdue	Vanderbilt	7-0
12.	Washington	Harvey Grant	Oklahoma	6-9
13.	Milwaukee	Jeff Grayer	Iowa State	6-5
14.	Phoenix (from Cleveland)	Dan Majerle	Central Michigan	6-6
15.	* Seattle	Gary Grant	Michigan	6-2
16.	Houston	Derrick Chievous	Missouri	6-7
17.	Utah	Eric Leckner	Wyoming	6-11
18.	Sacramento (from Atlanta)	Ricky Berry	San Jose State	6-8
19.	New York (from Chicago)	Rod Strickland	DePaul	6-3
20.	Miami (from Dallas)	Kevin Edwards	DePaul	6-3
21.	Portland	Mark Bryant	Seton Hall	6-9
22.	Cleveland (from Detroit via Phoenix)	Randolph Keys	So. Mississippi	6-9
23.	Denver	Jerome Lane	Pittsburgh	6-6
24.	Boston	Brian Shaw	Cal-Santa Barbara	6-6
25.	LA Lakers	David Rivers	Notre Dame	6-0

*Traded to Clippers
#Traded to 76ers

Sel. No.	Team	Name	College	Ht.
	SECOND ROUND			
26.	Portland (from LA Clippers)	Rolando Ferreira	Houston	7-1
27.	San Antonio (from New Jersey via Chicago)	Shelton Jones	St. John's	6-7
28.	Phoenix (from Golden State via Milwaukee)	Andrew Lang	Arkansas	6-11
29.	Sacramento	Vinnie Del Negro	N.C. State	6-5
30.	Detroit (from Phoenix via Sacramento and New York)	Fennis Dembo	Wyoming	6-6
31.	Philadelphia (from San Antonio)	Everette Stephens	Purdue	6-3
32.	New Jersey (from Philadelphia)	Charles Shackleford	N.C. State	6-10
33.	Miami	Grant Long	Eastern Michigan	6-8
34.	Charlotte	Tom Tolbert	Arizona	6-7
35.	Miami (from N.Y. via Chicago, Seattle and Boston)	Sylvester Gray	Memphis State	6-6
36.	Washington	Ledell Eackles	New Orleans	6-5
37.	New York (from Indiana via Chicago)	Greg Butler	Stanford	6-11
38.	Phoenix (from Cleveland)	Dean Garrett	Indiana	6-10
39.	Milwaukee	Tito Horford	Miami	7-1
40.	Miami (from Seattle)	Orlando Graham	Auburn-Montgomery	6-7
41.	Golden State (from Houston)	Keith Smart	Indiana	6-2

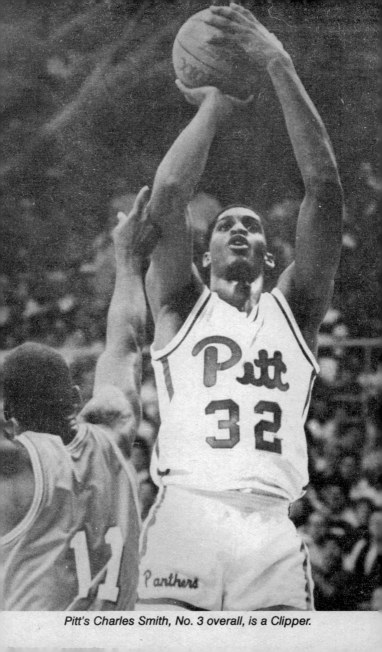

Pitt's Charles Smith, No. 3 overall, is a Clipper.

Nets made Auburn's Chris Morris No. 4.

Temple's Tim Perry got Sun-up call as No. 7.

No. 2 pick, Marist's Rik Smits, went to the Pacers.

Bradley's Hersey Hawkins, No. 6, is now a 76er.

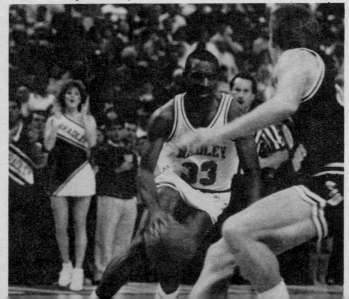

Sel. No.	Team	Name	College	Ht.
42.	Utah	Jeff Moe	Iowa	6-4
43.	Denver (from Chicago)	Todd Mitchell	Purdue	6-7
44.	Atlanta	Anthony Taylor	Oregon	6-4
45.	L.A. Clippers (from Portland)	Tom Garrick	Rhode Island	6-2
46.	Dallas	Morlon Wiley	Long Beach State	6-4
47.	Denver	Vernon Maxwell	Florida	6-5
48.	Detroit	Michael Williams	Baylor	6-2
49.	Dallas (from Boston)	Jose Vargas	LSU	6-10
50.	Phoenix (from LA Lakers)	Steve Kerr	Arizona	6-3

THIRD ROUND

Sel. No.	Team	Name	College	Ht.
51.	LA Clippers	Robert Lock	Kentucky	6-10
52.	New Jersey	Derrek Hamilton	So. Mississippi	6-6
53.	Portland (from Golden State)	Anthony Mason	Tennessee State	6-7
54.	Atlanta (from Sacramento)	Jorge Gonzalez	Argentina	7-7
55.	Phoenix	Rodney Johns	Grand Canyon	6-2
56.	San Antonio	Barry Sumpter	Austin Peay	7-0
57.	Philadelphia	Hernan Montenegro	LSU	6-9
58.	Charlotte	Jeff Moore	Auburn	6-7
59.	Miami	Nate Johnson	Tampa	6-8
60.	Washington	Ed Davender	Kentucky	6-3
61.	Indiana	Herbert Crook	Louisville	6-7
62.	Chicago (from New York)	Derrick Lewis	Maryland	6-8
63.	Milwaukee	Mike Jones	Auburn	6-6
64.	Cleveland	Winston Bennett	Kentucky	6-7
65.	Seattle	Corey Gaines	Loyola Marymount	6-3
66.	Denver (from Houston)	Dwight Boyd	Memphis State	6-3
67.	Utah	Ricky Grace	Oklahoma	6-1
68.	Atlanta	Darryl Middleton	Baylor	6-8
69.	New York (from Chicago)	Phil Stinnie	Va. Commonwealth	6-7
70.	Dallas	Jerry Johnson	Florida Southern	5-11
71.	Portland	Craig Neal	Georgia Tech	6-4
72.	Detroit	Lee Johnson	Norfolk State	6-9
73.	Indiana (from Denver via LA Clippers)	Michael Anderson	Drexel	5-11
74.	Boston	Gerald Paddio	UNLV	6-7
75.	San Antonio (from LA Lakers)	Archie Marshall	Kansas	6-7

1987-88
NATIONAL BASKETBALL ASSOCIATION

FINAL STANDINGS

EASTERN CONFERENCE

Atlantic Division	Won	Lost	Pct.
Boston	57	25	.695
Washington	38	44	.463
New York	38	44	.463
Philadelphia	36	46	.439
New Jersey	19	63	.232

Central Division	Won	Lost	Pct.
Detroit	54	28	.650
Atlanta	50	32	.610
Chicago	50	32	.610
Cleveland	42	40	.512
Milwaukee	42	40	.512
Indiana	38	44	.463

WESTERN CONFERENCE

Midwest Division	Won	Lost	Pct.
Denver	52	28	.659
Dallas	53	29	.646
Utah	47	35	.573
Houston	46	36	.561
San Antonio	31	51	.378
Sacramento	24	58	.293

Pacific Division	Won	Lost	Pct.
LA Lakers	62	20	.756
Portland	53	29	.646
Seattle	44	38	.537
Phoenix	28	54	.341
Golden State	20	62	.244
LA Clippers	17	65	.207

CHAMPION: LA Lakers

The ball was up for grabs and in the end the Lakers got it.

PLAYOFFS

EASTERN CONFERENCE

First Round
Boston defeated New York (3-1)
Detroit defeated Washington (3-2)
Chicago defeated Cleveland (3-2)
Atlanta defeated Milwaukee (3-2)
Semifinals
Boston defeated Atlanta (4-3)
Detroit defeated Chicago (4-1)
Final
Detroit defeated Boston (4-2)

WESTERN CONFERENCE

First Round
LA Lakers defeated San Antonio (3-0)
Denver defeated Seattle (3-2)
Dallas defeated Houson (3-1)
Utah defeated Portland (3-1)
Semifinals
LA Lakers defeated Utah (3-2)
Dallas defeated Denver (4-2)
Final
LA Lakers defeated Dallas (4-3)

CHAMPIONSHIP
LA Lakers defeated Detroit (4-3)

1987-88 INDIVIDUAL HIGHS

Most Minutes Played, Season: 3,311, Jordan Chicago
Most Minutes Played, Game: 55, Johnson, Boston vs. New York, 11/18 (2 OT)
    48, 16 players
Most Points, Game: 59, Jordan, Chicago vs. Detroit, 4/3
Most Field Goals Made, Game: 21 Jordan, Chicago vs. Portland, 12/26;
    Jordan, Chicago vs. Detroit, 4/3
Most Field Goal Attempts, Game: 42, Wilkins, Atlanta vs. LA Lakers, 2/19 (OT)
    39, Wilkins, Atlanta vs. Washington, 2/13
Most 3-Point Field Goals Made, Game: 7, Wood, San Antonio vs. Portland,
    12/20; Bird, Boston vs. Dallas, 4/3;
    Evans, Denver vs. Portland, 4/22 (OT)
Most 3-Point Field Goal Attempts, Game: 15, Adams, Denver vs. Utah, 3/14
Most Free Throws Made, Game: 21, Barkley, Philadelphia vs. Atlanta, 2/9
Most Free Throw Attempts, Game: 26, Barkley, Philadelphia vs. Atlanta, 2/9
Most Rebounds, Game: 35, Oakley, Chicago vs. Cleveland, 4/22
Most Offensive Rebounds, Game: Oakley, Chicago vs. Cleveland, 4/22
Most Defensive Rebounds, Game: 19, Eaton, Utah vs. Denver, 11/17;
    Oakley, Chicago vs. Cleveland, 4/22;
    Cage, LA Clippers vs. Seattle, 4/24
Most Offensive Rebounds, Season: 385, Barkley, Philadelphia
Most Defensive Rebounds, Season: 740, Oakley, Chicago
Most Assists, Game: 26, Stockton, Utah vs. Portland, 4/14
Most Blocked Shots, Game: 10, Nance, Phoenix vs. Philadelphia, 1/4;
    Bol, Washington vs. Golden State, 1/22;
    Benjamin, LA Clippers vs. Milwaukee, 1/29;
    Olajuwon, Houston vs. San Antonio, 4/21
Most Steals, Game: 10, Jordan, Chicago vs. New Jersey, 1/29
Most Personal Fouls, Season: 322, Ewing, New York
Most Games Disqualified, Season: 11, Brickowski, San Antonio; Sikma,
    Milwaukee

Charles Barkley: Most FTAs, FTMs in a game last year.

INDIVIDUAL SCORING LEADERS
Minimum 70 games or 1,400 points

	G	FG	FT	Pts.	Avg.
Jordan, Chicago	82	1069	723	2868	35.0
Wilkins, Atlanta	78	909	541	2397	30.7
Bird, Boston	76	881	415	2275	29.9
Barkley, Philadelphia	80	753	714	2264	28.3
Malone, Utah	82	858	552	2268	27.7
Drexler, Portland	81	849	476	2185	27.0
Ellis, Seattle	75	764	303	1938	25.8
Aguirre, Dallas	77	746	388	1932	25.1
English, Denver	80	843	314	2000	25.0
Olajuwon, Houston	79	712	381	1805	22.8
McHale, Boston	64	550	346	1446	22.6
Scott, LA Lakers	81	710	272	1754	21.7
Theus, Sacramento	73	619	320	1574	21.6
McDaniel, Seattle	78	687	281	1669	21.4
Cummings, Milwaukee	76	675	270	1621	21.3
Thorpe, Sacramento	82	622	460	1704	20.8
J. Malone, Washington	80	648	335	1641	20.5
Chambers, Seattle	82	611	419	1674	20.4
M. Malone, Washington	79	531	543	1607	20.3
Ewing, New York	82	656	341	1653	20.2

REBOUND LEADERS
Minimum 70 games or 800 rebounds

	G	Off.	Def.	Tot.	Avg.
Cage, LA Clippers	72	371	567	938	13.03
Oakley, Chicago	82	326	740	1066	13.00
Olajuwon, Houston	79	302	657	959	12.1
Malone, Utah	82	277	709	986	12.0
Williams, New Jersey	70	298	536	834	11.9
Barkley, Philadelphia	80	385	566	951	11.9
Tarpley, Dallas	81	360	599	959	11.8
M. Malone, Washington	79	372	512	884	11.2
Thorpe, Sacramento	82	279	558	837	10.2
Laimbeer, Detroit	82	165	667	832	10.1